RHYTHM IS OUR BUSINESS

JAZZ PERSPECTIVES
Lewis Porter, Series General Editor

Open the Door: The Life and Music of Betty Carter
By William R. Bauer

Jazz Journeys to Japan: The Heart Within
By William Minor

Four Jazz Lives   By A. B. Spellman

Head Hunters: *The Making of Jazz's First Platinum Album*
By Steven F. Pond

Lester Young   By Lewis Porter

The André Hodeir Jazz Reader
By André Hodeir   Edited by Jean-Louis Pautrot

Someone to Watch Over Me: The Life and Music of Ben Webster
By Frank Büchmann-Møller

Rhythm Is Our Business:
Jimmie Lunceford and the Harlem Express
By Eddy Determeyer

OTHER BOOKS OF INTEREST

Before Motown: A History of Jazz in Detroit 1920–1960
By Lars Bjorn with Jim Gallert

John Coltrane: His Life and Music   By Lewis Porter

Charlie Parker: His Music and Life   By Carl Woideck

The Song of the Hawk:
The Life and Recordings of Coleman Hawkins
By John Chilton

Rhythm Man: Fifty Years in Jazz
By Steve Jordan with Tom Scanlan

Let the Good Times Roll:
The Story of Louis Jordan and His Music
By John Chilton

Twenty Years on Wheels
By Andy Kirk as Told to Amy Lee

RHYTHM IS OUR BUSINESS

Jimmie Lunceford and the Harlem Express

EDDY DETERMEYER

The University of Michigan Press   Ann Arbor

Copyright © by the University of Michigan 2006
All rights reserved
Published in the United States of America by
The University of Michigan Press
Manufactured in the United States of America
⊗ Printed on acid-free paper

2009   2008   2007   2006   4   3   2   1

A CIP catalog record for this book is available from the British Library.

Library of Congress Cataloging-in-Publication Data

Determeyer, Eddy.
    Rhythm is our business : Jimmie Lunceford and the Harlem Express /
Eddy Determeyer.
        p.   cm. — (Jazz perspectives)
    Includes bibliographical references (p.   ), discography (p.   ),
and index.
        ISBN-13: 978-0-472-11553-2 (cloth : alk. paper)
        1. Lunceford, Jimmie.   2. Conductors (Music)—United States—
Biography.   3. Big band music—History and criticism.   I. Title.
II. Series: Jazz perspectives (Ann Arbor, Mich.)
ML422.L86D48   2006
781.65092—dc22
    [B]   2006015261

CONTENTS

PREFACE

Once upon a time in Memphis, a bunch of schoolboys started a band. The road they traveled took them from starvation to stardom. In its heyday the Jimmie Lunceford Orchestra drew such crowds that occasionally dances had to be canceled, the mass of bodies threatening the integrity of the building. During the swing era, roughly between 1935 and 1945, most of the better bands did that: they provided swing music. Jimmie Lunceford's Harlem Express bounced you into bad health. For many years, it was the best-loved dance band in the South, attracting eight to ten thousand dancers to big tobacco barns that had been turned into makeshift ballrooms.

Superior musicianship, dynamic control, and an irresistible beat were Lunceford's strong selling points, but showmanship was another pillar. The various sections of the orchestra moved in perfect unison to the groove; the trumpeters, when not screeching to the high heavens, would throw their instruments in the air, to catch them on the beat; even the handling of the mutes was strictly choreographed. On its tours, the band brought along the best professional dancers. Lunceford was the man who put the show in black show business. Most of the great swing bands and rhythm-and-blues acts took some inspiration from his Harlem Express.

Jimmie Lunceford was an innovator, introducing the electric guitar and the electric bass to jazz music. Cutting-edge arrangements by Sy Oliver, Eddie Durham, Gerald Wilson, Tadd Dameron, and Billy Moore put the band in the vanguard, where it bridged swing and bebop. The hip Lunceford style left its mark on numerous other bands, both black and white. Swing-era symbol Glenn Miller was one of Lunceford's staunchest admirers, stating, "Duke is great and Basie is remarkable, but Lunceford tops them both." With their impeccable, glamorous appearance, their infectious rhythms, and their jivey vocals, the musicians became role models for a generation of young African Americans.

Yet for many years the band remained virtually invisible to the white public because the band was constantly on the road to play black dances. Unlike most of the other top bands, the Lunceford orchestra seldom played the big New York hotels with their radio outlets.

Nevertheless, Lunceford's band played an important part in breaking down the color barrier. Not only was Jimmie Lunceford one of the first black leaders to hire white arrangers, a white singer, and white musicians, he also shunned segregated dances. His appearances at white colleges and other venues that up till then had featured white artists exclusively opened the door for other black acts.

Jimmie Lunceford was the first to teach jazz music at any school, and later, after his hit recordings and his successes at the Cotton Club in Harlem had made him a wealthy man, he financed several school bands and sport teams in order to fight juvenile delinquency. When his band really started to make money, he fulfilled an old dream and bought himself an airplane. And when, after just two months, he crashed that one, he replaced it with two new planes, including a state-of-the-art twin-engined Cessna. Shortly before his death he was developing plans to fly his band to Europe, to tour the continent in style—in a Dakota, to be flown by the leader.

Jimmie Lunceford and the Harlem Express brought a sense of glamour, class, and excitement to a people who were still recovering from the Great Depression. It was the kind of band one would spend one's last dollar on. So there's no use waiting: check your coat and join the crowd, because it's time to jump and shout!

ACKNOWLEDGMENTS

Piecing together a puzzle can be a lonely occupation; it is much more fun to do it in the company of friends. I think the first friend to show me that there was a Jimmie Lunceford puzzle was singer and jazz historian Babs Gonzales, who used to cram days and nights with his stories, starting at breakfast and finishing after everybody had gone to sleep. I should have followed him around with a tape recorder. Old Babs would be around forever, I figured. His adventures on the road as assistant band boy with the Jimmie Lunceford Orchestra constituted a considerable part of these stories, and after the third or fourth glass of wine he'd invariably cock his head slightly backward, close his eyes, grab my arm, and smile, "Hey Eddy, I know you've got Mr. Lunceford. Put on *For Dancers Only, nigger!*" Little Gonzi sure would have enjoyed a book about the Lunceford band.

Over the years Lunceford's name kept popping up in interviews I did with different musicians for various Dutch publications, and gradually I started digging deeper into the man's career and achievements. I realized that the history of his music was more complicated than available books told us. I had amassed about four inches of documents on Lunceford, which I regarded as quite an achievement, when Han Schulte of the Jazz Documentatie Centrum, one of the largest private jazz archives in Europe, sent me a box full of information, including the results of Franz Hoffmann's systematic coverage of the African American press between 1910 and 1950. At that point, there was simply no turning back.

Librarians and historians have become my buddies. They include the respective staffs at the Amsterdam Dutch Jazz Archive, the Universiteitsbibliotheek in Groningen, the Stockholm Svenskt Visarkiv, the Smithsonian Institution in Washington, DC, the John Hope and Elizabeth Franklin Library at Fisk University in Nashville, the Gaylord Music Library at

Washington University in St. Louis, Indiana University, the Warren-Trumbull County Public Library, the San Antonio Public Library, the White Plains Public Library, the Greenburgh Public Library, the Seaside Museum and Historical Society, the Fulton, Missouri, Historical Society, and *Down Beat* magazine.

Then there are the numerous private researchers and jazz enthusiasts who delved into their personal files. I do not wish to exclude anyone, and certainly not Roel Abels, who was the first one to grasp the significance and scope of this book, Frank Bonitto, who was a fan and a friend of Lunceford's ever since he first heard the band's nightly broadcasts from the Cotton Club, Robert Veen (who not only provided me with useful technical information, but got so carried away that he had his Beau Hunks orchestra study and perform the original Lunceford charts), Carl A. Hällström, Michael Arié, Rainer A. Lotz, Richard Palmer at Jazz Journal International, Donald R. A. Uges and Rogier Smits at the Laboratory for Clinical and Forensic Toxicology and Drug Analysis of Groningen State University, Mark O'Shaughnessy and the staff at BB's in St. Louis, where the last of the original blues trains roam, Ate van Delden, Ky Jennings, Arne Neegaard and Jim Gallert of the Jazz Research Group, Val Don Hickerson, Ernst Bruins, Bertil Lyttkens, who still regrets he missed the second show in Helsingborg, March 6, 1937, the editorial staff at *Orkester Journalen*, Wendy Prins and Lo Reizevoort, who helped me out with the Swedish articles, David Levering Lewis, Hugh Foley, and the gentlemen who desperately tried to mold my rather sad English into more or less readable matter, corrected factual errors (all remaining errors in the book are mine, of course), and added some useful information, Herman te Loo, Kurt Weis, John McDonough, and, last but by no means least, Walter van de Leur.

The musicians and dancers who were willing to share their memories of the Lunceford band and the swing era were invaluable. They include Emerson Able Jr., Rashied Ali, Benny Bailey, Butch Ballard, Art Blakey, John Carter, Arnett Cobb, Honi Coles, Buddy DeFranco, Von Freeman, Joe Houston, Hank Jones, George Kelly, Jackie Kelso, Freddie Kohlman, Milt Larkin, Jim Leigh, Willie Mitchell, Jimmy Oliver, Kathryn Perry Thomas, Bobby Plater, Eddie Randle Jr., Red Richards, James Flash Riley, Little Jimmy Scott, Horace Silver, Sun Ra, Sir Charles Thompson, Earle Warren, Frank Wess, Gerald Wiggins, and Don Wilkerson.

I was able to track down Jimmie Lunceford's closest living relative, his nephew Al, who saw his uncle just once, but was able to provide me with some information on the family.

When Chris Hebert of the University of Michigan Press saw my book proposal, his email reaction read, "I like the looks of this very much," and he, Lewis Porter, and the rest of the staff at the University of Michigan have been supportive ever since.

Finally, I dedicate *Rhythm Is Our Business* to the musicians who were members of the great Jimmie Lunceford Orchestra, some for one or two nights, others for six years, and whom I had the pleasure of interviewing. They are, in order of appearance: Jonah Jones, Gerald Wilson, Snooky Young, Truck Parham, Dave Bartholomew, Russell Jacquet, Benny Waters, Jerome Richardson, Connie Johnson, Russell Green, Al Cobbs, Al Grey, Joe Wilder, Billy Mitchell, and Aaron Bell.

The streamlined rhythms of the Harlem Express may have ceased to inspire and move a dancing nation, but the memory lingers on.

{1}

GO WEST

In Denver you weren't a sissy if you played music.
—Paul Whiteman

In 1901, 105 confirmed lynchings took place in the United States, and for a black man the chance of being lynched ran seven times higher in Mississippi, Jimmie Lunceford's birthplace, than the nation's average.[1] That year, a disillusioned George H. White, a lawyer from North Carolina, and the sole African American U.S. congressman, gave up his seat. It would be twenty-seven years before another black man, Oscar DePriest, was elected to Congress. It would take more than one hundred years before the U.S. Senate finally acknowledged and apologized for not passing anti-lynching legislation.

For a few years, the abolition of slavery had instilled a new hope in African Americans. But racial tensions had risen during the last three decades of the nineteenth century. At the turn of the century, peaceful coexistence between blacks and whites seemed as unrealistic as it had been before the Civil War. The future looked menacing, rather than bright.

James Melvin "Jimmie" Lunceford was born June 6, 1902, on the family farm in the Evergreen community, west of the Tombigbee River, in the northeastern part of Mississippi. The nearest town is Fulton, the seat of Itawamba County, which was formed in 1836, four years after the Chickasaw Session, when the Chickasaw nation was ordered to move to Oklahoma.

Over the years, the Luncefords would become a relatively well-to-do family. Daniel and Elisabeth ("Gracy"), Jimmie's paternal grandparents, were born in slavery and were brought to Itawamba County from the Smithfield area of Johnston County, North Carolina, during the late 1850s. Gracy was named after her former North Carolina owner, a Mr. Michiner. Their new owner was David Lunceford, formerly of Johnston County, who operated a farm east of Fulton. After the Civil War, Daniel and Gracy moved to a farm in nearby Abney, where Daniel worked as a field hand. After fifteen years he had gathered enough capital to be able to purchase 320 acres of land near Mobile, Alabama. The couple raised ten children; James Riley, Jimmie's father, was the sixth. He was born April 14, 1869, in Abney, and during the 1890s Daniel deeded James fifty-three acres of his land. James worked as a farmer, and in 1900 he married Idella ("Ida") Shumpert. Ida was born March 1, 1883, in Oklahoma City. She was the daughter of Sammie and Matilda Williams Shumpert. Ida Shumpert was an organ player of more than average ability.

One year after their marriage, James and Ida deeded their fifty-three acres to James's brother, Daniel Henry, and took over seventy acres from the Shumpert family, in the Evergreen community. Seven months later, James Melvin was born. Shortly after his birth, the parents felt the lure of the West and moved to Oklahoma, where Ida's family was living.[2]

Oklahoma City was fast rising at the time: the Santa Fe, the Rock Island, the Frisco, and the Katy lines were all constructed between 1889 and 1904. These railroads connected Oklahoma City with the prairies and with the rest of the world.

Oklahoma's cattle industry had started right after the Civil War. Attracted by the rich lands, settlers from across the nation and from abroad put pressure on the government to open the Indian territory to non-Indians. Between 1820 and 1842, the "Five Civilized Tribes" (Choctaw, Chickasaw, Cherokee, Creek, and Seminole) had forcibly moved westward to the eastern part of what was to become the forty-sixth state. With them along this "Trail of Tears" traveled many Indian-owned black slaves. And thus a curious kind of "plantation culture" had emerged on the grounds of the different Indian nations, where spirituals, work songs, and early forms of the blues developed much along the same lines as in other parts of the South.

The federal government decided that the Indian villages stood in the way of progress, and confiscated the land. From 1889 to 1895, five so-called land runs were held, with the participation of former slaves. Pamphlets were distributed throughout the southern states, urging blacks to come to Oklahoma, and establish their own businesses there (and possibly, it was hinted, even a first black state). In 1889 the first two hundred black citizens had settled in Oklahoma City's Sandtown, east of the Santa Fe tracks, along the north bank of North Canadian River. By 1910, more than seven thousand black people were living in Oklahoma City's Eastside. All over Oklahoma other black communities developed. Eventually, the state boasted twenty-seven African American towns, more than the total in the rest of the country.

In 1928, Charles N. Gould had described Oklahoma's cultural landscape as "a meeting place of many different peoples. Nowhere else is there such a mingling of types. Practically every state in the Union and every civilized nation on the globe is represented among the state's inhabitants." The *Oklahoma Music Guide* specified that

> this vast array of people and their music includes the song and dance music of the American Indian from the southeastern United States and western plains, northeastern woodlands, Great Lakes, and Ohio Valley; Anglo-Celtic ballads from the upland South, country blues from the Mississippi Delta, black and white spirituals from the lowland South, European immigrant music from Italy, Germany, and Czechoslovakia; polka music from the upper Midwest, and Mexican *mariachi* from the Rio Grande Valley.

According to Rogers State University's Hugh W. Foley Jr., an expert on Oklahoma's music, melting-pot features were visible in the development of the state's musical landscape, stimulating experiment and innovation. "Within this Oklahoma cultural mosaic, music knew no color. Black, white, and red musicians borrowed freely from each other, exchanging repertoires and musical ideas, and adopted new techniques and styles." Two bands that would set new standards in popular dance music were born in Oklahoma: Walter Page's Blue Devils in 1925 and, eight years later, Bob Wills's Texas Playboys.

Jimmie Lunceford was always reticent about his past and his personal life. The Lunceford family never set much value on diaries, scrapbooks, or any such records. Even musicians who worked under the man for many years had to admit they did not really know him. Accordingly, we do not have much information about his early years. We do know that his main interests were sports, aviation, and music. Jimmie's earliest musical experiences in all probability were his mother's organ playing and the singing in the Baptist church. He also heard the occasional brass band in the streets, and the blues songs drifting from the bars and brothels lining Oklahoma City's Second Street, such as Rushing's Café. Jimmy Rushing, the son of owner Andrew Rushing, was trying his hand at the piano and the violin during the period when Jimmie Lunceford started dabbling with the guitar and the banjo.

Second Street, a few blocks north of Bricktown (the entertainment district in today's Oklahoma City), was known in vernacular as "Deep Deuce." Apart from Rushing's Café, major venues in the Deep Deuce area were the Aldridge Theater, where all the big shows played, Slaughter's Hall, home of the dance orchestras, Ruby's Grill, Honey Murphy's, and Halley Richardson's Shoeshine Parlor. Second Street would eventually develop into one of the most prominent black entertainment strips west of Kaycee's Twelfth Street and east of L.A.'s Central Avenue.

It is possible that Jimmie heard Hart A. Wand, a white violin player active in Oklahoma City during the 1910s, who won a place in history by having copyrighted one of the first songs with the word "blues" in it, *The Dallas Blues,* beating W. C. Handy and his *The Memphis Blues* by just two days.[3] It is not unlikely that Jimmie also saw some of the traveling medicine and vaudeville shows that were popular all over the South at this time, and which featured singers, dancers, and their accompaniment.

James Riley insisted that his sons and, later, his grandchildren, attend church regularly. He also impressed upon his descendants the virtues of good education. His grandson Al recalled,

My grandparents really pushed education to me, they used to brag of me all the time. Because I can remember them telling people, "Watch Al spell this." I was only two or three or four years old, but I would spell. That was the tool they had—was education. I mean, you must have education. And I can see where it truly did me some good, you know, what I have done, in my endeavors in my life. It all goes back to really my uncle Jimmie and my grandparents. Every year, uncle Jimmie would always send me a United States Saving Bond because he wanted me to be sure to go to school and go to college. It was a twenty-five-dollar bond, sixty-dollar bond, back then. I ended up giving it to my father, so he could buy a car.

James Riley and Ida had two more sons besides Jimmie: Cornelius, or "Connie," Jimmie's junior by two years, who would move to New York and become road manager of Jimmie's fledgling dance orchestra after Connie had finished his own studies at Fisk University, in 1931. Later he became a teacher. A third brother, Al's father, appropriately christened Junior, was born in 1921. According to Jimmie, Junior was "a gifted piano player."[4] After studying at the Dana School of Music and Youngstown State University, Junior went into the music business on a part-time basis, playing piano and saxophone. Junior led bands in and around Warren, Ohio, where he and his family lived with his parents. He wrote arrangements for, among others, his big brother's orchestra. For a living, he worked as a sales serviceman at Alcan Aluminum.

Back in 1876–77 the so-called Reconstruction era had been concluded with the election of Republican congressman Rutherford B. Hayes to the presidency. Hayes gave the white man's fear and hatred toward blacks free reign by withdrawing the protective northern troops from the South. In 1889, just four years before Jimmie Lunceford's birth, the first of a long string of race riots erupted, coloring the former Confederate states red with black blood. The lull between the end of the Civil War and the beginning of the officially endorsed "separate but equal" doctrine had lasted a little over thirty years. From the 1890s on, racial segregation was the new line of thinking in Washington, giving local legislators the formal backing to start segregating all kinds of facilities. In 1910, the City Council of Baltimore approved the first city ordinance designating the boundaries of black and white neighborhoods. Its example was followed by Oklahoma City and seven other cities. The new line of thinking also encouraged white southern segregationists to disregard any law whenever a black man was suspected of a criminal act.[5]

In response to the rising number of riots and lynchings, Dr. W. E. B. DuBois, the leading African American writer and commentator, called a conference, and in July 1905 thirty prominent black militants met to discuss racial matters. The gathering became known as the "Niagara Movement," and it led directly to the formation, four years later, of the NAACP (National Association for the Advancement of Colored People). In every issue of *The Crisis*, the NAACP's monthly, its editor DuBois reported the lynchings and the riots, and wrote blazing editorials.

There is little doubt that an upwardly mobile man like Jimmie's father read either *The Crisis* or the Chicago-based *Defender*, the two most widely circulated black periodicals. In its heyday, *The Crisis* sold close to one hundred thousand copies each month,[6] and the *Defender*'s circulation was even larger; "in an era of rampant illiteracy, when hard labor left Afro-Americans little time or inclination for reading Harvard-accented editorials, the magazine [*The Crisis*] found its way into kerosene-lit sharecroppers' cabins and cramped factory workers' tenements," wrote David Levering Lewis, adding that "in middle-class families it lay next to the Bible."

Because he reached so many homes, DuBois had a huge influence on how both educated and common black people thought and acted. The Lunceford family was no exception. DuBois even was to play a direct and painful role in Jimmie's personal life.

Born in 1868 in Great Barrington, Massachusetts, William Edward Burghardt DuBois was of "Hudson River Dutch" and "New England Puritan" descent, with a dash of Bantu blood acquired along the way. DuBois was, even by WASP standards, extremely well educated. He held a bachelor's degree from Fisk University, a master's and a doctorate from Harvard, and had completed his education with two years of postdoctorate studies at the University of Berlin, Germany. With degrees in history and sociology, he wrote about a great variety of subjects, including the pan-African movement, women's suffrage, and Japan's victory over Russia in the 1904 territorial war (which, he declared, set an example for all black people), and he was the author of the *Encyclopedia of the Negro* (1933–45). His best-known work was *The Souls of Black Folk* (1903), a collection of essays about the condition and the future of the former slaves. He taught Greek, Latin, economy, history, and sociology at various universities, and the establishment of higher education facilities for African Americans was an issue he never tired of writing and arguing about.[7]

Educational issues would play an important role during Lunceford's later life. He would also develop clear-cut ideas about racial matters and, more specifically, the black man's image. However, as a young man his interests were far less political.

Sports played an important role during Jimmie Lunceford's high school years. Like most of his fellow students, he was fascinated by the achievements of heavyweight champion Arthur John "Jack" Johnson, the first black superhero. Jimmie became an avid boxer, in addition to running track, and playing football, basketball, and baseball.

Jimmie also took notice of developments on the dance floor. In 1911, the tango was all the rage in Paris. It was at the local Café de Paris that a couple of struggling professional dancers, Vernon and Irene Castle, witnessed the new dance craze and decided to take it to New York. "Castle is an acquired taste," wrote one critic, "but once acquired, his fantastic distortions and India-rubber gyrations exert a decided fascination."[8] In a matter of months, Manhattan's socialites were gathering at the Castle House School of Dancing, desperate to master the new steps.

The Castles are also credited with the popularization of the fox-trot, a dance so simple that in the Western world it soon became the standard movement on the dance floor. During intermissions, James Reese Europe, the black leader of Castle's house orchestra, used to sit down at the piano. His improvisations on *The Memphis Blues* and other slow tunes intrigued the dance teachers, and together the Castles and Europe designed a new step to fit them. (Some sources say vaudeville actor Harry Fox actually "invented" the new step for his act at the New York Theatre.) The fox-trot proved to be an even bigger hit than the tango: around 1915, when their popularity was at its peak, Vernon and Irene Castle were able to command $4,500 for a personal appearance. By that time "Castle" had become a brand name, the entertainers able to license it to a great variety of manufacturers and entrepreneurs.[9]

The success of the Castles and their syncopating Society Orchestra inspired countless others to start their own modern dance ensembles. One of those was Art Hickman, a native of San Francisco, who assembled a group of musicians in 1915, including two saxophone players, thereby laying the foundation for the swing bands of the future.

In 1915 the Lunceford family moved to Denver, where James Riley landed a job as a janitor, and it was at their house on Ivanhoe Street that Jimmie spent his high school years. In Denver, Wilberforce J. Whiteman—father of the future "King of Jazz" Paul Whiteman—became Jimmie's music teacher. The elder Whiteman was the conductor of the Denver Symphony and, from 1894 on, the director of music education in the local public schools as well. A grant from a Maecenas had enabled him to buy instruments and to start building a choir and an orchestra in the public schools of Denver. At this time Jimmie was already seriously involved in the guitar, and had tried his hands at several woodwinds, the violin, and the trombone. It was Whiteman who introduced Jimmie Lunceford to the fundamentals of music, including harmony and counterpoint, and during his high school years the young musician mastered an incredible array of instruments: trombone, clarinet, the complete saxophone family, violin, and piano, in addition to guitar and banjo.

Figuratively speaking, Wilberforce Whiteman was father of two future kings: Jimmie Lunceford was crowned "King of Syncopation" by Fats Waller, when the former started to make his mark on the music scene in the mid-1930s. By that time Wilberforce's son Paul was the world's highest-paid dance band leader and already known to the general public as the "King of Jazz." Another one of Whiteman's students, tuba player Andy Kirk, was also destined to become a famous jazz bandleader. Whiteman's influence is all the more remarkable considering his personal distaste for jazz. In his old age, he was asked by a reporter what he thought of his son's music.

> When it comes to "swing music," you can have my portion. I have always been addicted to frank speech, and I say plainly that I do not like swing or jazz or ragtime or whatever you choose to call it . . . they say swing started with the savages back in the wilds of darkest Africa. As far as I am concerned, they can have it right back. I am not a jungle chieftain, and I don't see why I should have to listen to jungle music any more than I have to eat jungle food.[10]

Despite his old-fashioned tastes, Whiteman Sr. was noticeably popular with young people in Denver. According to Paul Whiteman, "Every kid in Denver was crazy for a trombone or a French horn. In Denver you weren't a sissy if you played music." Yet there was no local music scene to speak of. The sole full-time black dance orchestra in Denver was led by violinist George Morrison. In early 1920, Jimmie made his professional debut as an alto saxophone player at the local Empress Theater with the nine-piece Morrison Jazz Orchestra.[11] Up to then, sports had been Jimmie's first love, and music a mere pastime. The balance had tipped after his experience as saxophonist in an amateur ensemble, one year earlier. "I trained him right here in this house in rehearsals, when he first started playing engagements with me," remembered George Morrison, forty-two years later.[12]

Morrison, a graduate of Columbia Conservatory of Music (Chicago), also played guitar, and wrote the arrangements for his band. He once had applied for the position of concertmaster of the Denver Symphony, but even praise from Fritz Kreisler, one of the most famous violin soloists of his time, was not enough to earn a black man a post such as this. Pragmatically, George Morrison decided to start a dance band.

The Morrison Jazz Orchestra was in existence from before World War I until after World War II and consequently became the longest-running big band in the Southwest. The orchestra was a favorite in Wyoming, Utah, and New Mexico, and it toured extensively, from Mexico to Canada, and from California to New York.[13] The leader told historian Gunther Schuller about his early influence: "At that time I was so very fond of the Art Hickman band out at the Fairmont Hotel in San Francisco. He never did come to Denver, but I heard his records."[14] George Morrison was the featured soloist in his Jazz Orchestra. The leader, who had worked his way up from playing crude dances at mining camps to Denver's elite parties, offered a varied repertoire: light classical music (showcasing his violin), popular songs of the day, ragtime, folk, show tunes, and sentimental ballads, all played in a gentle two-beat style. Sideman Andy Kirk later recalled that the band sounded a little stiff: it played sweet music, but with a beat. George Morrison explained,

> We had arrangements, of course—simple arrangements. I helped to make the arrangements and all the boys—together—we worked them out. We never wrote them down, just talked about them— what we call head arrangements. Whatever riffs came to mind we'd work out right here in this room. The other players too, like the trombone player, they'd occasionally take solos on tunes like *Dardanella* and *Royal Garden Blues* and *Ja-da*.

Traces of Morrison's musical approach, repertoire, and rhythm popped up later in Lunceford's own style. The former played syncopated versions of light classical works by Ruggiero Leoncavallo and Henri Vieuxtemps; the latter used compositions by Riccardo Drigo and Jules Massenet as a basis for saxophone showcases. Morrison's book contained perennial favorites *After the Ball Is Over*, *Silver Threads among the Gold*, and *Darktown Strutters' Ball;* these were comparable to such Lunceford recordings as *Jealous*, *Down by the Old Mill Stream*, and *Swanee River*. George Morrison's *Just a*

Dream is, however, not the same tune as *You're Just a Dream*, recorded by Jimmie Lunceford in 1939. (And neither one is related to Big Bill Broonzy's comical blues song *Just a Dream*.)[15] Announcing a 1946 dance ("Overflow Crowd Expected at Library Aud, Wednesday, to Hear Lunceford"), the *San Antonio Register* stated, "Masters of swing and sweet tunes, the [Lunceford] orchestra is also equally famed for torrid tempoed tunes as well as waltzes and rhumbas."[16] There is, however, no evidence that the Lunceford band ever played waltzes, and the only Latin-tinged tune it recorded was the 1939 *Shoemaker's Holiday*, a Sy Oliver arrangement on a bolero rhythm.

George Morrison's regular base during the early 1920s was the Empress Theater, 1615–21 Curtis Street. The Empress was primarily a movie theater, but it occasionally hosted other events as well, such as boxing contests. In December 1925 it was destroyed in a fire.

For many years, the Morrison orchestra was also the house band for the so-called Million Dollar Trip, an annual journey by train from Denver to Cheyenne, Wyoming, home of the largest rodeo in the world. The leader remembered,

> I have played that job, sponsored by the *Denver Post*, for fifty years. I remember when it started in 1912, we would carry four coaches, and one baggage car, and probably 150 men on the train, all guests of the founders of the *Denver Post*. There were about fifteen girls, and food and drink, and my band, made up of about six or seven pieces in one car. And we played, and the guests would dance with the girls. Then it grew each year. And soon we had 150 girls, and we'd have two baggage cars. And that augmented my band to fourteen pieces. And I'd direct both bands, one in each baggage car, going from car to car, playing all the way from Denver to Cheyenne.[17]

A remarkable number of Morrison sidemen later became bandleaders themselves: in addition to Lunceford, Jelly Roll Morton, Sonny Clay, Andy Kirk, and Johnny Otis. For a while, Alphonso Trent was Morrison's piano player, after Trent had dissolved his own big band. None of these sidemen became as famous—and as rich—as the band's vocalist, Hattie McDaniel. But that was later, when she had become a star of the silver screen.

Whenever Morrison faced two jobs on the same day, he hired extra musicians and commissioned either Andy Kirk, saxophonist Leo Davis, or Jimmie Lunceford to lead the other dance. Jimmie made his first, hard-to-find recording with Morrison's Jazz Orchestra in New York for Columbia on April 2, 1920. The issued title was *I Know Why*—not the same tune as the better-known Glenn Miller song, of course. *I Know Why* was put on the flip side of a Ted Lewis single. A second selection, *Royal Garden Blues*, was not issued at all. The same thing happened to two numbers, *Jean*, and, again, *Royal Garden Blues*, that the band recorded for RCA Victor, eleven days later.

The orchestra had traveled to New York to be part of a big show that was being prepared for a European tour. But when Morrison learned that he was supposed to be just one of the featured acts, and would not headline the show, he lost interest in the enterprise and did not go overseas. During the band's stay in New York it played a six-week engagement at the Carlton Terrace, at 100th Street and Broadway. This was Jimmie's first taste of the big city. By this time, Harlem had become a large black neighborhood, with music everywhere. It had not yet been discovered by the white downtown elite. Among the Harlemites, dancing, gambling, and whoring were favorite pastimes. Jimmie Lunceford, the seventeen-year-old country boy, liked what he saw, heard, and smelled.

A VERSATILE VARSITY MAN

If you don't come from Fisk, you ain't nothing.
—Anonymous musician

Urged by his parents and bandleader George Morrison, Jimmie Lunceford left for Nashville in 1922 to enroll at Fisk University, one of the oldest and most prestigious black educational institutes in the United States. After living in Denver, where both the mayor and the state governor served as Grand Dragons in the Ku Klux Klan, the liberal atmosphere at Fisk must have appealed to the freshman.[1] Right from the start, he immersed himself in an astonishing variety of varsity activities, among them the establishment of a small campus dance orchestra.

When Jimmie went to Fisk University, the Luncefords moved to Warren, Ohio. There his father purchased a three-thousand-dollar house on Oak Street, in the southwestern part of town, where a lot of Finnish people were living. He started working for the Halsey Taylor Corporation, a company that manufactured drinking fountains. James Riley also became an active member of the local Grace AME Church, where he led the choir.

People in Warren got used to the sight of James Lunceford riding his over-sized bicycle down Oak Street.[2]

"I can remember some of the other big bands coming through, like Duke Ellington. I mean, they would come to my grandparents' home and stuff, cause of Uncle Jimmie," his nephew Al said, adding, "The house is still standing. Now it is in a bad neighborhood, I mean, I don't go much down there anymore, because it's become such a bad neighborhood. The matter of fact, they've gotten so bad, I had to get my parents out of there because of worry about the drugs and stuff."

Fisk University was founded in 1865 under the auspices of the American Missionary Society, the Western Freedmen's Aid Commission, and the U.S. Bureau of Refugees, Freedmen and Abandoned Lands. The founding fathers were all white and included Reverend Erastus M. Cravath, who would become the first president, Reverend E. P. Smith, General Clinton B. Fisk, head of the Kentucky-Tennessee Freedmen's Bureau, Professor John Ogden, and businessmen Nelson Walker and Richard Harris. At the end of the Civil War, in response to the sudden demand for the education of the free blacks, they pooled sixteen thousand dollars of their personal resources to purchase a former Union army hospital in the vicinity of Nashville. The barracks were transformed into classrooms, and by October 1865, the Fisk Free Colored School had opened its doors. Two years later Fisk was chartered as a true university, and in 1872 Fisk became the first African American college to receive a class "A" rating by the Southern Association of Colleges and Secondary Schools.

Fisk University has always been associated with liberal causes and the arts. It produced noted thinkers and artists, such as W. E. B. DuBois, scholar James Weldon Johnson, Sen Katayama, the Japanese revolutionary, singer Roland Hayes, painter Aaron Douglas, and pianist Lil Hardin, who later married Louis Armstrong. But not all was rosy: the fact that the school's board was white became a source of resentment. In 1911, student protests broke out against the discharge from the school of twelve black teachers. In 1924–25, students came out against what they saw as suppression on the part of university president Fayette McKenzie, whom they called "Tsar" and "Tyrant." In response to demands by sponsors, McKenzie had developed a policy of suppression. The students forced the end of segregated concerts by the school choir and dances featuring the campus orchestra (led by Jimmie Lunceford), they demanded the end of restrictions concerning dating and even talking between male and female students, and they insisted on the restoration of the student parliament and return of the *Greater Fisk Herald,* the campus magazine. After an eight-week student strike, the revolt resulted in the resignation of McKenzie.

From the beginning, financial problems plagued Fisk's administration. Funding its building program proved to be nearly impossible. Coincidentally, George L. White, the first head of the Financial Department, happened to be a voice teacher as well, and shortly after the opening of Fisk he started a Sunday school singing class, from which he selected the best voices to build a small choir. At first, the eleven singers, six male and five female, were known as A Band of Negro Minstrels Who Call Themselves Colored Christian Singers. They soon changed the name to Fisk Jubilee Singers.

The spring 1867 debut of the Fisk Jubilee Singers marked the first time African American music in any form was publicly presented (not counting the contents of black minstrel shows, or the even earlier singing at the so-called Great Awakening gatherings). The reception was favorable, so the following year, another recital was staged. These successes at the campus prompted White to develop a plan whereby the singers would tour and help raise money for the university's building program. On October 6, 1871 the Fisk Jubilee Singers embarked on their maiden voyage. The choir was an almost immediate success. Invitations poured in, and the singers' fame was firmly established when they took part in the World Peace Jubilee at the Boston Coliseum in 1872, on the occasion of the end of the German-French war. About one hundred thousand spectators watched a massive two-thou-sand-man band, directed by the renowned conductor Patrick S. Gilmore, which accompanied twenty thousand vocalists. But disaster loomed when the mammoth orchestra started *The Battle Hymn of the Republic,* also known as *John Brown's Body.* The song was played too high for the vocalists, which left the first verses virtually impossible to sing. At that moment, the young men and women from Fisk broke away from the choir and saved the day. "Every word rang through the great Coliseum as if sounded out of a trumpet. The great audience was carried away with a whirlwind of delight," noted one observer. "Men threw their hats in the air and the Coliseum rang with cheers and shouts of 'The Jubilees! The Jubilees forever!'"

The choir's repertoire consisted of religious songs and secular material, such as *Home, Sweet Home, Old Folks at Home,* and even *An der Schönen Blauen Donau.* At this early stage, no recordings could be made, but from contemporary reports one can conclude that the choir's approach was essentially European rather than African American. Still, a Boston newspaper reported that the songs were "rendered with a power and pathos never surpassed." Some of the spirituals were genuine compositions; others had gradually emerged as collective creations, so to speak, comparable to the head arrangements of the big bands to come. The Fisk Jubilee Singers introduced songs such as *Steal Away, Swing Low, Sweet Chariot,* and *The Bells,* which have become standards.

In 1873 the singers' reach was extended considerably when they sailed to England. This tour lasted for about a year, and other European trips followed. Through these exhausting voyages, the Fisk Jubilee Singers raised a total of over $150,000 for the university's building program. On July 6, 1878, the group gave a farewell concert and subsequently disbanded, but one year later George White and bass singer Frederick Loudin decided to reanimate the choir. This time, it no longer had any formal connections with the university.

Several configurations of Fisk Jubilee Singers kept touring and performing both in the United States and Europe for the next decades, and other schools and churches followed Fisk's example, establishing touring choirs. The emergence, in the early part of the twentieth century, of gospel quartets and quintets was largely due to the efforts of the Fiskites.

There is little doubt that Jimmie Lunceford's stay at Fisk deeply affected his character. Taking music and Spanish as minor courses, he enrolled in the sociology department, the discipline that had enabled his spiritual role model, W. E. B. DuBois, to write his epochal studies of the history and the fate of the black man. DuBois's influence can be measured from the number of students in Fisk's sociology class, the largest one in the entire university. Sociology drew two and a half times as many students as the next largest department, education. During the 1924–25 unrest, students had broken windows and furniture, chanting the name of their hero: "DuBois! DuBois!" Seven months later, DuBois addressed the president, the trustees, students, and alumni in the university's chapel, and had thundered, "I have never known an institution whose alumni are more bitter and disgusted with the present situation in this university."[3]

According to DuBois's theory, the "Talented Tenth," the cultural elite, was destined to lift its brothers and sisters out of their ignorance, despair, and humiliation. This elite was supposed to excel in the arts and science, thereby establishing role models. "Progress in human affairs is more often a pull than a push, a surging forward of the exceptional man, and the lifting of his duller brethren slowly and painfully to his vantage-ground," Du Bois wrote in *The Souls of Black Folk,* adding that "it was not enough that the teachers of teachers should be trained in technical normal methods; they must also, so far as possible, be broadminded, cultured men and women, to scatter civilization among a people whose ignorance was not simply of letters, but of life itself."[4]

However, even the national General Education Board had serious misgivings about the establishment of higher education institutions for African Americans, arguing that the black man "should not be educated beyond his environment." The prevailing idea was that blacks were unfit for abstract thinking, and that the best way to educate them would be to create opportunities to become bricklayers or carpenters. By the time he graduated, with a bachelor's degree in sociology, Jimmie Lunceford was one of just twelve thousand black students in the entire country—out of a total population of about eleven million black Americans.

The curriculum of Fisk's sociology department encompassed courses in the Principles of Sociology, Practical Sociology, the Methods of Social Care Work, the Problems of Negro Life, and Advanced Practical Sociology. The textbooks included studies by noted scholars such as Lester Ward *(Applied Sociology)*, Arthur Bowley *(An Elementary Manual of Statistics)*, and Mary Ellen Richmond *(Social Diagnosis)*. Sociology, Richmond pointed out, is at the root of all social work. She was raised by her grandmother, who was a radical suffragist and a spiritualist. Domestic discussions about these topics, racial problems and liberal religions, social and political beliefs, formed the basis of Richmond's intellectual development. Jimmie Lunceford, who was not an outgoing personality himself, may have felt empathy with this withdrawn, shy scholar, who suffered years of poverty and rejection, and was known to prefer the companionship of books over people.

Arthur Bowley's book gave the students in general, and Jimmie in particular, serious headaches. Sir Arthur Bowley was a mathematician. His *Elements in Statistics*, published in 1901, was the first such textbook in the English language. Bowley strived to quantify all economic parameters and developments. In later years he attempted to compute the British national income, and conducted one of the first empirical studies of consumption behavior.[5]

As a music student, James Lunceford attended classes in Elemental Theory, Music Appreciation, Music History, Sight-Singing and Ear-Training, and Methods of Public School Music. Given his interest in the black cause, he probably attended the Negro Music and Composition class as well. Students were expected to be present at all recitals given at the university. They were to study the lives of the major composers and the various musical styles and genres, "the latter illustrated by use of the Victrola and player piano." Music Notation and Terminology, Child Voice, and Conducting also were subjects in Lunceford's curriculum.

Books to study included *Essentials in Music History* by Thomas Tapper, and *What We Hear in Music*, by Anne Shaw Faulkner. Faulkner's work was subtitled *A Laboratory Course of Study in Music History and Appreciation for Four Years of High School, Academy, College, Music Club or Home Study.* Published by the Victor Talking Machine Company, this was in fact an educational catalog and graded list that accompanied classical Victor 78 rpm albums. The series eventually ran from 1913 to 1943. Faulkner was regarded as an authority on both classical and folk music, and since she wrote monthly columns for popular magazines such as *Better Homes and Gardens*, the *Ladies' Home Journal*, and *Child Life*, her influence was significant. In 1921, she joined the international discussion about the merits and dangers of the new dance music called jazz in an article for the *Ladies' Home Journal*, titled "Does Jazz put the Sin in Syncopation?" Faulkner was clear about the origins of jazz music:

> Jazz originally was the accompaniment of the voodoo dancer, stimulating the half-crazed barbarian to the vilest deeds. The weird chant, accompanied by the syncopated rhythm of the voodoo invokers, has also been employed by other barbarian people to stimulate brutality and sensuality. That it has a demoralizing effect upon the human brain has been demonstrated by many scientists.

Her definition of jazz in this article was "that expression of protest against law and order, that Bolshevik element of license striving for expression in music." And so her answer to the question raised by the headline was a heartfelt and unequivocal yes.

Lunceford was, no doubt, influenced by noted music pedagogue Karl Wilson Gehrkens, three of whose books he had to read. Gehrkens stated that "teaching is an art and the teacher must be an artist to succeed in the classroom."[6]

In order to make ends meet at Fisk, Lunceford applied for a job as pianist in the house band of Nashville's Andrew Jackson Hotel. There he fell victim to a case of stage fright for the first time in his life. One night he noticed with horror that his fingers had grown stiff; he had no idea what he was playing and only knew that the band was on a completely different track. Shamefully, he chugged along until somehow he and the band teamed up again, which gave him a feeling of utter relief. After the set he went to the bandleader to apologize. "I'm sorry for not having been able to follow the band during the first half of the first fox-trot," he stuttered. "Oh, don't worry," was the answer, "I followed you during the second half— you played in three quarter time, and the whole band had to adjust to you, since you did not notice."[7]

After working with the hotel band on Saturday nights, Jimmie quite often had to content himself with a short night's rest, for on Sunday mornings he used to lead the choirs in Nashville's largest black churches. He was a true chip off the old block: he had often watched his daddy directing his choir in Warren.

At this time developments in aviation kept stirring Jimmie's imagination. Back in 1910, the first "Air Meet" at Dominguez Field, near Los Angeles, had drawn between 250,000 and 500,000 spectators, and was hailed by the *Los Angeles Times* as "one of the greatest public events in the history of the West."[8] The subsequent air war over western Europe furthered general interest in aviation, and the adventures of "Lieutenant" (or, when the occasion called for it, "Colonel") Hubert Fauntleroy Julian, M.D., the most famous black aviator during the 1920s and 1930s, were widely publicized. "M.D," by the way, stood for "Mechanical Designer." Julian's parachute jumps over Harlem were the talk of the town, and his attempt at crossing the Atlantic, even though it turned out a dismal failure, made him a folk hero among African Americans.

While he had to delay his yearning to become a pilot for almost twenty years, Jimmie invested a lot of time and energy in his other love, sports. We do not have a record of his athletic achievements prior to 1925, the year the *Greater Fisk Herald* resumed publication. But when it reappeared, the magazine called Lunceford one of the sharp shooters of the university's baseball team, a fielder "with bullet-like arms." An analysis of the 1926 team revealed that "the staff will be built around the battle scarred 'Piggy' Lunceford, server of submarine slants." He was an excellent football player as well. In the *Herald*, "Piggy" (Lunceford himself insisted his nickname was spelled "Piggie," not "Piggy") was singled out as one of "four of the most remarkable individuals (Bragg, Lunceford, Perry and Harris) to be found on college floors. All have been members of the same class team for three years, which should give them the added inestimable advantage of teamwork." Lunceford was awarded "F" for his achievements in football during the varsity year of 1925–26. (Contrary to the usual university grading system, an "F" in sports was synonymous with excellent.)

In December 1925 James M. Lunceford was elected as president of the university's Athletic Association. Charles S. Lewis portrayed him in the *Herald:*

In the fall of 1918 [actually 1922!] a man who addressed even the lowly preps as "Mister," and answered "Sir" to the aforementioned preps, appeared on Fisk campus. He was as green as the grass on Jubilee lawn and thought that senior classification was only one step short of the "Happy Hunting Grounds" unattainable except by the chosen few. But with courage born of a desire for the best, humbleness born of a realization of distance between himself and his goal, with a supple body and an active brain and a smile that never wore off—"Piggy" began to go forward. Truly he had the possibilities of a good fellow, a good man. My first years in Fisk recalled, I can see the musical, gymnastic, mentally active "Piggy." I see a conglomeration of summersaults, basketball, handsprings, flips, hash-slinging, and the U.L.S. [Union Literary Society] Club. I can hear the Bennett Hall Orchestra—a terrible aggregation—prep French, English "10"—and Piggy Lunceford.

Lewis gave an account of young Lunceford's other activities: member of the Extempo Club, Mozart Society, Glee Club, captain-elect of the varsity football squad, baseball team, track man, president of the class of 1925, coauthor of the *King of Uganda* revue, headwaiter, and leader of the Fisk Orchestra. The writer concluded, "Lunceford has always given his best. Versatility was and is one of his strong qualities. Fisk could choose no wiser, nor give herself more honor than by choosing and honoring one of her favorites. His energy and fire, his honesty and loyalty, manliness and strength all guarantee an honest administration."

The very first act of the newly elected president was tossing a field goal in the very first minute of the basketball match between the Tennessee State Collegians and the Bulldogs clad in Fisk's gold and blue. Fisk won that first game of the intercollegiate basketball season 39 to 14. One week later, the Fisk Bulldogs beat Walden College; Lunceford, John Harris, and Captain Bragg were praised and dubbed the "Three Musketeers" by the *Herald*'s Walter P. Adkins. The Tennessee State College team tried to rehabilitate itself in a return match two weeks later. To no avail—the final score was even more humiliating: 41 to 11. Of the team's forty-one points, thirty-nine were scored by the tried-and-true team of Harris, Bragg, and Lunceford. "A big house was out to see the old machine run away with the game," commented Adkins, "State College started like a house afire, but the pace that kills soon took them under as before. The Bethlehem Center was the scene of the carnage, and the date was January 30." In the next issue of the *Herald*, Lunceford's abilities were put in perspective, in a review of a match against Simmons University. Again, the gold and blue won—six out of a total of nineteen points were scored by "the versatile Jimmy Lunceford."

The March 6, 1926, match against Roger Williams College was saved by Piggie. "The Fiskites play their best when there is an audience, but this time spectators were scarcer than fast trains in Arkansas. Roger Williams took advantage of Fisk's apparent drowsiness and ran up three baskets and a foul making the score: Roger Williams, 11; Fisk, 8. Soon the dependable Jimmy Lunceford rallied and saved the day for his faltering team-mates, running up nine points," wrote Walter Adkins. The final score was Fisk 17, Roger Williams 14. Even when Fisk occasionally lost, as was the case in a game against Howard University, one week later, Lunceford stood out, as the review by Walter Adkins demonstrated: "Lunceford, jumping higher than the well known cow that jumped over the moon, batted in a pair of baskets. . . . The end of the great Fisk rally came when the gong sounded as Lunceford worked the ball under the basket for a set-up shot."

That 1925–26 season, the Fisk Bulldogs scored 213 points, their adversaries a total of 132, and James Lunceford was awarded another "F." Along with baseball, football, basketball, and track, Jimmie also excelled at boxing. According to Russell Green, Lunceford's trumpet star during the mid-1940s, Jimmie at one time won the lightweight championship in Tuskegee.[9]

Lunceford's presence and proficiency in the classroom, the gym and onstage did not go unnoticed. There were, in all probability, more than a few female students who watched the tall young man with more than a fleeting interest. One of these fellow students was Nina Yolande DuBois, the only daughter of Dr. W. E. B. DuBois.

Before her tenure at Fisk, Yolande had been a student at an English prep school. Apparently, she had not inherited her father's intellectual gifts: her grades were mediocre, and she was much more interested in Fisk's social life. As the president of the Decagynian Society, the university's female students club, she was responsible for a pageant in March 1923. There Nina Yolande DuBois fell for the lanky, dark sociology student with the tiny mustache and the smiling face, who conducted the orchestra for the pageant.[10] She also knew he was as strong as a bear, could outrun just about everybody, and was a fast pitcher. Before long, the whole campus buzzed with the news: "Have you heard about Yolande and Piggie? They' like glue!" Before long, even Harlem matrons started to gossip over their tea about DuBois's daughter and her boyfriend, who was her junior by two years.

Her father was not amused. In *The Souls of Black Folk* and *The Crisis* he had written about the arts, notably spirituals, literature, and the theater. In his vision, the arts were a potent force in black emancipation. So any form of art had to have a message; it had to reflect the *condition humaine* of the black man. To his mind, sports or syncopated dance music did not qualify. DuBois had condemned Claude McKay's explicit novel *Home to Harlem*, remarking, "After the dirtier parts of its filth I feel distinctly like taking a bath."[11] In a letter to the editor of *The Crisis* McKay wrote, "nowhere in your writings do you reveal any comprehension of esthetics, and therefore you are not competent to pass judgment upon any work of art."

In the public eye, DuBois was anything but a frivolous, outgoing fellow. When Claude McKay first read *The Souls of Black Folk*, the book shook him "like an earthquake." However, meeting the author turned out to be a disappointment for McKay: "he seemed possessed by a cold, acid hauteur of spirit, which is not lessened even when he vouchsafes a smile. Negroes say that Dr. Du Bois is naturally unfriendly and selfish. I did not feel any magnetism in his personality."[12] A stiff, formal man, devoted to his work and the black cause, Du Bois as a rule did not partake in Harlem's nightlife. Trumpeter Buck Clayton's mother was a civil rights crusader, and as a young boy he came in contact with DuBois, when the latter stayed at the Claytons'. "I considered him to be a real hero and I was fascinated by his beard guard that he would put on every night to keep his beard neat. Every morning when he would arise his beard was just as neat as it was when he went to bed," recalled Clayton.[13]

"I am not taking Jimmie very seriously," Yolande's father wrote in one of his letters to his daughter. The student-bandleader, not yet twenty-one, might develop into "a fine man but that is yet to be learned. Nothing is more disheartening and idiotic than to see two human beings without cultivated tastes, without trained abilities and without power to earn a living locking themselves together and trying to live on love."

It is difficult to overestimate the effects of DuBois's rejection on his daughter's sweetheart. Here Jimmie was in love, deeply, madly, deliriously, with the daughter of his and everybody's hero—only to be rudely embarrassed. It left a bitter spot in his heart and fueled his determination to show his worth to the whole world and Dr. William Edward Burghardt DuBois in particular. Though Jimmie and Yolande met only sporadically after they left Fisk, they never forgot their romance. According to David Levering Lewis, biographer of the elder DuBois, "Lunceford was Yolande's enduring passion, the man about whom she would spend much of her life dreaming, wondering how different things could have been if they had married." That feeling was reciprocal. Many years later, Yolande's daughter met the bandleader backstage at Baltimore's Royal Theater. She was allowed to finger the keys of his saxophone, and told David L. Lewis, "Tears came down his face like you wouldn't believe, and he said to my mother, she should have been mine." Jimmie Lunceford, who, seven years after his affair with Yolande, would marry Rose Crystal Tulli, a fellow Fisk graduate, never had children.

In April 1928 Yolande stepped in the spotlight when she married Countee Cullen, one of the most distinguished poets of the Harlem Renaissance movement. Though Cullen was his daughter's junior by three years, this was an engagement W. E. B. DuBois wholeheartedly approved of. Cullen's first poems had already appeared in *The Crisis* and had met with critical acclaim. The groomsmen at the wedding included Harlem Renaissance luminaries Arna Bontemps and Langston Hughes. The marriage at the time was viewed as a fairy tale of the new negritude. "Not since the convening of the Estates-General at Versailles at the eve of the French Revolution had such a rainbow of hats, bonnets, feathers, and gowns, waistcoats, jewelry, and gleaming footwear been seen," wrote David L. Lewis. Yet the state of matrimony was unhappy and short-lived—Cullen was homosexual.[14] Ironically, within six years, Lunceford, the rejected lover, was gaining international acclaim, while his rival's star was already on the wane. "Cullen has faded away, true, but he may return someday," an optimistic Lewis commented.

Nevertheless, Lunceford's acquaintanceship with DuBois's daughter had put him in touch with most of the major characters of the Harlem Renaissance. When he met Yolande, this new tide of black novelists, poets, and artists in Harlem, "the colored capitol of the world," was still gaining momentum. The position of the black man in the United States was of great concern to black leaders. Only two generations back, the vast majority of black people were still living in slavery. In the years right after the Civil War, the future had looked uncertain, yet full of promises, but life had turned into a nightmare well before the century was over. If "the Race" could ever foster any hope for improvement, the opinion leaders argued, it had to prove that the black man was equal in every respect to the white man, and to show that the latter's loathing and fear of black people were a result of ignorance and superstition. That was the general consensus among black intellectuals. So on March 21, 1924, black upper-middle-class sages, including DuBois, Charles S. Johnson, and Alain Locke, met with a group of influential black and white editors, liberals and philanthropists at a dinner party in New York, an event that became known as the Civic Club Gathering. At the time, the Civic Club was the only prominent New York cabaret where race or gender restrictions were nonexistent. This meeting resulted in a stream of articles and books, triggered by prizes and awards, which drew massive attention to the new young black artists of America.[15] Arna Bontemps, for instance was "twenty-one, sixteen months out of college, full of golden hopes and romantic dreams." He had resigned his job in the Los Angeles post office in order to move to New York, "God willing, to become a writer." He remembered,

> We were shown off and exhibited and presented in scores of places, to all kinds of people. And we heard their sighs of wonder, amazement, sometimes admiration when it was whispered and announced that here was one of the "New Negroes." Nothing could have been sweeter to young people who only a few weeks or months earlier had been regarded as anything but remarkable. In Harlem we were seen in a beautiful light. We were heralds of a dawning day. We were the first-born of the dark renaissance.[16]

Though African American music, theater, and dance had proven their universal appeal and influence for decades, the Harlem Renaissance leaders emphasized literary activities. Probably those involved realized that the majority of the American public considered music and dance "low," even "lewd" activities, unless these forms represented the European tradition. For his part, DuBois cared only for art that was functional. "I do not care a damn for any art that is not used for propaganda," he wrote in *The Crisis*.[17]

Jamaica-born poet Claude McKay was skeptical about the movement.

> Each one wanted to be the first Negro, the one Negro, and the only Negro *for the whites* instead of for their group. Because an unusual number of them were receiving grants to do creative work, they actively and naïvely believed that Negro artists as a group would always be treated differently from white artists and be protected by powerful white patrons.[18]

In retrospect, it seems that only Langston Hughes, with his fine, jazzy sense of rhythm and his bold use of meter, Sterling Brown, who incorporated blues forms and everyday street expressions in his poems, and perhaps a small handful of other poets were the true innovators, the true original black voices. The majority of the Harlem Renaissance poets and novelists, though young in years, merely represented and continued older—European-American—traditions.

Meanwhile, Jimmie's student orchestra played at the Fisk campus as well as around Nashville for door money, or tips. Among its members were, at one time or another, saxophonist Willie Smith and pianist Edwin Wilcox, who were to become key figures in Lunceford's future professional orchestra. Nothing is known about the orchestra's repertory. It probably consisted of stock and head arrangements (scores that one could order from a music publisher and arrangements that were devised on the spot, respectively), with possibly a few originals added, penned by Wilcox and Lunceford. In 1923, during the summer vacation, the school band played an engagement at a hotel in Belmar, New Jersey; the following year, it performed in a ballroom in Ashbury Park, a larger city on the Atlantic seaboard. These summer jobs paid well and spurred the musicians to think of music as a career. Though we know hardly anything about the orchestra's whereabouts during its existence, these undertakings suggest that Jimmie Lunceford was endowed with entrepreneurship, and that his dance band had already attained a semiprofessional level.

At Fisk University, Jimmie, a Kappa Alpha Psi member, developed from a shy country boy into a composed and dignified personality. Here he formed his standards for moral and social behavior. As a modern-day

Renaissance man, he also expanded his capacity for sports and music, quenched his thirst for knowledge, and learned about organizing a band of men, whether an orchestra or a sports team. One embittered musician later commented on Lunceford's attitude: "If you don't come from Fisk, you ain't nothing."

Yet Jimmie Lunceford was not satisfied when in the spring of 1926 he graduated as a sociology major. There was, he realized, still more to be learned.

DOWN AND OUT IN CLEVELAND

There's two beats missing.
—Jimmy Crawford

After graduation, Jimmie Lunceford went east for one year of postgraduate studies at New York City College, and there he refined his knowledge of pedagogy and business. During his college vacations, he worked in various local bands, respectively led by John C. Smith, Wilbur Sweatman, Elmer Snowden, Deacon Johnson, and, according to some sources, Fletcher Henderson. It is interesting to note that Sweatman three years earlier had led a dance band that became the nucleus of the Washingtonians, Duke Ellington's first ensemble. With Snowden Lunceford worked at the Bamville Club, in a lineup including Bubber Miley on trumpet, Glyn Paque, Castor McCord, and Lunceford, reeds, either Count Basie or Claude Hopkins, piano, Snowden, banjo, Bass Hill, bass, and Tommy Benford on drums. Before Basie joined the band, Lunceford alternated on piano and trombone.[1]

Having finished his studies, and after an abortive attempt at forming a band of his own, in 1927 Jimmie set out for Memphis, where he applied for the quadruple post of English, Spanish, music, and athletics teacher at Manassas High School, one of the two black schools in the city. Since his clothes were shabby, the white board of education entered the interview with some misgivings. The board soon discovered that the interviewee was a fast and eloquent talker, and that his knowledge and views surpassed their own. So from that year on, James M. Lunceford taught at Manassas and was the school's football coach. At the time, Manassas High had between eight hundred and a thousand students, a number that would eventually grow to three thousand. The school is still at the same location, though back in the 1940s the old stucco building and the wooden cafeteria were replaced by a new complex.

The main problem the new music teacher faced was the same that most black schools had to deal with: the lack of instruments. There were, for instance, four potential saxophone players, yet not one single usable saxophone, apart from some antique models with keys that either leaked or were stuck. One or two parents were able to buy instruments, and some kids delivered newspapers until they had gathered the money.

The teacher soon became friends with a local alto player by the name of John Williams, who was leading a band featuring his young wife Mary Lou on piano. John and Jimmie spent a lot of time playing checkers. "Usually John won the games, but Lunceford used to say he'd get a band and beat John with that. He was forever kidding about building up a combo that would make us look sick," Mary Lou Williams later recalled. "Jimmie went ahead, and we had to admire the way he taught the young musicians in his school."

When John received a telegram from orchestra leader Terence Holder in Dallas with an offer to join his band, Williams in turn asked Lunceford to sub for him, working under Mary Lou, who was his junior by eight years.[2]

Lunceford proved to be an adroit organizer, and pretty soon the Manassas school orchestra was a reality. It varied from fifteen to twenty students, who played various horns and percussion instruments. The orchestra performed at school functions and the usual dances and recitals in town. Graduation celebrations were held at nearby Gospel Temple Church on North Manassas, three and a half blocks south of the school. That is where the school's yell "Manassas, Manassas, ra-ra-ra!" sounded. At that time, there were no other school bands in Memphis, apart from an all-female drum-and-bugle corps.

During the 1920s, Memphis was a great town for jazz, blues, gambling, and dancing. Beale Street was jumping around the clock. "There was jazz in every Beale Street doorway," according to Lunceford, who added, "I can't say very much about Beale Street and its jazz places because I had little opportunity to visit them. Being a school teacher, it wasn't considered dignified for me to visit such spots, much to my regret, except on very rare occasions."[3]

The Mississippi waterfront was the location for various steamers and their dazzling bands. These included Eddie Johnson's brass-oriented Crackerjacks from St. Louis, flashy drummer Floyd Campbell's eight-piece outfit, and the Alphonso Trent Orchestra from Dallas. "There were few dance halls in those days," Lunceford explained. "The river boats were the main outlet for jazz and that's where you'd really hear it." Trent's dance orchestra at the time was considered the best in the Southwest. It had no trouble battling better-known bands, among them Fletcher Henderson's and Casa Loma.

The phenomenon of band battles in all probability had its origin in New Orleans, in the early years of the twentieth century. Bands used to advertise their appearances playing on trailers, and when two (or more) ensembles met in a street, they proceeded to "cut" one another. The audience was the final judge: its applause determined the "winner." Promoters soon realized the publicity value of these encounters, and before long they started to stage them. During the swing era, a couple of band battles gained near-mythical proportions, such as those between Chick Webb and Benny Goodman; Chick Webb and Count Basie; Lucky Millinder and Charlie Barnet; and Lionel Hampton and Louis Jordan. Reputations were indeed made and broken during the course of these relentless swing struggles. The name and fame of the bands were really at stake. It was also a matter of personal pride and honor. Consequently, musicians doubled their efforts, and managers and leaders sometimes resorted to the meanest kind of tactics and tricks in order to beat their opponents. None of these numerous musical fights were ever recorded.

Alphonso Trent's recordings prove that he had an attractive, smooth, yet strong style. They did not tell the full story, though. "Everybody who really heard that band talks about how great they were, even though the records could never do them justice because of the inferior quality of recordings in those days," maintained pianist Sammy Price, who as a sixteen-year-old Charleston dancer worked with Trent.

There was, in other words, both a great cohesion and a powerful drive in Trent's band, which, together with sophisticated voicing, gave it a modern touch. This must have appealed to Lunceford, who was also impressed by the band's comedy skits, its vocal trio—which sang in unison—and by the way the musicians dressed. He praised soloists Stuff Smith, Snub Mosley, and Hayes Pillars. In retrospect, Smith remarked, "When we played in Memphis, Lunceford used to come and stand right under the band, and that was when his band was still in college." In 1928 Alphonso Trent's outfit battled drummer Floyd Campbell's band, fronted by Louis Armstrong, on the steamer *St. Paul*, near St. Louis. Some five thousand dancers rocked the boat until it all but capsized, and it had to limp back to the quay in order to prevent disaster.

Generally speaking, the 1920s were a prosperous time for dance bands, and Trent's musicians did even better than most. In salary and tips, the earnings of the sidemen sometimes amounted to seventy-five dollars a night, an unheard-of sum at the time. Only musicians in white top bands made such fortunes—in a week. The Dallas stars drove Cadillacs, wore silk shirts and camel hair overcoats, and played gold-plated instruments. In the 1947 edition of *Esquire's Jazz Book*, Jimmie Lunceford wrote that "Trent's band gave inspiration to more young musicians than any other." The most daring charts were penned by Trent's trombone player Gus Wilson.[4]

Prominent musicians in Memphis at the time included Charles Holmes, who played saxophone and trumpet, trombonist Charley Hunt, and trumpeter Johnny Dunn, who was the first to "growl," and who would later gain fame in Europe. The trumpet was the most popular instrument in Memphis, probably on account of both Dunn's and Joe "King" Oliver's work: "Our local musicians would make regular trips to New Orleans to hear Oliver and were greatly influenced by his style," the teacher wrote. "Jazz was very big in Memphis, and I included jazz in my teachings to cover all phases of music. At Manassas we had a very modern and broad-minded principal, who was in full accord with everything constructive. In short order my students were picking up jazz in great fashion, so well, in fact, that we organized a jazz band at the school."[5]

Some of Trent's originality, the clever use of dynamics, and the fine-tuned cohesion, especially in the reeds, rubbed off on Jimmie Lunceford and his new dance band. Snub Mosley, who played in Trent's trombone section, gave Jimmie one of his band's arrangements to copy. Jimmie's old boss from his Denver days, George Morrison, also had sent in some charts.

The students called themselves the Chickasaw Syncopators, after Chickasaw, the black neighborhood where most of Manassas's pupils lived. (Scutterfield was the other area from where the school drew its students.) The Chickasaw are a Native American tribe, who originally inhabited northern Mississippi and Alabama. The independent, aggressive spirit that characterized the tribe probably appealed to Lunceford and his pupils. The Chickasaw's inclination to provide shelter for black fugitive slaves might also have been part of the reason for this tribute. And, lastly, Itawamba County, where Lunceford hailed from, had been Chickasaw land originally. His family, like the Chickasaw, had made the trek from Mississippi to Oklahoma.

Jimmie Lunceford taught his students jazz history, dance band harmony, dynamics and blending, the use of mutes, how to build a solo, and rhythm. He used a Victrola to have them analyze how other, well-established dance orchestras performed. In all probability, the teacher also had Arthur Lange's new book *Arranging for the Modern Dance Orchestra* at his disposal. It had been published in 1926, and was an instant success: within a year it was already in its tenth printing.

In 1927 Lunceford was one of the world's first, if not *the* first to teach jazz at a school. He beat cellist, conductor, and teacher Mátyás Seiber, who is generally credited with developing the very first jazz course, at the Hoch'schen Konservatorium, in Frankfurt am Main, Germany, by one year. While working in ocean liners' orchestras, Seiber in the mid-1920s had heard American jazz, and subsequently incorporated what he had experienced in his *Jazz-Klasse*.[6] It would take New York City's board of education another ten years before it invited popular musicians, ranging from Rudy Vallee and Wayne King to Duke Ellington and Benny Goodman, to conduct courses on swing music in local high schools.[7]

One of Lunceford's students was Annie "Baby" White, who played piano and guitar. Later she got a job at Piney Woods Country Life School in Mississippi, where in 1937 she was instrumental in forming a legendary all-women jazz band called the International Sweethearts of Rhythm. In the 1940s this big band would develop into the finest female swing orchestra in the States. Its style was a combination of the respective musical approaches of Lunceford and Erskine Hawkins—the latter's Bama State Collegians were more blues-oriented. During this period, Eddie Durham, who had worked for Lunceford as trombonist, guitarist, and arranger, became the Sweethearts' musical director.[8]

Another Lunceford student and early band member was Dickie Hopson, who would later train aspiring musicians at Douglass High School, in the northeastern part of Memphis. Eventually, they would form the Dozen Swingsters, for a long time the only regular black dance orchestra in the city, once the Chickasaw Syncopators had left Memphis.

Lunceford, who was popular with his students, staged annual spring revues, which featured his pupils in acting and dancing roles, and had them sing the popular Tin Pan Alley tunes of the day, such as *Tea for Two* and *Tiptoe through the Tulips*. "I would rate him very high," said pianist Kathryn Perry Thomas, who, like her brother, saxophonist Andrew Perry, studied under Lunceford (she still plays the latter's 78 rpm records on an old phonograph that has to be cranked).

The skill of those musicians was just perfect. I'd rate him high in the land as a great professor of music. Sure would. Because the crescendos and all that, you know, beautiful music. Beautiful music. You see, I would call a man of that stature, a man of more than one talent. And that is, being able to give to the youth a sense of direction in life, you know what I mean. He was patient, a hard worker. For him to build up an orchestra as he did, I would call that a very high achievement. And being able to teach sports, both those talents reached out to the youth, to the young, and built up the desire to become what they did become. If you are a teacher, you work hard to bring out their talents and character. He used psychology to build these fellows to achieve what they wanted to do. That's a whole lot.

Tuba and string bass player Moses Allen and drummer Finas Newborn were members of the early dance band. The pianist was a young woman named Bobbie Brown, and Lunceford played the alto saxophone. Within a matter of weeks, the band had grown into eleven pieces, Newborn was replaced by Jimmy Crawford, and on December 13, 1927, the Chickasaw Syncopators made their first recordings. The lineup of this primeval Lunceford orchestra was Charlie Douglas and Henry Clay (trumpets), H. B. Hall (trombone), Lunceford, George Clarke, Christopher Johnson, and Allen Williams (reeds), Brown (piano), Alfred Kahn (banjo), Allen (tuba), and Crawford (drums). They recorded two originals, *Chickasaw Stomp* and *Memphis Rag*, both probably composed and arranged by the leader. Stylistically, the two sides do not differ much from what other jazz-oriented dance orchestras were playing during the late 1920s—although the band at this stage still sounded amateurish, playing out of tune. This was hardly surprising, since the Syncopators at the time of the recording had been in existence for just two or three months. Still, there are points of interest. Moses Allen's preaching vocal on *Chickasaw Stomp* was a novelty. The music teacher played alto and soprano sax on these titles—he is heard in a piercing solo in *Memphis Rag*.

"He would do some arranging, Jimmie would, hand it to us and we would make it out and everything," band member Allen Williams recalled.

> One time a fellow in the band kept on playing his part wrong, Jimmie rode him pretty hard, then he snatched the music off his rack and threw it on my rack and said, "Play that for him, Allen." I played it, I transposed it. He [Lunceford] said, "you mean to tell me you can transpose tenor music on an alto!" I said, "yeah, I can transpose any kind of music on any kind of instrument, as long as it's a reed."

Clearly, Allen Williams was ahead of the rest of the students, since he had received intensive training from Professor Hunt, a local music teacher, and had played in the Knights of Pithas Brass Band. He was the first one to leave the Chickasaw Syncopators, in 1929. Williams had to go to the hospital to have his tonsils taken out, and he did not come back.[9]

"All the bands in Memphis in those days ranged in instrumentation from five to nine pieces at most," wrote Jimmie Lunceford. "There were no vocals in those bands, with one exception, Alphonso Trent's band, which had a couple of its members doubling on vocals. With my first band, I had the largest in the entire South, eleven pieces. We also did the first radio broadcast from a night club or ballroom in Memphis when we were at the Silver Slipper."[10]

Drummer Jimmy Crawford was not a great soloist, not in the class of a Chick Webb or a Buddy Rich. Nor was he an innovative drummer, devising new rhythms or accents or whole concepts, like Kenny Clarke or Jo Jones would. For the Jimmie Lunceford band he was the perfect anchor man, though. His timing was rock-steady: whenever the band recorded two takes of a song—it seldom required more than two—the difference in duration rarely was over one second. He could also slightly retard or speed the band to build climaxes. Crawford, known by the band members as "Craw," was a master of dynamics, and he could roll his drums to thunderous effect. He was an ideal section man. As a teenager, clarinetist Buddy DeFranco first saw Craw with the Lunceford band in a Philadelphia theater, when an uncle ("he was a fan") took him and his brother to go hear it. "You wanna hear a band really do something, this is it, this is the Lunceford band," had been his recommendation.

> My brother and I had the habit of going to different theaters around Philadelphia, where the big bands were playing. They would play five shows a day. We'd stay all day. One show after another, and just listen. Fifty cents, sixty cents. Sometimes we'd bring a sandwich along, sat there for the whole day, watch all the shows. He [Crawford] was not only one of the best rhythmic drummers, but he could influence this feel, the feeling of the band. And he was the greatest showman. He was marvelous to watch. I actually loved to go to stay at the theater, and watch the stage shows of the Lunceford band. You could spend a whole concert or a show, watching Jimmy play the drums. He would throw the sticks in the air, behind him, do all sorts of fancy things, but never, never ever missed a beat. Maybe the closest I can remember of the feeling would be Sid Catlett.

Didn't Lionel Hampton take after Crawford, juggling his sticks and showing off? "Yes, he had it. But Hampton was a little coarse. Jimmy Crawford was positive, smooth, his technique was a wonder to watch. And of course, there again, that deep-seated feeling that made people dance to the band, gave it a swing appeal, and half of that emanated from Jimmy at the drums."

Jimmy Crawford was the band's spark plug in more ways than one: his contagious happy shouting spurred both his fellow musicians and the dancers to great heights of abandon and expression. In a couple of early Lunceford recordings, Craw is heard hollering in the background. This band clearly liked its work.

The secret of swing lies in timing, in the way the musician's personal beat interacts with the rhythmic pulse. Timing gives life to rhythm, so to speak. Crawford's timing was impeccable. The typical Lunceford timing was slightly behind the beat. This almost imperceptible difference between, say, the rhythm in one's head and the one in one's body made it impossible not to tap one's foot from the moment the band played its first bar.

Like so many musicians, Jimmy Crawford got his start in an amateur band of youngsters. His aunt used to take him to the local Palace Theater, where he saw the stars appearing on the TOBA circuit. (The Theater Owners Booking Association, or TOBA, was an early booking office for black talent, which catered to a large theater circuit, mainly in the South.) The Palace pit band accompanied artists such as blues singers Ma Rainey and Bessie Smith, and the comedy team Butterbeans and Susie. Young Jimmy was duly impressed by the drummer, Booker Washington, who had a theatrical way of playing, throwing his sticks twirling in the air, shooting pistols, blowing horns, and a host of other musical antics.

At seventeen, Jimmy was in Lunceford's large school orchestra at Manassas High. He told writer Stanley Dance, "I was always interested in drums, of course, but I was just too poor to own a drum outfit, and whoever was well enough off to afford a set of drums played in the band. I borrowed one of the school horns, a peck horn, just to be in the band. When eventually the drummer left, the school acquired drums, and I sat behind them." Crawford stayed in the Chickasaw Syncopators, which evolved into the Jimmie Lunceford Orchestra, until, tired of the endless traveling, he finally left in 1943.

When in 1933 Sy Oliver became the staff arranger, Crawford had a hard time getting adjusted to the two-beat feel Sy wanted. The drummer thought it was old-fashioned, corny. "What's wrong with this two-beat thing, man," Sy would ask. "Well, there's two beats missing, that's all," was the invariable reply.[11] But before long, Craw's two-beat rhythm became one of the trademarks of the orchestra.

It is important to note that around this time, the early 1930s, the general trend in jazz was away from the old two-beat rhythm. The changes in the rhythm section, from the tuba and the banjo to the more agile double bass and the guitar, was responsible for a shift towards a more even four-four rhythm.

The orchestra's two-beat rhythm even prompted certain record stores to file its discs under the heading "Dixieland"! Writer Barry Ulanov regarded the typical Lunceford bounce as "the most effective utilization of two beat accents discovered by any jazzman; it made a kind of impressive last gasp for dying Dixieland, with its heavy anticipations, its almost violently strong and whisperingly weak beats, its unrelenting syncopation."[12]

Their conflicting ideas about the usage of 2/4 or 4/4 meters caused Sy and Jimmy to have quite a few rows. Jimmy felt that when he really turned loose in 4/4 during the middle part of the number, which felt like doubling the tempo, it was no use getting back to 2/4 for the finale. However, they always made up after the rehearsal or the show.

An important asset of his drum kit was a twenty-five-inch Chinese sizzle cymbal that seemed to contain all the sounds, shadings, and effects any percussionist could ask for. Craw used to hammer his fellow band members into high levels of commitment during the ride-out chorus of a number. The outcome, according to bass player George Duvivier, a fan of the orchestra, could give one goose pimples. He compared listening to the band to "breathing pure oxygen."[13]

Crawford had a sharp eye for the needs of both the dancers on the floor and the chorus line. In a letter to Stanley Dance he wrote, "I could tell when the band had the crowd in their hands, so I would holler to Lunceford between two numbers, 'don't quit now! We have 'em! And don't call trash like *White Heat* or any other flagwavers! Just call medium-tempo numbers, because we're ahead now and don't want to be unjointed!' "[14]

Crawford's idiosyncratic style did not go unnoticed by other drummers. Butch Ballard worked in trumpeter Cootie Williams's band, later graduating to Count Basie and Duke Ellington. He remembered his colleague well: "Everything was right there. Jimmy Crawford's laying that two-four beat, you know" (he demonstrated this by clapping his hands and singing enthusiastically), "and coming out of that two-four, and going to four—*ooh-ooh-ooh!* And the walls come tumbling down. Oh man, that Crawford was a tremendous drummer." Art Blakey was another admirer of the Lunceford bounce: "That beat! You know, that tempo, ways of tempo. That's hard to do. I tried it, but they got something masterful about it. It's that tempo." He shook his head, still amazed after all these years. "*Hm, hm, hm!* Not too fast, not too slow. Just right. They were masters at that."

The Chickasaws got their first press notice February 4, 1930. The *Chicago Defender* wrote, "The Chickasaw Syncopators ply their art in and around Memphis, Tenn., where they have built up a fine reputation. They broadcast over stations WMC and WREC, Memphis, and also play at the Hotel Chisca and the Memphis Country Club. During the coming summer they plan a tour with the orchestra. In the combination are 11 musicians, who all sing and double on different instruments."[15]

During the summer vacations they indeed used to venture further in the country, and by now the students could pay their college tuition from the money they made playing. The orchestra got its first semi-professional break as early as the summer of 1928. Dr. Crow, a Memphis physician, whose children were Lunceford's students, owned a dance hall in Lakeside, Ohio, and invited the school band to entertain his clientele. Apparently the engagement was a success, and the following summer the doctor asked them back for a fourteen-week engagement. Pianist Brown and trombonist Hall couldn't keep up with the pace and were replaced. The leader went off to Nashville, to his old alma mater, and recruited reed player Willie Smith, first, and pianist Edwin Wilcox, next, who had been freshmen when he was a senior and had played in his first band at Fisk. In addition, Smith, who had majored in chemistry, and Wilcox, a music major, supplied the Chickasaws with arrangements. Since jobs for the student band at this stage were not too plentiful, Ed Wilcox, too, took a teaching assignment at Manassas.

As a youngster, Willie Smith had relished studying the clarinet. By the time he was fourteen, he was proficient enough to play recitals, accompanying a coloratura soprano. A bright student and voracious reader, he had skipped several grades, so he was ready to enroll at Fisk University at this tender age as well. At the university he became a member of a campus chamber music ensemble. Through trial and error he learned to improvise. When in 1929 Lunceford wanted to reinforce his band, Smith, who by now played most of the reed instruments, was ready. He had taken some courses in harmony, and with the assistance of Edwin Wilcox he was able to write charts.[16] His preference for music over chemistry was not, however, shared by his parents, who "were very strait-laced people, and they were completely disgusted. To be a saxophone player was about as low as you could get at that time. They didn't allow card-playing in the house, and even after college, I didn't have nerve enough to light a cigarette there."[17]

In *Jazz Hot* magazine, French critic Hugues Panassié compared Smith as a soloist to Barney Bigard (on clarinet), Johnny Hodges (alto), and Harry Carney (baritone). Bigard had been his role model when Willie first started listening to jazz. The critic remarked it was a curious coincidence that this man should resemble Duke Ellington's three great mainstays on three different instruments, adding that he must be rated just as high as them. Panassié elaborated:

> The volume of his sound is phenomenal, it's mightier than most tenor saxophonists'; among alto players I know just one, Benny Carter, whose volume is comparable to Willie's. Willie Smith's playing is powerful to the point that the full orchestra is able to keep on playing fortissimo without overshadowing his solo just once.

Willie Smith, however, suggests both Johnny Hodges and Benny Carter. Like Hodges he has a hard intonation, thin inflections, and certain melodic turns; like Carter he has a sparkling sonority, a poignant vibrato and still other melodic turns. But of all the saxophone players, he is the only one who possesses as voluminous a sonority as that of Benny Carter; and the only one who can make his instrument sing as much. His imagination is no less vast than Johnny Hodges's and Benny Carter's. But what is most astonishing in him is his powerful execution and his indomitable fire. As soon as he gets into a solo he is seized by an impetuousness and a burst of force and ideas. He swings ferociously, far more than either Benny Carter or even Johnny Hodges.

Panassié mentioned Willie Smith's arranging and singing capabilities, and concluded that this musician belonged among the top in hot music.[18]

But Willie's main task was getting the reeds in line. By applying the same rigorous discipline he put on himself, he succeeded in making the saxes sound like one. Breathing, shading, dynamics, everything was consummate. When the reeds played unison, the resulting trademark sound was smooth as butter and huge as a hangar. When the baritone saxophonist played lead, they sounded like a formation of B-9s in a flyby. The leader of the saxophones instilled feelings of pride and craftsmanship in his section. Musicians in other bands mockingly called them "the trained seals," adding that Lunceford's reeds went to sleep dreaming of an extremely difficult etude.

Before long, Smith's standards were adopted by the entire orchestra, and when somebody made a mistake, he actually felt very bad about it. For a while, the musicians had the habit of stamping their feet out of time and hitting the music stands with their derby mutes when somebody goofed, regardless whether they were having a rehearsal or were playing a theater. Eventually the leader had to put an end to this ritual, since it interfered with the band's broadcasts from the Cotton Club in Harlem, where it resided in 1934 and 1935.

Smith was the one who called for endless rehearsals.

The saxophone section used to rehearse all by itself, and we'd play some real difficult music. "Later, for you," we'd tell the brass. We might rehearse just three numbers all day. Started in the morning, go out for lunch, and rehearse all the rest of the afternoon. There was no compulsion about it. We just wanted to have the best saxophone section in the world, and we did have. We worked on it, so it sounded like one guy playing five saxophones. Everything had to be marked, breath had to be taken at the same place, and all the crescendos were rehearsed over and over. So far as worry was concerned, the notes were the smallest part of it. The brass rehearsed in the same way. We'd join up and put it all together the next day. I may be prejudiced in favor of the reed men, but I don't think the brass quite reached our level, although they included some outstanding musicians and great showmen. [Trumpeter] Tommy Stevenson was about the first to start making all those screeches and high B-flats.

Joe Houston was an aspiring saxophone player when he first saw the band. The overpowering impression was that the reeds stood out. The band played the Cotton Club, Eleventh Street in his hometown Austin, "where all the bands played." It was a big ballroom with good acoustics, and little Joe used to go there all the time, practicing his horn. He was allowed to use the sound system of the house band. So he was familiar with the venue, though he had never seen a name band playing the Cotton Club before.

Lunceford, that's my big band, that's my . . . oh man, they used to swing, first band I saw in my life. They would breathe—they had been so long together. They was the greatest band that I ever heard in my life. The reed section sounded like some horses running, they was so close. First time I ever heard a reed section sound—and they played real soft—but they was so *strong*, like when Dan Grissom would sing. I remember it clear as a bell.

Later, in 1951–52, when he led Duke Ellington's reeds, Willie Smith used to upset his colleagues by insisting on regular section rehearsals. This was a regimen unknown to Duke's band. But Ellington's saxes really did seem to shine with a new sparkle, sounding fuller and richer, during the time Willie was in the orchestra.

As a soloist, Willie Smith was a stylist as well. Willie's raucous, yet fluent approach and his big sound were an inspiration for both Earl Bostic and Charlie Parker. "Oh yeah, he told me, he liked Willie," said Joe Houston. "Because I asked him, when I first met Bird, I asked him, 'Who's your favorite cats?' He told me, 'Pete Brown and Willie Smith and Benny Carter.' Those three, he named nobody else." Willie Smith and Johnny Hodges formed a mutual admiration society. Asked which alto players he preferred, Hodges answered, "Oh, Willie Smith. I always did like Willie Smith."[19]

Willie Smith was one of the loudest alto saxophonists in the history of jazz. Lunceford's reeds had no trouble competing with the shouting brass. In fact, Sy Oliver stated, "We brass men have to blow hard not to be outdone by those saxes." Depending on the acoustics of the hall, Lunceford sometimes even had his saxes sit behind the brass, in order to level the band out dynamically.[20]

Though Willie Smith supplied a couple of very interesting arrangements—*Mood Indigo* is a case in point—he later lost interest in writing charts. Eddie Wilcox, on the other hand, became a prolific writer. He probably produced as many arrangements for the band as Sy Oliver. The bulk of the book during the last few years of the band's existence was written by Wilcox. But Sy penned most of the vocal tunes, and those tended to be the successful ones, the ones put on record. That's why Oliver is generally viewed as the architect of the typical Lunceford sound. However, any Lunceford tune with an exceptionally beautiful chorus for the saxophones has to be Wilcox's.

An early hit was *Sleepy Time Gal*, of 1935 vintage. This work can be seen as proof of Wilcox's mastery. It features an adventurous reed chorus that requires the utmost from the musicians. In his study *The Swing Era*, Gunther Schuller remarked that "no modern 'Super Sax' group can equal or top its hair-rising roulades and careening twisting turns. The last chorus offers an early example of the entire orchestra in well-balanced eight-to-eleven-part block harmonies, a seemingly obvious idea but nonetheless at the time still little used (except by the Whiteman orchestra and its arrangers, Ferde Grofé and Bill Challis)."[21]

Wilcox was renowned for writing beautiful lyrical works like this one. This kind of daring, extremely difficult exercise was one of the orchestra's trademarks. In a way, they harked back to the saxophone choirs of the 1920s, when conceptual bands such as the Six Brown Brothers wowed their audiences with their dexterity. Throughout the 1930s and into the 1940s, Paul Whiteman continued to showcase his Sax Soctette in astonishing tours de force.

Even in his first work recorded by the Chickasaw Syncopators, the 1930 *Sweet Rhythm* (the tune's title suggests a manifesto), Wilcox displayed a mature and creative mind. It shows in a nice, lively passage for the muted trumpets, with out-of-tempo bits, and an impressionistic sax chorus. By the time the band made a test recording for the American Record Company, three years later, the self-assurance, the imaginative horn parts, and the compelling rhythms heard on the two sides left no doubt that at this point it was primarily Wilcox who had lent the orchestra its individuality.

Six months before the aforementioned hit record *Sleepy Time Gal*, another remarkable Wilcox arrangement, *Jealous*, was released. Here the arranger surprises with an all but imperceptible passage by the saxes behind singer Henry Wells's part, which follows the contours of the vocal like a shadow. One day later, the orchestra recorded *I'm Walking through Heaven with You*, again with a smooth, clever saxophone chorus. The 1940 remake is even more impressive than the 1934 original. The introduction of the new version is in multi-part harmony, and whispering saxophones provide the background behind vocalist Dan Grissom, soft enough not to overpower the acoustic guitar.

A most unusual trademark of the orchestra was the use of short sign-off ditties. When the band finished a set and wanted the dancers to know it was intermission, the saxophones played a fast, capricious lick of cascading notes, with large intervals, for one or two bars. One would expect that Wilcox was the writer of these brilliant little tags, and maybe he did have a hand in some of them, but Lunceford's musicians tell us they were essentially heads, played without music. Some were based on the structure of existing songs, like *That's All*, others more abstract. It seemed the band had an endless variety of these little gems in stock, and some musicians went to see it specifically to hear those sign-offs. None of them were ever recorded.

Edwin's classical background was responsible for his exceptional way of writing for the saxes. "When he wrote his scores, he wrote them with a pen. He didn't make any mistakes. He was one of the greatest saxophone chorus writers in history," claimed Gerald Wilson, who joined the Lunceford band in 1939 as trumpet player and arranger.

Wilcox had gone to Fisk to study both medicine (at the urging of his mother) and music (his sister's idea). His father, who owned a cotton plantation near Method, North Carolina, offered his son three hundred dollars if he would drop the music and devote his time to agriculture. Instead, Edwin abandoned medicine, eventually graduating with a degree in music.

While at the university, Edwin became interested in jazz by listening first to Fats Waller records, then Earl Hines, James P. Johnson, Willie "The Lion" Smith, and other strong piano players of the period. After he joined the Chickasaw Syncopators, he was assigned the bulk of the writing. He had studied orchestration, harmony, and counterpoint, but "little of it meant anything where dance bands were concerned. It was leveled at the symphony, and the difference is like day and night," he remarked. Working on a forty-eight-bass accordion, Ed discovered various cross-sectional ways to orchestrate, in order to obtain specific sounds. The hardest parts, he thought, were those for the baritone saxophone. He claimed the typical Lunceford style was developed

> between Willie Smith and myself. We didn't really hear bands that gave us ideas. It was what we wanted to do. The melodic quality I had came from studying classical piano. That was how I wanted to sound. If you have a good classical teacher, melodic structure is implanted in you so strongly that even when you find yourself wanting to do something else you don't lose it.[22]

This originality is open to debate: it seems obvious that at least Alphonso Trent was a model for the early Lunceford band. Duke Ellington's influence could hardly have been ignored either, especially after Duke had recorded *East St. Louis Toodle-Oo* and similar tone-poems. But it is true that Lunceford did give his arrangers a free reign; he did not wish to put a specific stamp on the music. This policy proved to be pivotal in the development of the band's unique style.

Wilcox told writer Stanley Dance about a tune arranged by Willie Smith, *Runnin' Wild*. It was in the book for a while before it was recorded, in May 1935. "He wrote the whole arrangement with the pickup inside, instead of outside. He couldn't figure it. He didn't get the downbeat at the right place. We played it all right, but it felt wrong all the way." Apparently, this disgusted Willie so much that he no longer felt the desire to arrange for the band.

In the same year that Wilcox and Smith joined, 1929, Henry Wells, who sang ballads and played trombone, was the next Fisk graduate to become a Chickasaw Syncopator. After Fisk, he had delved deeper into music at the Cincinnati Conservatory.

In late 1929 the Chickasaw Syncopators decided to try their luck and became professionals. Lunceford and Wilcox devised a five-year plan—and whether by coincidence or by plan, 1934 happened to be the year when the orchestra finally struck gold. Jimmie took a ninety-day sabbatical from his school, to be safe. If the entire enterprise failed, he could always fall back on his old teaching job. The provision proved unnecessary. Lunceford never saw the classroom again, at least not formally. Later on, after he had become famous, he used to bring his orchestra over to Manassas every time it played the Beale Street Auditorium. That way the students at Manassas could meet the band members, and ask them questions. And the bandleader would lecture, and exchange pieces of news and gossip with his former fellow teachers and his successor in the music department, Eddie Love.

The first job of the Chickasaws as a professional unit was at the local dance hall of the Men's Improvement Club on Hernando, between Beale and Gayoso, for a fee of fifty dollars. Not fifty dollars per person: this sum had to be divided among the full band. In early 1930, the Men's Improvement Club engagement was followed by a six-week stint at the Silver Slipper nightclub out East, off Poplar. After the Silver Slipper, the orchestra moved into the Showboat in West Memphis.

At the Silver Slipper the band started a weekly radio program for WREC, called the *Beale Street Hour*, "which was broadcast from the WREC studios every Tuesday afternoon from 4 to 5 p.m.," recalled the leader. "This particular program became one of the biggest radio features in the South, and remained on the air for almost ten years after we left Memphis." This called for special arrangements, which were ordered in New York. In the book now were two semi-classical numbers, *Drigonesque* and *Drigo's Serenade*, written by the popular Italian composer Riccardo Drigo. The band ran them down a couple of times in rehearsal before going on the air. Lunceford played the violin part on alto sax and Crawford started it off in waltz tempo, as indicated. At the first ending, Craw erroneously shifted to fox-trot, and the band finally got through the arrangement after much confusion. Lunceford later fondly recalled the outcome. "Well it seemed that our listeners thought the piece was arranged that way and several critics wrote it up as a 'musical innovation.' Guess that was one of the first, if not *the* first, example[s] of change-of-tempo arrangements!"[23]

The inclusion of light classical works in the book was not unusual. It was done by more bands at the time; the Fletcher Henderson and George Morrison orchestras being cases in point. Like his two mainstays, Wilcox and Smith, Lunceford had had a thorough classical training.

Like all bands, the Chickasaw Syncopators from time to time worked with replacements and guest artists. One such musician was trumpeter and composer W. C. Handy, who already was a famous artist at the time. Soon, in 1931, Handy was going to be honored by the city of Memphis with a park that bore his name. In his autobiography he recalled,

> In Memphis the Chickasaw band played for a barbecue and it rained all day. One of the shrewd members of the band figured that we would not get our pay and decided to take his in barbecue without letting us know. Some of the fellows asked him what he was doing with so much meat, but he didn't tell them until after we all got paid. The he tried to sell his meat back to the barbecue man and he got mad at us because we wouldn't buy it.[24]

The Chickasaws were formed to be a cooperative or commonwealth group, after the examples set by the Casa Loma Orchestra, and, as a matter of fact, by many territory outfits. So all proceeds were split evenly and all decisions were made in a democratic way. Pretty soon, the musicians agreed that Memphis was not the ideal base for the band, even though by now the Chickasaw Syncopators had made quite a name for themselves locally. The Syncopators knew their radio broadcasts had carried their name to places as far as Chicago, Cleveland, and even Buffalo. They decided to go north, and thought Cleveland looked good. Among musicians, Cleveland was renowned for its nightlife. Trumpeter Benny Bailey was born there, and he stated, "Cleveland was a place, I mean, you didn't have to have that much money to live actually, you know. There's a lot of broads around. Musicians always look for the chicks, oh yeah, they always made it—waitresses, you know, after the waitresses. Free meals and stuff."

First stop was Cincinnati, where the Memphis musicians met eleven other dance bands that had gotten stranded. The Chickasaw Syncopators survived on odd jobs, finally landing a four-week engagement.[25] Cleveland proved to be the acid test for the band. Although Lunceford was a good businessman, the organization ran into a series of bad bookings and alarmingly long stretches of layoffs. Promoters used to invite the band for so-called tryouts and auditions and, after all kinds of promises, run off with the money, never to be heard from again. To make matters worse, the Great Depression entered its grimmest phase. Local nightlife suffered from a strike of waiters and musicians, and during that winter of 1929–30, the city experienced some of the worst blizzards it had ever seen. On top of that, the depression had created a vogue for smooth, bland bands. It seems that in precarious times, such as a war or a deep economic crisis, people seek shelter and comfort in music that is reassuring, not too extravagant. Blues and hot music, so characteristic of the jazz age, now definitely were on the wane. Bessie Smith suddenly was old-fashioned, and Fletcher Henderson replaced *King Porter Stomp* with *Somebody Loves Me*. In fact, the nation's universities and colleges were the only havens where undiluted hot dance music still prospered. These institutions were fast becoming a major factor in the dance band business: the shortage of jobs stimulated young people to study and to spend more time at school. In the early 1930s the percentage of young adolescents between the ages of fourteen and eighteen who enrolled at colleges rose from fifty to seventy-five.

McKinney's Cotton Pickers, a Detroit band that had hit the big time, were in Cleveland, having themselves a big Thanksgiving dinner, with plenty of food, drink, and women. The men from Memphis, confronted with this temptation, looked on helplessly. Wilcox spotted the bandleader, Don Redman, and wanted to strike up a conversation, just to be able to boast that he had talked to the great arranger. But he was brushed aside by Redman, who told him, "Oh, kid, I ain't got time to talk."

Meanwhile things got worse. The musicians lived in two hotel rooms on a daily diet of a piece of cake and a glass of milk. Rent was constantly overdue, and the men shared two overcoats between them. Whenever somebody happened to secure a little job, he split the money, so they could buy their next piece of raisin cake, or a handful of peanuts. Jimmy Crawford spent his last dollar to see the Fletcher Henderson band. The Chickasaw Syncopators, who by now had changed their name to Jimmie Lunceford and His Tennesseeans, for three agonizing months were down and out. When the folks back home wrote to find out how they were doing, they replied, "Just fine."[26]

Lunceford had been elected nominal leader of the band, since he was the oldest, most respected, and most business-minded man in the group. As there was no manager, the leader was directly responsible for all the bookings, logistics, and promotional work. In *Esquire's 1947 Jazz Book*, Lunceford recalled, "There were no such things as booking offices and agents in those days. The bands booked their own jobs, and, of course, their fees were most nominal compared to the figure a top band commands today. But then, it didn't cost but a few cents for admission."[27]

Stubbornly sticking together, the band survived the hard times, and it is safe to assume that this gruesome experience boosted the mutual camaraderie and musical cohesion. The orchestra's sorry state hadn't interfered with the rigorous practicing and rehearsing schedules. The old school discipline had carried over into the band, and its team spirit became one of the orchestra's trademarks. A musician recalled, "The unity of direction, the togetherness the band essayed, gave a feeling of oneness that is seldom, if ever, found in the bands of today. This band had real personality."[28] Critic Hugues Panassié added: "To me, the urge to use the expressions: the orchestra plays 'like one man' and it is constantly 'gone' was never as evident as with this ensemble. One would have a hard time finding the slightest imperfection. Jimmie Lunceford's orchestra may be the only one that is giving its best all the time. Never does one get the impression that the musicians try really hard to get 'in the groove.' They're right there, without trying, so to speak, and all the time."[29]

The orchestra continued its grueling string of one-nighters and badly paid engagements along the shores of Lake Erie, ending up in Buffalo completely broke. But fortune at last smiled on them when they landed a four-week engagement at the local Hotel Vendome. As a rule, the Vendome presented local talent. Tenor saxophonist Joe Thomas worked there—he had not yet joined the Lunceford band. Stuff Smith, Jonah Jones, and Helen Humes all were regulars.

Returning to Memphis, the Lunceford band recorded once more at the local Civic Auditorium, for RCA Victor. On June 6, 1930, *In dat Mornin'* and *Sweet Rhythm* were waxed. On these sides one hears an orchestra that already makes a tight impression, and sounds fuller than the earlier outfit. Especially the reeds, probably Lunceford and Willie Smith, altos, George Clarke, tenor, and Christopher Johnson, baritone, sound pure and silky. Yet these performances on the whole still are largely interchangeable with the styles of most other bands at the time. The inclusion of Moses Allen's tuba and Alfred Kahn's banjo was responsible for a slightly dated flavor, though Lunceford had devised an integrated, orchestral, and modern-sounding role for the tuba. In *In Dat Mornin'*, the tuba plays both in counterpoint and in harmony with the brass, and Moses's mock-ecstatical, roaring vocal in that tune, a reworking of his earlier effort in *Chickasaw Stomp*, shows an astonishing breath control. This tune can be seen as a tongue-in-cheek reference to the gospel influence in American secular music—an influence that was to grow stronger and stronger in the years to come.

Bassist Gene Ramey, who witnessed the ensemble in its early stage, said that "Lunceford's rhythm section was very good, too, and with their two-beat rhythm they were the first movement towards the churchy feeling."[30]

It has been suggested that the alto soloist in these two 1930 titles might be the leader himself. There does not seem to be enough evidence to support this claim. The altoist is more likely Willie Smith, who at this time was still under Johnny Hodges's influence. Anyway, the record sales boosted the band's morale, and justified the decision to go pro. "We didn't return to Memphis until 1934 when we came in for a one-night stand at the Clark Park Auditorium for $500, a far cry from our first engagement for $50," noted Lunceford.[31]

{4}

SHADING WELL

The sharpest band in the world.
—Joe Houston

By the fall of 1930, the band was beginning to catch the attention of young black dancers all over the Midwest. The *Pittsburgh Courier* headlined "Lunceford And Bunch Sensation," and continued,

> Oct. 2—Jimmie Lunceford and his Tennesseeans, reputed to be the latest sensation out of the South, are touring the country and are making a big hit wherever they appear.
>
> The orchestra, composed of 11 college boys every one of whom is a master with his instrument, have "sold" themselves to the Middle West and Ohio.
>
> The orchestra recently played a number of engagements in Cleveland and so well did they register that after their first appearance capacity crowds were the order of the day.
>
> The orchestra at present is in this city [Cincinnati] and are proving satisfactory.

Following their Ohio engagement they are scheduled to appear in several large Pennsylvania centers before they invade New York.

One enthusiast, commenting on the caliber of the orchestra, declared they would be as big a sensation in a year as any of the larger bands now touring.[1]

It would take another three years before the New York invasion finally materialized. But in the spring of 1931 the musicians decided to try their luck once again in Buffalo, at the time a town teeming with bars, dance halls, and gambling places. They worked their way to Buffalo via Louisville, Indianapolis, Cincinnati, Dayton, and Toledo. In Cincinnati they played a six-week run at the Green Mill.

In the course of this last engagement the Lunceford men ran into the Speed Webb Orchestra, which led to their first band battle. Over the years, the Lunceford crew took part in a number of these collisions, and though it won the majority of them, there were a couple of close shaves and even defeats. At this early stage, Lunceford's Tennesseeans were no match for the more seasoned Speed Webb organization. Teddy Wilson, Webb's pianist, claimed their orchestra was comparable to the early Basie band. Among the name bands the Speed Webb Orchestra battled and conquered were McKinney's Cotton Pickers and Cab Calloway's unit.[2]

Lunceford managed to find a booking agency in Buffalo that could back the orchestra financially. A couple of important changes in the lineup were made while the band played a six-week return engagement at the Vendome Hotel in May–June of 1931. Trumpet player Paul Webster, who had joined the band earlier that year, had left the organization temporarily. His replacement was Jonah Jones, who had been working with a local quintet. Jones remembered this early experience: "This was before Sy [Oliver]. I joined when Doug was there, Charlie Douglas I think, plus another guy. It was the three of us. Henry Wells played trombone—there was just one trombone. In a later stage he [Lunceford] hired my brother-in-law, my wife's brother, who got the second trombone chair—Russell Bowles." The addition of Bowles released the leader from his occasional need to strengthen the brass on trombone when Wells had to sing his chorus.

"I was always fighting because we never made any money," Jonah Jones continued. "But you just wanted to play in a band. It didn't make any difference whether you made something or not. However, there came a day that I had to say, 'I can't make it any longer, I can't pay my room, I gotta go.'"

By that time, the summer of 1931, Jones had learned how Lunceford used to keep his men in line. Every now and then, a member of the audience would express his or her appreciation for a certain musician by handing him a bottle of liquor. In such cases, the lucky fellow was obliged to show the gift to the leader, who decided just how much the man was allowed to drink. In some cases, the sideman got nothing.[3] This procedure was not entirely without reason. Willie Smith, for instance, developed a serious drinking problem, one that was to haunt him for the rest of his life.

After Jones's departure, Jimmie tried to lure him back, telling him he had a feeling the band was going to make it. But Jones decided to go with violinist Stuff Smith, who had a job. He came to regret his decision, though. "The next thing I knew . . . those cats were in the Cotton Club, broadcasting nightly over the radio, and I was up in Buffalo, monkeying around for peanuts and no fame. . . . Was I sick!" he told *Down Beat* magazine.[4]

By the late 1930s, the Lunceford spell (cast by precision, harmony, and a two-beat bounce) had become virtually inescapable for a major part of the country's swing bands. But according to one source, as early as 1931, four years after the start of the Chickasaw Syncopators, they had made their mark on the Blue Ribbon Syncopators, a popular band in the Buffalo area. The incessant rehearsing of the Tennesseeans and the appearances at major local venues such as the Hotel Vendome apparently rubbed off. The Blue Ribbon Syncopators had recorded for Okeh and Columbia, in 1925 and 1927, respectively. The fact that the former Syncopators from Memphis had put their stamp on their brothers in Buffalo indicated that by now the Lunceford band not only had acquired professionalism, but also a degree of individuality. It is a pity that due to the deepening depression, the Blue Ribbon Syncopators did not enter the recording studio again after 1927, so there is no evidence of Lunceford's influence.

All through the varsity year 1931–32, the band commuted between Fisk University in Nashville and the Hotel Vendome in Buffalo. The leader had decided that a college education was indispensable for his musicians. He obtained a job as instructor and had nine of them enroll at the university. For a while Jimmie waited tables to help his pupils out financially. The job held no surprises for him, since he had supported himself as a waiter while still a student.

During a 1932 tour, two more college men entered the orchestra ranks. Lead trumpeter Eddie Tompkins, who replaced Douglas, and Earl Carruthers joined in Kansas City. Both men had already gained experience

with the renowned Bennie Moten Orchestra. Before that, the new trumpeter had studied at Iowa University. Willie Smith remembered Tompkins
as "one of the best first trumpet players I ever heard. At that time, if you
took a first-trumpet part away from a first-trumpet player, he was insulted
and ready to fight you. Nowadays, they say, 'well, you play this, while I get
my chops straight, and the other guy can play that.' Eddie Tompkins
played first parts all night."[5]

Jock "Earl" Carruthers, like trumpeter Paul Webster a Fisk graduate,
played the baritone saxophone. Before him, Christopher Johnson had
played the baritone in the band. To a certain extent, the baritone was still a
novelty, since at that time only Duke Ellington used it on a regular basis. It
would take another ten years before the bari finally found a permanent
place in the reed sections of the swing bands. Carruthers's role with Lunceford was roughly comparable to Harry Carney's pivotal position in Duke's
organization. Lunceford's arrangers put Jock's deep, sonorous "voice" to
good use, giving the band an extremely powerful bottom. Sometimes,
when both Carruthers and Smith played baritone, the band was liable to
tear up the floor. On the other hand, when Earl switched to the alto saxophone, the reed section took on a wonderful airy quality.

An important addition to the Jimmie Lunceford Orchestra was Joseph
Vankert Thomas. Joe Thomas had started out on alto saxophone in a local
band in Columbus, Ohio. In 1929, just nineteen years old, he had jumped at
the possibility of becoming a professional musician when pianist and
arranger Horace Henderson, Fletcher's brother, was in the city, in need of
an alto man. Joe was the proud owner of a Hudson Super-Six; this spacious
automobile may have helped in getting the job. After about nine months of
working in the Philadelphia–New York area, the Henderson band got
stranded in Buffalo. For two years Thomas stayed there, working with violinist Stuff Smith at Club Harlem. During the summer months, Thomas
played on a boat that cruised the Great Lakes. Its ports of call included Buffalo, Detroit, and Duluth. As a member of drummer Guy Jackson's band he
switched from alto to tenor. Jimmie heard Joe in early 1933, during the final
engagement of the Lunceford orchestra at the Vendome, which had
become the band's virtual home base.

Jimmie Lunceford admired Joe from the start. The tenorist's energetic,
soulful style appealed to the bandleader, and he did not hesitate to ask him
to join his own dance orchestra, where Joe replaced George Clarke. A
handicap was that Joe Thomas didn't read music, which had escaped his

new boss's attention. At first, Joe tried to fake his way, rambling through the notes, hitting and missing them as he went. Willie Smith was a tough section leader and wouldn't put up with sloppy part playing. So although Joe was a fine hot soloist when he joined the band, with Smith sitting next to him, his reading naturally got better.[6] Smith, Wilcox, and Lunceford were three of a kind: they believed in perfection.

Joe's first recorded solo was in *Flaming Reeds and Screaming Brass*, the 1933 American Record Company test pressing that remained on the shelf for thirty years. This showcase performance already possessed the characteristics that made him famous: enthusiasm, pushing power, and an irresistible rhythmic feel. Though clearly a Coleman Hawkins man at heart, Thomas deviated from his model, playing less rhapsodically and more staccato than Hawk. This booting quality and his sonorous, rough sound in the bottom register of the horn were to remain strong points of his style. These distinguishing features never failed to rouse an audience. "I remember when he used to get up to play a solo people just hollering and screaming," confirmed tenorist Joe Houston. Sometimes, arranger Sy Oliver wrote charts with Joe Thomas as lead voice. This resulted in a much deeper sound, as witness the 1935 recording of *Babs*.

"Wild Man of the Tenor Sax" Arnett Cobb summarized Joe Thomas's approach in one word: *"Simplification.* He was very simple, had drive, not a lot of notes, and that's why I took to [him]. Out of all the tenor players, I liked a lot of them, but Joe was my man. For the way I wanted to play."

Chicago's Von Freeman has been one of the city's vanguard tenor man ever since he made his debut in Horace Henderson's band, in 1940. He saw the Lunceford orchestra "hundreds of times." Freeman noted another quality of Joe's: "He's from that hard-blowing school. Joe Thomas, to me, was valuable because he was the next saxophone player to Coleman Hawkins that had this presence. Because he had a presence very similar to Hawkins. Man, he sit there and he overpowered the reed section almost!"

When Ben Webster left Ellington in the summer of 1943, Duke asked Joe Thomas to replace him. Joe refused, just as he had politely turned down Basie's advances. Although it was true he had toyed with the idea of starting a band of his own at an earlier stage, he simply could not desert his boss.

The addition of the hot Thomas helped the orchestra to steadily enhance its name value. At the formal annual Navy Ball at Cornell University in May 1933, Jimmie Lunceford and His Twelve Talented Tennesseeans played opposite Guy Lombardo and His Royal Canadians, the

leading "sweet" band at the time. The date had originally been meant for
McKinney's Cotton Pickers, but they couldn't make it. Lombardo occupied
the main stage, decorated with flowers and props. The Tennesseeans had to
content themselves with a smaller and less lavishly decorated stand. From
the ARC test recordings made earlier that month, we know how well and
exciting the orchestra sounded at this stage of its development. The college
kids, hearing the band for the first time, were just flabbergasted—they
almost started a riot. Commented Wilcox, "I don't know whether it was
our music or because we were so happy, but we made a hit with the crowd."
The next day the bookers in New York had heard the news about this band
of unknowns that had cut Lombardo. "That is a night we'll never forget,"
Jimmie's wife Crystal Tulli Lunceford recalled, twenty-four years later. "It
was Jimmie's first break in the big time."[7] It's true: after Cornell, the band
went on to play campus dances at Colgate, Western Reserve, Syracuse, and
Rochester. America's white students were among the first to embrace the
Lunceford sound and style.

The secret was the way the music moved, and the way the band moved
with it—especially in the fast numbers. Hollywood choreographer Busby
Berkeley had shown the world the power and beauty of precision movement by large groups of chorus girls and boys. New high-note trumpeter
Tommy Stevenson, nineteen, was the primary architect of the orchestra's
visual appearance. It soon became a trademark attraction of the Jimmie
Lunceford Orchestra: whole sections rocking backward and forward, or
from side to side, while the other sections moved in the opposite direction.
The trombonists pointed their instruments toward the ceiling, to let their
slides slip back simultaneously. The brass fanned its derby mutes in perfect
unison. At the end of an exceptionally heated version of *Le Jazz Hot*, one
enthusiastic radio announcer commented, "Well, if you're listening down
here, and could see the gyrations and gymnastics that go on in this band,
when they really get to sending—everybody starts with sort of a wave at
one end, and they swing back and forth until the whole place takes it up."[8]
In contrast to all these movements, pianist Ed Wilcox acted as if he were on
the verge of falling asleep, slumping backward or sideways. "His only rival
for looking blasé was Johnny Hodges!" claimed writer Ralph Gleason.[9]
Bass player Mose Allen carried on, slapping and leaping and shouting and
spinning his instrument as if it were a giant humming top. One could tell
that Jimmy Crawford had been a promising athlete in his high school days,
the way he danced and jumped in his seat, and twirled his sticks. All the

musicians grunted with joy as they cheered one another on, laughing and clapping. "It was probably even more important than the music," commented Von Freeman on the visual impact.

Most of these choreographed movements had originally been products of Tommy Stevenson's creative brain. The problem was, when it was time to execute the maneuvers "Steve" had designed for the band, the originator more often than not was the one who forgot them.[10]

Tommy Stevenson's other specialty was a flashy high-note style, based on the famous breaks of Satchmo, his idol, which added considerably to the appeal of the band. Stevenson hit notes that were higher than Armstrong's notorious high C's. Steve's high B-flat screeching was considered "in bad taste" by a lot of critics—but the audience couldn't get enough of it. Of course, the student could not match the phrasing that characterized the master Louis, not to mention the latter's magnificent tone quality.

By early 1935 Stevenson was drawing so much applause with his stratospheric exploration that he demanded equal billing with the band. Lunceford at that time never put the names of his soloists or vocalists on marquees or posters, and so Steve quit. It must have immensely grieved Lunceford, a man of high standards, to learn that his former trumpet star, who like his section mate Eddie Tompkins also was a qualified physician, never regained his momentum and became one of New York's first musician junkies.[11]

The Jimmie Lunceford Orchestra pioneered the use of choreography in black music. Its musical style, however, was clearly built on some of the other leading bands of the period. Apart from the aforementioned bands of Ellington and Trent, the Sunset Royal Serenaders, directed by Bob Saunders, exerted an important influence on the early Lunceford orchestra. The Sunset Royal Serenaders were a versatile territory band based at West Palm Beach, Florida. They could swing hard, but their fame rested also on their showmanship. Sax man Benny Waters, who played with Lunceford during 1942, commented, "I think that Jimmie Lunceford not only copied that band in the style, but in dress, too." Though the Sunsets did not record prior to 1941, it is probable that their riff-based idiom and their timing were aspects that appealed to Lunceford. Some of their recordings sound like head arrangements, comparable to the way tunes like *Well, All Right Then* used to originate and develop in the Lunceford orchestra.

No survey of the early stages of swing music is complete without mentioning Glen Gray's Casa Loma Orchestra. During the early 1930s, when sugary sweet bands ruled, it was the premier hot band, a favorite with college students. Arranger Gene Gifford's flag-wavers and the precise execution left a mark on Lunceford and his men. Traces of the Casa Loma approach are clearly audible in some of the early, swaggering recordings by the Jimmie Lunceford Orchestra, notably *White Heat* and *Jazznocracy*. Writer Barry Ulanov stated that "ensemble spirit as it was never known before, and perhaps never since, was the identifying mark of the Jimmie Lunceford band. Here all that was mechanical in the Glen Gray Casa Loma organization was carried through to something approaching perfection, with the machine oil all but visible."[12]

However important Alphonso Trent's orchestra, the Sunset Royal Serenaders, and Casa Loma may have been during the formative years of the Lunceford band, it would be Duke Ellington who eventually put the biggest stamp on the emerging orchestra. The musicians in Lunceford's band were crazy about Duke's original themes, the bold dynamics and dissonances, the wonderful shadings, and the all-out sophistication and creativity of his work. Arranger Sy Oliver, for instance, remembered that *Birmingham Breakdown* and *East St. Louis Toodle-Oo* were the first records that had made an impression on him while still a teenager. Ed Wilcox's piano intro for *I'll See You in My Dreams* (1937) is pure Duke.

It was no coincidence that the Lunceford band on its first studio date for Decca, on September 4, 1934, recorded three Ellington tunes, *Sophisticated Lady*, *Mood Indigo* and *Black and Tan Fantasy*. A fourth number, *Rose Room*, also was played regularly by Duke. Ellington's influence is evident. At the same time, it must be said that Lunceford's band undeniably had something all its own, and in one or two cases even surprises us. But still, Sy Oliver as a growl specialist showed less personality, less nuance than Cootie Williams, and the Ellingtonians sounded easier and more spontaneous, less contrived than the Luncefordeans.

In *Sophisticated Lady*, arranger Willie Smith projects the image of an easygoing female, more lassie than lady. The result, however, has a slightly dated sound. Lunceford unmistakably still has something corny going on in here. Compared to Ellington's Victor version, two years earlier, Sy's arrangement of *Black and Tan Fantasy* sounds merrier. Behind his own opening solo he has the band play a skip-time rhythm: every couple of bars the horns play a bar in double time. Eddie Tompkins molds a long trumpet note that gradually builds in strength, closely following Barney Bigard's original high-pitched solo on clarinet. In *Rose Room* the difference in warmth between Smith and Bigard, two years earlier, is striking. The lagging timing is typical of the Lunceford bounce. The song is played in a brisker tempo, but it is the imaginative arrangement, by Smith, that catches the attention. *Rose Room* sounds as if it is a harmonized solo; much like Eddie Durham's treatment of the tune *Avalon*, one year later. It gives *Rose Room* a far more modern sound than Ellington's conception.

The most unusual arrangement of this September session undoubtedly is Willie Smith's version of *Mood Indigo*. Again, the tempo is livelier (the clarinet choir punctuates a staccato countertheme behind the opening statement by the trumpets) than in Ellington's original from 1930. Duke, too, would over the years alter the tempo of *Mood Indigo*. But then, in the third chorus, something very strange happens. Like a submarine that disappears in the waters, the reeds seem to "submerge" in the sagging song—an effect that continues to amaze.

The year before they recorded their Ellington tribute, the Tennesseeans were still scuffling in the Midwest. The sidemen had their visions of the Big Apple, where Ellington and Henderson and Calloway reigned. A job there would spell the difference between lasting success and ultimate failure. Every bandleader dreamed of making it in Manhattan—or Harlem. Finding a job there was supposedly less difficult than in smaller communities; the city was the seat of the major hotels that offered live music. New York also was the hub of the recording business, the network chains, and the press. There also was less racial prejudice than in much of the rest of the country. Nightlife was still brewing, although a little less exuberant than before the depression struck.

"You could smell 'em," said actor and dancer James "Flash" Riley about the Harlem cabarets he passed in the streets in the early 1930s, when still a youth. Later on he would dance with the Lunceford band "in its prime, in Boston, The Southland."

Go by and smell that cheap perfume down in there. The cheap perfume was everywhere. But the music was coming out the walls. You know, there were rehearsals. An orchestra here, a basement was jumping, there was a piano in the window, trying to sell song sheets, and over here's another rehearsal, on the street was a tramp band [he imitated the sound of taps] trying to make a little dollar, down where all the actors gathered. Over the Lafayette was two rehearsal halls, bands were rehearsing material. You know, there were no radios, no jukeboxes either, you got music from the source.

In May 1933, everything seemed to click for the Jimmie Lunceford Orchestra. A job at the famous Cotton Club, in Harlem, was waiting. However, after auditioning, the musicians learned that the management in the end preferred the tried-and-true Duke Ellington Orchestra. Disillusioned, the leader tried to save the trip by applying with the American Record Company for a recording session. The studio accepted, but the resulting two sides, *Flaming Reeds and Screaming Brass* and *While Love Lasts*, remained on the shelve for three decades.

At this point, the organization acquired its most valuable member. Trumpeter, singer, and arranger Melvin "Sy" Oliver rejoined the orchestra. He made this decision not so much because he had the ambition to play the trumpet, sing, and arrange for the band, but because he saw it as an opportunity to hitch a ride to New York, to fulfill his ambition to study law. This had not been possible earlier, on account of his father's passing, which had caused financial obstacles that Oliver tried to overcome by making money in the music business. To Oliver, being in that business was just a temporary and easy way of making a living. When he joined, he wasn't even actively playing the trumpet, but taught a couple of students and concentrated on arranging.

Oliver had already been in the band for a while in 1931, after Jimmie had spotted him in Cincinnati. "I heard them rehearsing in the Stirling Hotel," said Oliver, "and their rehearsals were meticulous. Lunceford conducted a rehearsal as though it were a classroom, and I was very impressed." He had written a few charts for Lunceford and joined the orchestra in Columbus. But Oliver's stint had been a short one, and for the next two years he had been wandering in and out of territory bands around Ohio.[13]

Wilcox was instrumental in getting Sy Oliver to rejoin the band. Initially, Jimmie didn't particularly like the cocky youngster. "Look Pops," the pianist said, "you've got to admit the kid's got something special." He argued that Sy played enough trumpet, both open and with the plunger, to be a valuable addition to the brass, and that as an arranger he was a natural, an unusually talented artist. As Sy was mainly interested in writing jazz and jump tunes, Edwin coached him in the direction of popular music. It took some time before Oliver mastered the craft. Sometimes Wilcox had him write three different arrangements of the same tune, which resulted in as many arguments.[14] But after a while, Sy became just about the best editor of trivial and folksy material, as exemplified by little jewels such as *Swanee River* (1935), *He Ain't Got Rhythm* (1937), or *Annie Laurie* (1937).

Reportedly, Oliver never in his life took a formal music lesson, even though both his parents worked in the music business. His father was a singer and a music teacher who traveled all over the Midwest and along the East Coast with his Junior Choir and as a saxophone demonstrator for the Conn Company. His mother played and taught the piano. Oliver told writer Stanley Dance, "My parents started me on piano when I was quite young, before I went to school, but I didn't like it, didn't like to practice, and they didn't insist. My father taught practically every kid in southeastern Ohio but me! I can't remember when I couldn't read music. It seems as though I'd be able to read it all my life."

Melvin liked to write comparatively simple structures, leaving a lot of space, which gave his charts an airy quality and transparency. "One thing that I've always believed in, as far as arranging is concerned, is white space," he said. "Take advertising: You take a whole page of paper and put three words on it and everybody sees it. Then when you make a statement, everybody hears it. People can't hear but one thing at a time."[15] He was attracted to jazz through recordings by Ellington, Henderson, McKinney's Cotton Pickers, and Jelly Roll Morton. He knew the Cotton Pickers from the time they were still working in Springfield, Ohio, before they moved to Detroit.

Melvin took up the trumpet because that way he could stay out at night, rehearsing with a local band, Cliff Barnett's Club Royal Serenaders. His dad showed him the fingering and how to run a scale. "I learned to play the thing very quickly. I guess I have some innate talent. In a matter of months, I was ready to play with the band." Little Melvin was all of fourteen years old. He was a bright, enterprising youngster. When he started playing with Barnett, he already had close to four thousand dollars in the bank. "I was thirteen years old and I had grown men cutting grass for me in what I called Oliver's Horticultural Society. I'd get around, get the jobs, supply the tools, and take fifty percent of the take," he told Stanley Dance.

After finishing high school, he joined Zack Whyte's Chocolate Beau Brummels, a professional band based in Cincinnati. Sy described the sidemen as "a bunch of idiots that didn't understand anybody that spoke English." The only way to make himself clear was quite often by means of a fistfight. At eighteen, he started boxing for money between spells with the Beau Brummels. He'd already gotten his nickname at that time. The Whyte musicians, bewildered by his intellectual capacities, first started calling him "Professor." But since he was just seventeen, and professors, they all agreed, were over sixty and bald, the name did not stick. Then the drummer came up with "Psychology." This was the most difficult word he knew. It was abbreviated to Sy, and Sy it remained.[16]

The records Zack Whyte made for Gennett in 1929 are not quite as impressive as, say, Alphonso Trent's. The ensemble sounds tight in *West End Blues*—the orchestra clearly is on a Louis Armstrong kick—but apart from that, there is nothing outstanding about the Beau Brummels. In all probability, Oliver did not arrange any of these six sides. However, he later revealed that some of the arrangements he wrote in 1933 for Lunceford were just rehashes of the things he had made for Zack Whyte. Tenor saxophonist George Kelly played with Whyte for three or four months in 1938, and he recalled that the orchestra was still performing these Sy Oliver arrangements. "In fact, some of the arrangements that we played, when I got back to Miami, from Richmond, Kentucky—I heard these arrangements, and I said, 'I played that!' The Jimmie Lunceford band I heard. That's when I found it was Sy's arrangements."

In 1930–31, Sy Oliver had worked with Alphonso Trent as well. After the Trent band had lost its library in a fire, he was asked to rewrite the book, and he subsequently started traveling with Trent. In a sense, the orchestras of Whyte, Trent, and Lunceford were musically related through Oliver's arrangements. For instance, there is a remarkable resemblance between Trent's 1933 tune *Clementine,* a Gus Wilson arrangement, and Sy's adaptation of *What Is This Thing Called Swing?,* recorded six years later by Lunceford. This suggests Oliver put his stamp on Alphonso Trent's arrangers, even after he had left the organization.

To avoid the daily arguments and fighting in Whyte's band, Sy began spending his spare time writing for the twelve-piece orchestra. He dressed up the band's head arrangements with intros and endings and backgrounds in between. To Oliver, the Whyte band's way of playing was "harmonically ass-backwards." With Whyte he developed his arranging skills, including his distinctive approach to rhythm. His first score was *Nobody's Sweetheart,* and it became one of the band's successes. It took him one month to complete this opus, "from Maine to Florida." It will come as no surprise to learn that Oliver did not use a piano or a guitar when he composed or arranged a piece. Everything was right in his head. Sy also claimed that his characteristic preference for two-beat rhythm was more or less inborn, just as a person is either left- or right-handed.

Andy Gibson, who later also became a renowned arranger, sat next to Sy in Zack Whyte's trumpet section. He maintained that no band played Sy's arrangements better than Zack Whyte. Oliver reluctantly agreed: "Well, yes, I think that was so. In that band we were more or less playing for the love of it, and I just about knew how each of the guys breathed!" He added that in Lunceford's band the emphasis sometimes was too much on virtuosity.[17]

Sy rejoined in the summer of 1933, when Lunceford played a date in Boston. He was hired primarily as arranger, but competently filled the third trumpet chair, and his vocal contributions were often hip and funny. Though the style of the band, as designed by Ed Wilcox and Willie Smith, by now had settled, "Sy turned it around a little," according to Jonah Jones. "He had that good two-beat. He had worked with Zack Whyte. *This 'n That* was a tune he had written when he was still very young. That two-beat was there, all right."

That two-beat was mostly played in a very specific tempo that became known as the "Lunceford bounce." It was slower than a regular medium swing tempo, and faster than the average ballad. This kind of tempo is hard to play, and even harder to hold. The interaction of the instruments in the rhythm section is crucial. The pianist plays stride, alternating between bass notes on the downbeats and off-beat chords, which results in an *oom-pah* pattern. The bass player amplifies the bass notes played by the pianist. The guitarist strums his chords in four-four, which "mellows" the two-four pattern played by piano and bass, and lends a steady flow to the rhythm. Using various parts of his kit, the drummer supports his colleagues. The sum total is a deep, warm pulse that never overpowers the horns. The open character of the beat enables the arranger to write charts that can be fairly complicated rhythmically, often suggesting double time.

Sy Oliver carried his moods and his reputation with him, and soon found out that his new boss never sided with him when he, Sy, had a row with one of the musicians. So finally one day he told Lunceford that he was getting fed up with the way things were going on.

> I told him I was trying to build the damn band, and every time there was a problem, he would side with the members of the band. I asked him why he had hired me in the first place.
>
> He replied, "I'll tell you why I hired you, Sy. The reason I side

with the fellows is because I understand what they are up against. They don't understand what you're doing all the time. The things that you're doing are new to them and they just can't follow them. And you are extremely impatient. You don't give them a chance to learn. They'll get the idea eventually. Let it sink in. Give them a chance. If they all thought like Sy Oliver, they all would be Sy Oliver, and I wouldn't have had to hire you. You know, I always investigate everybody carefully before I hire them, and you are the only person I have ever inquired about that nobody ever had a good word for, and I thought that anybody who could alienate the world must have something special, and I thought I could control you."

One of Oliver's problems with his fellow musicians was that when a record became popular, Sy insisted they had to memorize their solos, or else the audience would start complaining. Sometimes, the new arranger even went as far as writing out entire solos.[18]

One can hear the result of this policy by following the development of, for instance, *For Dancers Only,* a popular Oliver composition, which remained in the book until after Lunceford's death. The tune could be expanded considerably on certain nights, but the arrangement basically remained the same. Over the years the tempo was sped up slightly, and while the solos did not remain identical, they stayed roughly similar. Usually, when a musician was replaced, the new man inherited his predecessor's solo spots. So it is remarkable that Kirt Bradford, Willie Smith's replacement, did not inherit his solo in this tune. After 1942 it was Joe Thomas who had a regular solo slot in the arrangement. Not a bad choice: his contributions tended to be even more effective than Smith's. "He had a powerful sense for making an effective entry and seldom lapsed into repetition in his work," the writer Albert McCarthy points out, and that description fits Joe's solo turns in *For Dancers Only.*[19]

Sy found out that musicians were never satisfied. Quite often they suggested he should mold a tune in the style of some other band. He would reply that for him, it was just a small effort to emulate that style, but they better realize their own orchestra recently had had a couple of hit recordings. Accordingly, they were paid better than the other band that still was scuffling at Harlem's Savoy Ballroom or some other place that paid just a fraction of what they were getting. Now did they want that?

Sy later emphasized the fact that their band's sound was just as unique as

Ellington's. But there was an important difference. Any band of established character, be it Duke, Basie, or Henderson, had a definite style. Each had a certain sameness about anything it would play, which made it instantly recognizable. Not so with his band, claimed Oliver. "Darn near every number Lunceford did was different from the one which preceded it and the one which followed." Oliver hit the nail on the head. One does not need a trained ear to recognize the Lunceford band after a few bars, just as one would easily spot Ellington or Glenn Miller. Yet amazingly, unlike the other great stylists in jazz, Jimmie Lunceford couldn't be identified with one specific style. His arrangers had their own personal approaches: Eddie Wilcox's scores were markedly different from Willie Smith's or Eddie Durham's or Gerald Wilson's. Though the typical Lunceford style was staccato, Wilcox always included legato lines, mostly in the reeds. Durham emphasized the wah-wah trombone sound; Wilson was the first to apply modern augmented and diminished chords. And Sy Oliver himself could best be described as multi-stylistic. He was the musical forerunner of the present-day conceptual artist, who changes his approach and material from painting to sculpture to an installation to a lecture to an ad or a mass-producted multiple. In a way, Lunceford's legacy can be compared to an entire school of art, like the pop art movement.

Sy must have loved the band a lot, because the financial rewards were meager: he was paid two dollars and fifty cents for masterpieces such as *Four or Five Times*, *Swanee River*, and *My Blue Heaven*. This included copying all the parts! Later, the leader doubled the scale to five dollars.

Oliver's charts are characterized by subtle dynamics and a clever juxtaposing of the various voices in the band. Contrasts form the heart of most of his arrangements; he uses the various colors in the orchestra to their fullest advantage. Sy introduced flügelhorns, in order to create a slightly warmer sound. The effect of these contrasting themes and vamps could be funny or dramatic. "Though Sy frequently orchestrates for three trumpets in a very high register, he almost always writes an accompaniment or countermelody in a low register to be played by either the trombone or the baritone sax. As a result the orchestra is well-rooted and marvelously balanced," noted Hugues Panassié.[20]

Oliver's writing was fueled by a unique and seemingly inexhaustible creativity. The way some of his intros develop, Oliver could easily have dug up a completely new melody. His charts abound with little mischievous twists and turns and sudden rhythmic spurts that last for a half bar or so, and everything is anchored by a very hip timing that reflects his absorption of Harlem's way of rapping and capping, walking, and dancing. An utterly logical and peaceful development in the melody might be alternated with sudden dynamic leaps and screaming brass. It is obvious that Oliver's little masterworks were the result of Lunceford's policy not to restrict his arrangers. Oliver's arrangements always were precise and balanced to the point where one could clearly distinguish each and every single voice, down to the acoustic guitar. One wonders how the writer realized the subtle shadings and dynamics in this pre-electronics era. It could, no doubt, only be achieved through incessant rehearsals. In *Because You're You*, of 1934 vintage, the muted trumpets behind Henry Wells's vocal sound just as soft as Al Norris's guitar.

Next to Ellington, Eddie Sauter, and Fletcher Henderson, Oliver was without doubt the most gifted and original of the jazz arrangers in the 1930s. To him, as easy and casual as it appeared to be, arranging was creative work. "Where does the introduction come from?" he once asked rhetorically, and gave the answer: "It's composition. Where is the background behind the vocalist or soloist? It's composition. The countermelodies? It's all composition. The modulation to go to the next chorus?"[21]

In the meantime, during a performance at the Dewitt Night Club in Syracuse, Lunceford had met impresario Harold Oxley. Oxley was impressed by Lunceford, and offered to become the band's manager. He was the son of Benjamin Oxley, co-founder of the American Federation of Musicians. Nicknamed "The Gaffer," or "Brains," Harold Oxley had been a violinist and conductor of traveling chamber music ensembles in the 1920s; in the summer of 1924 he had made a couple of recordings in New York, for Paramount and Okeh, leading his Post Lodge Orchestra. By the early 1930s he had decided to try his hand at talent managing. Lunceford was his first big asset and for a while his only one. The leader and the manager formed a company called Lunceford Artists Inc. Previously, Oxley had worked for both Irving Mills and Tom Rockwell, the most powerful businessmen in the New York dance band scene. So initially he was regarded as their rival, but in the event they cooperated. Mills and Rockwell could not be ignored; they controlled many ballrooms and theaters, even chains of venues.

In an interview, the stocky manager once mentioned that he loved Jimmie, four years his junior, like his own son. Oxley and Lunceford became mutual owners of the orchestra, and during the eleven years of their cooperation they entertained a most unusual symbiotic partnership, which was truly unique in the business. At his Manhattan office at 17 East Forty-seventh Street Harold Oxley developed what must have been the country's most extensive direct mail system at the time. Eventually it covered every venue, from the largest ballroom in Los Angeles to the most ramshackle barn in South Carolina. Every major appearance or move of the orchestra was announced in stenciled flyers. Special brochures were distributed during the holiday seasons. Oxley's system even contained every birthday in the business, so everybody received appropriate greeting cards, signed jointly by manager and bandleader. "No promoter ever lost a nickel booking Jimmie," was Oxley's favorite adage.[22]

During the summer of 1933 the band played an engagement at Lake Caroga, a resort near Gloversville in upstate New York. All summer was spent polishing the orchestra. Rehearsals were held around the clock, and in early September the long anticipated wire arrived. Frank Schiffman and Teddy Blackman, the managers of the Lafayette Theater, 2227 Seventh Avenue in Harlem, informed the orchestra that it had obtained a four-week engagement starting Saturday, September 30. This time it was for certain. The band was to play several shows a day, starting in the afternoon and finishing after midnight, accompanying singers, dancers, and vaudeville artists.

The Lafayette had opened twenty years earlier, advertising itself as "America's leading colored theatre" and "The cradle of the stars." The two-thousand-seat venue exuded a refined, nineteenth-century atmosphere, and quickly became one of the centers of black culture. The theater was recognized as the hub for African American plays, which prospered at the time. Those were the days of the *Darktown Follies* and other revues that first showed the world the power and elegance of black dancing, singing, and acting. Wilbur Sweatman's orchestra, which included Otto Hardwick, Duke Ellington, and Sonny Greer, had topped the bill back in 1923. This engagement, incidentally, marked Ellington's introduction to New York and Harlem.

It would take another three years before *Nigger Heaven* got published, Carl Van Vechten's controversial book that would focus the attention of the white elite on Harlem. Before *Nigger Heaven* it was not fashionable for the New York jet set to spend the night in Harlem, in order to enjoy a few hours of delicious and delirious "primitive" entertainment in ermine and pearls. After 1926, celebrities poured into the Cotton Club and Connie's Inn night after night.

The Lafayette was part of this never ending merry-go-round. Like the Apollo Theater, the Lafayette catered mostly to a black clientele. The Lafayette competed with the Apollo with lavish shows and the best orchestras. Three doors from the Lafayette Theater was Connie's Inn, where one could catch Harlan Lattimore, crooning *Lazy Bones,* accompanied by Don Redman's Orchestra.

When tap dancer Charles "Honi" Coles moved from his native Philadelphia ("where everybody could dance. Most of the good tap dancers came out of Philadelphia and Baltimore") to New York two years earlier, he noticed nobody in Harlem seemed to have heard about the depression.

> My first impression when I came to New York was that after six o'clock in the evening you didn't see anybody in the street without a shirt and tie on. I mean, there was an aura of . . . of *glamour*—glamour is not really the word. . . . But glamour *is* a good word. Everybody was neatly dressed. Seventh Avenue was like—I can't describe it to you, every other place was a jazz joint, every other place somebody was playing. Somebody was playing piano, somebody was singing.

Lunceford and the guys burned with desire. They knew that only last month Chick Webb had played the Lafayette. The musicians could hardly wait to become part of that wonderful slice of heaven known as Harlem. They were blissfully unaware of the fact that out of New York's fifteen thousand professional musicians, twelve thousand were unemployed.[23]

{5}

COTTON CLUB PARADE

People were dancing and swinging so hard the floor went down six inches.
—Gene Ramey

It was a disaster. The day the Jimmie Lunceford Orchestra, introduced in the advertisements as "One of America's Greatest Bands," made its debut at the Lafayette Theater, as part of Addison Carey's revue "It's a Knockout," everything went haywire. The tempos were wrong, the band stopped playing before the chorus was through, and it ruined Hannah Sylvester's singing. The other acts included headliner Jack Johnson, the famous fighter and entertainer—and Lunceford's childhood hero—singers Joyner and Brisco, and vaudevillian Gallie De Gaston.

It was so bad, the musicians didn't dare to stir a limb when the movie screen came down to show *Sing, Sinner, Sing*, based on the life of torch vocalist Libby Holman. They just sat there in the dark, stricken with a bad case of what you would call stage fright if it happened before a performance. They had messed up Ristina Banks and her Flying Colors Girls, also known as the "Number One Chorus," so named because it was the toast of Philadelphia. The Number One Chorus had danced with the cream of the big bands, including those led by Duke Ellington, Fletcher Henderson, and Bennie Moten. "That was a classy bunch of girls with very high standards, and if you didn't measure up, they just didn't pay attention to you," said Count Basie, Moten's pianist. Those girls told the new band from Memphis in no uncertain terms what they thought of the sad bunch. Willie Smith remembered, "Jimmie had goofed the show up, too, because he had been excited—the first time on a stage like that, in New York, the greatest place in the world. But it wasn't just his fault. The whole band was scared, because before that we had only played dances."

But the musicians had not worked so hard for nothing. After the initial horrors had worn off, the band immediately set out to get the demanding show material straight. The group launched a double-barreled attack, with its trademark drive and precision, and such was the audience response to remaining shows that the management decided to hold over the band for an extra period, which in the history of the theater was unique. This time, the band was the main attraction, supported by a revue cast of forty-two.[1] It became obvious to the trend-watchers in the dance band world: the Jimmie Lunceford Orchestra was definitely heading for the major league. In December, the theater asked them to return, an unprecedented move and further proof of the band's success.

That fall, everything went right during the opening night. To close the show, the musicians lined up along the edge of the stage and sang an a capella ballad in glee club fashion that "absolutely left the audience spellbound," according to Sy Oliver. Next day, the band and its vocal performance were the talk of the town. The fact that trumpeter Tommy Stevenson could hit those high notes just like Louis Armstrong did was duly appreciated, but twelve musicians who sang like a regular choir were definitely a novelty. There was one man who kept his mouth shut during the vocal performances. Jimmie Crawford, reported Sy Oliver, "could not carry a tune if you bottled it." Nevertheless, the band proved to be just as perfect vocally as it was instrumentally. That night lingered on in the memories of those who were there.[2]

In a way, the glee club routine was a triple legacy, from James Lunceford Sr.'s choir, from Jimmie's own experience as a member of Fisk's glee club, and from the tradition set by the Jubilee Singers. The Fisk Jubilee Singers style went back to British male three-part choral practices in the eighteenth and nineteenth centuries, characterized by a countertenor as lead voice. No examples, alas, of the band's glee club during this period have been preserved. From time to time, the full orchestra sang on records, but those renditions in general were vocal interjections rather than full-fledged vocals. *Blues in the Night*, its 1941 film hit, *Pistol Packin' Mama*, of 1944 vintage, and *I Need a Lift*, one year later, came closest. But the Lunceford glee club gained fame originally with its interpretations of *It's the Talk of the Town*, *Don't Blame Me*, *I Hate Myself for Being in Love with You*, *The Continental*, *Cheek to Cheek*, and other ballads.

Every major black orchestra in New York was owned by music mogul Irving Mills: Duke Ellington, Cab Calloway, Lucky Millinder, Fletcher Henderson, Benny Carter, Willie Lewis, Don Redman. "Owned" is the right expression: they were his, copyrights and all. His artists's songs were exploited by his publishing firm Mills Music, Inc. Mills Artists Bureau had all the right contacts. It had connections with the RCA staff and the Cotton Club, and so through Mills's effort the Lunceford orchestra entered the recording studio on January 26, 1934. This was its first regular session since the Chickasaw adventure, almost four years earlier. The first two selections of the RCA date, *White Heat* and *Jazznocracy*, were flag-wavers that soon would dazzle the audience at the Cotton Club. The musicians did not like the fast, exhibitionistic tunes much, but to their amazement, both *White Heat* and *Jazznocracy*, written by Will Hudson in a style that borrowed elements from Casa Loma and Fletcher Henderson, became hits, their first. The tunes were clearly designed for agile dancers. The acrobatic variant of the Lindy Hop was not yet en vogue—that would take another three years—but fast-paced tunes like *White Heat* (advertised at the time as "The fastest tempo ever recorded")[3] formed the blueprint for the Lindy's sound-track. The furious nature of these arrangements would no doubt present even today's big bands with problems, considering the precision interlocking of the sections. Memphis saxophonist Emerson Able had a vivid memory of the time when he performed *White Heat* in his high school band.

That's the hardest tune I ever played in my life! Ooh, man! And I had a raggedy saxophone. [Hums some rapid phrases.] Lot of tonguing. Oh man, that raggedy saxophone just wore me out! God, believe me. I couldn't make any of the low notes, and that bottom note that we had to pop was an E-flat concert. Yeah buddy, man, man, man! During these times you could get from the music store orchestrations that were—what? Like a dollar, seventy-five cents, or two dollars at the most. But they were exact copies of the tunes.

Some even had the solos written. But we were just always encouraged to disregard the solos and try to get on at there on your own.

Jazznocracy became Lunceford's theme song and would remain so until 1940, when he replaced it with *Uptown Blues*. For a long while, the orchestra would be associated with such rip-roaring flag-wavers. Their choppy tutti choruses are reminiscent of mid-1930s Paul Whiteman. Both bands used this technique, resulting in effects that could be either wild or funny, yet the music in both cases remained transparent.

In retrospect, the songs *Leaving Me* and *Chillun, Get Up*, also from this first RCA Victor session, were at least as interesting as the fast-paced hits. The way the brass is laying back in *Leaving Me*, a Wilcox score, is a typical example of the famous Lunceford bounce. So are the punching horns after Henry Wells's vocal, contrasting beautifully with the smoothly waving reeds that follow. *Chillun, Get Up* was another tune the band was currently rehearsing for the "Cotton Club Parade." The vocalist was once again Henry Wells, subbing, as it where, for Cotton Club star Adelaide Hall.

Harold Oxley, the band's new guide and organizer, arranged a string of appearances in New England. And then, after New York, Chicago was the next metropolis that fell for the Lunceford bounce. In 1933 and 1934, the orchestra played engagements at The Top, the College Inn, and the Regal Theater in that city.

The Cotton Club was the most famous nightclub in the United States. Mills had managed to secure an engagement at this venue, where the Lunceford men were rejected just a couple of months earlier, as a direct result of the business Lunceford had generated at the Lafayette. A job in the Cotton Club was a passport to heaven. An artist, act, or orchestra that had been offered a spot in this lavish Harlem club knew that the next step was, indeed, immortality. There was the bonus of live radio broadcasts from the club, six times a week. Radio exposure, through the syndicated networks, was a vital condition for success, as Duke Ellington and Cab Calloway, the band's predecessors in the Cotton Club, could attest (and as clarinetist Benny Goodman was soon to discover.) By the early 1930s radio had become the nation's most prominent source of entertainment. Between 1925 and 1931, the number of listeners had quadrupled. Quite often, a wireless set was the only article of luxury in a home. Lunceford's two runs at the club gave him national exposure. All over the country people were hearing the band before they'd had a chance to see it.

The club was very much a product of Prohibition. During the early 1920s, the Owney Madden gang, looking for a place in Harlem where it could sell Madden's Number One Beer, stumbled upon the Club DeLuxe, a restaurant at 644 Lenox Avenue, between 141st and 142nd Streets, run by heavyweight champion Jack Johnson. His business was not exactly thriving, and the gangsters took over the place, enlarged its capacity from five hundred to seven hundred seats, and maintained Johnson as front manager. In reality, Madden was the one in charge—even though at the time he was locked up in Sing Sing, serving time for murder. Herman Stark, his lieutenant, was the de facto manager.

Initially, the Mob imported both its employees and the entertainers from Chicago, people they felt were more trustworthy. The name was changed to Cotton Club, which supposedly evoked associations with the idyllic or primitive life at the good old plantations down South. The interior featured loads of fake palm trees and "African" murals. It did not take long before the kitchen gained fame for its soul food and its Chinese and Mexican plates.

It was, however, mainly because of the dazzling shows that New York's upper crust flocked to the Cotton Club. Even more so when the management in 1927 decided to sever its artistic bonds with Chicago, replacing Andy Preer's Cotton Club Syncopators with Duke Ellington's Washingtonians. This was the start of a golden era. Before long the depression ruled everywhere—but not at 644 Lenox. These were the times of *Jungle Nights in Harlem, Black and Tan Fantasy,* and *Jungle Jamboree.* Within a matter of weeks, the bandleader had dropped the "Washingtonians" tag, and rechristened his orchestra as Duke Ellington's Jungle Band.

In the summer of 1930, when Ellington traveled to Hollywood for his first movie, *Check and Double Check,* featuring the popular blackface team Amos 'n' Andy, Duke was replaced by Cab Calloway. Like Duke, Cab was launched on a meteoric trajectory. The night he introduced *Minnie the Moocher,* the clientele demanded six encores.[4]

Dan Healy was the producer of the twenty-fourth edition of the "Cotton Club Parade," which started Sunday, March 11, 1934, and ran through November of that year, except for the summer break. During this interlude, the Lunceford band worked at the Savoy Ballroom and the Lafayette Theater, in June, and the Harlem Opera House, in August. The show's long run is an indication of its popularity. It was a greater success than its predecessor, which had starred singer Aida Ward and Cab Calloway's orchestra.

Harold Arlen and Ted Koehler, who had worked for earlier Cotton Club revues, were hired to write the songs. Adelaide Hall was the star, singing *Chillun, Get Up, Primitive Prima Donna,* an instant hit, and *Ill Wind,* which took longer, but in the event became a standard. Bobby Connelly, Gluck Sandor, and Elida Webb were the choreographers. Webb had been involved in the legendary show *Runnin' Wild,* the one that had launched the Charleston, ten years earlier, at the Colonial Theater on Sixty-second Street.

The Cotton Club Boys were a novelty. Before this edition of the "Cotton Club Parade," the chorus line had been exclusively female ("tall, tan and terrific"). Una Mae Carlisle, who would later gain fame with the song *Walking by the River,* was part of the show girls troupe. For this version of the *Parade,* ten young male dancers were added. The Cotton Club Boys moved in perfect unity and were a smash hit with the clientele. The Boys, however, proved to be a fast-living pack as well. They were fond of sharp clothes, liquor, and ladies, and turnover was high.

Juan Hernandez performed his exotic voodoo dance and Bessie Dudley, "the original snake-hips dancer," strutted her stuff to the strains of *Black and Tan Fantasy.* In *As Long as I Live,* Avon Long danced with a breathtaking beauty of sixteen, who had been with the chorus and at the last moment had replaced Long's original partner. Her name was Lena Horne.

Pops and Louie and Dynamite Hooker did their tap routines.[5] Having worked with Duke Ellington and Cab Calloway as well, Dynamite used to dance to fast tunes. He went into a very powerful and fast kind of jittery dance, with his arms all spread out and his whole body, except for the hands, vibrating like a syncopated jackhammer. Pops and Louie, who would work with Lunceford off and on into the 1940s, used to improvise a lot. Pops Whitman was considered the top acrobatic dancer. One of his trademarks was a kind of very fast spin, during which he moved down into a squatting position and up again, with his ankles locked. Pops and Louie used to interact intensely: whatever Pops would think of, dance-wise or song-wise, Louie Williams tried to top, and vice versa.

The orchestra backed all these acts for three shows nightly, starting at midnight, and as an independent act performed *Jazznocracy, White Heat, Breakfast Ball,* and *Here Goes (a Fool).* *Here Goes* and *As Long as I Live* were arranged by Tom Whaley. Lunceford himself had discovered Whaley and had recommended him when the Cotton Club management had asked the orchestra leader whether he knew an arranger who had experience with shows. This was his first big-time job, and Tom Whaley would end up as copyist for the Ellington band. *Breakfast Ball,* also in the show, contained references to the hi-de-ho craze started by Cab Calloway at the Cotton Club three years earlier. Sy had arranged the song and played an Armstrong-inspired trumpet solo.

Reporter Louis Sobol listed the VIPs who attended the opening night:

> Among the folks present this night I noted Irving and Ellin Berlin and in their party movie producer Samuel Goldwyn and spouse; playwright Sam Behrman; Gregory Ratoff; Paul Whiteman and Margaret Livingstone; producer George White; man-about-town Jules Glaenzer; harmonica virtuoso Borrah Minevitch; Cobina Wright; Marilyn Miller; Lillian Roth; Lee Shubert; Miriam Hopkins; Jo Frisco; Ted Husing and Eddie Duchin.

And this was only a partial list: Sobol did not mention bandleaders Abe Lyman, Vincent Lopez, "Little" Jack Little, Fred Waring, Don Bestor, Jack Denny, Glen Gray, and Ozzie Nelson, who were also in the audience—a clear indication of the growing reputation of the former Memphis school band.

The orchestra was a hit with both the clientele and the management. Herman Stark told Lunceford that there had never been a band at the Cotton Club with a precision comparable to his outfit. The *New York Amsterdam News* called the twenty-fourth "Parade" "one of the best." Irving Mills had the orchestra record its Cotton Club repertoire in three sessions, in order to capitalize on the furor the band created at the club. The first came in January, the session that produced *White Heat, Jazznocracy,* and *Chillun, Get Up,* followed a few days after their stormy opening by a date that produced two more tunes featured in the "Cotton Club Parade": *Breakfast Ball* and *Here Goes a Fool.* Finally in September *Black and Tan Fantasy* was also put on record.

Echoes of that first Cotton Club show rang for a long time. Pianist Red Richards recalled,

> Man, them chicks would get out there and dance for twenty minutes like there was no tomorrow! Them days, it was a regular Broadway production. And they played that so perfect, they got a reputation immediately. There they started to be going so big. They were forc-

ing it into the recording game right quick, you see. Them days, didn't waste a lot of time to record.

But that was their break, to come into the Cotton Club. See, because then people would come from downtown, all the movie stars and things: "Say man, heard this band, this is in the Cotton Club now," and things like that. See, so playing that terrific show put them on the map, because you had the buzz people coming every night, you know, to see the show.

Right after it finished the first leg of its Cotton Club engagement, the Lunceford band, backing a selection of the other Cotton Club entertainers, went into the Lafayette Theater. Since by that time the Victor 78s had become popular in Harlem, black New York was ready. It should be remembered that black people were not welcome at the Cotton Club unless they worked there. It was at the Lafayette that Red Richards first saw the orchestra in action.

The "Cotton Club on Parade" opened at the theater on Seventh Avenue on Saturday, June 9. The Lunceford band headlined the show, which featured song stylist Lena Horne and dancers Pops and Louie, Avon Long, Bessie Dudley, and Dynamite Hooker, plus the chorus line. The musicians themselves paid their dancing dues as well. That year the Shim Sham Shimmy became popular, a tap dance routine consisting of three different shuffles and slides, straight and cross-legged. Willie Bryant's sidemen had performed the Shim Sham in a previous revue at the Lafayette Theater. Lunceford copied the routine with great success.[6] Apart from the Shim Sham Shimmy, choreographed for six members of the orchestra, there were individual musicians who held their own on the floor. Jock Carruthers, who wore the biggest smile in the band, like Joe Thomas was given to rocking to and fro to the beat in his seat. From time to time he rose to cut a few steps with his baritone as a partner, much to the delight of the audience.

Pianist Red Richards vividly remembered the effect Jimmy Crawford had on the chorus line.

To work in that Cotton Club you had to play that show. They had these chorus girls, Lena Horne was a chorus girl during them days, Louis's wife Lucille, all of them chicks, man. And they loved to dance. So Craw, he be chewing that gum: "Okay, old girl, let's go now! All right!" He be talking, man. And that band swinging. Aw boy, it was something! That Jimmy Crawford, I can see him now, talking: "Okay, old girl, I gotcha!" Jimmy Crawford is the one, really, to me—he made that band. Because they had the real type of drummer to fit a band of that mold. Craw and I, in later years we'd always talk about that band, boy, Jimmie Lunceford's band, boy. That was—*aaah!*

The "Cotton Club on Parade" was a winner. Lena Horne was undeniably the new star, as she proved she could sing as well as dance. She captivated her audience with her good looks and her cool, sensual voice.

The second-floor hall next to the Lafayette, around the corner on 131st Street, over a rib joint called the Barbecue, became the band's regular rehearsal room. All the major bands—Armstrong, Duke, Cab, Basie, Erskine Hawkins—used these upstairs halls for rehearsals. If you managed to make it past Jimmie's brother Connie Lunceford, who was the doorman, you were in the sanctuary supreme. Pioneer jazz writer Robert Goffin happened to attend several rehearsals. "Lunceford, sitting on a trunk, was giving directions with his baton. In one corner, Sy Oliver was busy rehearsing the brass section, in another, Willie Smith was training the reeds. The tune was *'Tain't What You Do*." As a youngster, aspiring bass player George Duvivier used to beg Connie to let him in. "Eventually, they just got used to seeing me around. When the weather was good, they kept the window in the second floor rehearsal room open, and the sound of that band literally stopped traffic! I was one of the ones in the studio hollering, *Well all right then!*"[7]

In 1934 a general feeling of dissatisfaction arose among Irving Mills's bandleaders. Fletcher Henderson complained about the loss of a job at the Cotton Club that had been promised to him. Instead the engagement was now going to be filled by the Mills Blue Rhythm Band, an ensemble everybody in the business considered inferior to Henderson's orchestra. Like Lunceford, both these bands at the time were heavily influenced by Duke Ellington, which must have been a factor in the club management's consideration. But though the band swung and had an appealing sound, Mills Blue Rhythm was like a poor man's Duke. Henderson displayed far more variety and depth.

Benny Carter and Willie Lewis felt the agency did not look after their interests sufficiently. The Lunceford crew, dissatisfied with the attention Ellington and Calloway were getting from the agency, and used to having its business run according to its own rules, was the first to buy its contracts with Mills and sever all connections, one week after the start of the Cotton Club's summer break. In order to do so, the musicians had taken salary cuts to save money for the buyout. Sensing that the Lunceford orchestra was becoming hot property, Mills sued the band and its new manager, but the parties ended up with some kind of settlement.

One week after Lunceford's departure, Fletcher Henderson followed his example. Cab Calloway was next in line. It took Duke Ellington five years. Only after he discovered that Irving Mills four years earlier hadn't spent the amount of money they had agreed on for the tombstone of Duke's mother, did Ellington, too, leave the fold.[8]

When the Lunceford cooperative bought its contracts with Irving Mills, it was faced with a double dilemma. Mills immediately had the band black-listed. And since Mills cooperated closely with William Morris, Joe Glaser, and other leading agencies and representatives, this meant that Lunceford was virtually excluded from playing the better venues, such as the big hotels and the major theaters. Unlike other top black bands, Lunceford was restricted to the African American circuits. This situation lasted until 1939. When an interviewer asked Sy Oliver whether this constant struggle frustrated the musicians, he answered that he "could never explain [it] if I talked for 1,000 years—there's just no explaining it. People live in a world and accept the world the way it is, or else they're going to knock their brains out."[9]

Then there were the problems with the musicians union, Local 802. Any band that wanted to work in New York (or any other big city, for that matter) for a stretch of time was supposed to be composed of union members. Even when one was a union member in another city, one had to apply for membership of Local 802. One had to be transferred, a procedure that took three months. Then followed another three-month incubation period. During this time, one was allowed to work in the city, but only with orchestras whose musicians were Local 802 members. When this band happened to go on tour, one had to obtain special permission from the union. After this period, one was considered a full-fledged member, with full rights and dues.

For some reason, Lunceford had not complied with these rules. Maybe he found them just plain stupid. This was not an issue as long as he was working for Irving Mills at the Cotton Club. Mills, of course, entertained a warm relationship with the union, and the union did not want to mess with the Mob.

All this changed in mid-1934. The musicians no longer worked under the protection of Irving Mills, nor the Mob, so Lunceford was forced to embark on a never-ending string of one-nighters. This constant touring deprived him of the opportunity to broadcast regularly, and the lack of exposure partly accounted for the band's underground-like reputation.

New York City remained the home base, even though the orchestra was constantly touring the South, and after 1936 its West Coast gigs were growing more plentiful. The first of Harlem's ballrooms to give the band a break was the Renaissance Casino, 138th Street and Seventh Ave. Lunceford, down to his last buck, debuted at the "Rennie" Saturday, December 30, 1933. The occasion was a "Cocktail Cadence," thrown by the Meteors, a social club, and admission was sixty-nine cents.[10]

Lunceford returned the favor by appearing there every Christmas Eve, playing "breakfast dances." Whenever its tight schedule permitted, the orchestra played the Rennie on Easter Sundays, Labor Days, and New Year's Eves as well. It was a tradition that Lunceford played for the same fee as at the original Cocktail Cadence. Fourteen years after the Renaissance debut, *Down Beat*'s Michael Levin recalled,

> Henry Wells knocked off one of those pash crooning vocals which slayed the fans, a ditty entitled *Remember When*. Worthy to add, the tune is still good enough to make a hit today. When Lunceford used to play it on his famed Christmas Eve Renaissance ballroom dates, the crowd would quiet down, dancing would stop. Wells would sing and the gals would quietly collapse in their date's arms.[11]

Willie Smith cherished these memories: "There were times with Lunceford when we'd go on the road for 364 days and play in New York one night—at the Renaissance. That night, you'd have to be somebody special to get in, and there would be a whole lot of famous musicians sitting along on the back of the stage listening to us."[12]

Vernon Andrade and his Society Orchestra, the house band at the Renaissance Casino, seem to have been one of the first New York ensembles to reflect the Lunceford touch and sophistication. Pretty soon, Andrade's book contained tunes like *White Heat*, *For Dancers Only*, and other Lunceford hits. Andrade's Society Orchestra worked at the intimate, plush Renaissance for twenty-seven years.

Robert Williams, manager of the Rennie, once booked no less than fifty-odd bands in one night at his medium-sized hall. At the first Annual Grand Ball of the Bert Hall Rhythm Club, on Thursday, February 26, 1935, Lunceford found himself in the company of Fletcher Henderson, Duke Ellington, Luis Russell, Don Redman, Claude Hopkins, Benny Carter, and Chick Webb, to name just a few.[13]

Frank Bonitto, a fan who back in 1935 had befriended some of the musicians in Lunceford's band, remembered a later dance at the Renaissance Ballroom, when he was in the army.

> The dance hall was just full of GIs, young men, you know, young kids with their girlfriends. The place was packed. There were about thirty rows of people in front of the bandstand, and the floor was full of people. And I came in, said, "Well, my God, I came in here to dance . . ." Joe Thomas spotted me from way back where I was, and he stands up and he says, "Bonitto!" Waving at me to come up. Just like the Bible story, the crowd just parted so I could pass right through it! Joe sat me down, right near Dan Grissom, the singer. I spent the whole night up on the bandstand. It was a new experience. I was much better off than out there on the floor. I felt rather proud.

The Jimmie Lunceford Orchestra held the ballroom's attendance record. At the Christmas midnight dance of 1938, a mob of over four thousand tried to get in, smashing the doors.[14] And one of Lunceford's last New York appearances, on Easter Sunday, April 6, 1947, was at the Renaissance Casino.[15]

After extensive structural remodeling the Apollo Theater, 253 West 125th Street, a former "whites only" burlesque house of 1913 vintage, reopened as Negro Vaudeville Theatre on January 26, 1934. Four months later, on Saturday, May 29, the Jimmie Lunceford Cotton Club Orchestra made its debut there. The occasion was a mammoth Midnite benefit for the NAACP-*Courier* Defense Fund. The lineup, staged by Maurice Dancer and emceed by Ralph Cooper, was impressive, to say the least: forty-two acts, including the orchestras of Cab Calloway, Fats Waller, and Fletcher Henderson, singers Adelaide Hall, Ethel Waters, and Tiny Bradshaw, and hoofers the Nicholas Brothers, Bill "Bojangles" Robinson, and Henry "Rubberlegs" Williams. The benefit netted over one thousand dollars.[16]

This was the first time Jimmie met Bill Robinson, who was known as "The Mayor of Harlem." The dancer was also known for his unpredictable

character, and his fits of ill-temper. Nevertheless, the two artists took a lik-
ing for one another and became friends. Later, in 1941, Bill presented Jimmie with an album of little gold leaves on which were the pictures of the latter's parents and wife.[17]

In the course of nine years, Lunceford played no less than nineteen
return engagements at the Apollo, most of them lasting a week, which was
something of a record. (During the same period, both Cab Calloway and
Duke Ellington played the Apollo twelve times.) With four runs 1937 was
a top year. On New Year's Eve, one year later, a double riot squad had to
be called in to control the mob. That night the Lunceford band set an attendance record that stood for many years.[18]

A regular audience member was Ralph Gleason, who at the time was a
student. He lived on Lunceford records, initially, and live shows, a little
later. Lunceford was the reason he went into jazz journalism. He maintained that the Lunceford band had a specific character, just as Duke Ellington's band always had character. Any hot jazz buff would know Jimmie
Lunceford's sound immediately. Once you hit that sound on the radio, you
knew it was him, without even needing to recognize the tune or the soloists.
Gleason explained, "Later, of course, there were little Luncefords, now and
then, but in the beginning there was really the one sound and that was the
way it really stayed because the imitations never made it."[19]

Under the management of Harold Oxley, the band got a new recording
contract. Decca Records, the American branch of the British firm, at the
time in operation for just a couple of weeks , would soon become an aggressive enterprise, specializing in hot music at cut-rate prices. One month earlier, Isham Jones had also signed with the new company, and Fletcher Henderson and others would soon follow. Decca founder Jack Kapp had
worked for Brunswick, and he had enticed big stars such as Bing Crosby,
Guy Lombardo, the Mills Brothers, and the Dorsey Brothers to come with
him. In the course of the second half of the 1930s and the 1940s the label
would develop a treasure trove of African American music. Virtually every
influential black musician, from Louis Armstrong, Billie Holiday, and
Count Basie to Louis Jordan, Ella Fitzgerald, and Buddy Johnson, plus
loads of blues and gospel singers, recorded for Decca or its subsidiary
Brunswick. Apart from the periods he was under contract with RCA Victor
(1934), Columbia (1939–40), and Majestic (1946–47), Lunceford's studio
recordings were to be found on the Decca label.

At its first Decca sessions, September 4 and 5, 1934, the band recorded its already mentioned tribute to Duke Ellington, consisting of *Sophisticated Lady, Mood Indigo,* and *Black and Tan Fantasy.* The last tune on this double date, *Stratosphere,* warrants closer attention. Its title referred to the contemporary exploration of the atmosphere's envelope by professor Auguste Piccard and others, a subject that must have appealed to Lunceford, with his penchant for all aspects of aviation. It was a tune composed and arranged by the leader, one of the few that can claim this distinction. Lunceford proved that his writing abilities by no means took second place to the work of his regular arrangers, Ed Wilcox, Willie Smith, and Sy Oliver. (Provided the leader did write the tune: in later years, Eddie Durham claimed that his former boss had arranged virtually nothing for the orchestra, but tried to wriggle his name in the credits on several occasions.) *Stratosphere* is fairly typical for the band's style. High over a vast, luxurious bed, spread out by the reeds, the trumpets play a simple staccato one-note riff, sounding like a bugler not yet awake, who's swaying in front of his tent, trying to remember the melody of his call. In fact, the brass are so tight that it is hard to determine whether the theme is played by one, two, or (probably) three trumpets. This must have been a tune of the kind the audience drank in breathlessly: full of unexpected turns, tempo shifts, percussive effects, crescendos, four-tone clusters, bitonal harmonies, and contrasts. Musicologist Gunther Schuller, on the other hand, in *The Swing Era* asserted that the opus didn't have a chance in terms of public acceptance: "As its title *Stratosphere* suggests, it was too 'far out there.' Perhaps fifteen years later, in the Stan Kenton era, it would have been acclaimed a 'breakthrough masterpiece' by *Metronome* magazine."[20] The composition, however, remained in the books until at least 1937: it was performed during the band's Swedish tour. So were *Rhapsody Junior* and *Bird of Paradise,* Eddie Durham's vanguard 1935 arrangements for the band.[21]

In contrast, Sy Oliver's *Dream of You,* from the third Decca session, was simple yet delightful, one of his first masterpieces. The tempo is relaxed. The tune begins delicately, the intro as intricate as a miniature painting, the various parts opposing one another in deliberate ways. Oliver's muted trumpet, backed by a softly moaning clarinet choir, establishes a dreamy mood. The glissandi behind Oliver's vocal are effective, and one is left with a feeling of bliss. The arranger had found a clear form for *Dream of You.* This was Oliver's first composition to become an evergreen.

Two months earlier, on September 5, 1934, the band had recorded a Sy

Oliver arrangement that first unveiled his mastery. *Nana* starts with the theme played in alternating short and long notes, with unusual timing and accents. Oliver pulls back the rhythm until its tension becomes irresistible. Carruthers's baritone sax plays an important role in the total sound, and it seems the arranger has Willie Smith play a second baritone in unison.

The November 3, 1934, issue of the *Pittsburgh Courier,* announcing a tour through the East and the Midwest, mentioned that "the band is winning favor both because of the smooth and finished quality of its playing and as a result of the clean-cut, well-trained young gentlemen who make up the ensemble."[22] In due time the adverse conditions in New York City, where the band had trouble finding suitable venues, were turned into an advantage: one-nighters, with the band playing against a percentage of the door, proved to be an inexhaustible gold mine. In his column "In the Groove," *Courier* reporter John Barker stated that the Lunceford orchestra "grossed $3,700 in one night at Old Orchard, ME, in 1934 and did it again last year at the same ballroom!"[23]

Jazznocracy, White Heat, Swingin' Uptown, Miss Otis Regrets, Rhythm Is Our Business, and *Sleepy Time Gal* all rang the cash register. *White Heat* was probably the very first "killer-diller" in the history of jazz to go over with the public. It outsold the 1939 re-creation for Vocalion, and was still in the catalog at the time of Lunceford's death.

In the course of eight months, twenty-seven thousand copies of *Rhythm Is Our Business* were sold—an amazing feat, considering the general dip in the recording business: around 1935–36, after a 1931 peak, the manufacturing of records had come to a virtual standstill. It is significant that 1935 was the last year in the history of the recording business that not one single record sold over a million copies. Apart from that, one can safely assume that at this stage Lunceford's disks did well mainly in the "race" market. As a result of the success of *Rhythm Is Our Business,* a Wilcox arrangement, Lunceford was asked to pen a sequel. But *If I Had Rhythm in My Nursery Rhymes,* recorded six months later, did not sell nearly as well.[24] Today the catchy, humorous *Rhythm Is Our Business* is still in the books of many swing-oriented bands.

The Oxley office employed secretary Alice Murphy and Dave Clark. Clark was a former musician and bandleader whose school orchestra from Jackson, Tennessee, had been the first to play on a black radio show in the South. After graduation, he had become a writer for *Down Beat* magazine, the first black man hired there. "Swing Row Is My Beat" was the name of his column. The Oxley office hired him as a front man, a job requiring traveling to the places where the band was scheduled to play and putting up posters, placing advertisements in the local press, and making sure the jukeboxes were fed with the latest releases. Since there were no black radio shows yet, and only the major cities had African American newspapers, this was the only way to break new records and publicize appearances.[25]

Sometimes Oxley's one-man advertisement department had to resort to unusual tactics. One night in 1935 Clark walked into the lobby of New York radio station WNEW, where Martin Block aired a brand-new program, called *Make Believe Ballroom*. It was a revolutionary format: there was no studio orchestra; Block spun records and was one of the first to do so. The program was launched February 3, 1935, originally as a filler broadcast between coverage of the Bruno Hauptmann trial, which writer H. L. Mencken had dubbed "the greatest story since the Resurrection." Attorney, prosecutor, jurors, judge, and millions of people all over the world relived the kidnapping and subsequent murdering of Charles Lindbergh's baby by Hauptmann, a Bronx carpenter.

Since the sound quality of 78 rpm records was generally considered too poor for use on the air, stations relied on live music by house bands and guest artists. Up until the 1940s, the sales of sheet music far exceeded the distribution of records; accordingly, the songs themselves had always been more important than any specific performer. So all the new (sheet music) hits were played by radio orchestras. Small stations, unable to sustain a house band, used special high-quality recordings made available by transcription services.

Dave Clark wanted Block to play a recording by the Lunceford band, a beautiful ballad, arranged by Edwin Wilcox, called *I'm Walking through Heaven with You*, with a vocal by Dan Grissom. It contained a gorgeous saxophone passage, a Wilcox trademark. The problem was, up to then Block rarely had records by black bands in his program, favoring popular tunes by white artists instead. As a rule, blacks were not even allowed to enter the studio. Errand boys, however, could deliver their messages in the lobby. So Clark had put on a chauffeur's uniform, and told the doorman he brought a record that the station's manager, Clark's boss, was eager to hear on the air, adding that the owner was at home, listening. The trick succeeded, and so Jimmie Lunceford was one of the first black artists to have his records played on the air.[26] From that night on, Martin Block featured disks by black acts on his program on a more regular basis. The ironic part is that in the event Block's show became so popular that, at the urge of the sponsors, he was forced to water down its contents, and play more and more ballads and the like.[27]

Now the one who was not enchanted with the idea of the record being played on the air was, strange as it may seem, Decca's Jack Kapp. Decca was fiercely protective of its records. During the 1930s, radio had become big as a means of entertainment, and was seen as a threat to both live music and the recording business. People who listened to records heard on their wireless set were not inclined to buy them, went the general way of thinking in the record-manufacturing business. Consequently, all Decca 78 rpm singles bore a warning, printed on the record label, between the company's 3D logo and the hole. It said, in tiny golden letters, against a dark blue background, "Not licensed for Radio Broadcast." It took the companies years and two famous court cases, involving Fred Waring and Paul Whiteman, before they realized it was just the other way around: radio could be a potent force in promoting their wares. Decca was one of the last to finally yield, in the early 1940s.

Lunceford's records did so well that the Decca company decided to concentrate on its gold mine, sacking some of its other black bands who sold less. Fletcher Henderson, Earl Hines, and Claude Hopkins were direct victims of Lunceford's successes.

Red Richards remembered that Lunceford went on the road right after *Rhythm Is Our Business* started to hit that winter of 1934–35. That was the first big-time tour, covering the southern states, the eastern seaboard, and southern Canada. "They used to draw like eight to ten thousand people a dance, through the South," maintained Richards. At that time, Fats Waller and Cab Calloway were the only black artists able to draw that many people. (In 1940, Waller played for 120,000 swing fans at Chicago's Soldier Field.)[28] Lunceford's drawing power was a result of his first hits on recordings and the broadcasts from the Cotton Club. Word-of-mouth also was an important factor. At the Lafayette Red found out that the band already had a vast repertory. Lunceford always tried out tunes on the road before he recorded them.

The tour Red referred to was called "Harlem Express." It started February 1, 1935, and lasted four months. Under the auspices of the Columbia Broadcasting System, the fifty "Jazz-Mad Stars" worked the major black theaters and dance halls in the country. At that time, one got a complete package for one's fifty-cent admission. First, there was the newsreel, fol-

lowed by a comedy short or a music short, and then the trailers for the coming movies. This was only the introduction to the live show, which ran for
at least sixty minutes. It was all designed to crank up expectations for the
feature movie, starring Clark Gable or Deanna Durbin. This format did
not change for years, but in the course of the late 1930s kids started to come
specifically for the live band. They could not care less for Charles Boyer—
they came to be sent by Charlie Barnet!

The Harlem Express show, produced by Paramount man Harry Gour-
fain, also featured contortionist Brady "Jigsaw" Jackson, vaudeville artist
Apus Brooks, singer Babe Matthews, and comedian Sandy Burns, plus
other dance and vocal acts. The Jimmie Lunceford Glee Club got a separate
billing, which proved the choir was a valuable attraction. The fact that in
certain theaters the musicians played acting roles during the first half of the
evening, accompanied by the house band, may also be considered unusual.
The show carried a pair of electricians, "to operate the switches, so that
'moods' may be accented by varying intensity of light," according to a contemporary newspaper report.

There were four new faces in the orchestra. High-note specialist Paul
Webster, who had been in the band three years earlier, had come back in
January, replacing Tommy Stevenson. Elmer Crumbley and Eddie
Durham arrived to reinforce the trombone section, and Laforest Dent from
Minneapolis was added to the reeds.

The strenuous tour required discipline from the musicians, both on and
off the stage. Whenever a man was late for a rehearsal, he had to buy the
band two bottles of liquor. If the bus was scheduled to leave at eleven, it left
at eleven. Anyone who happened to miss the bus was supposed to make the
gig on his own. In eighteen years, nobody ever missed a show, unless he
was sick.

The drawing power of the Harlem Express package was astounding.
Complete families crammed into their Model T Fords and traveled one
hundred miles or more to see the acts. When a thousand people turned out,
it was considered a slow night. Quite often it was over four thousand. Bass
player Gene Ramey told how as a youth he went to a dance in Woodland.
The venue was the old Masonic Auditorium. "He had the whole house
jumping. The people were dancing and swinging so hard the floor went
down six inches, and they had to cancel the dance!"

Both the press (the black press, predominantly, but not exclusively) and
the audiences raved. "Here is one of the new 'big' bands in the making,"

prophesied the *Warren Tribune Chronicle*. At Detroit's new Michigan Theater, formerly Orchestra Hall, the show shattered the attendance records set by Cab Calloway and George Olsen. (Olsen, a star since his 1925 recording of *Who?*, was a popular society bandleader.) During the week it played the theater, 12,389 people saw the program. The success was in part triggered by the shrewd manipulation of the local media and instrument retail shops by the orchestra's new manager, who had proclaimed a Support Jimmie Lunceford Week in Detroit.

Fisk University was another stop. The musicians had not seen their alma mater for three years, and returned at the request of Fisk's student body. Jimmie and Crystal Lunceford donated five hundred dollars to the endowment campaign of the university, and the orchestra members expressed their enthusiasm over the improvements made at Fisk since their day. The students responded with a statement about their prominent alumnus: "Fisk students feel that this Fiskite has been constantly making new friends for Fisk throughout the world. He has been ever willing to do his part to stimulate Fisk clubs and aid them in their program throughout the country."

During the last leg of the Harlem Express tour, in early May, Jimmie Lunceford was at the Palace Theater in Memphis, and it was here that Fats Waller crowned him "King of Syncopation." Both bands were appearing there, and though it was probably just a little thing cooked up by their managers, for a while the title stuck.[29]

In Boston, just before the band returned to its home base, the chorus line needed two or three replacements, and Mae Buzzelle, eighteen, was one of the hundreds of young, eager dancers who auditioned. She won the spot and became one of the musicians's favorite dancers, as well as one of their favorite cooks. Arranger Billy Moore Jr., in particular, raved over her sweet potato pies. Her boyfriend and future husband, Frank Bonitto, was working at the post office in Cambridge, Massachusetts, and had considered himself a fan since the broadcasts from the Cotton Club. Just like other listeners, music fans and musicians, he had questioned the management's decision to replace their beloved Duke with this band of newcomers. And just like the management and the other music lovers, he had discovered that this unknown band really had a style all its own. So when the Harlem Express tour started, he already was a dedicated follower. Now that his sweetheart was dancing with the show, he struck up a friendship with a couple of members of the orchestra.

"Jimmie and Sy and all the guys liked my wife as a person," said Frank, after all these years still proud of their friendship. "I guess they were used to theatrical types. My wife was sort of intellectual, was always reading, spoke good French. She used to be an entertaining person herself. I just came in on her back. That was right up my alley, of course. She danced locally, around Boston. You know, it was during the Depression, and she was sure making a hell of a lot more money than I was making."

Once, when a package show included the Lunceford band and comedian Dusty Fletcher, Mae Buzzelle acted as the "straight girl" in Dusty's "Open the Door, Richard" routine. She peeked out of the cardboard house that Dusty was trying to invade. This was long before Fletcher put it on record. It became a hit for Dusty and a dozen other artists who covered the song. Lunceford's version, by the way, was never released—probably because at the time it was recorded, 1947, the "Open the Door" craze had died.

Jimmie Lunceford, Sy Oliver, and Frank and Mae Bonitto would remain friends. Whenever the band played the Boston area, Frank and Mae were present. And New York was not too far: a weekend round trip by train was five dollars. They continued to be fans long after the Jimmie Lunceford Orchestra had ceased to exist.

The Bonittos were just two of the thousands of young jazz adepts who had discovered the Lunceford bounce when the band broadcast from the Cotton Club, and subsequently saw the Harlem Express when it toured the nation. These dances heralded the era that became known as the Swing Craze.

{6}

SWING BEGINS

What kind of dance is that, man?
—Earle Warren

Jazz lore has it that Benny Goodman started the swing craze. At the end of a grueling cross-country tour, he hit gold with an ecstatic reception at the Palomar Ballroom, on Vermont Avenue, between Second and Third, in Los Angeles; the date was August 21, 1935. The resulting publicity triggered a hype that lasted well over a decade, and made Goodman "King of Swing." To dedicated jazz and dance fans, his music sounded familiar. All over the country, black bands had been playing these rhythms and riff-laden grooves for four or five years. But the style was first heard on a truly grand scale months before Goodman arrived in California, during the February–May tour of the Harlem Express. Lunceford's drawing power had been markedly greater than Goodman's. The white press, however, did not pay much attention to Lunceford's successes. So it can be argued that it was Jimmie Lunceford, not Benny Goodman, who put the spark to the tinder. Apart from that, some contemporary fans felt that Goodman did not start to really swing before he acquired the services of tenor man Vido Musso, a full year later. For them, the tune *Jam Session* (recorded November 5, 1936) marked the beginning of the clarinetist's Kingship of Swing.

There are interesting similarities and differences between the two bandleaders. Goodman's roots were Jewish. His family was poor, of Polish-Lithuanian descent, and at fourteen little Benjamin, a child prodigy, was earning enough money playing clarinet in dance orchestras to be able to support the family. Not long thereafter he really started to make a lot of money when he became a much-sought-after studio musician in New York.

Lunceford, Goodman's senior by seven years, was black. His family had become relatively well-to-do, and he mastered an impressive array of instruments, including the clarinet, without really excelling on any of them. Before he started his own band, Lunceford had been a teacher.

Both leaders were good businessmen and strict disciplinarians, but whereas Benny was perceived by many as being cold, absent-minded, and egotistical, Jimmie, though introverted, possessed a warmer personality. Both men achieved their initial fame through series of radio broadcasts. Goodman did so with the *Let's Dance* show (1934–35), and Lunceford when he resided at the Cotton Club, just a couple of months earlier. Both their reputation were solidified during extensive tours.

Benny Goodman's role in breaking down the color line has been well documented. Few people are aware that Jimmie Lunceford, too, did his share to integrate the music business. From 1933 on, two years before Goodman's integrated trio made its debut, the Lunceford orchestra played white colleges, the first black band to do so. Lunceford was one of the first black leaders to hire white arrangers, a white singer, and white musicians. The orchestra's drawing power enabled musicians and management to be fastidious about the venues they played: as a rule, the Jimmie Lunceford Orchestra did not perform in segregated dance-halls.

So while Goodman was hailed as the King of Swing by the white press, Lunceford had achieved a similar status in the black community ("King of Syncopation"). This happened seven or eight months before Benny Goodman's coronation.

There were other black pretenders for the swing throne at the time when Lunceford was touring with the Harlem Express revue, bands that drew capacity crowds wherever they played. Fats Waller's music teemed with exuberance and humor; his appeal was broad, and he could turn any silly song into a sparkling jewel. Cab Calloway, like Waller, was a crowd-pleaser; his band sounded tight, and he was able to reach both the black man in the street and the white Park Avenue crowd. One of the most popular black bands of this era was the Mills Blue Rhythm Band, led by singer Lucky Millinder. It could swing hard and had a good rhythm section, exciting soloists, original arrangements, and a string of hit records. Fletcher Henderson's band swung just as violently as Lunceford's—though it would have had a hard time competing with the Harlem Express in the flag-waver department. The problem was, Henderson was busy rebuilding his orchestra after his last outfit had deserted him in November 1934, after quarrels over money. He did not record at all in 1935, was involved in a series of hassles with the musicians union, and was also busy writing material for Benny Goodman's *Let's Dance* radio show.

Duke Ellington's Famous Orchestra was superior to all these bands, but catered to predominantly white audiences. Moreover, for Ellington 1935 was a year full of grief. His mother died and he sank into a deep depression.

In hindsight, the most likely candidate to have started the swing era was Louis Armstrong, who virtually "invented" swing. Armstrong's dexterity, both as a singer and as a trumpet player, was undisputed, and his creativity, enthusiasm, and spontaneity were infectious. But the trumpet pioneer had spent most of the early 1930s in Europe, and was recovering from an over-stressed lip while Lunceford toured the United States.

None of these popular black acts displayed Lunceford's versatility and finesse. None of them was able to swing as violently as the Harlem Express. The ability to play romantic ballads next to novelty numbers and hard-swinging killer-dillers or flag-wavers put the Lunceford band in the van-guard with both the dancers and the listeners. This versatility, combined with its unique stage show, sold the band.

The rise to fame of the early swing big bands coincided with a number of changes in American society. At the time of Lunceford's successful runs at New York's Cotton Club, his first large-scale tours, and the initial hit records, the music world was about to boom dramatically. Not only the music reached a boiling point, but the entire United States was in for some fundamental changes.

When the second half of the 1930s got on its way, the first results of President Roosevelt's New Deal program, his answer to the stagnation and the poverty caused by the Great Depression, became tangible. A general feeling of relief, of cautious optimism, began to emerge. This dawning of a positive change showed itself in politics as well as in everyday life, in the arts of the period, architecture, design and fashion, movies and shows, even in the futuristic way some automobiles, trains, and airplanes, those symbols of the modern times, were shaped. The notion that America was indeed rapidly becoming the world's leader in business matters, technology, and popular culture was once again beginning to jell. The nation had made impressive strides in this respect before the Great Depression, and observers realized that the economic crisis might just be a temporary hiatus in that process. A strong collective sense of forward motion hovered over America.

However, the lean times were not over yet. Poverty was still everywhere. Furthermore, this was a period of political turmoil. The American Communist Party achieved new heights of acceptance and impact, fueled, among other causes, by the strong sentiments aroused by the Spanish Civil War.

The big bands furnished the soundtrack for the era. Swing music spread like wildfire in 1935. There had been a baby boom around 1920–21, in size comparable to the more famous one of 1946–47. It was the first time the annual increase of the national population had passed the two-million mark.[1] So there was a tidal wave of fresh fourteen-year-olds, eager beavers looking for action.

The kids got their action from Benny the King, they got it from Tommy Dorsey, from Casa Loma, already a favorite at the college circuit, from Lunceford and in no time from hundreds of other dance orchestras turned into swing bands. And remarkably swiftly, these youngsters had developed an extensive youth culture. Jazz musicians's slang, dating back to the 1920s, was adopted as their official *jive lingo*. Smoking marijuana, which had been common in musicians' circles and metropolitan high schools for years, became a favorite pastime among part of the *hep cats*. During the early 1940s, the *zoot suit* was popular among those who were "in the know." Frank Sinatra, the coolest crooner of the time, Cab Calloway, Lionel Hampton, and Louis Jordan were four important role models to popularize the new oversized look. It consisted of a generously padded, wide-lapeled jacket that reached down to the knees, high-waisted, baggy pants, tapering down to the ankles, and two-tone shoes, topped by a wide-brimmed fedora. In a zoot one looked like a cross-breeding of gangster, clown, and gorilla. If a loud-colored zoot suit alone was not enough to attract the attention of the opposite sex, there was nothing else left to do but to directly attack the object of one's affection with a serenade. In olden days this was done with the help of a guitar; now you put your nickels in the jukebox, trying to find out what band or singer happened to be the girl's favorite.

Coin-operated music machines were not a novelty in 1935, for they had been around since the beginnings of the recording industry. But that was the year the jukebox phenomenon really obtained a foothold in American society. In 1933, during Prohibition, some 25,000 jukeboxes were in operation, a large percentage of them in speakeasies. The next year AMI, Seeburg, and Mills, the most prominent manufacturers of jukeboxes, turned out a total of 15,000 machines. This was just before Wurlitzer and Rock-Ola arrived on the scene. Before the end of 1936, 63,000 Wurlitzers had been shipped to distributors. One year later, Wurlitzer was selling $2,000,000 worth of jukeboxes monthly. By then, approximately 225,000 public venues, ranging from bus terminals to ice cream stands, featured these hot slot machines.

The jukebox was largely responsible for the recovery of the 78 rpm record: from 1936 on, sales went up, year after year. In 1932 the recording industry had hit rock bottom, with total sales of a mere $5,000,000. Sixteen years later, this figure had risen to $250,000,000 annually.[2]

In black neighborhoods, 78 rpm singles by Cab Calloway, Chick Webb, Fats Waller, Blind Boy Fuller, and Lunceford were in jukeboxes constantly. Between the mid-1930s and the late-1950s, one would have had a hard time finding a jukebox in Harlem that did not have its share of Lunceford disks.

Swing music triggered specific dances, such as the Suzy Q and the Lindy Hop; the latter was the most acrobatic, energetic, and elegant swing-era dance. It also challenged one's creativity: couples used to draw up new steps, leaps, and turns in their homes, to show off at the Saturday dance. The Lindy Hop was not taught in dancing schools, like the earlier craze, the fox-trot, but developed spontaneously, in private homes and on the floors of the ballrooms.

In 1937 Earle Warren joined Count Basie's band as its lead saxophonist and ballad singer. When he made his debut with Basie at New York's Savoy Ballroom that year, he was "just flabbergasted."

I didn't know what the people was doing, swinging there, throwing them over their heads and everything. It was the Lindy Hop. And I said, what kind of dance is *that*, man. They didn't dance that way in my part of the country, it hadn't gotten that far yet. Nobody did that at my dances! But here—they were throwing each other out, she's kicking this way and he's kicking that way, you know. It was just like I left to go three hundred miles, and I'm in a different world!

When I got to the Savoy, there was top people. They created what you call circles. I remember there was a circle there and a circle here, and there's a circle down the hall. Farther on the dance floor, everybody was doing their thing. I mean, these three couples, they were extra special dancers. That's the first time I saw a guy throwing a chick over his head and do a split. I was just flabbergasted.

Ballrooms grew bigger, and their numbers rose as well. After the so-called Roaring Twenties, the era when hot dance music first flowered, the dance hall business had suffered significantly during the Great Depression. The repeal in 1933 of the Volstead Act, which prohibited the manufacture, sale, or transportation of alcoholic beverages in the United States, had reversed the situation for the dancings, and between 1936 and 1941, their number doubled.[3]

The aforementioned youth subculture of habits, looks, and expressions started in the African American and Latin neighborhoods of New York, Los Angeles, Kansas City, Memphis, and other urban areas. From there it filtered into the mainstream. As such, it had a unifying effect: the sons and daughters of older American families mixed with kids from recent immigrants and, in New York and other northern cities, even with blacks. They were all united by a common "belief" in swing.[4]

It should be borne in mind, however, that this process of acculturation worked differently in the white world, where dancing and dance music were perceived to be of little value. Some opinion leaders even proclaimed that jazz and dance music were harmful to the mental health of America's youth. This was, in effect, a repetition of the situation in the early 1920s, when clergymen and political leaders declared jazz a threat to young people's morals.

Among blacks, music and dancing always had been held in high esteem. In New Orleans, for instance, the number of pianos and phonographs per capita was higher in black neighborhoods than in the white sections. This was in spite of the belief among a not insignificant minority of traditionally religious African Americans that jazz and blues must be considered and condemned as "the devil's music." The many excellent music departments at black high schools, colleges, and universities stood as testimonial to the high regard with which music was held. Consequently, when the dance band phenomenon started to flower in the mid-1930s, leaders were able to pick musicians who already had a thorough training in the classics.

This whole shift in popular culture was about to happen when Lunceford hit the big-time. For twelve or thirteen years, roughly between 1933 and 1946, the Jimmie Lunceford Orchestra was the most exciting and best-loved all-round dance band in the African American community. No other orchestra combined such precision, dynamics, and rhythmic punch with a flashy show. No other swing big band exerted so much influence on other ensembles. Yet no other orchestra seems to have drifted further into the mists of collective oblivion. "It really has become sort of a cult band," mused San Francisco trombone player Jim Leigh. "It's funny, people who heard Lunceford's orchestra all say it was the greatest big band, better than Duke Ellington or Count Basie. Now if you ask me, you can't tell from its records."

It's true: most eyewitnesses agree that the band made a far more profound impression live than on any of its recordings. (That, of course, goes for many good live acts.) Radio air checks suggest the Harlem Express not only played looser—and faster!—at dances, but tended to enhance its arrangements and stretch out on tunes. It is also true that the sound quality of the band's recorded output during the mid-1930s varied from passable to dubious. (The vinyl reissue program from around 1980, in the French Jazz Heritage series, suffered from poor mastering and pressing. Only occasionally can one catch glimpses of the full dynamics, the subtle coloring, and the power. More often than not, one has to guess as to what the orchestra's actual sound and impact might have been.) The French Classics CD series does more justice to the Lunceford band, but for a taste of the full spectrum the best choices are the scattered compilations on American Decca/GRP and Columbia. Radio transcription recordings, pressed in the 1940s on sixteen-inch, 33 rpm hi-fi vinyl disks, manufactured for distribution among smaller stations, were reissued on the Circle label. These sessions show Lunceford's organization in all its splendor, as if the orchestra is sitting in one's living room. Apart from these two CDs, some of the *Jubilee* shows, recorded during the war by the Armed Forces Radio Service, were reissued with good sound quality.

Lunceford believed that in order to build a sizable following, he had to combine swing and sweet: screaming instrumentals alternated with soft crooning. Henry Wells, who played the trombone and handled the ballad singing, departed in early 1935, to go with the Claude Hopkins band. Just prior to that, Elmer Crumbley had broken up his own band in Omaha in order to join Lunceford's trombone section. Wells was replaced by Eddie Durham, who did not sing, and Dan Grissom, who did not play the trombone. The latter sang and got around on the saxophone. So although Lunceford's regular reed section numbered just four saxes, with Grissom and, occasionally, the leader himself added, it could expand into six horns.

Grissom's saccharin-sweet crooning did not go over well with hardcore swing buffs. He was nicknamed Dan Gruesome by his detractors, and not entirely without reason, though this kind of crooning does have some period charm. "Dan was the Bing Crosby deal," chuckled Benny Waters, who served in the 1942 reed section, "for the chicks." Waters has a point: the band and its crooner definitely had a strong appeal with the females. This appeal was a major factor in Lunceford's success in the black community.

Grissom, however, could and occasionally did sing in a more attractive ordinary tenor voice. He built a solo career after he left the Lunceford organization in 1943. Though the rhythms and the actual sound have changed, Grissom and colleagues like Pha Terrell and Bill Kenny (of Ink Spots fame) can be viewed as forefathers of the so-called R&B crooners, sixty years later. Maxwell and D'Angelo may not be aware, but they had grandpas in the swing era.

Probably as a result of the band's success at the trendy Cotton Club, more and more emphasis was being put on showmanship. When the orchestra members mounted the stage, they successively saluted the audience, their leader, and one another in a set way.[5] The band had even rehearsed four different bows to the audience. Apart from the dancing and the choreographed movements of the musicians, now comedy bits were added, like Willie Smith putting on a silly hat and singing a nursery song, or Eddie Tompkins doing his Louis Armstrong impersonation. In the theaters the Lunceford orchestra specialized in doing imitations of popular bands such as Paul Whiteman's, Duke Ellington's, and Guy Lombardo's. Sometimes the orchestra would perform certain ballads or a hit like *For Dancers Only* behind a screen, in backlighting, the shadows on the screen enhancing the drama of the tune. "That was all novelty and I liked it," said

Eddie Durham, referring to his first encounter with the Harlem Express at the Apollo, shortly before he joined the band.[6]

"Lunceford was the onliest band that had showmanship, during that time," stressed saxophone player Joe Houston. "Everybody in there, like, the horns would do this, saxophones do that. That's what made them. All what Lunceford do [was] stand there, direct."

Eddie Tompkins sometimes played the role of the band's straw boss. Whenever the orchestra found itself entangled in a particular difficult passage during rehearsals, it usually was Tompkins who told his fellow musicians how to phrase or articulate.[7]

During the 1930s and 1940s, it was quite common for black sport stars such as Jack Johnson, Joe Louis, Jesse Owens, and the Harlem Globetrotters to appear on the same bill with touring dance bands. Johnson had been the headliner when the Lunceford orchestra first performed in New York, at the Lafayette. Owens traveled with Skeets Tolbert's Gentlemen of Swing, an early jump band. During intermission, Owens used to put up hurdles around the dance floor and then gave demonstrations of his athletic skills.[8] In the summer of 1935 Lunceford accompanied Joe Louis, the future heavyweight champion. At the time Louis was a promising talent, who one year earlier had become pro, after winning some important fights. The show was presented at, among other places, Chicago's Savoy Ballroom and the Rockland Palace in New York. As a result, the popular fighter declared, "Lunceford is my favorite band." "To the average person, reared within the refined cloisters of the Whiteman-Kemp-Duchin cult," writer Edward Stein pointed out, "Jimmie Lunceford's band carries a tremendous 'sock,' the music parallel of Joe Louis' gloved fists."[9]

The "Cotton Club Parade" had been a hit, but for the winter season the club's management hired the Blue Rhythm Band, directed by Lucky Millinder. Lunceford was asked back for the 1935 show, which again proved to be successful. This was the "Truckin'" program, named after the song and dance that were introduced in it. "Keep on truckin'" had a bitter relevance in mid-1930s Harlem, which was suffering from an unemployment rate of 80 percent. The club's management used to hand out food baskets at Christmas time, for the poor. This was, of course, good publicity as well. In the "Truckin'" show, the Jimmie Lunceford Orchestra played an even more dominating role, supplying the bulk of the vocals and comedy.[10]

Touring helped to establish Lunceford as a household name. In Texas future rhythm-and-blues tenor star Joe Houston saw the traveling orchestra and maintained that Lunceford "had more class than everybody. He had more class than Duke. Duke got the credit for having class—but Lunceford *had* class. They cared for themselves, they were the sharpest band in the world. I remember Willie Smith told me, he'd say they was the only band that gave Duke trouble." "They walked and they talked and they played like men who had been touched with a very special thing," confirmed Ralph Gleason, who saw the band many times when he was a student in New York.[11]

Joe Houston continued, "He [Willie Smith] say, they was recording a hit, and both sides were hits. The record man tells them, 'Man, just record one hit, save the other one for the next session.' They's that hot, man! Two-sided hits!"

By now the records were indeed selling like hotcakes. Lunceford sold better than most other black orchestras. There were times when Lunceford had three records in *Billboard*'s pop charts simultaneously. He was in the same category as Ellington, and only Fats Waller and Bumble Bee Slim fared better in the juke joints down South. At this time, the mid-1930s, any record that sold over five thousand copies was considered a hit.

Jimmie Lunceford's first successes, *Jazznocracy* and *White Heat*, had been issued on separate 78s in 1934. The following year, the band scored four back-to-back hits: *Avalon/Swanee River* and *Running Wild/Four or Five Times*. This was continued in 1936 (*Sleepy Time Gal/Organ Grinder's Swing*), 1937 (*For Dancers Only/Coquette*), 1939 (*'Tain't What You Do/Cheatin' on Me*), and 1940 (*What's Your Story, Morning Glory/Swingin' on C*). In this period between 1936 and 1940, Lunceford's disks were continuously on the Roll of Honor in *Metronome*'s annual Records of the Year selections.

The first single successes proved to be just a prelude. In the second half of 1935, during its return run at the Cotton Club, the orchestra scored two "classic" hits, *Swanee River* and *My Blue Heaven*, both tunes arranged by Sy Oliver. *Swanee River* opens in a way not unusual for the band: the muted trumpets play Stephen Foster's melody staccato against a background of slowly moving, soft yet full-sounding reeds. In the next chorus, the theme is transformed by the saxophones. They stretch it, compress it back into shape, and are followed by the brass, which continue this process in a more overt way. Then a trio of aggressive trombones partake in the conversation. The solos by Crumbley, Smith, Wilcox, and Oliver are modest but functional: subservient to the overall orchestral sound.

Sy Oliver's conception of *My Blue Heaven* is even more adventurous. He designed a sophisticated arrangement, not just for the band, but also for the vocal Trio, consisting of himself, Willie Smith, and guitarist Al Norris. In this recording, the latter also plays the violin in the background. This clearly is not your ordinary vocal trio with instrumental accompaniment. The vocals are orchestral in character, and their timing and phrasing are utterly hip. Starting with a simple yet dramatic introduction by the piano, evoking a wealth of expectations, the arrangement proceeds with inevitable logic and a pleasant impact. Bass player Mose Allen seems to carry the band in his fingertips with his irresistible bouncy two-beat swing. Willie Smith plays an attractive countermelody on the baritone sax. *My Blue Heaven* is a classic big band performance, and it had mass appeal as well. Hundreds of amateur vocal groups must have tried to emulate the Lunceford Trio in gymnasiums or cellars, trying to blend and phrase just like their idols.

Even critics who were skeptical about Lunceford's ideas of polished swing, claiming it was "commercial," had to conclude it worked, both in box-office terms and as an artistic concept. Dutch reviewer Willem van Steensel van der Aa wrote under the *nom de plume* of Will G. Gilbert in *De Jazzwereld*, a monthly magazine. After stating that Lunceford's music in general "is too artificial for my taste, there is too much filing going on, too much planing, too much sanding, too much polishing," he admitted, "to be honest, *My Blue Heaven* is an exception to the rule in more ways than one," praising the band's timing and modulations and Joe Thomas's tenor work.

The same critic reviewed the singles *Swanee River/The Best Things in Life Are Free* and *Nana/Miss Otis Regrets*. He compared Lunceford's style with contemporary assembly-line products and wondered "whether this is a virtue or a deplorable spiritual impoverishment. Lunceford's process mirrors the general spiritual regression of our time."

The reviewer stated that because of Lunceford's standardization of orchestration and execution, he was not able to distinguish among the titles. Which is remarkable, to put it mildly, given the totally different nature of *Swanee River* and *Nana*.[12]

The Lunceford beat is worthy of closer examination. We have seen that it is essentially a two-beat rhythm. But unlike the choppy modern-day Dixieland variant, it is more even and doesn't cut up the flow. In the course of the 1940s, this two-beat rhythm was to evolve into a regular backbeat, which became the standard drum pattern of rhythm-and-blues bands.

While the beat was provided by the rhythm section, the horns furnished their share of the pulse, accenting the second beats, giving the rhythm an elastic quality. Arranger and bandleader Buddy Baker explained, "He [Oliver] created that rocking feeling by having the various sections play rhythm while playing the melody. For example, he would have the trombones playing a pattern that really laid down a beat. Then he would have the saxophones going against that."[13] Whenever Sy Oliver wanted the brass or the reeds to play a really snappy note or chord, he put the term *hop* in the score. Al Grey had some enlightening remarks about this subject. He switched from Benny Carter's trombone section to Jimmie Lunceford's brass:

> Benny Carter, his band played everything long. When I went into Jimmie Lunceford, see, everything was played short. The rhythmic feeling, the line itself. For instance, like, Jimmie Lunceford would say [hums the famous intro of *For Dancers Only*]. Benny Carter would have said [hums the same phrase legato]. You see? Then when you go into a new band like that, and here you have been playing things long, and here there is chopping and shortening, you have to reacquire yourself. So I feel it's still good, from going from long to short. It enabled me to really stay up on top of the playing of the music.

Al Grey had inherited Trummy Young's position as lead trombonist and soloist. Trummy, in turn, had replaced Eddie Durham, who had been the most important new face in the 1935 band. The latter had moved over from Willie Bryant's orchestra in the early part of that year, and was a three-way asset—he strengthened the trombone team of Russell Bowles and Elmer Crumbley, played amplified guitar, and wrote highly original charts.

Durham's background was the thriving Kansas City scene: his buddies Eddie Tompkins and Paul Webster both from that city, had recommended him to their leader. His rhythmic feeling was closer to K.C.'s standard 4/4 than the prevailing 2/4 in his new environment. However, as a musician with roots in old-fashioned minstrel shows, Eddie Durham had no problem getting adjusted to the more archaic rhythm. Yet his dynamic arrangements always stayed closer to the mainstream groove than Sy Oliver's. One of his trademark devices was the use of wah-wah mute effects by the brass—a style element that was not unusual in big band swing and that was picked up by Glenn Miller later.

One of Eddie Durham's first tasks was writing a new book for vocalist and part-time sax player Dan Grissom. Up to then, Grissom had played Joe Thomas's parts. Now he was put on fifth alto.

For his first recording session with his new employer, Durham, supervised by Ed Wilcox, arranged two little-known Ellington pieces, *Bird of Paradise* and *Rhapsody Junior*. Duke himself never recorded these compositions for a commercial label. *Rhapsody Junior* is an architectural wonder of modulations and moods, with an end result that is more pointillistic in character than Ellington's impressionistic style. In fact, it was indebted to Don Redman's 1931 *Chant of the Weed* just as much as to, for instance, Duke's original version of *In a Sentimental Mood*, recorded one month before *Rhapsody Junior*.

Like the other arrangers, Durham was allowed to stretch out, and there were no boundaries. That way, he felt he was able to stay ahead of the audience all the time. The contrasts in his arrangement of *Thunder* bear this out. The introduction is pure avant-garde "noise." Then the storming horns lay themselves to rest behind Dan Grissom's vocal. The arranger used multipart block harmony in *Count Me Out* and employed the double-barreled unison baritones of Carruthers and Smith in *Running a Temperature*. He could write quite complex arrangements, but Durham was, perhaps, at his best when he did not waste any notes, as in *Swingin' on C*. In this piece he managed to generate a maximum of swing with the barest melodic material. It was a precision operation: Earl's baritone punctuated notes with the assured perfection of a seasoned surgeon.

Like Sy Oliver, Durham was fond of changing the key halfway through an arrangement, as *Oh Boy* testifies. Note also the twin baritone lead in this tune, in unison and two-part voicing. Here one hears how the arranger had the horns play decrescendo toward the end, only to come back full throttle for the last bar. (Four years later, he would milk this little trick when he arranged *In the Mood* for Glenn Miller, thereby establishing swing music's anthem.) The amazing, very visual *Pigeon Walk*, which sounds like it was written for a cartoon, was full of modulations. Contrasts abound; the muted trumpets after Durham's guitar interlude are a real find—and a mark of fine craftsmanship. Raymond Scott, who did his share of cartoon writing, called these kind of atmospheric pieces "descriptive jazz." *'Frisco Fog*, from the same session, but arranged by Leon Carr, is another example. These intricate tunes, with their unusual modulations and surprising contrasts and effects, were daring for their time. They gave the repertory a distinctive character and have not become dated.

Eddie Durham's *Harlem Shout* is an example of the kind of exciting, yet restrained flag-wavers Sy Oliver also was good at, with Paul Webster screaming high above the ensemble. Sometimes, in *Avalon* for example, Durham's free-flying charts sound as if they are harmonized solos. After the theme, the trombone trio play a chorus that is imaginatively timed and as varied as any hot solo created on the spur of the moment. Willie Smith's alto solo, by the way, shows why he was cherished by Earl Bostic.

When he was with Bennie Moten's band, around 1930, Eddie had introduced the National resonator guitar. It was an ordinary wooden Spanish model, with a built-in conical tin resonator, about ten inches in diameter.[14] This gave its sound a peculiar loud, sharp, metallic quality, halfway between the banjo and the electric guitar of the future. Resonator guitars and the related all-metal steel guitars and smaller dobros were manufactured by the National String Instrument Corporation in Los Angeles. These guitars were originally designed for dance orchestras and Hawaiian ensembles, and since Hawaiian bands in the 1920s enjoyed a vogue in traveling vaudeville shows, their instruments "crossed over" to hillbilly outfits. In blues and especially jazz, these amplified guitars remained rarities.

It is clear from the abundance of guitar solos in Lunceford's 1935–37 output (Eddie managed to put a guitar solo in just about every chart he wrote) that the leader, who had started out on guitar, was very fond of the instrument. During live performances Lunceford used to hold the solo microphone near the F-shaped sound hole of the guitar. Everything was fine until early 1937, when the instrument broke down, and Durham learned that he could not get a new one. That's when he changed to an electric model.

Electric guitars were a novelty back in 1937. Only a few artists in jazz (George Barnes) and blues (Memphis Minnie) had dabbled with early models and home-built contraptions. In the early 1920s "mad professors" such as Lloyd Roar had built experimental electric instruments, and the Gibson company had tried to put them on the market, but it had been, quite simply, too early. In 1935 Gibson unveiled its first electric production model, a metal body Hawaiian guitar. One year later, the famous ES-150 appeared, the first regular electric Spanish model to hit the market.

By that time, Jack Miller had already amazed patrons of Orville Knapp's show orchestra with a home-built electric steel guitar. Bob Dunn, with Milton Brown's Musical Brownies, a pioneering Western Swing outfit, excited 1935 Fort Worth audiences with his rapid-fire excursions on the electric steel. He is regarded as the first electric guitar soloist in the history of music. Still, it would take another couple of years before the new instrument really caught on.

The swing craze was instrumental in this development. The ballrooms grew larger, and since public address, or PA, systems were still in their infancy, the bands had to grow in size to accommodate the halls. An ad in the *Baltimore Afro American* of August 8, 1938, announcing an Elks Grand Ball at the Fifth Regiment Armory, with music provided by Jimmie Lunceford and His Famous Orchestra, specifically mentioned a special amplifying system.[15] In New York, the Savoy Ballroom was one of the first dance halls to be equipped with a PA system. But before that, the poor acoustic guitar was drowned out in the violent roar of trumpets and drums.

Eddie Durham's first electric guitar was not a factory model, but a contraption he had designed himself. Originally, he had a friend remodel a standard microphone, wired to a PA system, to be inserted in the F-hole of the instrument. This apparently did not entirely satisfy the guitarist, so he designed a movable bridge, connected to a metal wire coat hanger. By manipulating the coat hanger with his finger, he could produce a resonating effect. His electric model confronted Eddie Durham with a couple of problems. It was not unusual for his guitar to overload the mains of the hall, causing the lights to blow fuses. He almost electrocuted himself a couple of times. An even bigger problem was that his custom-built amplifier used alternate current, whereas most of the country still ran on direct current.

Early in 1937 Durham, on the road with the Harlem Express, met a talented seventeen-year-old guitarist in Oklahoma City, named Charlie Christian. Charlie of course was still playing acoustic guitar, and Durham showed him how he could get a crisper sound by hitting the strings in downward strokes only. He also showed him that by getting his instrument electrified, he could play at the same level as the horns. (Later, Christian was to devote a tune to their current problems: *AC/DC Current*.)

During the same tour Durham came across Floyd Smith, guitarist in the Jeter-Pillars Plantation Club Orchestra, a meeting that resulted in Smith's adapting the electric guitar.[16] *Floyd's Guitar Blues*, recorded two years later (on an electric lap-model) with Andy Kirk's Twelve Clouds of Joy, became the first electric guitar hit. Durham's own early electric guitar work was recorded only after he had left Lunceford. It probably took the studio technicians some time before they had figured out how to handle the electric model.

In March 1936 the band played dances at Cornell, Duke, Michigan State, Indiana, Fisk, and Purdue. During this campus tour, the musicians got stranded. On March 18, the radiator of the bus broke down near the small town of Smithville, Ohio. There had been a sizable snowstorm that night that paralyzed all traffic; schools were closed, and most outdoor activities were suspended. Alice Dunn was a little girl of nine who had accompanied her mother to the small family restaurant on the town square. She was playing with the salt and pepper shakers, pretending it was *her* lunchroom, when she noticed a black man outside, sitting on a radiator. Black people were not a common sight in Smithville. Years later she recalled,

> He was well-dressed, wearing a cashmere topcoat, a slouch hat and unbuckled galoshes—and by the way he sat on the radiator, it somehow seemed likely that he had been wet and cold for a long time.
>
> I watched as the man removed his hat and asked my mother if she'd be able to fix him a sandwich.
>
> "Sure will, what will it be?" Mother replied, telling him the choices on the menu.
>
> "The Western sounds real good, Ma'am."
>
> When my mother finished fixing the sandwich, she called out, "come and get it." The man, who was still next to the radiator, turned toward her with a surprised look on his face and said, "y'all mean I can come in here and eat?"
>
> "No reason why not," Mother said.

Whereupon the man replied, "I'll be right back," only to return a little later with about fifteen of his friends. One of them seemed to be their leader. He walked up to Alice's mother and introduced himself. "My name is Jimmie Lunceford and these men are members of my band. Our bus is stuck in the snow and in need of repairs. Would you mind if the men ate here in your restaurant and stayed in out of the cold?" That was no problem and so the entire Jimmie Lunceford Orchestra ate "as though they hadn't had food in a week. With Mother and Dad taking orders as fast as they could, it was like watching a three-ring circus, so much was happening at once. There wasn't room for everyone to sit, but I heard no complaining, no bad language and no griping about the long delay." Little Alice was sitting behind the cash register and she remembered that one of the musicians had a $100 bill in his wallet. In those days, this was a small fortune, and the man allowed Alice to feel the bill. She was surprised to discover it felt just like an ordinary dollar. After the meal, the men thanked the Dunn family—in their own way. "Some of the men had taken food to Jimmie Lunceford," recalled Dunn,

He had gone back out to stay with the bus. When they returned to the warmth of the restaurant, they brought along their instruments and an autographed photograph. The music they played that afternoon was unlike anything I had ever heard. The man called Moses brought his stand-up bass. He slapped that bass around, pulling a throbbing rhythm from the strings and singing along in a deep voice that filled the room with a sound like thunder rolling across the hills in summer.[17]

LIFE WITH LUNCEFORD

The greatest person that I've ever worked for.
—Truck Parham

He did not need an introduction. When Jimmie Lunceford entered a room or appeared on a stage, you just knew he was The Man. Six feet four, weighing 198 pounds when he was in his early thirties (210 at the time of his death), athletically built, impressive looking, dark and handsome. Trumpeter Joe Wilder joined the orchestra in early 1947, and remembered Lunceford as "a guy who was the epitome of what we say: he's a leader. He was definitely that."

A journalist thought he looked more like a prizefighter, or even a bear, than a musician.[1] Yet the former schoolteacher was clearly an intellectual. He spoke Spanish fluently, and was ready to discuss scientific matters, as well as sports.[2] Everything revolved around that man, who could be wearing a broad smile, but often stood brooding, absent-minded, looking placid, waving his three-foot baton. The leader was a good sight-reader, he could arrange, and he was proficient on a remarkable array of instruments. "But he also had a flair for conducting," maintained Gerald Wilson. "He had this long baton—you never saw him, huh?" "Well, he wasn't a classical conductor," Joe Wilder explained, adding, "I think that he sort of tried in some ways to emulate Paul Whiteman. I think that's one of the reasons he used the big long baton. He was a big guy anyway, as was Paul Whiteman." Sometimes, when a new arrangement was on the music stands, the leader tucked his baton under his arm and conducted with his hands. That way he made sure the musicians did not miss out the subtleties that specific parts of the arrangement required.

Tenorist Von Freeman remembered the orchestra at the Regal Theater and the Savoy Ballroom, in his hometown of Chicago. "We'd all go and listen to Lunceford, and he was always immaculate. You know, in tuxedo. And he would wave his baton, and he'd direct." Freeman made subtle movements, suggesting minute details in an arrangement. "And then when he got tired he'd go sit over behind the piano—closes his eyes and just listens to his band."

James Melvin Lunceford was no Cab Calloway, who was often clowning and dancing and yelling, and turning cartwheels, back flips, and somersaults. He did not possess the sophisticated charm of the suave Duke of Ellington. And he was not one of the boys, as was Basie. After a show, the various band members might go slumming, sitting in, getting high, or looking for girls, but the leader seldom took part in his men's nightlife. "Jimmie was funny, you see. He remind me of Fletcher [Henderson]," stated Benny Waters.

> He don't laugh much. He looked like a teacher and he act like a teacher. So he was up there standing up like this [Waters put on an aloof, serious face], and anything he liked, he'd get a little, *just-a-little-smile* on the corner of his mouth. Like a real teacher. Like a teacher in school, you know what I'm saying. Something amuse him, he's afraid to laugh, afraid to say, "That's fine." I don't know, he was a very quiet man, kind of withdrawn.

As a rule, the leader never talked about himself, his background, his upbringing, or other personal issues. "That's another thing that's very strange," said Joe Wilder. "I wasn't in the band that long and, you know, he died so suddenly, there were few opportunities to sit down and talk about his personal life. It was just difficult. I know really very little about him." Even musicians who worked under him for many years admitted that they did not really know the man. Lunceford kept a safe distance most of the time. Yet this shyness was not caused by feelings of insecurity; it was rather a natural disposition. The often extroverted character of his music obviously did not mirror his mind. Still, most people thought Jimmie Lunceford was a charming man. Perhaps his inclination toward modesty was a family trait. Jimmie's nephew Alfred, Junior's son, remembered, "Dad was pretty much kind of a very quiet, shy person. Very humble. But he was also ahead of his time, too, in his own way. He wasn't as aggressive as Uncle Jimmie was. My father was about a step and a half from really being proficient. But he just did not have the desire or drive. Uncle Jimmie had the drive, obviously, and the ambition, where Dad didn't. But Dad was quietly a tremendous musician."

Uncle Jimmie got married, probably in 1934, when his band was finally catching momentum. He had started dating Rose Crystal Tulli—the daughter of a newspaper owner—when they both studied at Fisk University. Jimmie and Crystal graduated together in the spring of 1926, he as a major in sociology, and she as a major in education, and she too had ended up in Memphis, as a teacher in English literature at Booker T. Washington High School.

A popular fund-raising event in Memphis during the late 1920s and 1930s was "The Ballet." "The Ballet" was a periodical dance show at the Palace Theater, patronized by the well-to-do, and staged to raise money for Booker T. Washington High School. The school's principal, G. P. Hamilton, used the money to buy typewriters for his school. "The Ballet" was produced by Crystal Tulli, herself an amateur ballet-dancer. Rufus Thomas, who later would become a famous disc jockey and singer, made his debut as a tap dancer, portraying a frog, at the 1932 edition of "The Ballet." As a result of her marriage to Jimmie, Crystal was forced by the school to give up both teaching and "The Ballet." At the time, female teachers were not allowed to marry.[3]

Both Luncefords were dedicated to the arts. One of Jimmie's ambitions was to elevate jazz music, to bring it on the same level as Western art music. He was convinced that it was necessary to play the sweet songs alongside the hot numbers, if only to build and retain an audience. Jimmie admired Fred Waring's Pennsylvanians and the Casa Loma Band, calling them the world's greatest orchestras. Fred Waring led one of the most popular, yet arguably one of the dullest, orchestras of the 1920s and 1930s, and he was known for his glee club, which carried from six to twenty-four singers! Waring made more money than Duke Ellington and Jimmie Lunceford put together. On account of the latter's own glee club, he was sometimes referred to as "The Black Fred Waring."[4]

From this one might conclude that Lunceford himself wasn't really a hard-core jazz buff: hot dance music and swing merely happened to be the fad when he was in the band-leading business. His favorite author was Joseph Conrad; one is tempted to draw analogies between the work of this novelist, full of storylines and rich in detail, and Lunceford's music. The orchestra leader was also interested in sociology, the profession he abandoned when he got his teaching assignment; he detested mathematics.[5]

Looking back on his time with the organization, Sy Oliver showed mixed emotions about the leader. During their six years of day-to-day traveling and working together, he resented the man. Or, rather, there was a complex love-hate relationship. Oliver was an exceptionally bright man, who might have become a scientist or a thinker or a scholar, had he chosen that path. Yet he felt intellectually inferior in the presence of the leader, and could not help looking up to him, despite feeling Jimmie was a square. Still, Oliver had to admit, the moment Lunceford set foot on the stage, he was in charge. Without contributing much musically, he made the band. He was the boss.[6]

The animosity between the leader and his staff arranger was eventually settled in the boxing ring. According to trumpeter Russell Green,

> They had a little bad blood between them so they thought they would have it out, in a nice way you know. So they had this boxing match at the YMCA, and they went in there and the band was in there. And Jimmie never said a word, he never let out he was a boxer, had been a boxer. He won a championship, light heavyweight at Tennessee State, when he was in school. Sy got in the ring and when the bell rang they came out and Jimmie hit him once. That was all there was to it. That settled that feud there.[7]

Old comrades Willie Smith and Ed Wilcox were the only sidemen who regularly visited their boss at his home at 409 Edgecombe Avenue in Harlem, the most prestigious apartment building in that part of the city. The three of them had split leadership over the orchestra when it grew from the original eleven-piece cooperative to fourteen members—until financial

and organizational problems threatened to submerge the cooperative corporation and Lunceford became the sole leader. When Smith left in 1942,
only Wilcox remained. That was the year saxophonist Benny Waters
replaced Ted Buckner. Almost forty years later, the image of the two pals
was still etched on Waters's mind: "They were together all the time."
Waters never was invited by the Luncefords, who moved to White Plains
near New York that year, but remembered, "He had those chicks, though.
He wasn't sociable, no."

Like most young musicians starting out in the 1930s, future bandleader
Sun Ra was a declared Lunceford fan. Ed Brown, who played alto saxophone in the 1936–37 edition of the Harlem Express, had been his music
teacher. Sun Ra mentioned rumors circulating among musicians about
Lunceford's amorous life. The leader apparently had been involved in an
affair with another man's wife. And he supposedly had made a pass at one
of his musicians's ladies, which, according to Sun Ra, had caused "a lot of
hooey. I think her name was Billie." It may have led to a certain estrange-
ment between the leader and his wife. At the time of his death, their marriage seemed to be on the verge of breaking up, or at least that's how Joe
Wilder perceived the situation. And apart from that, Yolande DuBois, his
first Fisk sweetheart, was still in the back of Jimmie's mind.

During the first thirteen years of the orchestra's existence, Jimmie
Lunceford had been the oldest one in the band. The arrival of veterans like
Waters and Omer Simeon, during the Second World War, had changed
that situation. He was father figure of sorts for all the musicians, their security, their guide. On stage, discipline came first. Offstage, he was more
relaxed, more casual, especially when he could talk sports, aviation, or
music. "He was consistent in everything he did, and that gave the fellows in
the band a feeling of security," summarized Sy Oliver.[8] "He was a very
gentle man himself," Harry Carney, Ellington's baritone saxophonist,
added. "Quiet, nicely spoken and very gentlemanly."[9]

Sports always had a special place in Lunceford's life. The orchestra had
a softball team and played against other swing bands in the "Flute League."
Jimmy Crawford was the catcher. When Gerald Wilson joined, he became
his warm-up catcher. Russell Green, who during the mid-1940s played
trumpet in the band, testified, "Jimmie was a hell of a pitcher! He had a fast
ball, it was out of sight. That's right, we played against Harry James. It was
all the white bands that had a team. I think Basie had a team, I'm not sure."

"Don't you know about my baseball team?" Jimmie remarked during a radio interview. "Why, these fellows make up the greatest softball team in the band business. We can lick any band in the country, playing ball. We'll clean up," he added, stressing, "that's my favorite subject, baseball." And after the orchestra had played two of its popular tunes on the program, *'Tain't What You Do* and *For Dancers Only*, the leader dared the listeners to come out for a match against his team.[10]

"Oh, we came up winners one year, we came up second another year," remarked a modest Russell Green about the big band league. Added bass player Truck Parham, "We played, you know, we get to a place where we had, like, a week, two or three nights, and we had to fill in. Or a week lay-off," Joe Wilder pointed out that some of these other big bands had been together for quite a while, so they had pretty good ball teams. He also remembered one occasion in Birmingham, when they played basketball against a college team. Some of the young guys in the band had been bragging about what great basketball players they had been during their college days. Jimmie arranged with somebody at the college to have a match between his band and the college boys. Wilder laughed, "Those guys ran the band to death! It was so embarrassing, maybe our guys may have scored three baskets and these other guys had thirty! And they weren't even abusing us, they were just doing what they did! And Jimmie said, 'This is an embarrassment.' No, he didn't play, he was just sort of an observer. But he was expecting a lot more competition than he got from the guys in the band."

The leader did not drink, smoke, or curse; he was a paragon of wholesomeness. Joe Wilder commented,

You know, there was something else about him. He didn't like to gamble per se. But if the guys were betting on a big football game or automobile race or one of those things, and the guys were all be picking the top name they were almost certain would win. And there would be someone who would say, "Jimmie, you wanna take one of these," whatsoever, and he'd say, "Well, such-and-such a thing is left," and he would take whoever, whatever was left. And it would be some nondescript person, and he would invariably win! It was almost hysterical! He had no choice, he just took what they gave him, what nobody else had taken. And Jimmie would win, I mean, we'd say eight out of ten times he would win. It got to be a joke, almost, you know. He never picked his—[he'd] say, "Okay, I'll take whatever you got left."

At the end of the comical 1935 song *Hittin' the Bottle*, singer Sy Oliver commented, "Everybody, except Jimmie, hits the bottle." Lunceford's tough ways with liquor lasted right until his last days. Joe Wilder observed that

> he was a taskmaster. You know, he was very aware of the black image. And he had very little patience with guys who drank too much and came on the job and made it obvious they were in no condition to play. Jimmie would just sidle over to somebody if he saw some guy in the reed section and he was kind of in bad shape. Jimmie would just go over and say, "This one is on you!" That meant he wasn't going to pay him for that night. And then a little later, maybe about a month or six weeks later, Jimmie would say, "After the job tonight we gonna have a little party." And everybody'd say, "Ooh, that's nice." And we have this little get-together with some catered food, and the guys'd be saying, "Oh, thank you Jimmie, it's awfully nice." He'd say, "Don't thank me, thank . . . " and he'd point out the guy who had lost a night's salary, or two nights', or whatever. He's a nice man. A brilliant man, actually.

The leader used to finance several amateur baseball and basketball teams, in addition to youth orchestras, in order to fight juvenile delinquency. This practice appears to have started in May 1937, when Jimmie stayed at his parents' Warren home, and was entertained by the Thompson Band (later, the name was changed to the Sultans of Swing), a group of local high school boys. This was Warren's only black band. To show his appreciation, Jimmie presented the youngsters with a cash gift to purchase music.[11]

Another musician who benefited from his generosity was an aspiring Memphis trumpet player named Willie Mitchell. Later, during the 1960s and 1970s, he would become the most revered producer of soul music at Hi Records, and launched the careers of Al Green, Otis Clay, Ann Peebles, and other stars. But in the early 1940s he was a student at Melrose High School in Memphis, where Lunceford had helped build a band. The musicians of the school band heard young Willie, and he was invited to join their trumpet ranks. To get to the rehearsals, twice or thrice a week, took some effort. It took "about two hours to go there on the trolley. You had to go downtown, get another trolley, then walk two miles," Willie said, adding that he learned a lot in that particular orchestra.

Jimmie Lunceford was a man of high moral standards. "We didn't bother to curse in front of him," remembered Gerald Wilson. "Everybody says Jimmie was tough. He wasn't really like it. He was a schoolteacher, he was a coach, he was a football player. Fact, I went to school in Memphis where he had been a coach. I went there two years. He was always kind to me and everybody in the band." Joe Wilder confirmed this: "I was very fond of Jimmie. He treated me just wonderful." It is doubtful whether there were other leaders in the dance band world with as many nicknames: Lunce, Lunch, Pops, Piggie, Ol' Boopadoola.

He may have been kind, but nobody could make Lunceford do anything he didn't want to do. He was his own man and could be very stubborn when the occasion called for it. He especially did not like white men bossing him. That's how he got into trouble with just about every booking office in New York. It took years before his band was admitted to the stages of the really big theaters and hotels. Russell Green recalled that the band played Loew's State, the Paramount and the Apollo during the time he was in the band. But these jobs usually lasted one or two weeks. Real location jobs, such as Fletcher Henderson's at the Roseland, or Glenn Miller's at the Pennsylvania, were not available for the Harlem Express. Green: "Jimmie was a hard-liner. You couldn't make him do anything. You could ask him, but you couldn't make him. He's too damn independent. He was that way up until the time he died."

It bothered Lunceford and Oxley no end that the band, in spite of its growing popularity and versatility, had a hard time obtaining quality jobs and that it could get no location engagements with radio outlets in Manhattan. Spurred by the first hits, the triumphs at the Cotton Club, and the response during the tours, by early 1936 they decided to take command. If they were denied all the good venues in New York City, they'd better acquire a stage of their own. Consequently, they bought a restaurant, the Larchmont Casino. It was located on Boston Post Road, just outside the city. To finance the enterprise, every musician suffered a cut in his salary, and had to live on rent and board money for a while.

The roof of the Larchmont was not yet finished on the day of the restaurant's opening. "We couldn't disappoint our legions of fans," Willie Smith explained. "And it rained! There were inches of water on the floor, but all the people were there. They stayed and danced in the water. We got wet, too, but we didn't care." A novelty was Larchmont's moving stage, with the musicians seated on an elevated platform on rails. During the opening number, the exciting flag-waver *Jazznocracy*, it looked as if the whole orchestra was charging right into the hall, causing the audience to panic and flee to the back of the room.

To everybody's surprise, Harold Oxley managed to keep the Larchmont in operation for four years. From the very beginning, the operation was plagued by raids by the Mob and other harassments.[12] The Larchmont had radio outlets, and during the summer of 1936 the Lunceford band broadcast four nights a week over stations WJZ (Sundays, Thursdays, and Saturdays) and WEAF (Mondays), which greatly increased its rising popularity.[13] WJZ was the NBC Blue Network flagship; WEAF was the Red Network. The band's growing "visibility" prompted other venues, big movie houses such as Loew's in Times Square to hire it, and eventually, other black outfits as well, something that had never happened before. The orchestra played its Casino regularly, but during the summer of 1938, for instance, it was in such great demand that it was not possible to pay their own home base a visit.

During the last part of the 1930s, America witnessed a flirtation between hot music and red politics. Jazz and blues music were viewed by part of the liberal wing as the proletarian's songbook. The Spanish Civil War gave rise to many a benefit performance, in order to sustain the democratic forces and help the victims. Leading jazz musicians such as Duke Ellington, Benny Goodman, and his pianist Teddy Wilson were frequent participants in left-wing events. Wilson was one of the attractions of a November 21, 1938, benefit at New York's Carnegie Hall for the Spanish Children's Milk Fund. Under the auspices of the Committee to Aid Spanish Democracy, the "Jamboree for Spain" at the same time was a celebration of composer W. C. Handy's sixty-fifth birthday. Also on the bill were the Jimmie Lunceford Orchestra and the bands of Cab Calloway, Fats Waller, and Roy Eldridge. Admission ranged from eighty-three cents to $2.20.[14] But apart from this occasion, Lunceford seems to have been largely inactive as far as political causes were concerned. Two years before his death he donated $500 to the NAACP, and became a life member. He was the fourth bandleader to attain this status, after Basie, Duke, and Cab.[15]

Lunceford did look for respect and standing. In 1940 he was honored with the membership of the Crescendo Club of Negro Composers, whose members were a cross-section of the most prestigious black composers and songwriters, in jazz as well as concert music. Presided by its founder J. C. Johnson, the Crescendo Club included luminaries such as W. C. Handy, who acted as treasurer, Fletcher Henderson, Fats Waller, Clarence Williams, Will Vodery, Porter Grainger, J. Rosamond Johnson, Lucky Roberts, Edgar Sampson, Don Redman, Eubie Blake, and James P. Johnson. The members all held ASCAP (American Society of Composers, Authors, and Publishers) credentials.[16] Since Lunceford could hardly be considered a prolific writer, he might have felt a little out of place among the Crescent Club giants.

Two quotes may serve to illustrate the leader's Gemini nature, his inborn ambivalence. In November 1938 *Life* magazine was supposed to publish a portrait of the orchestra leader. When the weekly failed to do so, French writer Hugues Panassié, who was spending a couple of months in New York, expressed his disappointment to Jimmie. The latter's reaction was laconic: "I'm not surprised, I attract misfortune all the time."[17]

On another occasion, a fan asked him when he was born. "On my lucky day," was the reply. What was so lucky about it, the fan wanted to know. "Well, if I had been born on some other day, I might have been inclined to mathematics instead of music. Then I would have grown up to mathematics and the music would have gone scot free. Instead, I've been working at Swing and the 'percentages' have been working for me!"[18]

During the final stage of the leader's life, bass player Truck Parham was one of the musicians with whom Jimmie Lunceford was close, especially after the latter found out that his sideman, like himself, had a penchant for sports. Truck had been a prizefighter and played football, and the leader often sat with him on the bus, and told him intimate things about the band.

He said, "Truck, I tried to get the band during the war, in Washington, DC, . . . to save some, so we could have bought a whole block." He'd have taken half salary for a year. We'd have enough money to buy the whole block, and we could have put our own homes. He knew business. He knew. So he said, "Truck, you know, all these guys, I got them out, I brought them out of Memphis, taught them this and that. Do you know," he says, "they never did take me up on the altar." He told them, he says, "Look, we take half salary for a year." He'd heard about property was nothing, you know. The guy was hurt. He says, "The guys been with me and I got them from scratch, help them to be somewhere now." He says, "Truck, it really hurt me. They wouldn't trust me with any money." That was the big thing, there. He thought the guys really loved him. But when it came to investing some money with him to buy something for themselves in the future, they didn't trust it.

Joe Wilder confirmed Truck's story. The idea was to put the men's savings in an escrow account. As soon as their savings had grown to a certain amount, the band was supposed to have purchased property in both Washington and New York. Not only would the musicians have decent, cheap housing that way, they could let out the vacant space for hire, reaping a benefit. It was meant to be like a pension: then as now, jazz musicians as a rule did not have any kind of old-age provision. None of the big bands had such funds. "As the bands went along," Joe Wilder explained, "all they did, they lived from day to day, each day was another day's work and you got paid for that. You had to live that way, you know. There were no insurances or anything."

The investment in real estate actually was a forward-thinking enterprise. The problem was, around the time everybody finally agreed to the scheme, the leader bought a new car. And some musicians started to insinuate that it was their money that he had used to buy the vehicle. Wilder recalled, "He was really . . . he was so outdone by them—he was hurt by them! I remember he told me, he said, 'You know, the guys thought I was stealing the money from them.' He said, 'I want to buy a new car, and I bought a new car, and they saw it, making remarks and all kinds of innuendoes and whatever.'" In the end Lunceford got the books, showed everyone where his money was, went to the bank and paid each and everybody back. That was the end of a possibly brilliant plan. Joe added, "I think some of the guys were so embarrassed that they just began leaving the band—personally, I think, when they found out that what they had thought was untrue."

Truck Parham remembered another example of Lunceford's investment schemes:

Two months before he died we played Oakland. All around the Bay Area there, he had found out about some property, some land he could buy. So he told me, he says, "Truck, I'm telling you, cause I'm gonna invest in this land over here. I'm not gonna mention it to the guys, to hell with them." He says, "I got up to and buy this property. You got some money, put it with me, we'll get some of this property." I guess that was about May, and July 12, that's when he died. We'd have lived, we'd have owned property. Later on, I saw nothing but oil wells on the property. He didn't tell the rest, he told me because he knew I believed in him. I knew he was a man.

Even his old buddy Edwin Wilcox at this time had alienated himself from the leader. He was one of the musicians who did not support the idea of investing money. But this might have had something to do with the animosity that existed between Wilcox's wife and Mrs. Lunceford.

Truck Parham, on the other hand, cherished nothing but warm memories about his old boss:

Why I feel so great about him [is] because when I joined Jimmie Lunceford, my second daughter was a baby. She was four months old. I was home, we were laying off on a three-week vacation, and I was home. I had her in the front room, early in the morning, and I was looking at her and admiring her, you know. And I saw a little piece of, looked like quicksilver, near the pupil of her eye. I said, "What the hell is that? How she get that in her eye?" Till I called my wife. She tried to get it out. Two days later I had to go because we were opening in Miami, Florida. I was worried. I went on to Miami, and then my wife called me the next day. She had taken my daughter to the eye doctor, and he said, "It's very serious. It happens once in a thousand babies." A tumor. He was all nervous, gotta have an operation on it immediately. I didn't have any money.

Lunceford's just a humanitarian. He knew his men. He knew I was a happy player, and I wasn't happy. He asked me, "How you doing, Truck, everything all right?" I said, "Not really." Jim says, "When we get off, come by my room at the hotel, we talk about it." I went by and told him, said, "My wife called me and my baby needs an operation. It's very serious, and I don't have any money, and I need four thousand dollars at least, I know that." And I told him, said, "I don't know how I'm going to get it." I had some property. I said, "I don't know whether they give me that much for the property." So he says, "Call your wife, tell her to go ahead. Don't you worry." He paid. He went to a trunk to get the money.

And I paid him back. A hundred dollars a month. Sometimes more. When I gave him the last fifty dollars, he said, "Truck, you're the only man that been in my band that's ever paid me back to the penny. You need anything else, don't go to the road-manager, come to me."

So he was my man. Jimmie Lunceford was the greatest person that I've ever worked for. The two greatest people I ever worked was Art Tatum and Jimmie Lunceford. All he want you do is play his music, and combine each other like brothers—*brothers*. He had that brotherly . . . you know, he wanted to be like brothers. Not like guys, *brothers*. He was a man like that.

{8}

FOR DANCERS ONLY

<hr>

They could swing a band right off the pickup.
—*Garvin Bushell*

In recent years, a fragment on film of the Lunceford band in 1945, featuring singer Lena Horne, has surfaced. It was produced by the Army Pictorial Service, which advertised it at the time as "a real treat for overseas troops."[1] But since the release was just prior to the surrender of Japan, it is doubtful the film was actually shown. A couple of 8 mm silent movies, shot by amateurs at dances, are also known to exist. Apart from these snippets and a fleeting—and disappointing—appearance in the 1941 feature film *Blues in the Night*, a so-called bio-pic about a band and its amorous pianist, the only audiovisual document of the band is an item in the Vitaphone Melody Master series. Entitled *Jimmie Lunceford and His Dance Orchestra*, this vignette was probably shot in Brooklyn, in July 1936. Joseph Henabery was the director, a minor poet in his trade, who had started his career by playing the part of Abraham Lincoln in D. W. Griffith's *The Birth of a Nation* (1915), and from then on had directed his own films. After a 1931–32 series of

"Mystery" movies, he was assigned Vitaphone's music shorts, beginning with *Barber Shop Blues*, featuring Claude Hopkins and His Orchestra and the Four Step Brothers. Over the next six years, Henabery would document the early phase of the swing era with shorts on Ben Pollack, Don Redman, and Red Nichols, among others.[2]

In *Jimmie Lunceford and His Dance Orchestra* six tunes were played, barely totaling ten minutes. The selections are *Jazznocracy* (really just a fifteen-second introduction under the opening titles), *It's Rhythm Coming to Life Again*, *Rhythm Is Our Business*, *You Can't Pull the Wool Over My Eyes*, *Moonlight on the Ganges*, and *Nagasaki*. A remarkable fact is that among these five featured titles, only *Rhythm Is Our Business* had been issued on a 78 rpm record.

The movie short begins with the image of an unidentified singer in a devil's outfit (positively no member of the orchestra), on the brink of hell, who informs us that *It's Rhythm Coming to Life Again*. Drummer Jimmy Crawford is silhouetted, followed by images of the full orchestra, and its various sections, in a split-screen sequence. The band is dressed in shiny white (or silver) tails. Against a swirling backdrop of twisting staves, Willie Smith sings *Rhythm Is Our Business*, enlivened by Craw performing his "tricks with sticks," and topped by the brass section, who climb the chairs to form a semicircle around Paul Webster, who "hits 'em high." Guest singer Myra Johnson, introduced by Lunceford as "that personality girl," warns the viewer that "you can't pull the wool over my eyes." In *Moonlight on the Ganges* the band accompanies a rather bland and long-forgotten dance act named the Three Brown Jacks.

Apart from *Rhythm Is Our Business*, the most exciting (and longest) sequence is a tempestuous *Nagasaki*. During Eddie Tompkins's humorous scat vocal, Sy Oliver shouts, "What about this, papa," rubbing the palms of his hands. Tompkins and the rest of the band copy this rhythmic gesture, to great effect. Next, the brass performs a baffling choreography with the derby mutes, and the saxes sway their instruments simultaneously from side to side. Then it's Joe Thomas's solo turn, with Jock Carruthers and Ed Brown performing hip rhythmic hand gestures in the background that would put any hip-hop artist to shame. After his solo, Joe and Earl cut a few highly entertaining steps that send the pedestrian efforts of the tapping Brown Jacks to oblivion. During Paul Webster's closing solo, Sy Oliver and Eddie Tompkins take off their jackets, Jimmy Crawford throws them two mallets, and they proceed to hammer along on the seats of their chairs.

This is really the one tune that gives an idea of how this eager band had its tunes choreographed in live situations. It's a truly stunning document, and it was through this clip that a lot of black people became aware of the band's existence.

As far back as 1933, the band had started to make an impact on the white college campuses around the country. In due time, these would constitute an important circuit for the Lunceford orchestra, but back in 1936, "race records" (a common term the trade used to indicate disks aimed at the African American market), let alone dances featuring black bands, were still a rarity at the campuses. Bookers were keen on getting gigs at colleges, since they could charge as much as twice the money they were getting at regular dances.

After stating that, surprisingly, British dance band records by Ray Noble, Jack Hylton, and Bert Ambrose could be "termed 'most popular' among the general student body at New Haven," Yale's spokesman H. W. Wing reported in the trade paper *Variety* that Duke Ellington, "that peerless pater of the smoky fantasy," held first ranking among the black hot bands. "The Duke's men, with all their delicate instrumentation and intricate arrangement, still possess a beautiful danceability, which serves but to enhance their contrasting sallies of torridity. It is this same versatility that creates the surprising popularity of Jimmy Lunceford, whose lazy *Charmaine* or heatwavish *Rhythm is Our Business* are equally enticing. And Lunceford possesses an unique understanding of recording possibilities which makes his output attractive indeed to knowing disc doters."

One week later, Walter J. Dodd Jr. noted in the same paper that at Dartmouth, Lunceford was regarded as "the ace colored band of the day. Among colored bands he is certainly the favorite at Dartmouth." Dodd, incidentally, dismissed Ellington, claiming his "weird discords have grown stale."[3]

The question of who was the "best," Ellington or Lunceford, became a serious topic of conversation in hot circles, both in America and Europe. In the mid-1930s, a significant number of critics, musicians, and fans began to question Duke's achievements. Apart from some scattered theater engagements, the "peerless pater of the smoky fantasy" was not very visible in New York for a considerable while. His October 1935 appearance at the Apollo was the only one on this stage during that year. There were rumors about a feud with some mobsters. Then again, Ellington at this time was spending considerable stretches of time in Hollywood, appearing in movies, and was busy touring the United States. However, the main reason for Duke's relative obscurity was a severe and prolonged attack of depression, following his mother's death. This resulted in one of the masterpieces in jazz, the four-part *Reminiscing in Tempo*. Some critics had trouble hearing the true magnitude of this work, and accused Ellington of mannerism, of a *l'art pour l'art* attitude. People were beginning to feel irritated by what they conceived as a pretentious manner. Leading critic John Hammond characterized *Reminiscing in Tempo* as "complete sterility." To him, Ellington's music had "become vapid and without the slightest semblance of guts." In a 1935 article in the Swedish monthly *Orkester Journalen,* Lunceford lamented, "Ellington is, alas, beginning to repeat himself."[4]

In retrospect, it is hard to reconcile these negative comments with Duke's recorded output. Maybe the widespread initial elation about his forward-thinking scores was just wearing off.

In any case, their ranking compared to other groups clearly shows the high esteem in which both orchestras were held. Under the headline "Duke and Lunceford Lead in Poll For Favorite Swing Band," writer Franklyn Frank noted in the *New York Amsterdam News,*

> Two weeks ago, I left it up to you. Thus far, several have spoken— and they have named only Duke Ellington and Jimmie Lunceford. Benny Goodman has not been considered, nor has any other colored band.
>
> Here's the opinion of Chick Finney of the St. Louis Crackerjacks' rhythm section, one of the best dance bands in that section. Mr. Finney says that all eleven members of the orchestra will "tell you at once that Jimmie Lunceford has the greatest swing band in the world."
>
> He adds further, "every day we play Lunceford, Ellington, Kirk, Henderson, Waller etc. records" to improve their own style, and the consensus is that "Lunceford has the best all-round band we have ever heard."[5]

It is remarkable that one year after the Luncefords had moved to 309 Edgecombe Ave. in Harlem, Ellington, too, relocated to this most prestigious apartment building.

Needless to say, the Harlem Express left its mark on a variety of college bands. The most prominent of these were the Duke Blue Devils at Duke

University, formed in 1935 by reed player and arranger Les Brown. Their early recordings reveal a heavy debt to the Lunceford style. In due course, Les Brown would become the leader of one of the most consistently popular big dance bands of the nation, directing his Band of Renown well into the 1990s, and establishing himself as one of the most durable bandleaders of all times. It is interesting to note that some of the longest-running big bands—for example, Harry James and Ray Anthony—had a relationship to the Lunceford style, which showed in tight ensemble work, great dynamics and generous swing, and precise arrangements that featured kaleidoscopic shifts in angles and atmosphere.

During the height of the swing craze, 1938–42, Lunceford's was the only black band to place in the top ten of Billboard's Annual College Poll. It came in ninth in 1938 and eighth, three years later. (Goodman and Miller, respectively, occupied the number one slot in those two years.) Lunceford already dominated both *Metronome*'s and *Orchestra World*'s black popularity polls from 1935 on. The latter polls were established in 1935, when swing music really started to catch on. Other publications and radio stations followed suit. These polls were not always reliable: agents sometimes bought dozens or even hundreds of magazines that contained poll ballots, in order to magnify their client's worth. Magazines, on the other hand, tended to exaggerate all figures, probably just to impress rival publications—and advertisers. Still, poll results in general did give a rough indication of a band's or a soloist's popularity.

The reputation of the Lunceford band continued to soar. *Organ Grinder's Swing*, recorded eight months after the milestone *My Blue Heaven*, and a couple of weeks after the Vitaphone movie short, hit the jackpot, both artistically and financially. It delicately contrasts a softly moaning trio, consisting of muted trumpet, trombone, and clarinet (reminiscent of Duke's voicings for ballads), with full-throttled blasts from the orchestra. Arranger Sy Oliver makes clever use of Carruthers's boisterous booming baritone. He combines this with his own growling trumpet, and alternates these solo voices with whispering saxes, a discreet celesta and Crawford's characteristic temple blocks, the spherical wooden slit-drums on top of his bass drum.

How did he do it? Was there a system, a method to Oliver's effective arranging technique? According to the writer, it was all instinct. He never sat down to figure out certain voicings, or dynamics, or contrasts; neither did he analyze what he wrote. He told writer Dempsey Travis, "A simple tune like *Organ Grinder's Swing* was a great success for the Lunceford band back in 1936. It was my arrangement and I can't tell you how or why I wrote it. I took the nursery rhyme and wrote an organ grinding voicing for the brass and the reed section, and then added a two-beat rhythm and a Lunceford tempo, and the public responded."[6]

It was around this time that noted tenor saxophone player Arnett Cobb first saw the band and met his idol Joe Thomas. Cobb was a member of the Houston-based big band of trumpeter Milt Larkin. Lunceford played Houston once or twice a year. Larkin's men used to copy a lot of Lunceford hits, as many dance orchestras all over the United States were doing by now. Whenever Larkin's musicians played their hometown ballroom, the Harlem Grill, they went downstairs for the jukebox. Cobb stated, "We put Lunceford's records on and stood just listening, everybody, the whole band. And then we went upstairs, to go give it a try." That, no doubt, is how many a band tried to master the style.

Jimmie Lunceford's emphasis on appearance struck Cobb. "Jimmie was a guy that believed in them looking right. If they were supposed to wear brown socks, they all wore brown socks. When he catch them with the wrong socks—oh, didn't say anything, you know—that's a twenty-five-dollar fine. So he'd catch your eye, and that's the only thing. He wouldn't say anything! They pooled the money, and they had a party off of it, at the end of the tour," remembered Arnett Cobb.

Lunceford was strict. He was a diplomat. To some degree, he was a disciplinarian. That's all true. "But he would ride on the train with them, ride on the bus with them, when he didn't fly his own plane. And he kept everything in order," said Cobb. According to him, the leader was a very pleasant personality, but everything was business with him. "He stuck with that business attitude. He was just the leader, he was like glue, he kept everything stuck together," the saxophonist explained.

Although the band was constantly on tour, and by the early 1940s began spending more time on the West Coast than in New York, its popularity in Harlem did not diminish. Pianist Red Richards remembered Easter Sunday in Harlem,

a sight to behold. People would be walking down Seventh Avenue to go to church, and they come on, they be stroll 'em. They'd stop at some bars. There was a bar in this corner from Small's Paradise, that side [of] 135th Street, was the Big Apple. And people would go in, have a few drinks. But everybody loved to show up on Easter Sunday. Boy, that was a big event in Harlem. You talk about an Easter Parade! Then they wind up, they had another ballroom, not quite as large as the Savoy, on 138th and 7th Avenue. [Red referred to the Renaissance Casino, 150 West 138th Street.] And they have a senior church and Jimmie Lunceford and them would play an Easter Dance there.

Back in 1937, Jackie Kelso was an aspiring reed player of fifteen. In due time, he would become a busy man on the rhythm-and-blues circuit, playing dances all over the country with Lionel Hampton, Johnny Otis, and Roy Milton. There were only four bands Jackie cared about: those led by Ellington, Basie, Kirk, and Lunceford. The first lead alto saxophone player he heard and who impressed him was Willie Smith. "The Jimmie Lunceford Orchestra was so smooth and had so much showmanship. There are stories that Glenn Miller had his whole band go watch the performance," Kelso said. "You know, the *doo-da-doo-da-doo-da*, like, the fanning with the derbies." Miller once did state that Jimmie Lunceford had "the best of all bands," adding, "Duke is great, Basie is remarkable, but Lunceford tops them both."

Kelso was also impressed by the trumpeters throwing their horns in the air in *For Dancers Only,* and by the way the musicians dressed. He remembered how the glee club stepped forward and lined up at the edge of the stage. Whenever the orchestra came to the Paramount or the Orpheum in L.A., all the young musicians his age, Dexter Gordon, Buddy Collette, Chico Hamilton, and the rest, went to listen and watch.

Likewise, all the young New York musicians flocked to see Lunceford, especially when he was battling other name bands. When the battle involved drummer Chick Webb, who led the house band at the Savoy, opinions differed as to who was the winner. Chick's trombone player Sandy Williams felt that Basie and Lunceford could not beat them, because the crowd was loyal. But, he added, had they encountered those orchestras in other dance halls, the results might have been the other way around. Garvin Bushell, a member of Webb's reed section, held a different view. He remembered that Webb could not win when he faced Jimmie Lunceford. The Harlem Express simply had too much power. "They could swing a band right off the pickup. People would just coattail," he said, adding that Webb excelled mainly in the faster tunes, while Jimmy Crawford had a certain feel that his own boss could not match.[7]

In other instances, it was clear who was the winner. Arranger Larry Clinton, of *Dipsy Doodle* fame, led an orchestra patterned after the riff-laden Casa Loma Band. He recalled a horrible night at Dartmouth College, where he was hired to play the Green Key Ball, along with the Lunceford band. He told *Metronome*'s George T. Simon what happened. The Clinton band was early, and Lunceford pulled in at the last moment, since he had played somewhere in the middle of Pennsylvania. So Lunceford asked him to open the show, while the Harlem Express men washed up and got dressed.

They agreed, and for the first hour Clinton "trotted out all our flag-wavers with the trumpets playing high C's. Then Jimmie came on, and after he'd played just a minute or so of *For Dancers Only*, with that great beat his band had and the trumpets tossing their horns in the air and everything, I made up my mind right then and there that I could play nothing but sweet things if I were going to survive that night." Clinton added that this was the reason his band's style changed. From then on it concentrated on the pretty tunes.[8]

Occasionally, Harold Oxley put the band on a regular battling tour. This was the case in 1936 with the Joe Robichaux Orchestra from New Orleans. Robichaux played piano and led one of the hottest bands of the Crescent City, frequently touring the South. In the mid-1930s Robichaux, following the general trend, had enlarged his combo to big band size, styled after Fletcher Henderson's. The pianist had added another trumpet, so he now had three trumpets, and the reed section comprised of two tenors and three altos, including Earl Bostic. All the musicians were strong, heavy players, not untypical of New Orleans. Before long the band, fifteen pieces by now, had become even more exciting. Freddy Kohlman was Robichaux's drummer, and he remembered,

> We would travel from New Orleans to Houston, Texas, playing battles of the bands along on the way. *Joe Robichaux from New Orleans battling Jimmie Lunceford from New York*. When we get to Houston, that'd probably be our last battle with them. But Houston was a good dance town, Joe Robichaux was one of their favorites in Houston, so Jimmie Lunceford's so mad. The whole question is: one band plays, and then they'd break, and then the other band plays and had a break, and in the end the two bands play together. The people applauded and showed who they liked best.

When the Lunceford band traveled east, Oxley had the Lunceford and Robichaux bands battle in New Orleans, Biloxi, and Mobile. Joe Robichaux was a favorite in Mobile as well, since his singer was from that town. Kohlman explained, "Her right name was Daisy Lowell, but we used to call her Joan Lunceford. Daisy Lowell didn't sound so high when Joe hired her, so we gave her that name, Joan Lunceford. People used to ask her was she Jimmie Lunceford's sister. We played dances, you know, and all coming to the bandstand, 'Hey yo, miss, is you Jimmie Lunceford's sister?' "

The same tactics, enhancing a band's appeal by letting it travel with another orchestra, were applied to Oxley's other leading attraction, Edgar Hayes, who did battling tours with Louis Armstrong and Teddy Hill.

Lunceford's musicians were proud and loyal men. One night in 1936, bandleader Tommy Dorsey drove Willie Smith home after a performance of the Lunceford band at its brand-new own dance hall, the Larchmont Casino. When Dorsey dropped Willie at his house, he put out his checkbook, signed a blank check and handed it to the saxophone player, pointing, "You see this line up here, 'Pay to the Order of'?"

"Yeah," Smith said.

"Put whatever you want on that line and it's yours."

Willie didn't take the check, although at that moment he was earning no more than room and board. "I felt it would be a terrible breach on my part. That was the spirit we all had. Nobody would quit regardless of what happened."9

Though many people came to ballrooms primarily to listen to the band, the Harlem Express was tailored for the dancers. The unbreakable bond between music and dance can be illustrated by the genesis of *For Dancers Only*. This particular medium-tempo Sy Oliver opus, based on a Joe Thomas riff, became a classic. It was one of *the* tunes people associated with the band. During the writing process in early February 1937, the dancers of the Apollo chorus line got together with the composer and suggested the various accents they wanted. This way, an organic relationship between music and dance was established.

The effect was shattering. Bass player George Duvivier was a fan, and he recalled, "They used to use a silhouette effect to highlight the band. In conjunction with what you heard, the impact was incredible. The only time I saw a chorus line get five encores at the Apollo Theater was when they danced to *For Dancers Only*, with the Lunceford orchestra playing behind a screen."10

Led by Carruthers's baritone, the trombones stated the commanding intro, followed by a stop-time chorus, designed for the trumpeters who threw their instruments in the air. The tune is a series of lively, picturesque variations, spiced by Paul Webster's high-note screeching, rather than a full-fledged composition, based on a melody. At dances, it sometimes ended in a pagan ritual that could last for thirty minutes. The trumpet-juggling bit was a trick that always worked, leaving the audience in awe: three, and eventually five trumpet players simultaneously tossing their instruments exactly the same distance straight up towards the ceiling, catching them, and bringing the horns back to their lips on the beat and on the right chord. Pianist Nat Pierce saw Lunceford around 1943 in Symphony Hall in Boston: "His four trumpet players were throwing their horns up to the ceiling. It was a big, high hall, and they'd throw them up twenty or thirty feet, pick them out of the air, and hit the next chord."[11] Gerald Wilson added, "I always caught it. Except for one time at Loew's State in New York, I missed and I dropped my horn. But it was all right, no dents or nothing." His colleague Joe Wilder was not so lucky: "I threw mine up once and it came down behind me. Was looking in the wrong direction. Destroyed the trumpet."

The second variation of the *For Dancers Only* theme bore a remarkable resemblance to Horace Henderson's *Christopher Columbus*, written for brother Fletcher Henderson, who had recorded it March 27, 1936. This piece in turn was supposedly based on a riff Fletcher's tenor star Chu Berry used to play. Lunceford, who recorded *For Dancers Only* on June 15, 1937, sued Joe Davis, publisher of *Christopher Columbus*, claiming theft of his song. There is no record, alas, of the outcome of the lawsuit. One might speculate that Lunceford would have had trouble backing his claim with evidence. The little riff first popped up in the final bars of a Teddy Wilson recording with Billie Holiday, *Yankee Doodle Never Went to Town*, October 25, 1935, featuring Chu Berry. This is no irrefutable proof that it really was the tenorist's creation: it may have been part of the "public domain" even at that early stage. Later, in 1939, arranger Andy Gibson used the riff in Harry James's tune *Sugar Daddy*. To make matters even more confusing, Benny Goodman put it in his—or, rather, Louis Prima's—*Sing, Sing, Sing*. It is in this guise that most people know the tune.

For Dancers Only was one of the band's perennial numbers, and became its semi-official theme song, often replacing *Jazznocracy* (which was hated by the musicans). The piece stayed in the book until Eddie Wilcox's orchestra, successor of the Harlem Express, folded in the early 1950s. Eyewitnesses remembered that the piece could have a magical effect on the dancers. The tune could be expanded considerably, new riffs, licks, and solos popping up every minute, "grinding down the blues-ish sound and feeling in the growls and riffs and making the whole audience meld together into one homogenous mass extension of the music," recalled writer Ralph Gleason. "It wasn't just 'For Dancers Only.' It was for listeners and for viewers and for lovers, too. With Jimmie taking that little soprano up sometimes to play lead on a song and the rest of the time standing there—white-suited in summer—waving the baton like a magic wand over the heads of the dancers and smiling, the band produced a variety and volume and an ever-changing tapestry of sound that was really unique."[12]

Jack Kapp, Decca's president, saw the potential of *For Dancers Only* and urged other bands to record it. To its amazement, the Bob Crosby crew discovered in 1939 that its version of the Sy Oliver opus was in more jukeboxes than its own hit *South Rampart Street Parade*.[13]

Some of the songs in the Lunceford book could turn out markedly different in different performances. Though the band did not play nearly as many head arrangements as, say, the Count Basie Orchestra, there were certain numbers where the musicians were able to ad-lib, and where the lead players would devise new variations on the spot. At dances, for instance, soloists were allotted a full chorus or more, whereas in the studio or during radio broadcasts, they had to be content with just a few bars. Apart from *For Dancers Only*, selections such as *Dinah*, *Strictly Instrumental*, and *Wham* could, according to the circumstances, be stretched into six- or sixty-minute swing orgies.

The original tempo of *Stomp It Off* was much slower than that on the record: Sy had to speed it up so it would fit in the three-and-a-half minute slot, the duration of the 78 rpm single. Likewise, *By the River Sainte Marie* originally lasted eight to ten minutes, but for the recording, an entire sax chorus was omitted. The same thing happened to *Sleepy Time Gal*, which lost a clarinet choir. On the other hand, Gerald Wilson's piece *Hi, Spook* proved to be a little too intricate to be played at the tempo the composer had chosen, so the leader had to slow the tempo down for the recording.[14] Only occasionally, notably *Dinah* (1940), *Blues in the Night* (1941), *I'm Gonna Move to the Outskirts of Town* (1942), and *Back Door Stuff* (1944; a fine example of powerhouse swing at a very slow tempo!), were numbers issued on two sides of a single 78 rpm record.

The novelty of Eddie Durham's amplified guitar, in combination with the innovative charts by Oliver and, a little later, Gerald Wilson, Billy Moore Jr., and Tadd Dameron, plus the hip vocals and stage antics, gave Jimmie Lunceford's Express an outspoken modern touch. Apart from Ellington's and Red Norvo's orchestras, no other pre-bebop band sounded as hip (or rather: *hep*, or *solid*, to use the parlance of the day). Cab Calloway, with his fine-tuned sense of grassroots culture, may have popularized the zoot suit and jive talking, and his lyrics did refer to reefers and coke. But his 1930s arrangements were as pedestrian as any dance band's. Granted, the nasal vocals by Lunceford's crooner of romantic songs, Dan Grissom, sound dated to today's ears. But more often than not they were framed by rich, inventive arrangements. His 1935 hit song *Charmaine* is a case in point. The arrangement opens playfully with muted trumpets; then the theme is picked up by the saxes, sounding deliberately corny. Joe Thomas's straight tenor solo occupies the second chorus and sounds like it was written out by the arranger. Only then is it Dan Grissom's turn, and he is supported by Willie Smith, who plays a clarinet obbligato. The tune ends with Jimmie Crawford's evocative effects on the temple blocks, and a booting trombone solo by Russell Bowles. Like a lot of Sy Oliver charts, *Charmaine* is a study in contrasts: high versus low, soft versus loud, legato versus staccato, muted trumpets versus baritone saxophone.

Sun Ra, who was an aspiring piano player when Lunceford celebrated his greatest triumphs, went to see the band whenever he got a chance: "When Sy left [in 1939] they were really very futuristic. Those were nice arrangements."

Sun Ra did not exaggerate. He rarely did when he discussed music, and was not wandering off into outer space. "The deft employment of dynamics and the strength of the descending chord at the end of a tune were unusual then, though commonplace now," writer Ralph Gleason agreed.[15] In 1944, Billy Eckstine's bebop band, considered one of the most advanced jazz orchestras of its day, recorded Tadd Dameron's ballad *I Want to Talk about You*. This song was a note-for-note copy of Sy Oliver's *Living from Day to Day*, a tune waxed by Lunceford eight years earlier—a clear case of plagiarism. Four months after *Living from Day to Day*, the Lunceford men recorded Oliver's arrangement of *Linger Awhile*. Here, after Grissom's vocal, the trumpets played a passage that, if it was not full-blown bebop yet, certainly bridged Armstrong's vanguard recordings from the late 1920s and Dizzy Gillespie's work in the years to come. Oliver's concept of *Ragging the Scale*, also from 1937, was even more amazing. In this chromatic study the band modulated from G to E-flat. That itself was not unusual, but one is intrigued by the modern-sounding use of the higher notes—ninths, elevenths and thirteenths—in the chords.

It is, perhaps, significant that in 1936–37 the band was billed as "Jimmie Lunceford and His Streamlined Rhythm." Streamline was a phenomenon just being discovered, studied, and applied—although German engineers had already experimented with low-drag airplanes in the early 1920s. Twenty years before the Germans, an American inventor, Frederick Upham Adams, had designed the very first streamlined vehicle, a train he called the *Wind Splitter*, which was used on the B&O line and reached speeds of 85 mph. The vogue for streamliners, however, did not set in until the mid-1930s, when futuristic aluminum and stainless steel models like the *Flying Yankee* and the *Comet* were put into service on various lines.

The Schneider and Bendix air races had resulted in ever refined airplanes, culminating in the sleek P-39 Airacobra fighter. The fancy Auburn Speedster set a new standard in elegance and smoothness for automobiles. Even toasters, refrigerators, and vacuum cleaners were by now being streamlined. In order to get a good picture of this streamline era, one only has to take a look at the science fiction comic books of the time, such as Flash Gordon and Buck Rogers. Any kid who went riding along in his father's fire-engine-red Studebaker Dictator was bound to believe that he was the merciless Ming, chasing all earthlings.

As such, the Lunceford orchestra with its suave, immaculate appearance, cartoon-like movements and polished, crisp execution fit in perfectly with this new age and its appealing art deco aesthetics. The intro of *Rhythm Is Our Business* evokes the Zephyr 9900 leaving the Kansas City railway station for Omaha.[16] Tunes such as *He Ain't Got Rhythm, For Dancers Only, Harlem Shout, The Melody Man,* and *Annie Laurie* sound like some streamliner dashing by, especially in live situations, when, generally speaking, the tempos were sped up. The smooth saxes in *Honey Keep Your Mind on Me, Organ Grinders Swing,* or *I Can't Escape from You* suggest the seamless skin of the Hughes H-1 race plane. And didn't the meticulous way Sy Oliver put together the various parts in an arrangement remind one of the precision interlocking of a Pratt & Whitney engine? Durham's amplified guitar and Paul Webster's high-note screaming added to the cutting-edge image of the band, as did some of the charts by Oliver *(Ragging the Scale)* and others. The Harlem Express moved smoothly in the fast lane.

SWINGING IN SWEDEN

The whole place started rocking.
—*Nils Hellström*

By the mid-1930s, Lunceford's influence on other dance orchestras was beginning to be felt. The Blue Ribbon Syncopators from Buffalo and Vernon Andrade's Society Orchestra in New York already had absorbed elements of the style before the Lunceford band had started its rise to fame. There were, no doubt, other bands studying Lunceford's charts, but they did not leave recordings or even memories. Surprisingly, one of the first white dance bands known to pick up on Lunceford was James Kok's 1935 outfit in Berlin. Born in Romania, Kok had moved to Germany in the early 1920s and formed a dance orchestra. Casa Loma and Lunceford were his prime models, and he recorded Lunceford's *Jazznocracy* one year after the original version had hit the market. That same year he was forced to exit Germany, and he returned to Romania.

In the years prior to the Second World War, most of the prominent European dance band arrangers and musicians had started to listen to four

American models: Whiteman, Ellington, Henderson, and Lunceford. And like a lot of African American bands, even European amateur ensembles now had their share of Lunceford on their desks, in addition to the Ellington, Dorsey, and Goodman tunes.

Lunceford's impact was not felt by big bands only. Smaller outfits tried to translate his orchestral coloring, cohesion, and bounce as well. One of the first of these was a hip little group led by trombonist and slide-saxophone player Snub Mosley, who from 1937 on worked at the Club Afrique in New York. We have met Mosley before: he was the man who had handed Jimmie one of Alphonso Trent's arrangements, when the Chickasaw Syncopators were in their infant stage. Saxophonist, singer, and songwriter Louis Jordan, known as "The Father of Rhythm & Blues," was inspired by Mosley's Club Afrique crew. But Jordan also was an avid collector of Lunceford records, as John Chilton, Jordan's biographer revealed: "He bought most of the Duke Ellington small-band sides, and recent recordings by Benny Carter, Jimmie Lunceford, and Pete Brown."[1] Lunceford, in return, later covered a couple of Jordan hits, notably *I'm Gonna Move to the Outskirts of Town*, *Knock Me a Kiss*, *G.I. Jive*, *Slender, Tender and Tall*, *You Ain't Nowhere*, and *Caldonia*.

A third prominent medium-sized jump band in New York under the Lunceford spell was the nine-piece Savoy Sultans, who for a couple of years were the hot house band of the famous Harlem ballroom. The Sultans were notorious for being a serious threat to any visiting orchestra that had the misfortune to find itself entangled in a battle of bands. Every night admirers would be standing right in front of the Sultans' bandstand, wondering, where do these nine men get that much music? It was, of course, from the arrangements. Jack Chapman, guitarist of the Sultans, could voice the instruments beautifully. The Savoy Sultans had a sound similar to the Lunceford band's, and then they had a Count Basie kind of sound, too. They weren't playing Count Basie arrangements, but they were swinging like Basie. They did not play songs associated with Lunceford, either. Their tenor soloist, George Kelly, remembered one tune that Jack Chapman had composed, a thing called *Let Your Conscience Be Your Guide*. The saxophonist did the vocal on it, and that arrangement sounded like it was written for the Lunceford band.

The Sultans' recording output suggests that the Lunceford spell was more prominent than Basie's influence. A tune like *Second Balcony Jump* (an Al Cooper composition, different from the better-known Gerald Valentine work) has a Basie feel, but other songs, such as *Jump Steady, The Thing, Stitches, Jumpin' the Blues* (again, not the Jay McShann tune), and *Sophisticated Jump* definitely point toward Lunceford. Especially in *Jump Steady*, the contrasts between the muted trumpets and the reeds smack of Lunceford. Moreover, the way the arrangers use Al Cooper's baritone saxophone *(Jumpin' at the Savoy)* is reminiscent of the role Jock Carruthers plays in the Jimmie Lunceford Orchestra. In *Looney*, from 1938, arranger Al Cooper uses elements of Sy Oliver's *For Dancers Only*. Intonation and cohesion of the Savoy Sultans, on the other hand, were much rougher and more uneven than in the Lunceford band.

The Savoy Sultans not only borrowed musical style elements from the Lunceford men; their visual appearance also paid tribute to them. They swayed their instruments from side to side, and pointed the trumpets upward, just like their models. And George Kelly, who was with the Sultans from 1941 to 1944, recalled,

> They were funny, man. I will never forget the first time I joined them. They gave me a hammer. I said, "What is this," you know. Said, "I came here to play music." So I found out what it was. Oh man, they'd drive you nuts. Rudy Williams would take his alto solos, and, like, Al Cooper, myself, and the two trumpet players, four, had hammers. And when he started riding on his solos, we'd beat on the floor with the hammers, you now. In a frenzy, man!

This was another thing the Sultans had copied, as can be seen in the already mentioned Vitaphone movie short by Jimmie Lunceford and His Dance Orchestra.

Even soloists came under Lunceford's influence. In an interview, piano wizard Erroll Garner once revealed that he loved Lunceford and Ellington. Keeping time was a thing he had learned from Basie and Lunceford. "Those two bands really laid that on me and it was a thrill."[2] One might argue that Garner's typical two-beat style and behind-the-beat timing were a reflection of Lunceford's rhythmic concept. Furthermore, Garner's style was essentially orchestral. Very few pianists were able to use dynamics, changes-of-tempo, contrasts, and sumptuous chords, resulting in subtle colors, the way Erroll Garner could. One writer called him "the pianist who frequently sounds like a movie-palace orchestra."

Apart from Paul Whiteman, Duke Ellington, and Cab Calloway, no

major American jazz band had traveled the Old World. European jazz
record collectors had become aware of the Jimmie Lunceford Orchestra
soon after its RCA Victor 78s had become available, in 1934. Lunceford's
Scandinavian tour, in February–March 1937 was considered quite prestigious. Bandleader Frank Vernon had learned from an interview in the
English magazine *Melody Maker* that Lunceford would love to tour
Europe. A good friend of Vernon's worked at the newspaper *Folkets Dagblad,* in Stockholm. And yes, the *Dagblad* was willing to sponsor a Swedish
tour. Initially, five cities were scheduled to be visited. In addition, Norway,
The Netherlands, Denmark, England, Belgium, and France were on the
two-month itinerary. "Europe! Europe! Europe! Watch for those streamlined rhythms!" cried an ad in *Down Beat* magazine. "Jimmie Lunceford
will stagger Europe!" promised *Melody Maker,* which only two years
before had condemned Lunceford's records, claiming the ensemble was too
precise, too mechanical. The music weekly had predicted that Lunceford
never would attain the heights of Duke Ellington or Fletcher Henderson.
Now, *Melody Maker* had nothing but praise for the arrangements, the fine
soloists, and the terrific phrasing.

Sweden was not completely unaware of American jazz. As early as 1895,
the Fisk Jubilee Singers had visited the country. Black shows had toured
Sweden during the 1920s, and major soloists such as Louis Armstrong, Joe
Venuti, Coleman Hawkins, and Benny Carter had performed there, accompanied by Swedish musicians. But this was the first time a regular American
band would tour the country. A proud Jimmie Lunceford announced his
European tour on the air on Thursday, February 4, during the night New
York disc jockey Martin Block celebrated the second anniversary of his
popular record show *Make Believe Ballroom* on station WNEW. Dozens of
celebrities, including Andy Razaf, Teddy Wilson, Cab Calloway, Chick
Webb, Vincent Lopez, Benny Goodman, Glen Gray, and Charlie Barnet
attended. "Thanks a million for your invitation," Lunceford said on the air,
adding, "Yes, we are sailing for London but I don't know whether or not
we'll play for the coronation." Apparently, there had been rumors about
the band furnishing the music for King George VI's coronation ball. The
bandleader concluded the little radio interview by asking Martin Block to
play his recording of *My Last Affair.*[3]

Next night, the orchestra started its farewell week at the Apollo. Choreographer Clarence Robinson, of Cotton Club fame, had staged an elaborate
show, featuring many acts, among them cabaret star Mabel Scott, the Four

Step Brothers, the versatile Taps Miller, Pigmeat Markham, who danced, sang, and performed comedy skits, comedian Jimmie Baskette, and "Sixteen Dancing Beauties."

Apollo's 1930s audiences were spoiled with fast-paced, talent-crammed shows, but this "So Long, Jimmie" revue definitely was something else. "Standing room only," motioned the big man at the door. Decked out in blue, yellow, and red, his impressive appearance was enhanced by huge gold-filled front teeth. SRO meant over seventeen hundred people were in the Apollo.

Inside, the room was completely dark. Accordingly, one did not notice the stage nor the crowd, apart from a low-key, but excited murmur. Suddenly, the lights went on, unveiling the bandleader, who sat in an automobile, wearing a broad smile. While the orchestra played a fast tune, he was escorted by the chorus girls on motorcycles, who drove him off to the cardboard docks in the back, roaring their engines and ringing their sirens. The fast pace was maintained, the Step Brothers captivated the crowd with their routine, challenging one another into increasingly acrobatic steps and jumps. The band played a string of its favorites, closing with an absolutely devastating version of *Chinatown, My Chinatown,* crammed with solos. The ensuing applause, cries, and whistles lasted through six curtain calls.

At the back of the theater musicians and other well-wishers were assembled. After a couple of minutes, under a sign that said, "If your friends and relatives won't pay to see you, who will?" the backdoor opened. The leader emerged, in shirt-sleeves, wiping his head (the Satchmo way), grinning, as if embarrassed: "Sorry folks, I must look terrible. Just cooling down."[4]

Before the band took off for Europe, it played "the most sensational battle of bands ever to grace the mammoth Cornell University Drill Hall" (said *Down Beat*) on February 12. It was a triple battle: the Lunceford men were booked against the Hudson-DeLange band and the up-and-coming Bob Crosby group. Over four thousand swing fans watched, listened, and danced for five solid hours. As the battle evolved, the Hudson-DeLange aggregation fell to the wayside, leaving the battlefield to Lunceford and Crosby. *Down Beat*'s Ted Rowes was present, and he noted,

> Steve De Bann, Junior Prom Chairman, who was responsible for hiring the "unknown" Crosby, had his satisfaction when that great Dixieland band matched the terrific ensemble arrangements of Lunceford with equally terrific individual exhibitions of "out of this

world" swing genius and definitely proved themselves to be one of the greatest white swing bands in existence. . . . To expect a college crowd that listens remarkably well with its eyes to withstand the tremendous show of the Lunceford troupe is like expecting [Crosby's drummer] Ray Bauduc to muff a "jam session."[5]

It seems that the most satisfying battles put together bands of different styles. Ironically, Crosby's concept changed in the early 1940s, and his orchestra, playing in a Lunceford vein, became very much part of mainstream swing.

Two days later, the Streamlined Rhythm Band went to Hoboken to board a Polish liner, the new *Stephan Bathory*, a 287-ton, twenty-knot ship. After the orchestra had performed for Captain Berkowski and his party, on the last night aboard, Lunceford and Oxley were presented with the company's medal of honor.

The ensemble opened February 24 with a double concert at the University of Oslo. Next night the band gave a double performance at Oslo's Losjen auditorium. After the first show, Frank Vernon, who acted as the orchestra's guide, wrote a postcard to Nils Hellström at *Orkester Journalen*, the Swedish jazz monthly. On the postcard were three words and five exclamation marks: *What a band!!!!!*

Since the Americans were paid by the day, and their salaries were substantial, the Swedish promoters had been forced to extend the Swedish leg of the tour from the original five scheduled cities to sixteen dates. Hence, right after its European debut, the band continued with double concerts at the Göteborg, Sweden, Konserthuset (February 26), then Stockholm (the twenty-seventh and the afternoon of the twenty-eighth), Eskilstuna (the twenty-eighth), Jönköping (March 1), Örebro (the second), Göteborg again (the third), Boras (the fourth), Norrköping (the fifth), Helsingborg (the sixth), Malmö (three performances at the Realläroverkets Aula on the seventh and one more on the eighth), back to Stockholm (the ninth), Karlskoga (the tenth), Karlstad (the eleventh), closing at the Göteborg Konserthuset, March 13. A segment of one hour of this last performance was broadcast, and four numbers were recorded by a fan. These selections represent the earliest known live recordings of the Jimmie Lunceford Orchestra. The sound quality, however, is poor.

On this tour, apart from its well-known hits, the band played songs such as *I Hate Myself for Being in Love with You* (a glee club number), *Nagasaki,* and *St. Louis Blues,* and usually closed its performances with either *Tiger Rag* or *Bugle Call Rag,* selections never performed in a recording studio.

The Swedes turned out in the thousands (although the concerts in the smaller towns were far from sold out). "It was not full," remembered Bertil Lyttkens, who as a boy of sixteen saw the band at the Helsingborg Konserthuset. "You didn't have much money. Sweden was a poor country in the thirties. In Stockholm and Göteborg and Malmö it was full." Bertil had to travel by train from his home in Halmstad to Helsingborg, a distance of about seventy miles. "I started very early. I had to be free from school. It was a Saturday, and we went to school till four o'clock. I went to the head of the school and begged him to be free from some lessons, so I could take the train for Helsingborg at three o'clock. I telephoned a week before to reserve a place for me, and when I came there, there were a lot of vacant seats. I was amazed. I said, these are dull, silly persons here in Helsingborg!" Since he had to take the last train back, Bertil missed the second concert, something he regrets to this day. "It was said that the second concert was better than the first. They were warmed up. It was a wonderful evening! I remember only some details now; it's long ago. They did not play *For Dancers Only.* Dan Grissom—I think he did not sing in Sweden. Willie Smith and the Trio did the vocals, not Dan Grissom. He played alto sax; he sat in the second row, between Al Norris and Moses Allen. And Crawford sat on a table, over the piano. He had a lot of percussion. Yes, it was fantastic." Bertil drifted back to that very special night in 1937, and he repeated softly, "Yes, it was fantastic."

For the Malmö performances, more than one thousand jazz fans from nearby Copenhagen had crossed the Sont strait between Denmark and southern Sweden, a distance of twenty miles. At Berns Salonger, the fashionable ballroom in downtown Stockholm (dating from 1850, it is still in operation today), the admission price for the *Dans-Soaré* that lasted from 9:00 P.M. to 2:00 A.M. was three kronor (about seventy-five cents), tax and dinner not included. Five hundred people, the cream of the Swedish jazz musicians among them, danced to the streamlined swing music. "They went nearly crazy, hearing this clever band," Bertil Lyttkens chuckled. The audience listened and cheered when Karl Gerhard, a well-known comedian, during intermission satirized current events in Swedish life.

The tour's turnover totaled ninety-seven thousand kronor, at the time roughly twenty-five thousand dollars. A novel aspect of the tour had been that the orchestra had played concert halls, rather than the usual ballrooms and theaters, apart from the dance at Berns Salonger. "Swedish miles—they kill me," was the comment Paul Webster scribbled on a promotion picture, referring to the distances and the Swedish winter. "Tout à vous," added suave Sy Oliver.

"It is an extraordinary orchestra," wrote *Orkester Journalen*, "well-disciplined, funny, versatile, a lovely swing, good vocalists. The band has got just about everything." One enthralled fan wrote a letter to *Orkester Journalen:* "For one week, I was actually unable to work. In my head there was nothing but Lunceford." But *Orkester Journalen*'s review contained words of criticism as well. "Of course, everything was played with the utmost precision. However, it was a little boring to hear the soloists play exactly the same solos as they did on the records, though it is maybe asking too much to have them improvise on the same melody day in, day out, and for years at a stretch." In the next issue of the magazine, Nils Hellström elaborated,

> Even though many of Lunceford's arrangements—especially those where the brass is forced upward chorus after chorus—may not have much value in themselves, and are just tailored to address some kind of strange sport instinct, or whatever, in the audience (and they succeeded in doing just that!), the band does possess an incredible *swing*. Why is it that people at least do not react to the orchestra's vitality, even though the melodic and harmonic elements might not be really revolutionary? I just do not understand some people's odd sense of rhythm, since even the most unique rhythms are wasted on them. I remember for instance the moment when Eddie Tompkins started rubbing his hands (with his palms against one another), after his vocal in *Nagasaki*—something that is a traditional gesture in Harlem, by the way. This may sound very simple, but he did it in such a rhythmic way that I got the feeling the whole place started rocking with him! Rhythm may be just one of music's three elements, but witnessing it being ignored as completely as this is remarkable, to put it mildly.[6]

Apart from *Orkester Journalen*, there was little jazz expertise among Swedish music critics. Most of them wrote about either classical music or local show business. Under the headline "Negerjazz pa Realskolan" ("Negro Jazz at the High School"), Sten Broman wrote an extended review for the *Sydsvenska Dagbladet Snällposten*. After stating that "Negro records, up to and including Mr. Armstrong's original way of playing (i.e., his original way of jiving), all sounded like the loveliest of maidens chanting, compared with the primitive wails one heard the other night," he pitied the brass:

> One is astonished—one even feels the pressure in the head—when one hears these Negro trumpeters blow to the high heavens, into the clarinet or the flute register: my, my, this guy's lips and brain must be hurting when he goes way up. That was formidable—that was stronger even than Armstrong.
>
> Well, nobody will deny that this orchestra is special. How supple, how soft these saxophones play, and how unprecedented, how utterly capable the trumpets and the trombones that follow. Not to mention the visual aspects: the percussion man, who juggled the rhythms, his sticks, and himself. Or the string bass man, who looked like the world's jolliest missing link (both he and Mr. Lunceford would make excellent models for Stomatol ads [a weight-control remedy], but this is just a hint that is free of charge). Every now and then said link drew attention with some kind of good-natured, primitive falsetto singing, whereby he appeared ready to climb the bass violin. (He managed to restrain himself.)
>
> All in all it was quite fantastic. It was a splendid kind of madness. Rhythmically and acoustically, everything was heavy.

Broman concluded his review with "one went home with ears that echoed a most infernal roar. But it cannot be denied that it was fun witnessing this Triumph of Sound. Lunceford has realized all imaginable consequences of playing hot, and the audience, not surprisingly, was left ablaze."

Not every critic shared Sten Broman's positive view. In the *Nerikes Allehanda*, one "Geo" belittled the accomplishments of the American musicians in racially loaded terms: "It is unlikely that people who live in the Old World are enlightened by this kind of musical achievement. Only a band of gorillas, or possibly orangutans, would be able to outdo them, and they would look better, too. Sweep these Negroes out of the concert hall, Mr. Ribbe!"[7]

The Americans, not surprisingly, left a mark on Swedish big bands as well, not in the least part due to their willingness to share their knowledge and experience with their colleagues. Many drummers watched Craw's hi-hat cymbal in awe: at the time, this contraption was unknown to Swedish musicians. Likewise, Durham's electric guitar triggered curiosity. There were numerous parties, thrown by musicians and fans, after the shows. There was a lot of jamming. The American musicians even had to be forced *not* to play: "A Swede from time to time wants to look his neighbor deep in the eyes, in order to be able to bring out a toast," according to Nils Hellström, who added that the black musicians seemed to like nothing better than to just play.

Lunceford's influence on Swedish musicians showed primarily in the timing displayed by bands such as Sam Samson's and, later on, Harry Arnold's. Willard Ringstrand, like Arnold and Samson an arranger, leaned toward Dixieland, but in his 1940 composition *One Two Three Four* he cited Sy Oliver's daring arrangement of *Ragging the Scale*. Twenty years after Lunceford's visit to Sweden, noted trumpeter, bandleader, arranger, and publisher Thore Ehrling recalled in an interview that his encounter with the band at Stockholm's Berns Salonger was the most profound experience of his entire career.[8]

The effect of the Americans was, perhaps, felt even more in the provinces. The Whispering Band from Örebro was founded in 1933—and lasted over fifty years. Led by pianist Lars Johansson, it was considered one of the top amateur ensembles of the country. After Lunceford's concert in the local Konserthuset, musicians from both bands got together and jammed. The Whispering Band recorded an instrumental version of *Rhythm Is Our Business* one year after Lunceford's visit to Örebro.

A projected extension of the tour through England during the second half of March, as well as appearances in Denmark, fell through because of currency problems and fierce resistance from the British and Danish musicians unions, who wanted to protect their members. The official explanation was that the English concert halls failed to come up with the guaranteed one thousand dollars per concert, as requested by Oxley. It was rumored that the band even had turned down an invitation to play at King George VI's coronation ball—for a larger sum of money, of course—as a reaction to the hostile reception by the musicians union.[9]

Upon arriving in London, Harold Oxley immediately returned to New York on the *Queen Mary*. The Scandinavian experience prompted the manager to plan a second European tour for July, which was to include Paris and Monte Carlo. Probably because it was planned on such short notice, this tour did not materialize.

The rest of the party, including Crystal Lunceford and Jimmie's road manager-brother Cornelius, spent two days in London before sailing back to the States on March 20 aboard the German liner *Hansa*. (Scheduled appearances in The Netherlands, Belgium, and France had also been canceled; the Swedish promoters had encountered too many obstacles, involving working permits and the like.) The ship docked in New York on Thursday, March 25.

Three days after its return, the band, now advertised as Jimmie Lunceford and His International Orchestra, was top of the bill at an Easter Sunday dance at New York's Renaissance Casino which lasted twelve hours. The other bands were Edgar Hayes's and Vernon Andrade's. Admission was fifty cents, provided one entered the dance before 5:00 P.M.

Hayes had been the piano player and musical director of the Mills Blue Rhythm Band, which had broken up two months earlier; singer Lucky Millinder, who had fronted the Blue Rhythm Band, took half of it, and the remainder went with Hayes. The latter did not waste any time whipping his new band into shape, and it is a proof of his professionalism that within a couple of weeks the group sounded like it had been playing for years. The results of its first recording session, May 25, bear this out. Some of the arrangements—by the leader and by his saxophonist Joe Garland—had a Sy Oliver flavor: notably the way the writers juxtaposed sections, and the prominent role they gave to Crawford Wethington, who played baritone and bass saxophones. Other charts, featuring multi-part block harmony, referred to the work of Edwin Wilcox.

The Easter dance at the Renaissance proved to be the acid test for the new big band. It was a widely publicized affair, and on account of Lunceford's acclaimed European trip the place was packed with bookers, club owners, and other luminaries. Andrade's house band opened, but when one hour later Hayes took over, the party really got going. Clyde Bernhardt, Edgar Hayes's trombone soloist, remembered that they

opened with *Stomping At The Renny,* and I'm not bragging, but we blew Andrade away. Old Henry Goodwin, he was screaming on trumpet, Edgar was stomping, just playing his ass off, and the band was riffing like crazy.

Man, those dancing jitterbugs went wild—all hooting, hollering. People started standing up to watch the band.

Sy Oliver, who was working in the Lunceford band then, came over and asked who did the arrangement.

"Joe Garland," I said.

"Man, I'm telling you," he whispered, "you cats got something."

Next we did *In the Mood*, then let it all out with *Meet the Band* and other great swing numbers. We wrapped it up with *Swinging in the Promised Land*, and the audience was so hot they wouldn't let Vernon come back on. We had to do an encore and still had to beg off. Made such an impression that Andrade never did come back, and we alternated with Lunceford for the rest of the show.[10]

Oxley was present, and when somebody inquired who was booking Hayes, he quickly stepped forward, claiming he did. It was not true, but from that day on, the Edgar Hayes Orchestra was a new client. Ironically, Hayes and Wethington had already been haunting Oxley at his East Forty-seventh Street office, to see whether he was interested in booking the new band. But the manager had given them the cold shoulder, saying they needed more experience. Now Oxley got the band new uniforms, a week at the Apollo, and a recording contract with Decca. The Edgar Hayes Orchestra became Harold Oxley's second major asset.

The July 1937 night in Hartford, Connecticut, when the Luncefordeans encountered the Basie band for the first time, was an event to remember. It was staged by the *Pittsburgh Courier*. Lunceford had recently returned from Europe, and Basie was just beginning to make his presence felt. Basie had a dozen or so complete arrangements at his disposal, for the most part donated by Fletcher Henderson, and Lunceford boasted a treasure chest of three hundred charts to choose from. The Basie band, dead tired, having arrived from Pittsburgh in a raggedy old bus, was taking a rest, when the Harlem Express made its entrance in a grand way, aboard a spacious air-conditioned Greyhound bus. This bus was rented, and the band had its own regular driver. Al Norris and Russell Bowles also were qualified chauffeurs, so the sometimes substantial hops between venues were no problem.

Members of Lunceford's local fan club had set up a large banquet table on the floor near their idols' side of the stage. The band boy quickly moved the music stands, the instruments, and the chairs of their pitiful opponents to the other side of the battlefield, in order to make room for the main attraction. "Willie Smith was one of the warmest guys you could ever meet, and Joe Thomas was very friendly, but most of the guys in Lunceford's band didn't even speak to us," Basie's trumpet man Harry Edison remembered. This was the night, by the way, that Eddie Durham was scheduled to join Count Basie, his old buddy from the Bennie Moten days. Producer and talent scout John Hammond had arranged it, a couple of weeks before, at Lunceford's own Larchmont Casino. Durham said, "Willard Alexander [the booking agent] offered me $75 a week to play with Basie, and another seventy-five to write for the band, so it was $150 a week." Since he was making $70 a week with Lunceford, the decision had been easy.

The Harlem Express went on the offensive against the motley crew from Kansas City, bringing its singing Trio, the glee club, and all its other tricks into the battle. "When things got under way, that great Lunceford band was fantastic," Basie remembered. But the KC men fought like tigers. Basie elaborated, "I guess I can say our guys were swinging pretty nice in there, and Jo Jones was something else that night, too. He was on fire. Jo and Big 'Un [bassist Walter Page] were driving all the way. Considering what we were up against, I think we did pretty good. At least we didn't get chopped too bad." "Prez played like he'd never played before," was Edison's impression of tenor sensation Lester Young that night. He testified that Lunceford and his men could not hide their curiosity and interest and came up to the bandstand. He maintained that his band "washed Lunceford out of the dance hall." Basie was a little more modest: "We just weren't ready for Jimmie at the time. His band was too rugged for any of us." On another occasion he stated, "They'd start to rock, and they'd just rock all night long."

One must take into account that at this time the Basie band was still building. It had great potential, but undeniably sounded rough. The radio broadcasts from the Chatterbox, in Pittsburgh (in January and February), bear this out. Eddie Durham, playing his last gig with Jimmie, was positive. There was no dance orchestra in the world that could "wash Lunceford away at that time. Nobody!" Both bands stayed at the same hotel, so all the band boy had to do was move Durham's luggage from one side of the lobby to the other.[11]

With Eddie Durham gone, Al Norris now took up the electric guitar. Again, the instrument was not recorded for the next four years. It was only in 1941, with *Yard Dog Mazurka*, that Norris had his first amplified solo documented, not counting some earlier radio air checks.

When James "Trummy" Young took Eddie Durham's trombone chair in September 1937, he had to study Durham's parts for three weeks before he was able to perform with the orchestra. He had had offers from Chick Webb and Cab Calloway, and he was uncertain about the Harlem Express. "You think I should go?" he had asked his roommate Ray Nance. "To make sure you go," Nance had replied, "I'll put you on the train myself tonight."[12] Trummy considered himself the ignorant one in his new band. All the other musicians had college degrees, and the only thing he could boast of were his four years with Earl Hines's orchestra. He noted with amazement that the other band members were not only educated, but went to church and Sunday school. For swing band musicians, this was quite exceptional.

The new arrival proved to be an extremely powerful and harmonically forward-thinking player. Russell Bowles had been the prime trombone soloist in the band, but from now on Trummy had the solo chair. The trombones never sounded better. "Apart from Duke, the trombone section is the most perfect one I have ever heard," French critic Hugues Panassié wrote. "James Young is the big star here. His attack is incredibly forceful. He is one trombonist I rate very high. Russell Boles and Elmer Crumbley are good musicians as well, and I was surprised to hear the latter play choruses in the style of 'Tricky Sam.'"[13]

Trummy Young turned out to be a singer with a hip, casual inflection as well. His biggest success was *Margie*, a tune that had been a hit for the Original Dixieland Jazz Band in 1920. It became one of the best-selling Decca singles of 1938, and there were, in all probability, not many nights that year when Young did not sing it. Sy Oliver had written out the vocal to make sure it would blend in exactly. It was a nice arrangement, not one of Oliver's top charts, but simple and catchy. Drummer Freddy Kohlman, who by this time had moved from New Orleans to Chicago to work with Earl Hines and Jimmie Noone, remembered the night Lunceford appeared at the Windy City's Savoy Ballroom and Trummy wasn't there. When the band went on a break, the drummer went backstage to talk. From the battles with Robichaux he knew everybody in the band. He asked them, "What happened, where's Trummy?" "He's up in the hotel, sick, a case of pneumonia. He can't make it," was the answer. When the musicians went back onstage after intermission, the crowd insisted they play *Margie*, and almost started a riot because the bandleader wouldn't play the song *sans*

Trummy. Kohlman concluded, "They had to go get Trummy Young out of the hotel by ambulance and bring him over there, just to do *Margie*. And they went wild after he did that *Margie*."

It was clear to everybody in the business, swing fans and bookers alike: after its meteoric rise in 1935, the Jimmie Lunceford Orchestra by 1938 was firmly settled as a major attraction, on a par with established names such as Fats Waller and Cab Calloway. Its varied style, visual effects, and precision playing inspired and influenced countless bands. It is not too bold to judge that Lunceford had a direct hand in the raising of the general standard of swing music. All over the country, he had become a household name in the black community, and jazz fans all over the world cherished his recordings.

{10}

WHEN SY LEFT THE LUNCE

When Jimmie Lunceford came along, he upset everybody.
—Bobby Plater

All over the country the band broke attendance records, many of them long-standing. In Philadelphia, booker Reese DuPree was excited over the band's business at the Strand Ballroom. In addition to Lunceford, Willie Bryant and Lucky Millinder's Mills Blue Rhythm Band had drawn well there in early 1938,[1] prompting *Billboard* to publish an editorial under the headline "Colored Bands Becoming Big Biz." The magazine noted that despite the recession in music that year (partly caused by the fading of the typical Hollywood musical, and, probably, the "Second Roosevelt Depression" of 1937–38), the demand for black talent was rising. It was in this atmosphere of slowly but steadily growing opportunities that African American bands like Lunceford's worked, constantly hoping for better conditions and better venues, for fairer treatment, comparable to what their white colleagues were getting.

The same booker announced in 1943 that Lunceford had set a new record while touring the South. In the course of seven nights, more than thirty thousand people had danced to the music of the Harlem Express. Fans had been turned away at each performance; emergency firemen and police were called out. The band had outdrawn Basie, Calloway, Armstrong, Kirk, and Hines on previous, similar tours.[2]

Edwin Wilcox confirmed that the reason for Lunceford and Oxley to opt for endless strings of one-nighters, rather than the more comfortable location jobs, was mainly a financial one. Union scale for one-nighters was four hundred dollars—roughly five thousand dollars in today's money—but working against a percentage of the door earnings meant making twice as much—or more.[3]

The discipline that characterized the music and the visual part of the show was maintained on the road. Lunceford insisted on traveling together by bus, by train, or, occasionally, by charter plane or airliner. In October 1939, for instance, the entire orchestra flew from New York to Chicago and back, to play at a private ritzy debutante ball. Hence the men were back in time to have the dancers hopping at the Renaissance.[4] Nobody was allowed to use his own private car, not even for a fifty-mile trip. Jimmie's adage was: if something happens to one musician, it happens to the full band.

While their monetary success and fame may have caused the musicians to display traces of vanity when in the presence of rival bands, there was no stand-offish behavior toward the audience. When intermission came, the sidemen used to mingle freely with their fans. During the 1950s, Emerson Able was the music teacher at Manassas High School in Memphis. Before that time, he had been a student there, trying to master the saxophone, and he remembered that he always got Joe Thomas's full attention whenever the Lunceford band played the Beale Street Auditorium, and next morning visited his school.

All of the guys had personalities out of this world. They were very, very friendly, courteous, and they talked to you. Mingling with the performers was very much in fashion because, first of all, they didn't have any dressing room! Listening to those guys talk to us, you know—and we were kids. They had individual photos; they were about three by two-and-a-half. They handed those things out and autographed them to everybody in the audience. Little bitty small thing, you know. They were individual portraits of the guys in the group.

Lunceford was the king, man. They were neatly dressed, like Wynton Marsalis has required his musicians to do. You know, they just didn't look like the guy on the corner with the vest and the cap on his head. They were very, very professional.

During its performance most of the people stood in front of the band. They didn't dance, they just listened, because these arrangements were something else—*ooh!* Please! Please! Yeah, I mean, the little saxophone lines, the ensemble bits, and things that they used to play. Man, oh, they were something.

Proof of the band's popularity with the ladies are the many names and telephone numbers still legible on the backs of the original music sheets. Bass player George Duvivier, who in 1945 became staff arranger for the orchestra, had been a fan since the Cotton Club days. He stated that when the band arrived in certain towns, it was honored with a parade usually reserved for aviation heroes.[5] It was always party time. The way the band members got along with each other and their enthusiasm for the music was obvious and infectious.

"He played for the workers," singer Babs Gonzales emphasized. His mother ran a restaurant in Newark, where the Lunceford band sometimes ate. The cotton pickers down South, the workers, were Lunceford's target group. "He had to hire black hands to book venues, all over the country. Like tobacco barns where they had moved the tobacco to the back, for the workers to dance, you know. I saw all these things while I was the assistant band-boy."

Tenorist Von Freeman noted a similarity between Lunceford and Erskine Hawkins.

These two bands were sophisticated on a certain level. Well, the critics would say for instance, "Erskine Hawkins's band is out of tune" because they would play a lot of minor ninths and things. But it's bluesy, you know. And then they would say about Lunceford, "Well, he sounds like he has a concert band." But actually, it was just different levels that you're playing on, in my view. I noticed Lunceford was very popular, although I don't think too many people knew what he was playing . . . other than a few Sy Oliver arrangements he had, and they were like spirituals, sort of to speak, and they went over in the black neighborhood.

The working class formed the core audience for the band, but the Harlem Express had a sizable following among the black middle class as well. This had to do with the college background of the musicians. Education was one of the criteria when the leader screened new musicians. Back in the 1930s and 1940s, the black intelligentsia had a habit to stick together and support one another. "People loved Lunceford in Austin," Joe Houston recalled. The 1950s tenor star first saw the band when he was still in high school.

> When the band came to Texas, they made their headquarters in Austin. They come to Austin and stay, work out of Austin. They [would] go to Dallas and come back to Austin, San Antonio and come back to Austin. They'd stay there because Austin had two black colleges. And Lunceford went to school with some of the people that was teaching there, you know. They had some of the doctors that Lunceford had graduated in school with. All the musicians would stay in these people's houses. I used to go up to Trummy Young's house all the time because he lived close to me.
>
> They fit with everybody, because all the cats had college degrees. They were the only black band on the road with college degrees. Earl Hines and Duke, Ben Webster and all them cats, they didn't have no college degrees! Shit, *drinking* degrees! They would kill everybody, drinking! But Lunceford, you know, [they] were very talented; when they come to town they stayed with the biggest people in town.

Swing music, generally speaking, was frowned upon by the black intelligentsia. There was a tendency to revere forms of European art and music, and disregard African American grassroots culture. This attitude was encouraged by the black church; as late as 1967, Duke Ellington's *Concert of Sacred Music* was banned from Baptist churches in the Washington, DC, area. The reason for the boycott was given by the Rev. John D. Bussey, who, while admitting he had not heard the music, stated that Ellington's lifestyle "is opposed to what the church stands for."[6]

When you were a black middle-class youth, as a rule you weren't allowed to go to a dance. In case you had the good luck to have enlightened parents, they might make an exception for a so-called class act: Duke Ellington, Cab Calloway, or Jimmie Lunceford.

A marked difference between Lunceford and his closest rival Duke Ellington was the respective colors of their audiences. Though the blues, ironically, had a more prominent place in his repertory, Ellington always drew a lot of whites. From the beginning, his manager Irving Mills had marketed Ellington to the white intelligentsia, while this latter group usually formed a small minority whenever the Harlem Express pulled into a town. In his book *The Joy of Jazz* Tom Scanlan remembered that there were just a handful of whites present when he discovered the splendor of the Lunceford reed section in a Washington ballroom, just prior to World War II.[7] French critic Hugues Panassié, who spent five months in New York in 1938–39, observed that only musicians and black people seemed to appreciate the band.[8] Still, probably due to the orchestra's appeal at white colleges, which began early in the 1930s, there were pockets of affluent white people who revered the Lunceford band, as Buddy DeFranco remembered: "They were very popular with the high-level club, people who were in upstate New York, Connecticut, the upper echelon."

Meanwhile, the band's aspirations abroad met with little luck. A projected larger European string of performances during the early months of 1938 was canceled. According to the leader, "unsettled conditions abroad" were the reason for this cancellation.[9]

A look at the itinerary for mid-June to mid-July of that year will give an idea of how the Lunceford men used to work:

June 15	Beckley, West Virginia
June 16	Roanoke, Virginia
June 17	Winston-Salem, North Carolina
June 18	Knoxville, Tennessee
June 19	Columbia, South Carolina
June 21	Charlotte, North Carolina
June 22	Macon, Georgia
June 23	Asheville, North Carolina
June 24	Atlanta, Georgia
June 25	Savannah, Georgia
June 26	Charlotte, North Carolina
June 27	Savannah, Georgia
June 28	Charleston, South Carolina
June 30	Jacksonville, Florida
July 1	Daytona Beach, Florida

July 2	Fort Lauderdale, Florida
July 3	Miami, Florida
July 4	Tampa, Florida
July 7	Birmingham, Alabama
July 8	Memphis, Tennessee
July 9	Birmingham, Alabama
July 10	Nashville, Tennessee
July 11	Paducah, Kentucky
July 12	Hopkinsville, Kentucky
July 13	Owensboro, Kentucky
July 14	Evansville, Indiana
July 15	Columbus, Ohio
July 17	Cincinnati, Ohio[10]

Note the jumps between the dance halls, averaging 250 miles, and peaking at 400 miles. In the course of five weeks, the musicians had four nights off—provided there were no last-minute additions in the itinerary. Note also the fact that the band sometimes would alternate between cities. The Harlem Express and Andy Kirk's Twelve Clouds of Joy were considered the kings of the road. The constant traveling put its toll on both the musicians and their gear: wear and tear on the instruments alone cost management at least twelve thousand dollars yearly.[11]

New York critic George T. Simon wrote for *Metronome* magazine, and though he devoted far more space and praise for his buddy Glenn Miller, he also had an open ear for Lunceford. He referred, for instance, to an appearance in the summer of 1938 "up in South Norwalk, Conn., in Leo Miller's Roton Point spot, where Jimmie's boys settled into a groove so deep that they had to be chiseled out with a pick and shovel and shipped home."[12] Nonetheless Simon, too, on occasion cast his ears to the wind when, for instance, he wrote that in the mid-1930s the saxophone section was given to sloppy intonation: "This used to be a unit in which Willie Smith led as he pleased and the others followed as they pleased, with all of them tuning up as nobody pleased." This was a period when, according to Simon, the brass played better than the reeds. This assertion infuriated Sy Oliver, a brass man himself, whose verdict was that at no stage of the band's existence the brass were better than the saxes.

Simon complimented the band for its combination of vigorousness, joy, and swinging craftsmanship. Never had he witnessed a big band that swung

Jimmie Lunceford, ca. 1934.
(Jack Bradley Collection.)

Jimmie Lunceford Orchestra, ca. early 1934. *L. to r.:* Russell Bowles, Jimmie Lunceford, Willie Smith, Joe Thomas, Ed Wilcox, Al Norris, Jimmy Crawford, Moses Allen, Tommy Stevenson, Henry Wells, Sy Oliver, Eddie Tompkins, Earl Carruthers. (Bertil Lyttkens Collection.)

Cotton Club, 1934. *L. to r.:* Ed Wilcox, Jimmy Crawford, Moses Allen, Al Norris. (Bertil Lyttkens Collection.)

Jimmy Crawford at the Cotton Club, 1934. (Jack Bradley Collection.)

Jimmie Lunceford and Harold Oxley. (Bertil Lyttens Collection.)

Jimmie Lunceford Orchestra in Vitaphone movie short, ca. July 1936. *L. to r.:* Sy Oliver, Russell Bowles, Paul Webster, Eddie Durham, Elmer Crumbley, Eddie Tompkins, Ed Wilcox, Jimmie Lunceford, Jimmy Crawford, Willie Smith, Dan Grissom, Ed Brown, Al Norris, Joe Thomas, Moses Allen, Earl Carruthers. (Jack Bradley Collection.)

Lunceford Trio: Eddie Tompkins, Willie Smith, Joe Thomas. (Jack Bradley Collection.)

Glee club, ca. early 1935. *L. to r.:* Earl Carruthers, Sy Oliver, Russell Bowles, Ed Wilcox, Eddie Tompkins, Eddie Durham, Jimmy Crawford, Jimmie Lunceford, Willie Smith, Al Norris, Moses Allen, Joe Thomas, Laforest Dent, Elmer Crumbley, Paul Webster. (Svenskt Visarkiv Collection.)

Berns Salonger, Stockholm, March 9, 1937. *L. to r.:* Harold Oxley, Karl Gerhard, Crystal Tulli Lunceford, Ake Strauller. (Svenskt Visarkiv Collection.)

Al Norris, Moses Allen, and Jimmy Crawford at Berns Salonger, Stockholm, March 9, 1937. (Svenskt Visarkiv Collection.)

Berns Salonger, Stockholm, March 9, 1937. *L. to r.:* (standing) Russell Bowles, Gösta Törner, Elly Lind, Thore Jederby, Nisse Lind, Earl Carruthers, Britt Törner, Lizzie Eriksson, Moses Allen, "Sax-Jerker" Eriksson, Georg Vernon; (squatting) Al Norris, Sune Lundvall, Sy Oliver, Bengt Rydberg, Ed Wilcox, Yngve Nillson. (Bertil Lyttkens Collection.)

Elmer Crumbley, Trummy Young, Russell Bowles, ca. 1939. (Bertil Lyttkens Collection.)

L. to r.: Willie Smith, Ted Buckner, Joe Thomas, Earl Carruthers, ca. 1939. (Jack Bradley Collection.)

Gerald Wilson, Snooky Young, Paul Webster, ca. 1941. (Jack Bradley Collection.)

Put On Your Old Grey Bonnet, ca. 1937. *L. to r.:* Eddie Tompkins, Al Norris (hidden), Willie Smith, Joe Thomas, Moses Allen. (Bertil Lyttkens Collection.)

Brass section, ca. 1940. Russell Bowles, Trummy Young, Elmer Crumbley (trombones); Paul Webster, Snooky Young, Gerald Wilson (trumpets); Ed Wilcox (piano). (Jack Bradley Collection.)

Put On Your Old Grey Bonnet, ca. 1937. *L. to r.:* Eddie Tompkins, Al Norris, Willie Smith, Joe Thomas, Moses Allen. (Bertil Lyttkens Collection.)

Brass section, ca. 1940. Russell Bowles, Trummy Young, Elmer Crumbley (trombones); Paul Webster, Snooky Young, Gerald Wilson (trumpets); Ed Wilcox (piano). (John Hope and Aurelia Elisabeth Franklin Library Collection.)

Jimmie Lunceford Orchestra, October 1939. *L. to r.:* Jimmy Crawford, Earl Carruthers, Willie Smith, Trummy Young, Elmer Crumbley, Joe Thomas, Dan Grissom, Russell Bowles, Jimmie Lunceford, Ted Buckner, Dutch Williams, Moses Allen, Ed Wilcox, Eddie Tompkins, Gerald Wilson, Al Norris, Paul Webster. (Bertil Lyttkens Collection.)

Jimmie Lunceford (standing, second from left) and aviator friends, ca. mid-1940s. (John Hope and Aurelia Elisabeth Franklin Library Collection.)

Lunceford Quartet, ca. 1945. *L. to r.:* Russell Bowles, unknown, Bob Mitchell, Joe Thomas. (Jim Gallert Collection.)

Jimmie Lunceford Orchestra, ca. summer 1947. *L. to r.:* Ed Wilcox, unknown, Al Norris, Omer Simeon, Joe Marshall, Kirt Bradford, Bob Mitchell, Reunald Jones, Earl Carruthers, unknown, Al Cobbs, Russell Green, Elmer Crumbley, Al Grey, Russell Bowles. (Jim Gallert Collection.)

Jimmie Lunceford, ca. 1945. (Photo James L. Kriegsmann; Bertil Lyttkens Collection.)

Jimmie Lunceford, ca. 1939.
(Jack Bradley Collection.)

Bungalow
Ballroom,
Seaside, ca. 1943.
(Seaside Museum
Collection.)

Broadway, Seaside, ca. 1947. Bungalow Ballroom ("DANCE"), middle; Callahan's
Radio and Record Shop ("ORDS"), left. (Photo Christian; Ky Jennings Collection.)

so hard and with so much abandon as Lunceford's. For a man who during the swing years watched the performances of hundreds, and possibly even thousands, of jazz and dance orchestras, this praise cannot be dismissed as merely casual or dutiful. Lunceford himself once remarked, "A band that looks good, goes in for a better class of showmanship, and seems to be enjoying its work, will always be sure of a return visit wherever it plays."

George Simon's graded review of three appearances during the summer of 1938 rated A, the maximum. The only other bands to receive an A rating in the *Metronome* that year were Benny Goodman's and Red Norvo's. As a former drummer, Simon's judgment of the rhythm section warrants attention. He pointed out its almost telepathic togetherness, resulting in consistent lift and drive, in all tempos. "Heaps of credit go to drummer Jimmy Crawford—as one member of the band put it: 'man, sometimes before the job I feel beat, but just as soon as I feel Jimmy behind me, I'm right in there again swingin'!' "

Looking back in his best-selling book *The Big Bands*, George Simon noted that "it was the sort of band that no one with even the slightest feel for swing could stand in front of and stand still." He characterized its grooves as joyous, delivered by uninhibited and infectiously enthusiastic musicians.

French critic Hugues Panassié argued that

> *The Merry-Go-Round Broke Down*—a poor affair, in the hands of Jimmie Lunceford's orchestra became a splendid interpretation simply because the perfect tempo was found.
>
> Moreover the orchestra has a fire and a great enthusiastic power; it swings, not in a massive or heavy way, but in an alert, incisive, delicate and well-knit fashion which is sometimes supple and restrained as in *Margie* and *Organ Grinder's Swing*, and sometimes violent and tempestuous like *Runnin' Wild*, *Annie Laurie*, and *For Dancers Only*. In moderate tempos, the orchestra plays with an ease and indescribable nonchalance, in so unusual a fashion that the expression "Lunceford tempo" is used.[13]

The power, precision, and showmanship of the band actually inspired many music fans to actively pursue a career in music. Sixteen-year-old Paul Gonsalves was not even a music fan when his father took him to the RKO Theater in Providence. With his two guitar-playing brothers, Paul had to perform Portuguese folk music, hillbilly tunes, and Hawaiian songs at family gatherings, which interfered with his athletic aspirations. But his outlook changed that night. "The feeling that came over me when the movie ended, and all the lights went out, and the curtains parted, and I saw Jimmie Lunceford's band—man! Of course, I knew all their records, knew all Willie Smith's solos, and liked the band next to Duke's. When I went home that night I was so thrilled, and decided from that time on I wanted to play saxophone. So I worried my father until he went out and bought me one, a fifty-dollar tenor in pretty bad shape, but still a saxophone."[14]

Pianist Horace Silver, the prince of 1950s and 1960s soul jazz, was converted in the summer of 1939 in Norwalk, Connecticut, where he lived. Barely a teenager yet, standing next to his dad and peeking through the window slats of a ballroom, he saw "the uniforms, and they had choreography with the different sections, the saxophones and the trumpets and trombones, and the arrangements were so great and the soloists were great and the singing was great. I was just overwhelmed. I think that was really the first big band I saw. That's when I said to myself, that night, I said, that's what I want to be. I want to be a musician. So the Lunceford band turned me on, you know, it inspired me to become a musician." Silver went on to explain that this first encounter was a "whites only" affair.

> It was like a pavilion on the edge of the water, right near the ocean. It was like a dance pavilion. A summer night—it was hot. It was enclosed, but it had slats, where people outside could look in and listen from outside. Blacks were not allowed in there, those times of prejudice, you know. You couldn't go in. But the whites were dancing and enjoying the music. And there were some whites outside looking in, too. They did not want to pay the money to go in or something.

Turned on by Lunceford that summer night, young Horace went to the record store to buy as many records by the band as he could find, memorizing the soloists' names. And he started to follow the orchestra wherever he could. He saw it at the Paramount and Loew's in New York, and again in Connecticut. It became close to an obsession: he was so hung up on his idols that he did not pay much attention to either Ellington or Basie. In later years Silver "had to go back and backtrack and check them out, you know. Because I was just interested in Lunceford at that time. I could not see nobody else. The visual thing was nice, too, but the music far exceeded that in terms of influencing me." He met Edwin Wilcox one time at a dance in Connecticut. Horace stood near the piano player all night long. And during the break he had a chance to talk with him.

Horace had two left feet, and when he did go to a dance he went there to listen. Apart from the dancers, who enjoyed the music by dancing to it, there always was a group of people who could be found standing in front of the bandstand, just listening. "And," he said, "I was one of those."

When he was a student, writer Ralph Gleason used to dance to Lunceford's music, preferably "in front of the band, where you could see and hear it all as you danced along *very* slowly and watch the trumpets twirl and the trombones wave and see those eyes of Earl Carruthers look to his section mates as he rocked backwards in his chair, anchoring the sax section." Mesmerized by what he heard and saw, Gleason noticed "the sly look in his [Willie Smith's] eyes as he leaned forward to sing and get a good view."[15] The writer recalled the way the sets were programmed:

> The dance, of course, was the fox-trot and its acrobatic extension, the Lindy Hop. Lunceford programmed those sets to take care of the dancers. They began with the slow, dreamy ones and they ended with the uptempo stomps, and periodically towards the end of the night the whole house would be rocking and rolling to *Running Wild* or *White Heat,* after an interim period of the middle tempo groovers like *Pigeon Walk.* They would set up the whole evening with swinging versions of *Annie Laurie* or *Four Or Five Times* and then cut loose with a screaming version of one of their flagwavers.[16]

A visual innovation was the introduction of straight business suits, in addition to the usual dinner jackets, tails, and fancy custom-made uniforms. The bands of Ellington, Lunceford, and Hines were considered the best-dressed of the swing era. According to Gerald Wilson, the musicians had a wardrobe of seven different uniforms at their disposal. After he left, the emphasis on their visual appearance only grew. "You know how many uniforms we had?" third altoist Benny Waters exclaimed. "Eleven uniforms! Sometimes we changed three times a night. Pants, socks, shoes, cravats, everything. Eleven uniforms."

At a June 1938 prom at Baltimore's prestigious Johns Hopkins University (an institution at which no black orchestra had ever played), a new band uniform was unveiled. It consisted of a white shirt, a soft grey woven worsted suit, with tiny red and blue stripes, the high-waisted trousers featuring white woven silk belts, three inches below the top. Socks were blue and white, shoes white. When the musicians mingled with the audience, they changed into fine woolen gray slacks with white pencil stripes. To go with the slacks they wore white sharkskin polo shirts.[17]

The uniforms were manufactured by Fox Brothers Tailors at 712 West Roosevelt Road, Chicago. Fox dressed many of the top bands of the era, including Earl Hines, Stan Kenton, Dizzy Gillespie, and Lunceford. Under his alias Jimmy Dale, Harold Fox led a big band that used to play the arrangements of the bands his alter ego dressed, as it was customary for him to exchange his creations for these charts. It is rumored that Harold Fox also invented the zoot suit, but this is open to speculation, since the first zoots seem to have appeared around 1941 on Beale Street in Memphis.

On Wednesday, November 30, 1938, the Lunceford Orchestra opened the new Band Box club on New York's Fifty-second Street for a promising three-month engagement. The venue, however, turned out to be a little too stiff and formal to accommodate the exuberant swing machine. French critic Hugues Panassié and his party, Mr. and Mrs. Milton "Mezz" Mezzrow, kept a less than pleasant memory of the opening night. The club's fancy atmosphere notwithstanding, the party was denied access to the ringside table the orchestra leader had reserved for his three guests. On top of that, the employees of the Band Box tried to poison Mezzrow's wife Johnnie Mae, who was black. By chance, the clarinetist had swapped glasses with his wife, and so he was the one who suffered severe stomach problems in the taxi on their way home.[18]

The orchestra stayed at the Band Box for two weeks. After that, the club folded. It would take a year and a half before the band secured another location job in the city.

One year before the Band Box incident, Panassié had praised the ensemble in his *Jazz Hot* magazine: "Jimmie Lunceford's orchestra is the most important thing that has happened in jazz since the great period which produced Louis Armstrong, Bessie Smith, Bix, the Duke and the Chicagoans," he wrote. It was printed in bold type.[19] Now he saw the band with his own eyes and reported being knocked out by Joe Thomas, who riffed like a man possessed, and from time to time threw in appropriate body undulations.

For a long, long time, altoist Bobby Plater led the reed sections of Tiny Bradshaw (1937–39), Lionel Hampton (1942–64) and Count Basie

(1964–82). Earlier he had been a member of a little band called the Savoy Dictators, based in Newark, New Jersey. Herman Lubinsky named his Savoy record label after the band: it was the first act to record for the new firm. Around this time Plater visited New York for the first time in his life.

> I heard Fletcher Henderson and Duke Ellington and Jimmie Lunceford. I sat all day long, listening to Jimmie Lunceford. I never heard anything like that! What a stage presentation! Musicians of today don't know what they are missing. They haven't seen all these things! Everything was perfect—*perfect!* Dress impeccably, the music was perfect. Oh, gee. Course, Duke was in a class by himself—*until Jimmie Lunceford came on the scene!* Jimmie Lunceford came along, and it kind of shook Duke up. They had to start playing *good.* They was playing when they wanted, but sometime they was so great, they just do like what they wanted. When Jimmie Lunceford came along, he upset everybody.

In her column "Shadow" for the *Baltimore Afro American,* Lillian Johnson wrote, "Jimmie Lunceford, undoubtedly, stands at the top of the band business today. The only man vying with him is the great Ellington, but Lunceford, undoubtedly, has the greatest mass appeal today."[20]

Sixty-odd years later the question "Who is the best?" has quieted down, if only because Duke has become a sacrosanct icon and Lunceford has drifted into relative oblivion. Pianist Sir Charles Thompson worked with Lucky Millinder, Illinois Jacquet, and Charlie Parker, among others, and was known for his critical opinions. He said, "When you talk about Jimmie Lunceford, you're talking about an *institution.*" In Thompson's estimation, Jimmie Lunceford was as great as Duke Ellington. No doubt about it. The main difference was, Sir Charles added, that Duke Edward was not only the leader of his orchestra, but also the one who did most of the writing. Sonny Greer, Ellington's drummer, concurred:

> The band that came closest in competition, in my opinion, was Jimmie Lunceford's. He had class, talent, and variety, and his band was full of terrific stars. Count Basie's and Chick Webb's were top bands, but they never had the variety of material and presentation. Jimmie Lunceford was a good man; he believed in discipline, and he never caroused.[21]

The results of the first time when Duke Ellington and Jimmie Lunceford battled, December 26, 1938, at the Athletic Club in Philadelphia, are not quite clear. Harry Carney, Duke's baritone man, remembered, "They did some marvelous things on records and I think I was always among the first to buy their new releases." But Carney also stated, "On this occasion I'm happy to say the Ellington band came off the better." It must have been an extremely exciting event. Ellington's clarinetist Barney Bigard recalled,

> Lunceford and Duke were in their heyday, and Lunceford's guys had been running up and down Seventh Avenue telling everybody, "we got 'em now! We gonna cut 'em!"
>
> Lunceford went on first that night, and they played all Duke's numbers that they could, and, oh, boy, were they happy! Willie Smith played my *Rose Room*. "What are you doing, Willie?" I asked him. We were both laughing. So Duke is a funny character. He's going to play all slow tunes with no bounce to them, until Cootie Williams got angry. "For crying out loud, Duke, play something!" he said. "We got to get with this thing!" So Duke finally opened up—*St. Louis Blues, Tiger Rag,* and that was it! Lunceford and his guys were standing over by the window, and Sy Oliver, the arranger, came over and said, "I didn't think much of you guys before, but I take everything back. Have mercy on us!"

Ellington teased his opponents by pulling out *Le Jazz Hot,* which at that time was not yet recorded by the Lunceford band. Jimmie ended up by calling for *Dinah* and proceeding to play that tune for what felt like a full hour. Duke struck back with a full hour of *St. Louis Blues*! The tunes went through all imaginable movements and tempo changes, riffs were designed and executed on the spot, loads of soloists poured their hearts out, the crowd cheered and whistled. Hugues Panassié witnessed the war of the giants, and reported,

> Ellington's brass possesses a fuller, finer, and more expressive sound than Lunceford's, but the latter's reeds produce twice the volume, plus a richer sonority as compared to Duke's. In Lunceford's band the saxes are as strong as his brass; with Duke the brass drown out the saxes completely. So in Lunceford's band there's more of an orchestral equilibrium, which is counterbalanced by the extraordi-

nary personality of Duke, who knows how to ignite a fire and zest in his musicians that leaves no listener unmoved.[22]

Assistant band-boy Babs Gonzales may have been partial when he emphasized, "I witnessed nights when Duke washed Jimmie away and nights when it was the other way around. But more often it was Jimmie who bashed Duke! I've seen that, I sure have. Showmanship *and* musicianship, too. That's true."

"If there was a challenge of bands, Duke Ellington would have been obsolete, in my opinion," stressed singer Little Jimmy Scott. "It [Lunceford's band] was just that good, just that great. All the musicians knew it. Had the highest respect for them." Saxophonist and music teacher Emerson Able Jr. agreed. "I thought he swung more than Duke. I thought, as a youngster I did. You know, I did not have him, Duke Ellington that is, above Jimmie Lunceford's band, see, because I had heard Jimmie's band a whole lot of times. In fact, every time he came to Memphis."

When pianist Hank Jones first saw the Lunceford band, around 1941 at Flint, Michigan's IMA Auditorium, he was struck by the precision of execution. "Not many bands shared that precision. You may think that Ellington played precise, but that's not true. Duke was much looser. Lunceford swung harder than Duke, I mean not just the rhythm section, they were swinging all right, but I mean the band as a whole. Lunceford also offered a lot of variety. I remember a tune they played, called *'Tain't a Fit Night for Man nor Beast*. Now what band would play a tune with a title like that?"

Young Babs Gonzales and eight friends had formed a gang called Los Casanovas, and they were all trying to make it in the music business. They had made a deal with Oxley to put posters and flyers announcing dances on pillars and walls. First working in Newark, they later enlarged their territory to include Ashbury Park and Atlantic City as well. "He had the top band, ain't no problem. His records sold much better than Duke's," stressed Babs Gonzales, whose band-boy tasks included running errands for Trummy and other band members. After forty years, he vividly remembered the prejudice the band sometimes ran into, being called "nigger" and not being allowed to register at any hotel. "When the band finished at twelve, the whole orchestra, instruments and all, was supposed to have left the town by twelve-thirty. That's how it was."

Trumpeter and arranger Gerald Wilson knew from firsthand experience how difficult it was for Duke's Famous Orchestra to hold its own against the Harlem Express. One of these battles was at a university in New England. "And Jimmie Lunceford and them were so slick, the people just went for Jimmie Lunceford. *We wanna hear Jimmie Lunceford!* But you know, Duke and them were blowing." He added that Duke undeniably was a master of the music; you just couldn't go by that band. "But Jimmie Lunceford was *sharp*, and they play good, too."

In all fairness, it should be stressed that the reason Duke sometimes caused irritation, or did lose a battle, was usually due to simple sloppiness. When it was his turn to play in a battle, Ellington frequently found himself on the stage in the company of just seven or eight musicians, with the rest of his men still busy finishing their drinks at the bar, and slowly filing in during the first or the second tune. This was the case at a battle of the bands at The Mosque in Newark, when it took Duke thirty minutes to build his band from six pieces to its full strength. By that time his set was almost over. Jimmie had no trouble killing him quick: the crowd had lost its interest and drifted away.

Snooky Young, Lunceford's lead trumpeter in 1939–42, more than sixty years later still was a stunning lead man. "I don't think anybody ever topped Duke," was his verdict, adding that Lunceford's popularity at times was as great as Duke's, and, yes, a lot of people used to wonder which band was the "best." "But no band has ever topped Duke Ellington to me. I mean, that's just my personal feeling. Now that does not mean it's so true, one way or the other."

In spite of Lunceford's popularity, in 1938 only two recording dates were scheduled, and between April 12, 1938, and January 3, 1939, the band did not set foot in a studio. There had been six dates in 1937. And 1939 was a rich year with eight sessions, yielding no less than thirty-nine sides, including nine hits. By then Lunceford, dissatisfied with Decca's royalties payments, had switched from Decca to Columbia. *Down Beat* magazine called the argument "a nasty mess which was finally settled satisfactory."

Moving to Columbia meant not just more recording sessions. Columbia's recording standards were higher than Decca's, so accordingly Lunceford's 78s from the 1939–40 period were characterized by a more spatial, better-defined sound, which especially benefited the rhythm section.

The first record date resulted in two hits: *'Tain't What You Do* and *Cheatin' on Me*, plus gems such as *Le Jazz Hot* (a tribute to fan Hugues Panassié and his publication of the same name) and *Time's A Wastin'*. It was Joe Thomas who shone in these two last titles. Even more poignant was his solo in *Baby, Won't You Please Come Home?*, recorded four months later, with Thomas honking away like an Illinois Jacquet—whose opus *Flying Home* was to be recorded three years later. As he had proved before, Joe Thomas was the patriarch of all R&B tenor men.

Jimmy Oliver was one of Philadelphia's most prominent young tenor players in the mid-1940s. While still a student in high school, his first professional job had been accompanying singer Pearl Bailey. Joe Thomas, Lester Young, and, a little later, Charlie Parker all left their marks on the young tenor man. "I was a force to be reckoned with," he claimed without a trace of false modesty. Jimmy, in turn, was one of John Coltrane's role models. Fifty years after his heyday, he yearned for the good old times.

Not so long ago they had a recording by Jimmie Lunceford on the television. *'Tain't What You Do (It's the Way That You Do It)*. I was singing along with that song, and I told my son that Jimmie Lunceford had an orchestra that was out of this world. And you don't even hear his name *mentioned* no more. Duke and Count, those are the ones they mention, but not Andy Kirk, not Fletcher Henderson. That's why I think the *essence*, the core is gone. So I sang along with that song . . . the lyrics of those old songs . . . the essence, the *substance!* They were *real!* It really meant something!

Poet T. R. Hummer is editor of the *Georgia Review* and program director and professor of creative writing at the University of Oregon. One day, while he was studying a list of song titles on the back of a Jimmie Lunceford CD, it struck him that it read like a table of contents in a book of poems.

I have this little homunculus who lives inside my head who says perverse things sometimes, and they always come true. The little homunculus said, "You will write poems with those titles," and I said back to him, "No, I won't. That's just ridiculous. It's silly." So I set it aside, and you know, sure enough, then, about six months later, I thought, "He was right. I gotta try that at least to see what happens." And then I had to think about it further. What motivated me to want to do that? Well, what motivated me *really* to want to do that was that I wanted to play with that band. You know, I'm listening to that band and I'm thinking, that band just really kicks, you know. Wouldn't it be fun to play with them? Because the Lunceford band, it was an entertaining band. The kind of jazz he played was not like chamber jazz, you know; it was not art jazz. It was dance music, and it's actually closely related to jump blues and ultimately, therefore, to rock and roll. He was there to entertain. He was there to provide a context in which people would dance and drink and make babies.

That was the genesis of Hummer's *Lunceford Suite*. In his poems, he tried to evoke and convey something of the cultural world that the Lunceford band was part of. This was, Hummer emphasizes, a man's world. "It was kind of like ships, they would never think about taking a woman on the road with them, I don't think. I don't think Lunceford's band ever had even a woman singer."[23]

It is true that Jimmie Lunceford relied on his "built-in" vocal attractions, on individual singing musicians such as Trummy Young, Joe Thomas, and Willie Smith, plus the Trio, Quartet, and glee club, comprised of band members. But Lunceford did try to lure young Ella Fitzgerald away from Chick Webb, after she had scored with the song *Love and Kisses*, her 1935 debut on records. Though the singer was a fan of the Lunceford band, out of loyalty to Chick Webb, her boss and "father," she had to decline his offer. For a while in 1940 Lunceford featured the Dandridge Sisters, who recorded and traveled with the orchestra. And more often than not he had guest singers when the band was on the road. Drummer Rashied Ali, for instance, recalled that in the late 1930s his mother had sung with the band for a couple of nights, as a result of winning first prize in a vocal contest in Philadelphia. An even more intriguing addition was Billie Holiday, who in March 1936 made a short theater tour around New York with the band.[24] This, of course, was a tantalizing combination, and one wonders how Lady Day fit the band—and vice versa. The typical Lunceford bounce was just behind the beat; Billie used to lag even more. One year later the singer asked Lunceford men Eddie Tompkins and Joe Thomas for a record date that yielded the classics *Let's Call the Whole Thing Off* and *They Can't Take That Away from Me*. Joe played a radiant solo in the first tune, full of swagger, yet restrained and balanced.

That same year, clarinetist Mezz Mezzrow invited Sy Oliver and Jimmy Crawford for an RCA-Victor record date. These were rare examples of the bandleader allowing his sidemen to take part in somebody else's recording session. Most of the time there just was no room in the band's itinerary for extra work. In February 1945, reed player Omer Simeon was the first Luncefordean to record under his own steam, as The Carnival Three, together with James P. Johnson and Pops Foster, piano and bass, respectively.

During the week starting November 20, 1936, the band accompanied veteran blues singer Bessie Smith during an engagement at the Howard Theatre in Baltimore.[25] Bessie was a couple of years past her prime; however, it is a provocative thought: the Empress of the Blues, backed by the new King of Syncopation. In 1944–45, Effie Smith from time to time sang with the Harlem Express. Tina Dixon, billed as "A Bombshell of Blues," toured with the band during much of 1943–45, but never shared the recording studio with it. Velma Middleton, who later would gain fame with Louis Armstrong's All Stars, also traveled with Lunceford. In early 1946, Lunceford added Marilyn Kilroy to his roster of artists. So actually, the band was rarely without a female singer.

Apart from the Dandridge Sisters, none of these singers ever made commercial records with the orchestra. It seems that Lunceford used these female vocalists merely as added attractions. Unlike Ella Fitzgerald (with Chick Webb) or Helen Forest (with Harry James), the guest singers with Lunceford's band did not have a significant role in the arrangements; always, the orchestra came first.

Jimmie Lunceford's glee club appealed to all lovers of choir music; the vocal Trios and Quartets were dug by the younger generation. Starting with the Mills Brothers, vocal quartets were very, very big during the 1930s, 1940s, and into the 1950s, especially in the black community. In the Lunceford band, those vocal sequences were meticulously arranged by Sy Oliver and sound hip even today. He had refined his craft at a remarkably fast pace. His first vocal arrangement for a trio comprising Eddie Tompkins, Willie Smith, and himself had been *Chillun, Get Up*, in January 1934. It had sounded pretty straightforward, not unlike the vocal trios Paul Whiteman, Nat Shilkret, Jean Goldkette, and dozens of other dance bands had featured as far back as the early 1920s. Eleven months later, in December 1934, Lunceford recorded *Rain* and *Since My Best Gal Turned Me Down*. The Lunceford Trio clearly had developed. By now, it sounded self-assured, and the arranger had put more dynamics and a hip timing in the renditions, which integrated the vocal part in the orchestral backing.

One might even maintain that the highly rhythmic vocal performances by the Trio and the full band in *My Blue Heaven*, *'Tain't What You Do*,

Cheatin' on Me and *Ain't She Sweet* can be regarded as early predecessors of today's hip-hop vocalizing. Both styles have their roots in early urban black street "jiving" and southern Baptist preaching.

In his study *Jazz Singing* Will Friedwald comments, "Annexing trios and quartets to dance bands led to a dead-end street; bandleader Jimmie Lunceford made his already exciting records all the more terrific with vocal units drawn from the ranks of his sidemen. . . . On *My Blue Heaven* (1935, Decca), *Muddy Water* (1936, Decca) and *Cheatin' On Me* (1939, Vocalion), these Luncefordettes do an about-face from the frenetic dot-doot-dah peppiness of virtually every other singing group of the thirties and, instead, achieve a luxuriously laid-back sonority. On *Me And The Moon* (1936, Decca) especially, they could be three guys on the corner smoking tea."[26] Sy Oliver did not try to emulate the charming, yet intricate way of group singing as popularized by the Mills Brothers. His timing made the vocal efforts stand out. "Well," he said, "we were always compelled to sing in that manner, because none of us had voices and the idea was to sing softly to get a blend. If we had sang in our natural voices, in a robust fashion, it would have been terrible."[27]

Oliver's smooth voicings and his use of everyday, familiar melodies such as *My Blue Heaven* or *Annie Laurie* helped the band to bridge the gap between the hot bands from Harlem and the sweet white orchestras downtown. In 1939–40, the Jimmie Lunceford Orchestra definitely broadened its appeal and to a degree crossed over to white audiences.

Sy Oliver left two months after the recording of *Ain't She Sweet*, at a show in Brighton Beach, Brooklyn, because he felt that by now five dollars for an arrangement did not match his worth, and because he wanted to fulfill his old ambition to study law. On top of that, he was just plain exhausted. The night he put in his notice, Tommy Dorsey's road manager happened to be there. From Dorsey's two staff arrangers, Paul Weston and Axel Stordahl, the manager had learned that his boss had been working on the arranger for a while, and after some persuasion, he managed to get Sy in his car, just to drop by and say hello to the old man. When they entered Dorsey's hotel room, the leader was in the middle of shaving. Without even bothering to greet his visitor, Dorsey flatly said, "Whatever Lunceford gave you last year for playing and arranging, I'll top by $5,000."

"Sold," answered Oliver.[28]

A professional black musician, not working in a name band, at that time might average $4 to $5 a night, or up to $700 a year at most. A laundry man made $750; a postal worker $1,800 a year. Dorsey's offer was good money indeed.

Tommy Dorsey's dissatisfaction with the Dixieland orientation of his own orchestra had been mounting for a while. His biographer Herb Sanford, who in the late 1930s had produced Dorsey's radio show, remembered "a rehearsal, long before Sy's time with the band, when a new swing arrangement was being run through. The notes came out right, but it wasn't getting through with the right effect. Tommy was exasperated. 'Look,' he said, 'make it sound like Lunceford.' This was direct and clear. He was thinking about those Sy Oliver arrangements."[29]

Earlier in 1939, the Tommy Dorsey band had recorded a two-part version of *Lonesome Road*, written by an aspiring arranger called Bill Finegan. "It was not an easy chart to read. It showed that my main inspiration was Sy Oliver's charts for Jimmie Lunceford," Finegan recalled. "I like to think that my arrangement led to Tommy's wanting to incorporate Lunceford's kind of music into his band, and that's what caused him to hire Sy Oliver in the first place."[30]

Together, Sy and Tommy began to overhaul the book and the personnel of the Tommy Dorsey Orchestra. Critic John S. Wilson noted that within a few months after Sy's arrival, the Dorsey band had changed its character completely. Its denser harmonic approach made the ensemble sound richer, and it acquired a power it had not possessed earlier. Another few months and of Dorsey's original musicians, all but two (trumpeter Jimmy Blake and saxophonist Johnny Mintz) had left. Sy had created a completely new orchestra, as powerful and as versatile as Lunceford's crew—almost. "The feeling wasn't there," an honest Buddy DeFranco admitted, who during most of 1944–48 was in the Dorsey band.

> We all knew it. The subtle feeling. The obvious feeling of the Lunceford band that they did with the Dorsey band, or that Billy May did, the obvious things they did—but the underlining subtle feeling. . . . Even the singing: Trummy Young in the group, the way they sang, they just had a certain way of feeling. There again, it exemplified the mood of the band. As opposed to a lot of singers in a band who *sang*.
>
> He [Oliver] had trouble with bringing up that particular feeling, concept. He [Buddy Rich] was not the drummer that could convey that feeling, that wasn't him, you know. Sy tried to get that Lunce-

ford feeling out of the Dorsey band, and of course he was dealing with all white people. I hate to say that, but that happens, you know.

The new arranger had taken Dorsey's musicians to the Roseland Ballroom, to watch and hear his former band in action. This had happened before, as Buddy Morrow, one of Dorsey's trombone players, recalled. The leader had addressed his band: "'Guys, your rehearsal tonight is to go see Jimmie Lunceford at the Famous Door.' We went over to Fifty-second Street and listened. Tommy knew all about Sy Oliver, but he wanted everybody to see and get a sense of what his approach was."[31] There is, however, no evidence of the Lunceford band ever having played the Famous Door. Morrow probably mixed up this club, at 66 West Fifty-second Street, with the short-lived Band Box, 152 East, where Lunceford resided during the early part of December 1938, the time Morrow was with Dorsey.

Oliver also had brought with him some of his most successful Lunceford charts, including *Stomp It Off*, *Swanee River*, *Blue Blazes*, and *Mandy*. Apart from that, he helped Dorsey to score big new hits, like *Well, Git It!*, *On the Sunny Side of the Street*, *Opus One* and *Yes, Indeed!* Recordings of *On the Sunny Side of the Street* and *Yes, Indeed!* both sold over a million copies. The latter song was a tune originally rejected by Lunceford—he apparently did not think much of it.

After his stint with Dorsey, Sy went into the military, serving as bandmaster at Camp Kilmer, New York, during 1943–45. Next he started his own big band, touring and doing many studio dates, backing singers as diverse as Chubby Checker and Louis Armstrong. He became so busy that for lack of time he even lost his radio show in 1947, and had to hire outside arrangers for his own orchestra.

His friend Frank Bonitto remembered how Sy used to take him to all the after-hours joints and jam sessions in Harlem. One night they ended up at Minton's Playhouse, where they found saxophonist Sidney Bechet, who was blowing like a man possessed while walking around the tables and chairs. Frank noted that everybody seemed to know Sy and vice versa. "The place was full of people and smoke and music and everything else. Sy walked in big, everybody almost hushed, like he was a big shot, like a master or somebody walked in."

When Lunceford wired Gerald Wilson, twenty years old, asking him to replace Sy Oliver, the young trumpet player had to think twice. He liked his work in the Chick Carter band, but when he learned that this band was about to break up, he called back, and accepted the job. Wilson was no stranger to the Lunceford orchestra: he had been following it since its early recordings, and by coincidence had had his schooling at Manassas High in Memphis, albeit after Lunceford's teaching days. So he knew about the Chickasaw Syncopators. After Memphis, Gerald had moved to Detroit, to study music at Cass Tech High School. There he first saw the orchestra, at the Arcadia Ballroom on Woodward Avenue. This had been in 1937. Not much later he saw it again at the Graystone Ballroom and the Michigan Theater. Whenever the orchestra played the Graystone, the musicians allowed the ambitious youngster to sit on the bandstand, next to Sy. Trummy was the one who had hipped Lunceford to the trumpet player, who also sang and arranged.

> I arrived in New York in the morning and Eddie Tompkins, the great trumpet player in the band, met me. We made a stop at the tailor shop and they measured me up for all seven of my uniforms. It was a well-dressed band. After that we got a room for me at the YMCA for that night and we left the next morning for a tour. The first stop was Rocky Mount, N.C. The band was playing a June-teenth date. I didn't play that night. Sy Oliver, the guy that I was replacing in the band, was going to join Tommy Dorsey's band as his chief arranger, and Sy was playing that night.
>
> I got so frightened when I heard them play that night, I thought, I can never make it in this band. I'm not ready for this. I got sick to my stomach. Trummy Young had to put me on his back and take me up to my hotel room and put me to bed.[32]

The leader hired other top writers: they included Billy Moore Jr., Bud Estes, and, a little later, Tadd Dameron. Dameron, who in a couple of years would develop into the premier bebop arranger, got his New York introduction through the band. Wilson stressed: "Lot of people don't know, they think that Tadd Dameron came with the bebop. He was with us. He arranged for the Lunceford band, for a couple of years or so."

George Duvivier, who during the 1950s became the most sought-after bass player in the New York studio circuit, had been a Lunceford fan since the time the band broadcast from the Cotton Club. He also heard Cab and Duke, but "it was Lunceford's band that really caught my ear," he recalled in his biography *Bassically Speaking*. "I heard something there that I heard in no other band. The effects, the discipline, the shadings, the swing affected me deeply. If anything had an effect on me other than classical music, it was that orchestra." As a teenager he had played in a band called the Royal Barons, who were on a Lunceford kick. His colleagues included future greats Herbie Nichols on piano and Mike Hedley on tenor sax. The former wrote, "Around 1937 I was good enough to join a wild and precocious teen-age aggregation headed by a fellow named Freddie Williams. I can recall that each member of the orchestra used to write mystifying scores which had to be played—or else." Nichols's biographer A. B. Spellman added, "Herbie used to write some of the arrangements—they were so difficult that even he didn't want to sight-read them—but the band's primary arranger was Billy Moore Jr., who wrote for the Royal Baron orchestra until he left to join Jimmy Lunceford's band. The Royal Baron was an advanced group, and it showed a lot of promise; but most of its members never reached their promised potential." Moore worked in a butcher shop and studied orchestration and harmony under his neighbor Sy Oliver, eventually becoming his replacement as Lunceford's staff arranger.

Mike Hedley remembered,

I'll never forget the first night we played opposite Lunceford. It was at the Renaissance Casino on 138th Street and 7th Avenue. When we arrived, Lunceford had already finished and the house band was back on stage. While Lunceford's men were getting ready to leave, somebody told them, "why don't you stick around and listen to these kids?" We got set up and started playing. When we looked up, we saw that all the Lunceford men were back up on stage, listening to us! We gave a pretty good account of ourselves that night.[33]

Of Lunceford's new arrangers, Billy Moore in particular showed a lot of promise. Sy saw to it that Billy, twenty-one, got his first assignments straight. Apparently, these charts were hard for the band to play: for a while, the leader had Moore direct the first sets, which featured a dozen of his new pieces. However, from his first composition on, *Belgium Stomp,* a feud developed between Lunceford and his new employee, since the boss had wanted to be credited as co-composer. This feud was the reason Moore's contract was not prolonged one year later.[34] Oxley may have played a part in this story: he and Lunceford were partners in a publishing firm, H. F. Oxley Inc., and Oxley was said to have pushed Jimmie to put his name in as many credits as possible.[35]

Trummy Young and Ted Buckner were the authors of *I'm in an Awful Mood*, recorded three months after Billy Moore's debut as an arranger. Here Moore has the reeds and muted trumpets behind Trummy's vocal sound as if they were recorded in a modern-day multi-track studio: it seems physically impossible to play at these low levels in an acoustic situation.

When Moore later started writing for the Charlie Barnet, Jan Savitt, and Will Bradley bands, he carried a Lunceford flavor over into these popular dance orchestras of the early 1940s. He went on to work as arranger and pianist for the Delta Rhythm Boys. Still later, Billy Moore moved to Denmark, where he led the Danish Radio Jazz Orchestra. Moore's replacement in the Lunceford organization was Roger Segure, a white man who was a friend and admirer of Moore's.

Up until the early 1940s, the band had been remarkably stable. There were very few changes in its lineup, which accounted for the ensemble's cohesion, both musically and personally. This situation started to change in 1942. One by one, the musicians began to leave. The draft was an important reason, but so was the feeling among the musicians that they weren't earning the money they should be. Lunceford had always tried to hire educated musicians; but these craftsmen soon discovered that their jobs included constant traveling and staying at dire hotels. They noticed the crowded dance floors, they knew the records sold in huge quantities, and their salaries did not match their output, they felt. On top of that, their few vacations were in fact just non-paid layoffs, as opposed to the practice of some of the other name bands. They saw Jimmie buying and wrecking airplanes, and buying new ones. They also noticed that the leader was enjoying the lifestyle of the rich and famous. All this led to uncomfortable feelings among the musicians. Some sidemen had gotten offers from white bandleaders who paid better. "The places we played were still packed," explained Willie Smith, "but it got so that we never knew what money they made. Before that, we used to know." So one summer night in 1942 at the YMCA in Harlem, the musicians called a meeting and Smith, speaking on behalf of the band, asked for a raise. Lunceford was furious. He wanted to take out his anger on Willie, but after he realized the latter had spoken on behalf of everybody, he called it a mutiny. The leader emphasized the fact that his name and his name alone was out on the marquee, and he finished by bluntly stating he simply could not afford to pay more. (In the music trade it was a well-known fact that Lunceford restrained from hiring New York musicians as much as possible, because they were bound to complain about the money.)[36] The "mutiny" was the starting point of the band's deterioration. One by one, musicians began to leave, some because they had received their draft card; others were lured away by better-paying leaders.

Gerald Wilson denied that the pay was too low. Cab Calloway paid better, but he was the exception. He cited the example of the Erskine Hawkins band, who played the Savoy. Those guys got thirty-seven dollars a week. When Gerald joined, Willie Smith was the highest paid man in the band: fifteen dollars a night. Crawford took home fourteen dollars a night, same as Wilcox. Paul Webster, Trummy Young, and Joe Thomas got thirteen. "The lowest scale was eleven a night. Snooky Young and I got eleven." Finally one night in Boston everybody got a four-dollar raise.

Conditions for touring abroad seemed to look better in mid-1939, when Oxley, invited by the National Exhibition in Zurich, Switzerland, staged a six- to eight-week European trip for the late summer and fall of that year. In July the manager traveled to Europe, to arrange the tour. But he soon discovered it now was even more difficult to organize an extensive tour than it had been in 1937. The future was uncertain; promoters and agents were reluctant to pinpoint dates. "Everybody in America has told me I am nuts, making a business trip to Europe in this day and age," he told a reporter of the Dutch monthly *De Jazzwereld*. The manager was optimistic: weren't war and political unrest more or less the rule in Europe?[37]

According to the *Chicago Defender,* after completing the European tour the orchestra was to sail for Japan, no less, "where they, too, know the difference between a jitterbug and an icky."[38] But this Japanese leg turned out to be no more than a rumor. The band was to open September 1 in Zurich.

Billy Moore Jr. had turned in his first composition, *Belgium Stomp,* dedicated to the "Hot Clubs" in that country, which was also on the itinerary. It was one of the most intriguing proto-bop compositions in the orchestra's book. *Belgium Stomp* contained a passage for the trumpets that foreshadowed bebop conventions. "I never liked that term, *bebop,*" said pianist Hank Jones distastefully. When the new music started attracting attention, in 1944, he was playing an engagement in Buffalo, in a trio led by tenor saxophonist George Clarke—the same musician who had been in the Chickasaw Syncopators, before Joe Thomas had replaced him. "To me, it was just modern music," Jones resumed. "I don't know—I think the term originated from Dizzy's singing. They called it *rebop* first. But Lunceford's

Wham-Rebop-Boom-Bam really put rebop in people's minds. It became part of the street, the way people talked."

The Jazz Club de Belgique had staged a gala for "Jimmie Lunceford et son célèbre orchestre" at the Palais des Beaux Arts in Brussels, Saturday, September 9, 1939. The next day the orchestra was to perform in Scheveningen, The Netherlands, at a luxurious ballroom called the Kurhaus. Copenhagen, Oslo, Paris, Prague, and even London were also listed on the itinerary. In exchange, Jack Harris's English-Canadian-American band was to appear in the States. Again, nine Scandinavian venues were ready to welcome back the Harlem Express between September 17 and October 1. At the last moment, the Socialstyrelsen, the Swedish Health and Welfare Council, had given the green light. The musicians were to sail for Europe on the Holland-America Line on August 24.[39]

A couple of weeks prior to their departure, however, Oxley received a tantalizing offer from the prestigious Paramount Theater in New York's Times Square. To the music fans, this was swing heaven: Goodman and all the other white name bands celebrated their biggest triumphs at this spacious movie theater. Starting August 23, Jimmie Lunceford and His Hot Harlem Band were scheduled to appear at the well-paying Paramount, the first black ensemble to play there. Here a new vocal attraction, the Lunceford Quartet, was baptized. It consisted of the Trio (Willie Smith, Eddie Tompkins, and Trummy Young), augmented by new addition Gerald Wilson. The other artists on the program were Stump & Stumpy, the dancers, and the Peters Sisters, who harmonized on the ditties of the day.[40]

"They enjoyed the status of precision, they enjoyed the status of intonation," was the judgment of a proud Gerald Wilson about his new colleagues.

I tell you, we played Beethoven's *Sonata Pathetique*. When you hear it, you'll hear how precise the band was.

And we had hit records. We were a hit with our people, not only with our people, but with the other people too. At the time I joined Jimmie Lunceford's band, they could outdraw any band in the country. Benny Goodman?! We were more popular than Benny Goodman! We were the first black band that played the Paramount Theater, downtown New York. Not Duke Ellington, not Count Basie. Six weeks in a row, four or five shows daily, and it was packed every day, people lining up around the corner, constantly! We could outdraw any band in the country. They were the forerunners, between swing and bebop. They were right there. And their records prove this. One of the greatest bands of all time.

Wilson mentioned the head arrangement of *Uptown Blues*, and explained how that tune came about. It developed at the Paramount, the moment the stage slowly disappeared in the basement at the end of the performance. "It was just a little thing to keep the music going. So the trombones started doing this little thing, the three of them." Then Carruthers would come in with the baritone, followed by the trombones, who just made up some other notes. At first, there were no solos. Three months later, in the recording studio, the musicians decided to put alto and trumpet solos in, and the saxophones devised little background figures on the spot.[41] *Uptown Blues* became the band's new signature tune. When a dance was over, the band started playing it, and slowly, section by section, the musicians packed their horns and left the stage, until finally just Willie was left, whose big sound filled every nook and cranny of the place. This was, in fact, a routine the band had already been performing when playing its former sign-off tune, *Jazznocracy*.

Jazz Information, a small magazine aimed at record collectors, was focused on Dixieland and Chicago-style music. Its most thoroughly covered artist was pianist and composer Jelly Roll Morton. Its sour comments on contemporary swing band records were notorious, but the January 12, 1940, issue contained a review of Vocalion 5382, *Uptown Blues / Put It Away:*

> *Uptown Blues* is not only the best Jimmie Lunceford record we can remember, but a useful item to shove in front of anyone who can't see that this band, in spite of its polished commercialism, has real talent which sometimes takes over.
>
> The reason is that arrangement, here, is confined to a short introduction, a short conclusion, and background figures which are not too effective, but not intrusive either. For the rest, the side consists of two solo choruses each by Willie Smith, alto, and Snookie Young, trumpet. This is blues somewhat in the Ellington mood, though simpler, and Smith brings to his excellent solo a tone, attack, and invention quite similar to Hodges, but more feeling and spirit than Johnny has shown in late records. Young's trumpet has amazing range, clear tone and good attack, and in spite of some high-register extravagance, is very effective. In short, a real and pleasant surprise.[42]

Moses Allen had mixed emotions about the Paramount engagement. One night, his bass got caught between the rising stage and the floor. The instrument got crushed and splintered all over the theater. Gerald recalled the drama: "It was terrible, because there was nothing he could do. They did not stop the thing."

The Paramount engagement implied that the European trip had to be postponed by one week; now the musicians were scheduled to sail on the French liner *Normandie*. The luggage was packed, tickets for the boat trip were purchased. This time, eight wives accompanied the band members. The musicians were all eager.

The decision to abort the trip was made on the very day of their departure. The clouds that for a couple of years had been gathering above Europe by now were jet black. They burst on the very day the band was to leave New York—the day the Germans blitzed Poland. The *New York Age* called the canceled band "one of the first 'casualties' of the European war in this country."[43] The other side of the coin was that the band's success at the Paramount prompted the management to extend its engagement by five more weeks. Every day of the week, about fourteen thousand aficionados passed underneath the big billboards. After leaving the New York swing fans gasping for breath, the Harlem Express departed on a two-month tour.

Though the Nazis condemned *entartete Musik*, which included jazz and just about everything that had come after Richard Wagner, interest in modern music remained at a feverish level among that small minority of German youngsters who did not particularly sympathize with the Hitler Youth. In big cities such as Berlin and Hamburg, young swing fans, known as *Swing-Heinis*, gathered to listen to live music and records that were not approved of by the Nazi officials. It is remarkable that two of the best-loved big bands in that country, led by James Kok (originally from Romania) and Teddy Stauffer (originally from Switzerland) leaned heavily on the Lunceford bounce. At the time of the outbreak of the Second World War, among underground *Swing-Heinis*, Bing Crosby, Lunceford, Louis Armstrong, Chick Webb, and Teddy Wilson were favorites.

In 1945 those *Swing-Heinis* who had survived the war were grown men. *Down Beat*'s Mike Levin stated, "Young GIs in Europe after the war were constantly queried about a band they had heard only infrequently, and were always being lectured on its merits and superior ability."[44]

BATTLING ON

They used to hit some awful grooves.
—*Frank Wess*

Considering that Bechet, Armstrong, and Ellington had to go to Europe to first earn serious critical acclaim, it should not be surprising that the same was true for Lunceford. When in 1935 Jimmie Lunceford's fresh, imaginative style started to draw attention, *Down Beat*'s George Frazier called the band "horrible." John Hammond, the most influential American critic, talent scout, and record producer, also tended to speak and write negatively about the Harlem Express. He claimed the band played "stiff and out of tune," and simply didn't swing. On the other hand Hammond praised the leader's inventiveness, patience, and ability in decision-making. Evidently Hammond, who was hooked on Goodman's and Basie's four-to-the-bar beat, failed to feel and hear beyond that. John Hammond once stated that he "loved the whole feeling of small groups, and preferred them to big bands. All I liked about big bands was the power—and the fact they gave good soloists the wherewithal to eat. I liked best Fletcher's, Basie's and

Elmer Snowden's bands, for their looseness, and the opportunities they gave their soloists."[1]

It is significant, perhaps, to keep in mind that Hammond was no dancer. (Hammond usually entered a club carrying a stack of magazines. During the performance he leafed through them, bobbing his head and tapping his feet.) It is entirely conceivable that he did not notice the subtle rhythmic and dynamic shadings in some of the Lunceford band's ballads, resulting in a different kind of swing during the last part of these songs. Most dancers would feel this and consequently would respond to it.

When the band in 1939 switched from Decca to Columbia, Hammond became its producer. He had mellowed by now, and their cooperation ran smoothly. "I met John Hammond in person. He never said anything like that, always seemed very happy about the band," Gerald Wilson stated. Anyway, *Metronome*, the leading music publication, rated Lunceford's organization in that same year as being tops in both the dynamics and rhythm departments.

Probably less than half of Lunceford's repertory was recorded. It was the leader's policy to first test tunes in live situations: for instance, *Uptown Blues* was recorded in December 1939, nearly four months after its genesis at the Paramount. Only once the audience reaction had been proven favorable was a song fit for recording. Even a favorable reaction from the dancers was no guarantee that the song would be recorded. In December the leader announced in the press that he was ready to record twelve tunes he considered worthy of putting out. However, four of them (*Give Me a Swing Song, Home Cooking, Who'll Take My Place When I'm Gone,* and *Swing Little Indians*) apparently weren't fit after all.[2] Sometimes, a tune simply was too long for the regular 78 rpm record and could not be shortened, as exemplified by *Yesterdays* and *Body and Soul,* ballads that featured trumpeters Freddie Webster and Russell Green respectively. In other cases, it is hard to see why certain tunes did not get recorded. Selections like *Hallelujah, Little John* and *What a Difference a Day Made* were attractive and exciting, but exist in broadcast versions only. Wild man of the tenor saxophone Arnett Cobb gave another example: "I'm trying to think of a tune they played. It scare you to death, the way they put their horns into their hats, the brass section, and pop out a note real loud. Boy—and everybody jumped in the theater. Oh, I can't think of the name of the tune. It was an old standard. It was an old tune, but—oh! *Shade of the Old Apple Tree.*" Arnett hummed the melody, and then suddenly went "*Pow!*" He continued humming the arrangement: "And they come up with another *pop* and scare you, because you don't know what to expect. It was a gimmick, but a good one."

Anyway, Lunceford saw his records as promotion tools for the dances, not the other way around. He made his money doing one-nighters. In February 1940 the *San Antonio Register* reported "a surprising pre-dance sale so many days in advance of the dance itself." These tickets for the dance at the Library Auditorium sold for ninety-nine cents at drugstores and restaurants. The newspaper predicted "one of the biggest crowds for any occasion—barring none—of the fall and winter season," adding, "Indication of the interest in the dance may be gleaned from the fact that the Alamo Athletic Association has postponed its regular Monday games in the basketball league, to release players, and hundreds of fans alike, for the occasion of the Lunceford appearance."[3]

Gerald Wilson had come west with the Lunceford organization for the first time that same February. The musicians had left Chicago, where they had played the Regal Theater for a week, in the middle of a Windy City winter. When Gerald woke up in the Pullman near sunny San Bernadino, he made up his mind right then and there. The West Coast was the place for him. When the musicians left the train at Union Station in L.A., they were met by a big parade, an indication of the popularity of the orchestra in the City of the Angels. The band was marched from the railway station right to the elegant Dunbar Hotel on Central Avenue.[4]

The large numbers of dance-mad jitterbugs Lunceford used to attract sometimes caused problems. At a "Jimmie Lunceford Swingaroo" in March 1940 at the Shrine Auditorium on Jefferson Avenue in L.A., a mob of six thousand, reportedly provoked by a rival promoter, went berserk, smashing windows and breaking into fights. Seven people were injured.[5] Wilson remembered the incident: "It got started, and of course we got out very fast, we didn't play anymore. It was over once it started. We were gone." During this same tour, the orchestra had already played the Shrine Auditorium. "The first night we played at the Shrine, nothing happened. I mean, a lot of people were there, there was a great dance and everything. But the next time was the one in the Shrine, which where they had two places that they held concerts, you know. We were in the Exposition Hall, I think they used to call it at that time. I don't remember going back to the Shrine ever again with Lunceford."

The orchestra also played dates at the Glendale Civic Auditorium, the

Paramount Theatre in L.A. for a week, and six weeks at the Casa Mañana on Washington Boulevard in Culver City.[6] The Casa Mañana, owned by the Zucca brothers, was formerly known as Sebastian's Cotton Club, where Jimmie Lunceford and His Streamlined Rhythm Revue had appeared in October 1937; it could seat close to two thousand people. For a while it was the premier nightclub on the West Coast. It booked top bands for two- , four-, and occasionally six-week stands.

Joe Zucca was pleased with the business the Lunceford orchestra generated. In a wire addressed to Oxley after a return engagement later in 1940 he stated,

> I personally wish to advise you that since Jimmie Luncefords opening on August 15th at the Casa Mañana ballroom cafe in Culvercity California he has been the most outstanding organization we have ever had his musical arrangements and entertainments having broken all nightly and weekly attendance records of any band or attraction that ever played at the Casa Mañana Lunceford is still drawing capacity attendance.[7]

Tenor player Bill Perkins was one of the young musicians who witnessed the band at the Casa Mañana. He recalled, "With Ellington you took what you got and you never knew whether it was going to be absolutely brilliant or not. Lunceford's band with their white suits and showmanship was impeccable and swung so hard I remember the floor of the old Casa Mañana literally shaking with it."[8]

Wilson stated that the band continued to grow, to develop during the three years he was with it. He mentioned some of the highlights of this period: *Chopin's Prelude, Beethoven's Sonata Pathetique, Belgium Stomp, Twenty-Four Robbers, You Can Fool Some Of the People Some of the Time, Rock It for Me, Walking through Heaven, Lunceford Special,* and concluded, "The band was much sharper. The band was much more polished. I think it developed, yes, it developed."

Wilson is right. Before long he and Snooky Young, who replaced Eddie Tompkins five months after Wilson had joined, were recognized as powerful, modern soloists. Likewise, the attack of the trumpet section now became more ferocious, and *Twenty-four Robbers* proves the brass has no problem working in Lunceford's trademark high register. On the other hand, the phrasing of the trumpets in *Lunceford Special* shows a new hip subtlety. Chappie Willett's adaptation of Beethoven's sonata is an old-fashioned tour de force, not unlike *White Heat*. It was obviously not designed for the dancers, but rather meant to dazzle theatergoers. The 1940 Lunceford orchestra was still fully capable of tackling tricky charts like these. If anything, the band gained in smoothness, and in tunes like *It's Time to Jump and Shout* it impressed like a peacock parading.

Gerald Wilson remembered how an engagement in a posh Boston restaurant, where the band broadcast nightly over NBC, resulted in a change of style that became permanent.

> You know how that happened? We were at the Southland Cafe in Boston. It's a small supper club, and people would be eating. It's a society deal, where rich people came, you had to have a lot of money to come in there and dance and eat. So we couldn't play all these shout choruses, loud, like we were playing. So one night we decided to play the trumpets down an octave. I don't know how it happened, we did it, because it was too high to play soft. It doesn't make any difference where the harmony is, the notes are there. We played it— it sounds so good! So we left it in. We could play it real soft. Then we got out on the road, we did it that same way. We played it real soft . . . then we played it like it was! And then Wilcox started writing it like that.

Wilson also supplied state-of-the-art charts. He started to write after he had spent about six months in the band. "I made my first arrangement on *Sometimes I'm Happy*. And it wasn't too good. It didn't make it. Snooky always liked to kid me about that." *Honeysuckle Rose*, from a July 1940 broadcast when the band was playing Chicago's Panther Room, is Wilson's first chart that was preserved. It foreshadowed his best-known compositions from this era, *Hi Spook* and *Yard Dog Mazurka*. *Hi Spook* was chosen as the year's best record by *Down Beat* magazine. *Yard Dog Mazurka*, which was adapted by Stan Kenton's trumpet player Ray Wetzel and turned into *Intermission Riff*, featured the same kind of dynamic developments Eddie Durham used to love. Wilson explained, "The copyright laws let you take seven bars of a guy's number and use it verbatim. Just change that eighth bar."[9]

Apart from these originals, the new arranger turned in his versions of *Strictly Instrumental, Jersey Bounce, Rocking Chair*, and *On the Alamo*. He had also written a couple of original tunes that didn't have names yet, but were performed nevertheless. After Wilson left, from time to time he kept turning in fresh arrangements for the band. The old pop tune *Louise* was one performed by the Lunceford Quartet. "Jimmie asked me after I left, anytime I wanted to send in anything, just send it in."

Gerald was also involved in getting Snooky Young to join their trumpet section as its lead player. Snooky was one of the new first trumpeters the brass fraternity had just started to buzz about. One night in November 1939 at the Howard Theater in Washington, DC, Eddie Tompkins left the stage in the middle of a song, never to return. Wilson told the leader about his former section mate in Chick Carter's band, who was playing down in Dayton, Ohio. Lunceford first checked with one of his old school buddies, who worked in a local funeral parlor, and who happened to be the cousin of Snooky's wife. He told the leader, "Get Snooky. He can play trumpet." But Young's first reaction was, "I can't do that." His wife persuaded him to give it a try, and so he joined the band at the Howard.[10] Lunceford was Young's first big break. "So that's how I got my shot in the band," said Snooky. "And that's when my career really started and got me rolling."

It was a touring band, that was Young's predominant memory. With Lunceford's orchestra he saw every state in the United States, a great experience for an aspiring musician. "I was the kid in that band. I was the baby, nineteen years old."

The leader once summed up the working situation of his band: "We do a couple of hundred one-nighters a year, fifteen to twenty weeks of theaters, maybe one four-week location, and two weeks of vacation. All in all, we cover about 40,000 miles a year!"

Among the millions who saw the band perform live were many musicians. One of them was tenor sax man and future Basie star Frank Wess.

Every time they were anywhere near, I heard them. And I used to listen to all the records. You know, I had all of them, all the records. That was a hell of a band. Count Basie was telling me once that they had a battle of music up in Connecticut, say Lunceford washed them out! This was a swinging band, boy! If you'd walk in a hall, a dance hall, a big hall, you know, maybe a thousand people or so, and from the door, where you walk in, the floor is bouncing like this. The whole floor is bouncing.

Wess illustrated his remark by moving his hand up and down above the table. "That band—they used to hit some awful grooves, yeah," he continued. The thing that amazed him most of all was the size of the ensemble. Just six brass and four saxophones, sometimes five, when Grissom joined the reeds. "Yeah, it wasn't a big band, but they could hit, *ooh!*" Wess made a wry face, expressing a high degree of admiration and awe. He stressed the fact that it wasn't a matter of just playing clean: other bands, Cab Calloway, Chick Webb, used to play in a clean style. "It was a unique style. They used to do a lot of two-beat stuff, and then when they'd shift gears and go into four, it was always effective."

As Frank was a beginning tenor player, Joe Thomas was his idol. Actually, Lunceford was "his" band: "Yeah, before Basie, Lunceford, you know." But he added that at the time, late 1939, in the New York jazz community Chu Berry was considered *the* tenor player: hardly anybody knew Lester Young yet, and Coleman Hawkins had only recently returned from Europe. The latter's hit recording of *Body and Soul* had just started dominating the juke boxes. So to Wess, those were the big three: Chu Berry, Joe Thomas, and Andy Kirk's Dick Wilson.

During the late 1930s, Houston-based trumpet man Milt Larkin led what by all accounts was the best big band in the Southwest. Larkin's tenor star was Arnett Cobb. Cobb remembered,

> We were crazy about Jimmie Lunceford's band. Our piano player Cedric Haywood, who was our chief arranger until Bill Davis came on the scene, copied everything from Lunceford's records. He wrote everything out. And Lunceford loved our band till he came down to Houston, taking Sy Oliver with him, to introduce him to Cedric—to find out about our voicing, we sounded so heavy. Lunceford didn't sound as heavy as we did. He liked our voicing. Certain little things we played were identical to what they did, but we sounded a little heavier, a little deeper than Lunceford. So Lunceford came down to the Majestic Theater, called for a piano and sent for Cedric—he paid Cedric—because he wanted Sy to find out about our voicing. But Cedric was smart enough not to tell them everything. So what did they do next? They asked if they could *exchange* things. We had a little thing, *Nice Work If You Can Get It* [Arnett sang the arrangement in a sonorous, penetrating voice], and they

gave us *Battle Axe,* a Joe Thomas piece, in return. The purpose of this exchange was to be able to analyze the voicing.

Larkin and Lunceford "battled" at least twice, in Houston in 1936 and in Chicago, four years later. To Larkin's mind, it was an even draw. One of the secret weapons of the Texans was a little trombone man, Henry Sloane, who danced while he played. But the leader, who for many years was considered the pride of Houston, added that Lunceford was very cool, very sophisticated. And he stressed the point that these music battles were essentially good-natured events. "It was with love from me and whoever the other leader was. It wasn't malicious. You know, we teased each other. Sometimes we'd win, sometimes we tied."

Alto player Don Wilkerson (not related to the better-known tenor man of the same name) witnessed both occasions and held a more outspoken view.

Actually, that particular period in the Lunceford era, Milton had the best band. Milton Larkin, he had the best band. The only thing Lunceford had that Milton didn't actually have is that girl vocal group. At Lunceford's peak, he had a girl vocal group, the Dandridge Sisters. They only cut two records. I know the one main recording was *Little Red Wagon.* In that time, Milton had Arnett Cobb and Gus Patterson on tenor, and he had Frank Dominguez, Eddie Vinson, and Illinois Jacquet on alto. He had three altos, two tenors, and one baritone. The baritone player played clarinet. Now you're talking about *heavy.* Milton had the first amplified bass. Lawrence Cato played the first amplified bass in that area. It was a regular upright bass; it had a pickup on it. Pickups were something of the future, what Cato had.

They had the battle of bands in '36 and in '40. '40 it was up in Rhumboogie in Chicago, and '36 in Houston, Emporium Auditorium. I saw this with my own eyes: Lunceford walked off the bandstand, his handkerchief drying his eyes, he says, "It's a shame these boys down here, with no break no kind of way." *No kind of break.* He played the club, had the best band ever been in existence. Now Lunceford said this himself, I was listening to him, just like you and I. Now that's an experience I had. I didn't take it for what it is now;

at that time I didn't realize it was such a great band. But nowadays I look back and see how great it was. Here's a man who was supposed to have the best band in the country, and he's giving boys that I went to school with, that I grew up under, credit for having the best band.

Wilkerson must have referred to the 1936 encounter. By 1940, the Lunceford band had become very hard to conquer. At this stage, only Duke and Basie would have stood a chance. "As good as they were," Gerald Wilson said about Milt Larkin's band, "they would not have beat Jimmie Lunceford's band out, at that time. No way! *No Way!* It's a matter of opinion, but it's just no way. We were a sharp band, and we had great arrangements also. So there was no way they were gonna outblow Jimmie Lunceford's band."

According to Arnett Cobb, the orchestras battled in Dallas and Fort Worth as well. Actually, those were not real battles, but rather double bills, advertised as battles—which most "battles" were anyway. It seems that only when visiting orchestras ran into house bands did real battles evolve, with audiences actually participating.

Cobb found out how effectively a tune like *Dinah* could mess up an audience. "Joe Thomas and just a small group on the stand, playing *Dinah*, Dixieland. They gonna keep it in Dixieland and all of a sudden all the band is coming up, different sections, one by one. And then, when they turned that thing around, man, it went into something else, they got into the arrangement. And they played that thing for an hour!"

During the time Gerald Wilson was riding on the Harlem Express, it "battled a couple of bands. We battled Andy Kirk, which was no challenge. Teddy Wilson, we blew them away, too. The only persons we wouldn't had in a show were Duke and Count, that's all. The rest of them—no, we didn't even think about." The Lunceford-Wilson battle took place in New York's Golden Gate Ballroom, 142nd Street and Lenox Avenue, during the first weekend of 1940. "No band wanted to play opposite Lunceford," grinned George Duvivier. After the Golden Gate battle, it was reported that Lunceford went home with a fee that constituted "an all-time Harlem high for this attraction."[11]

Battling the house bands of New York's Savoy Ballroom on their own turf always was a tricky business. Haywood Henry, Erskine Hawkins's baritone saxophonist, claimed a victory over the Lunceford men. Hawkins was more blues-oriented and had a lot of crowd-pleasing tricks, which gave him the edge, according to Henry. On top of that, in some tunes the Lunceford band played too soft for the people in the corners of the hall to hear. The Twentieth Century Gabriel (Hawkins's nickname) was familiar with the acoustics of the Savoy and kept his horns open.[12]

On June 7, 1940, the Lunceford crew started a four-week run at the new Fiesta Danceteria, located in Times Square, on the corner of West Forty-second Street and Broadway. Clarinet player Joe Marsala's big band had opened the place in November 1939. Situated on the second floor of the Rialto Theater, the Fiesta Danceteria featured name bands exclusively. Lunceford was the first black band to play the plush downtown restaurant that was advertised as "the world's first self-service nightclub," and offered food, drinks, and dancing from 6:00 P.M. until 3:00 A.M. An advantage were the radio connections: both MBS and CBS and their affiliated networks broadcast nightly from the Danceteria. This also was the orchestra's first Manhattan engagement since the ill-fated Band Box adventure in 1938. Mae Buzzelle, the band's former chorus girl, and her husband, Frank Bonitto, decided to travel to New York to hear it. "We were the only black couple there," recalled Frank. "Everybody said, 'Oh, you can't go in there.' It was something somebody like my wife wanted to dig. Sure we did go in there—we never had any trouble. I'll never forget that place. All the guys were kind of surprised when they saw us, sitting at the table. Wasn't an exclusive club, you know, classy. It was just kind of ordinary; it was clean and nice. Wasn't anything special." He paused, and in a soft voice added, "When I think of that Lunceford band, it's just a shame a band like that can't exist now." Most of the live broadcasts from the first Danceteria run have been preserved, and on October 4 the Harlem Express returned for another month.

The supreme victory in the history of the Harlem Express was, perhaps, the night of November 18, 1940. No less than twenty-eight top-flight bands were scheduled for a mammoth battle of the bands at New York's Manhattan Center. The proceeds of this gathering of the tribes were intended for the Local 802 Medical Fund. The spectacle ran from 8:00 P.M. until 4:00 A.M., and was aired over WNEW radio. Its popular deejay Martin Block, of *Make Believe Ballroom* fame, emceed the night. Each band was allotted fifteen minutes and not one second more. The lineup included the finest black swing bands, Fletcher Henderson, Count Basie, Lucky Millinder, and Erskine Hawkins among them. On the other end of the spectrum were the best-loved sweet bands, such as Guy Lombardo and Sammy Kaye. Lunceford was scheduled round about midnight, appropriately sandwiched between Glenn Miller, who was still rising fast, and reigning "King of Swing" Benny Goodman.

The show ran smoothly, and when Glenn Miller finished, the six-thousand-plus audience showed its appreciation in no uncertain terms. As soon as the Harlem Express, straight from the Apollo Theater, got under steam, however, all hell broke loose. The audience danced and screamed itself into such a frenzy that the only thing the promoters could do was allow the band to play an encore, but even this did not satisfy the jitterbugs. The Jimmie Lunceford Orchestra capped its performance with a twelve-minute rendition of *Dinah*, starting out in the familiar Dixieland vein and then dissolving into a never-ending stream of riffs, building and building, with Joe Thomas growling and stomping and dancing away on top of that. Gerald Wilson remembered their victory with relish. "I'll tell you this: everywhere we played, we broke it up! We were not one of those bands that played good. *We broke it up, every time.* It was very nice, yeah, it was a great time, a great thing to be a part of it." After this demonstration of its power, the Harlem Express rolled back to the Apollo, to finish its show there.[13]

From 1941 on, the band was invited for annual Christmas holiday appearances at the Apollo Theater. Frank Schiffman, the manager, had hired Lunceford for the 1940 New Year's gala revue as well, since the band had proven to be the most popular attraction during the past year. Producer Leonard Harper coupled the orchestra with the Miller Brothers and Lois, a new acrobatic dance act, the popular comedy duo Apus and Stella, and the Apollo chorus girls, among others. "Lunceford is one of the highest ranking 'stand bys' in the amusement field and his appearances at the Apollo always bring out the old S.R.O. sign," noted the *New York Age*.[14]

Gerald Wilson stressed the fact that the band continued to have big hits after he joined. "Huge hits. Like in the hundreds of thousands, I should say. It sold even more than that." This was because by this time the market had started to change: not only were blacks buying the records, but also some of the white jitterbugs. The band began to play quite a few white dances in those days, something its diverse book allowed it to do with ease. From 1940 on, the Lunceford bounce was also felt in the big white ballrooms.

But in the meantime, new "jump bands" were beginning to draw the fickle audience's attention. Just as a couple of years earlier Lunceford had outstripped Fletcher Henderson and upset Duke Ellington, now younger bands, more attuned to the blues, began to take over. Lucky Millinder,

Erskine Hawkins, Count Basie, Lionel Hampton, and Buddy Johnson, were ringing the cash register in the early 1940s. The number one big band in the 1940 *Pittsburgh Courier* poll was Count Basie's, drawing 11,200 votes. Ellington and Hawkins placed second and third, respectively. The fact that Hawkins finished so high should come as no surprise when one thinks of his hits that year: *Dolimite, Five O'Clock Whistle, Junction Blues,* and *After Hours,* his biggest one. When Hawkins arrived in Harlem, in 1935, Lunceford reportedly told him, "We can't play like Goodman. We need a new beat." With 10,540 votes, Lunceford placed fourth in the poll.

In December Columbia decided not to renew the recording contract. According to the company's press release, the band's 78s weren't selling in proportion to the money paid to the Oxley-Lunceford organization. Oxley stated that during 1939 and 1940, the period they were under contract with Columbia, 448,000 disks had been sold.[15] This is hard to believe, considering the band's string of hits with *'Tain't What You Do/Cheatin' on Me, Baby, Won't You Please Come Home? Ain't She Sweet? Well, Alright Then, What's Your Story, Morning Glory/Swingin' on C,* and *Red Wagon.*

The band went back to its old company, Decca Records. Since Decca by now accounted for 90 percent of the records in the jukeboxes across the nation, and jukeboxes ate up about half of the total recorded output, this move clearly enhanced the band's "visibility." The first thing Decca did was reissue ten of the band's best-loved records in an album. It must have soured Columbia that the hits after 1940 sold even better. The two-siders *Blues in the Night* and *I'm Gonna Move to the Outskirts of Town* were huge successes.

During the winter months of 1940–41, a dispute between the radio networks and ASCAP about the new, almost doubled rates to be paid for broadcasting ASCAP material, resulted in a ban on ASCAP compositions, in effect on January 1. The networks went as far as to prohibit ad-lib solos, for fear of quotes of ASCAP songs. All solos had to be written out in advance and submitted to station officials for approval. The networks promoted their own BMI (Broadcast Music Incorporated) roster. In the music community, BMI was referred to as "a pain in the asscap." In the meantime, radio stations and their orchestras had to resort to public domain material, which resulted in a vogue for "jazzing the classics" and a revival of traditional folk material. *I Dream of Jeannie with the Light Brown Hair* and Claude Debussy's *My Reverie* suddenly found themselves side by side in the top ten.

Lunceford vented his frustration in an article in *Down Beat* magazine, arguing that his band had developed a highly individual style. He wondered whether the years of hard work after all were fruitless. Radio officials were now telling him what to play. It was not possible to perform indiscriminately and still keep the band original. "We have a definite following that likes our music, and if we have to change it, we lose that following," he said. The bandleader knew what he was talking about: his orchestra was fully booked ten months in advance, and radio always had been a valuable tool for promoting the band. In the same article, Harold Oxley stated, "Jimmie chooses his own tunes to play just like every other leader does. Then he allows a staff arranger to shape them up in the style which has made the band the tremendous success which it is." The bandleader added, "It has been impossible for me to have arrangements made in as short a time on the tunes published by BMI. As a matter of fact, some of the tunes just wouldn't suit my band anyway."

The music press reported that Oxley had considered a lawsuit against the CBS network, though he apparently dropped the idea.[16] Stubbornly refusing to cleanse his broadcast performances of ASCAP songs, Jimmie Lunceford lost valuable airtime. He lost his ASCAP theme song too: *Jazznocracy* was replaced by *Uptown Blues*. This turned out a blessing in disguise: the latter tune was more representative of the band's current, even more streamlined style, which was honed in incessant rehearsing and in battling other bands on the road. *Uptown Blues* also drew attention to the group's merits as an unadulterated jazz orchestra.

BLUES IN THE NIGHT

"Jumpin' with jive and joy."
—ad Metropolitan, Chicago

Around 1939–40, when his income shifted into a higher gear, Lunceford had taken flying lessons and gotten his license. In August 1941, after he had logged over 150 solo hours, he went to Pittsburgh and purchased a sleek, fast three-seater, a Bellanca Model 19-9 Junior. Its additional fins on the tips of its tailplane gave the twenty-thousand-dollar plane a decidedly contemporary look. When it was convenient, the leader flew to his engagements, alone or with his spouse, who would soon obtain her own flying license. Ed Wilcox became the next pilot in the organization: he got his flying lessons from Jimmie. Later, when sax player Kirt Bradford joined the band, he also got his wings.

All went well until September 9, 1941. Jimmie, en route from Pittsburgh to Columbus, Ohio, where he was to fill an engagement, crashed his brand-new Bellanca at Cherry Ford emergency field near Winchester, Adams County, Ohio. The still inexperienced pilot had gotten off course and run out of gasoline. Dr. Sam C. Clark, of Winchester, treated the orchestra leader for lacerations of the cheek. His two passengers were unhurt. The three continued their way to Columbus by car. But Lunceford didn't make it in time, and the band played without its leader that night. According to Lunceford, it was the first time in years that he had missed a job.[1]

The insurance covered about two-thirds of the Bellanca's value, and Lunceford decided to replace his crashed machine with two new planes. The single-engined Fairchild Model 24, which seated three, was a gift to his wife, and the twin-engined Cessna T-50, the forerunner of the line of luxurious executive planes of that company, became his own toy. The Fairchild's interior was styled by famous designer Raymond Loewy, and the plane had wing flaps, an unusual feature for such a light model. The extra lift generated by these flaps enhanced the plane's takeoff and landing characteristics, which made it relatively easy to handle.

The Cessna, a five-seater, was strictly a plane for the very well-to-do, who could afford the price, close to thirty thousand dollars, a small fortune at the time. First flown in 1939, only forty civilian models were built before the outbreak of the war. It was powered by two 225 horsepower Jacobs radial engines, which gave it a maximum speed of 200 mph and a range of 750 miles. Still, the T-50 had its drawbacks: the engines had trouble getting started in cold weather, and it had a hard time remaining aloft on one engine. In rainy weather the pilot had to seal cracks with chewing gum. The plane served in the American and Canadian air forces as a trainer for bomber crews, where it was known as the "bamboo bomber," on account of its partly wooden structure.

Lunceford even boasted of a private airstrip, and he took great pride in inviting his business associates for flying trips. Shortly after he had purchased the Cessna, he took young bandleader Stan Kenton, whose appreciation for the Lunceford bounce showed in his early recordings, and Kenton's manager, Carlos Gastel, up in the air. At this stage, Lunceford's inexperience apparently discouraged his passengers: Kenton and Gastel remembered their flight as pretty scary. Sometimes, the pilot took aerial pictures of the towns he played, and had them published in the local newspapers.

As a rule, the only musicians who were allowed to fly with Pops on a more or less regular basis were old comrades Smith and Wilcox. George Duvivier, who arranged for the band and rehearsed it, copied scores, and occasionally played bass in the orchestra, remembered,

One time we were soaring along and Jimmie leaned back and told me, "you got it!" I said, "I got what?" He answered, "the plane, friend!" That was my introduction to flying. It was an awesome feeling—having this heavy plane suddenly under my control. I had my hands against the wheel, my feet on the two rudder pedals, trying to keep everything in line with the artificial horizon. I was sailing along nicely, feeling pretty proud of myself, when Jimmie says, "don't look now, but we're losing altitude." I was so busy doing one thing that I forgot to look at something else. But all in all he was quite pleased with me, and I used to make trips with him often.[2]

From time to time, other musicians flew with the boss. "In fact, when my daughter was born, he flew me home to see my daughter," said trumpeter Russell Green. Lunceford once rang Mary Lou Williams's doorbell at four in the morning, "asking if I wanted to fly to Pittsburgh with him," she told writer Max Jones. "I said, 'What are we going to fly in?' and Jimmie said, 'Didn't you now I had a pilot's license and my own plane?' I hadn't known, but refused to go anyway, saying, 'It's too foggy there.' Pittsburgh with its hundreds of steel mills makes its own fog."[3]

Lunceford's passion for all things technical was not confined to his extra-musical activities. As we have seen, in 1937 his band introduced the electric guitar, and it also was one of the first in jazz to include an electric bass. The development of the electric bass got started not long after the first electric guitars were built. Gibson was probably the first company to dabble with an amplified four-string bass-mandolin, which they called the Mando Bass. Rickenbacker's Los Angeles–based Electro String Instrument Corporation developed its first model in 1935, based on the experiments George Beauchamp had carried out, using various parts of the family washing and sewing machines. Beauchamp had developed a pickup consisting of two horseshoe magnets and six pole pieces that concentrated the magnetic field under each string. A touch of the strings caused oscillating changes in the magnetic field, which were translated into sound. The Rickenbacker bass resembled a modern electric bodiless upright specimen, with a loudspeaker replacing the body, and it was fitted with an outrigger support for the player.[4] Pictures from 1941 prove that Moses Allen played what probably was a rare early model Rickenbacker.

Bass player Truck Parham left Earl Hines to replace Allen that year. In

April, Lunceford had heard him with Fatha Hines at the Apollo, "so he called me, and asked me would I like to join the band. He said, 'I like your rhythm.' So I said, 'I would love to'—it was one of the great bands when I started out with territorial bands." In August, Parham traveled to California, where his future colleagues were playing at the Trianon Ballroom on South State in Los Angeles. The bassist, who played the ordinary acoustic model, had to wait a week until Mose Allen's notice had expired. In the meantime, the band worked on the movie *Blues in the Night*. That week, Truck was already on salary.

The orchestra had gone into the Warner Brothers studio to shoot a film noir called, at the time, *New Orleans Blues*, directed by Anatole Litvak and produced by Hal Wallis. Robert Rossen wrote the script, based on the play *Hot Nocturne* by Edwin Gilbert, and the cast included Priscilla Lane, Betty Field, Richard Whorf, Jack Carson, and Elia Kazan, the latter portraying a clarinetist. The plot involves a raggedy, struggling band that lands a job in a club, actually an illegal gambling casino. The owner is a gangster, whose jealous girlfriend sets out to harass the band. Apart from the soundtrack, the atmospheric photography in black and white is memorable.

Lunceford got the job when Litvak and Warner executive Henry Blanke attended a dance, probably at either the Casa Mañana in Culver City, where the band resided from June 24 on, or at the Trianon Ballroom. They decided then and there that they had found their screen stars. "I think that making this picture will just about fulfill Jimmie's greatest ambition," the mother of the screen star said—though the musical action happened to be mostly off-screen, in the background, and behind dialogues. Will Osborne's band was the other musical attraction. In the movie, the Lunceford band performed two selections, *Blues in the Night* and *Hang On to Your Lids, Kids*. *Blues in the Night*, featuring Trummy Young and the glee club, was so promising that it became the new title of the movie.[5] The tune climbed to number one on the Harlem Hit Parade.

The *New York Times* wrote, "Here tunesmiths Harold Arlen and Johnny Mercer, with assists from the Jimmy Lunceford and Will Osborne Bands and a quintet composed of the film's leading players, have produced a melodious sound track. And, so far as this corner is concerned, that's just about all the film has to offer." *Down Beat* added, "Director Anatole Litvak got hold of it and injected just enough of those all-too familiar musical comedy routines to ruin it without improving its entertainment value."[6]

Frank Bonitto's reaction was not so mild.

The main thing is, there's these two guys, talking in this club: "You want to hear this band, you gotta hear this band, boy, they can play." And, course, it was the Lunceford band. Can you imagine Lunceford and that band, as slick as that band was, dressed so nicely, and sharp all the time, and Lunceford looking so great out there, next thing they put Lunceford on and [Frank's voice rose] I couldn't believe it! *He's in rags!* He's literally in rags. I'm not kidding, not joke about it, no quotations about it. He was in rags! Sitting up there, waving his baton. I said, what the hell is that, what sort of band? They're just as ragamuffin as he is. I said, what are they doing? Oh, I was so upset. Of all bands they'd do that to—some comic band like Louis Jordan or someone could have taken it a little bit better. Here's a band that was known for looking so beautiful and sharp and slick and playing so precisely and beautifully. Of course I ran out.

Yet the impact of the movie was unbelievable. Though *Down Beat* in February 1942 had decided that Lunceford's recording of the title tune was "too late to mean anything as a money-grabber,"[7] it shot right to the top of the charts. First in Lunceford's version, a two-sider, and almost simultaneously in cover versions by Cab Calloway, Glenn Miller, and Woody Herman, which sold even better.

Sponsored by Warner Brothers, the distinguished Chamber Music Society of America staged a *Blues in the Night* symposium, at the Waldorf-Astoria Hotel in New York. On November 6, 1941, Lunceford, Osborne, Goodman, the Dorseys, Glenn Miller, Ruby Smith, Teddy Wilson, Albert Ammons, and Art Tatum were among the one hundred guests who discussed their music before a critical board of longhairs. Headed by Eddy Brown, ·president of the society, such luminaries as Sigmund Spaeth (National Association of Composers and Conductors), Carlton Sprague Smith (American Musicological Society), Philip James (New York University), Leonard Liebling (writer for *Musical Courier* since 1902), Albert Stoessel (Juilliard School of Music), and Wilfrid Pelletier (Metropolitan Opera) listened to music that was alien to their ears—and that had almost nothing to do with the blues. The idea was to examine the possibilities of incorporating blues and jazz elements into the general body of American "serious" music. Some of the classic connoisseurs pontificated on jazz, thereby, according to reporter Dave Dexter, revealing "their ignorance, to a man, of jazz and everything pertaining to the subject."

The jazz authorities who followed their classical brethren "bellowed and shouted in worse taste than the older and wiser reps of the classical art." Joe Thomas and a pickup band closed the evening with music and thus "saved the affair from complete failure," Dexter reported. By the time the symposium was closed, about three in the morning, the band could hardly be heard over the chatter and the tinkling of the glasses.[8]

The orchestra's 1942 advertisements announcing live appearances sometimes tried to capitalize on the movie: the Regal Theater, at Chicago's Forty-seventh and South Parkway, invited music fans to come "all aboard for the Harlem Express! The one and only Jimmie Lunceford and his Orchestra of 'Blues In The Night' Fame and his world famous School of Jazznocracy."[9] The nearby Metropolitan Theater suggested "jumpin' with jive and joy! Jimmy Lunceford and Orchestra. My Mama done tol' me,"[10] citing the famous opening line of the title song.

One of the band's West Coast fans was Ray Heindorf, musical director at Warner Brothers. He had a hand in part of the arrangement of the movie's title track; the last few bars of the first half of the song, the bit that sounded like a quote from *Stormy Weather*, were his. When the band played the Casa Mañana, he was there every night. Knowing that Lunceford's musicians were excellent sight-readers, he a couple of times invited several of them to augment the studio orchestras he used in Warner movies. This may have sparked the contemporary rumors that the Lunceford band appeared in more movie shorts. Granted, it is a tantalizing thought that more Lunceford footage may be lurking in some forgotten archive, but as of yet no such treasure has been unearthed.

Truck Parham believed the band at this time was more popular than it had been in the 1930s: "The places we came, people just flocking at." The records, like *'Tain't What You Do* and the new version of *Four or Five Times*, were selling in large numbers. To Parham, the band was "the best." He especially appreciated the camaraderie, which manifested itself both on stage and after the performance: guys like Joe Thomas and Trummy Young were notorious for hanging out. "Lots of cats liked to hang out. I used to follow them around. They did a lot of drinking, getting high, and all that shit. But I didn't do that." The rhythm section used to go out and jam. Anywhere the band went, the guys grabbed every opportunity to sit in, to jam. This, for instance, was the case at a session sponsored by the San Francisco Hot Music Society, at the local Dawn Club, in February 1940. Willie Smith, Joe Thomas, Al Norris, and Edwin Wilcox joined forces with members of cornettist Lu Watters' Dixieland Band, the Ray Noble Orchestra, the Vernon Alley Trio from the Club Alabam, and Jerome Richardson, then nineteen years old, who played alto and clarinet. The rest of the Lunceford band, including its leader, was among the four hundred spectators. Jimmie delivered a short speech, complimenting the society on its efforts.[11]

A most remarkable composition from this era was *Yard Dog Mazurka*, which was attributed to the triumvirate of Gerald Wilson, Tadd Dameron, and Roger Segure. Actually, Gerald Wilson wrote it, and he stressed that

> Tadd Dameron had nothing to do with *Yard Dog Mazurka*. The reason there is another name on [it is] a fellow by the name of Roger Segure—who was an arranger with Jimmie Lunceford—I was at his home for dinner and I sat down at the piano and I played this phrase of music. And I said, "This is my introduction to *Stompin' at the Savoy*, what do you think of it?" He said, "I like it, it's fine. Why don't you put a bridge to it and you'll have yourself a composition." And I said, "Okay, I'll do that." I put a bridge to it and then I played it. I said, "Well you know, Roger, had you not made that suggestion, it never would have happened, because I was making an arrangement on *Stompin' at the Savoy*." That whole first eight-bar phrase was the introduction to go in the *Savoy*. So I says, "Just for that, I give you half of it." That's what I did. Then I sketched it all out, all over the harmony, every rhythmic figure. And Roger—who was working with us; he wasn't traveling on the road on one-nighters—I handed him my sketch. He just copied this off and give it to the copyist. That's all he did. All of it is mine, every note.
>
> *Yard Dog Mazurka* did real well, because it was new. It was a new progression. And also my *Hi Spook* had already been out, with the use of the minor ninths as we know it today, and the augmented elevenths as we know it today. I had already gotten into that, just heard it somehow.

"They had a hell of influence on a lot of bands," emphasized Frank Wess. "Stan Kenton's *Intermission Riff* was a direct steal from Gerald Wilson's *Yard Dog Mazurka*. If you listen to Thad's music, Thad Jones got a lotta Lunceford influence. Lunceford influenced a whole lot of people, believe that. It was a hell of a band," he added, shaking his head.

In *Jazz Panorama*, a collection of essays edited by Martin Williams, composer Bill Russo, who during the early 1950s was associated with Kenton, attacked the contents of a Lunceford reissue album: "The intonation is often bad (especially in the saxophones) and the section balance of saxophones or of trombones is rarely uniform (the fact that these were recorded before our era of Enlightened Stereophony will not excuse this). The drums are badly tuned throughout, and the drummer's playing is often sloppy." Connoisseurs of the Lunceford bounce surely will raise their eyebrows even higher when confronted with Russo's more specific criticism: "*Impromptu* is excellent writing, but too much writing, the result is confused." It is hard to see how writing can be both excellent and too much, especially since the arrangement (by Edwin Wilcox) evolves with great logic, subtle variations, and elaborations, and the writer has clearly paid attention to details. And talking about too much writing: the composer took a full solo chorus, accompanied by just the rhythm section. "The saxophone background on *By The River Sainte Marie* is worse than that on a stock orchestration," Russo commented, but he must have been listening to a different recording, since the phrasing by the saxes in the introduction is utterly hip, in sharp contrast to Dan Grissom's vocal that follows. Russo had more axes to grind. "The first two sections of *Yard Dog Mazurka* are excellently connected; the contrapuntal *pot pourri* is great. How sad that the guitar bridge was inserted. Even worse is the attempt (right after the guitar solo) to pick up where things left off." Perhaps it is a matter of taste, but one is tempted to think that the guitar solo stands in nice contrast to the busy arrangement, and the ensemble after said solo forms a delightful unity with the rest of the song. Likewise, Russo called *Hell's Bells* "the most uneven piece of music in the album," though arranger Sy Oliver had tried (and managed) to cram as much variation and humor in the unorthodox tune as possible, without losing its unity. The piece opens with the theme, played by Jimmy Crawford on glockenspiel, accentuated and contrasted by wah-wah effects by the trombones. A playful staccato clarinet choir takes over from Crawford, and the brass waves derby hats in front of its bells. *Hell's Bells* is as colorful and ingenious as a *Silly Symphony*.

For the same collection of essays, British writer Albert McCarthy supplied "Jimmie Lunceford: A Reply." He noted that the album under review (*Jimmie Lunceford and his Orchestra*, Decca DL 8050) actually represented a poor selection, adding that he had heard the Lunceford band a few times in person. He mentioned the effect of hindsight, which sometimes made things seem better than they actually were. But, he added, he had also heard Ellington, Teddy Hill, and Edgar Hayes in person, and these encounters had not left a comparable impression. He did not claim that Lunceford was "better" than Duke, but one expected a certain level of sophistication, a certain degree of brilliance from Ellington, and "Lunceford was a shock."[12]

One can only guess as to Russo's motifs for his harsh and unfounded criticism. His work for Stan Kenton, several symphonies, and his own ensembles indicates the composer essentially was a somber person who was committed to writing grandiose, authoritative works. Did he view the Jimmie Lunceford Orchestra as too frivolous?

As we have seen, the Lunceford style was imitated and absorbed by other bands almost from the start. By the late 1930s the swing craze was nearing its apogee, and it is striking that the best-known and most successful orchestras based their styles on Lunceford, including bands led by trombonists Glenn Miller and Tommy Dorsey and trumpet virtuoso Harry James. One could find typical Lunceford devices—dense, rich harmonies, resulting in sumptuous colors; original, daring arrangements; certain little riffs; the proverbial "bounce"—throughout their respective books. Miller was a declared Lunceford nut. He not only modeled his style after the Harlem Express's sweet side, but incorporated most of its visual effects as well. Swaying the saxophones from side to side, pointing the trombones skyward, juggling the brass's derby hat mutes in unison—it was all borrowed from the men from Harlem. Clarinet virtuoso Buddy DeFranco saw both bands (and in later years led the Miller ghost band) and declared, "Somehow when Glenn Miller approached that show, showmanship was fine, people loved it—but it was synthetic. Secondhand. Same with Jimmy Crawford on drums. A lot of guys showed off, but it was so natural with Jimmy. When the Lunceford band waved the hats, it was natural. A natural way. So it was more real and artistic. It wasn't contrived. Very nice, it was really nice to watch. It never upset the music."

Margie, Whatcha Know, Joe? Twenty-Four Robbers, What's Your Story, Morning Glory, and *Blues in the Night* are among the best-known Lunceford songs the Miller band covered. Initially, the Moonlight Serenader had some misgivings about this last opus: "that tune, with its ABCCA construction, will never make it," was his prediction.[13] Most of these arrangements could be bought or ordered in music shops—it should be borne in mind that before 1940 the sheet music sales still outnumbered the distribution of records. Sometimes, however, Miller turned directly to his idol, as Gerald Wilson remembered.

> In those days, see, the only people who could copy music were people who could write music. They didn't have copyists like they got people today to copy. So Jimmie comes up to me, calls me in his dressing room, say, "Gerald, want you to copy off *Jump and Shout* for Glenn Miller here. Drop it by the Chicago Theater tomorrow." So I'd go home, to the hotel, and copied this number all night for Glenn Miller. Stopped by the Chicago and gave it to him. It was Eddie Durham's tune. Jimmie sure gave it to him.

Miller in all probability would have loved to hire away Sy Oliver, who wrote roughly 60 percent of the Lunceford book, including about fifteen big hits. Miller's friend and rival Tommy Dorsey, however, was a little quicker and had a little more to offer than Glenn Miller, who at the time, the summer of 1939, was just on the verge of the big time. Miller might have missed out on Oliver, but he did attain the services of Eddie Durham. For the Miller band Durham wrote charts that rank among the most brilliant of the swing era. *St. Louis Blues, Hold Tight, Tiger Rag, Farewell Blues, I Want to Be Happy*, and, yes, *In the Mood* will not lose their irresistible swing and charm for ages to come. Miller led a good, versatile band (it has been unjustly dismissed as "commercial" and "bland" by most critics, who evidently never listened beyond *In the Mood*), with capable soloists. Its only weakness lay in its rhythm section.

Miller, James, and Dorsey were not the only leaders who admired the Harlem Express. Under the headline "Dorsey, Dunham & Others Indicate a Lunceford Trend," *Down Beat* noted "a growing tendency, possibly even a definitive trend, in style of dance bands in a Jimmie Lunceford groove." Young white bands, led by Sonny Dunham, Bob Chester, and Freddie Slack, emulated the style of the Harlem Express. Back in 1939, Chester had been the first to stylize his orchestra after Glenn Miller's, but now he "also has veered away from his Glenn Millerized type of danceaptation and in recent works has been playing the more Negroid Lunceford style of jazz. Freddie Slack says he is building a 'Lunceford band.'" *Down Beat* added that "not a little of Les Brown's stuff is patterned in the JL idiom, with chief arranger Ben Homer admittedly striving for Luncefordean 'mile-wide' voicing and melodic accents on first and third beat, letting rhythm section take care of second and fourth." Earl Hines and Jimmy Dorsey were established bandleaders showing more than a few traces of Lunceford's harmonic and rhythmic approach. *Down Beat* rated Jimmy Dorsey's "the most radical change."[14]

Lunceford's soloists also left their mark on aspiring musicians. Joe Houston, who with selections like *Worry, Worry, Worry, All Night Long* and *Shtiggy Boom* made a name for himself as a tough tenor tornado from Texas, remembered watching his idol Joe Thomas when he was still a youth. How did he know the band was scheduled to play in his hometown?

> They put placards out. They did that in Austin. That was the first
> name band that I saw. I had the money, dollar and a half. That was
> in them days, man. I saw Joe Thomas before I saw Arnett and . . .
> identical! First time I saw Lunceford, Joe Thomas and Willie Smith,
> all of them was there. I loved Joe Thomas. I had an alto and I liked
> the alto, but I always liked the tenor players. Some of the tenor play-
> ers did what I liked. I used to play like the tenor players on my alto.
> And Joe Thomas was . . . was beautiful. He was simply great. In
> Austin, where I lived, we had a place called the Cotton Club. They
> had those benches, like a church, you know what I mean. Man, I was
> the first one there, and I got me a seat and I never moved, not even
> during intermission. I'll never forget that, man. I'd sit right there. I
> wanted to see what everybody was doing. I'm right in front of Joe
> Thomas. Joe Thomas, he sit in his seat, he never sit like this man,
> he'd do this [rocks back and forth] *all* the time. You know, he was a
> showman. Mr. Lunceford was a good man. I asked him to play *Body
> and Soul*. And Joe played *Body and Soul* for me.

Considering the turmoil the Harlem Express as a rule would cause in band battles, it is perhaps ironic that one of the most remarkable defeats was the one against Claude Hopkins, in 1942, in a big barn in the South. Hopkins led a good band; its unobtrusive, muted sound was not unlike Lunceford's. In variety, musicianship, dynamics, power, and showmanship, however, Lunceford excelled. Hopkins's secret weapon was his crooner, Orlando Roberson, a falsetto tenor in the vein of Andy Kirk's Pha Terrell and

Lunceford's own Dan Grissom, only far better. Whenever the handsome six-footer opened his mouth to sing a ballad, all the women in the house started screaming and yelling, or quite simply fainted with a blissful smile.

But this defeat was an exception: during the early 1940s the Lunceford ensemble was virtually unbeatable. Its fleeting appearance in *Blues in the Night* and the subsequent eponymous hit single had greatly enhanced its visibility, and growing numbers of white swing fans were by now paying attention to the band. There was nothing that could stop the Harlem Express in its victorious journey through the land of swing—or so it seemed.

EXODUS

I became totally disinterested during the war.
—_Jackie Kelso_

Much has been written about the demise of the Lunceford orchestra over the course of the 1940s. Some writers, such as Gunther Schuller in his study _The Swing Era,_ even put the beginning of its deterioration as early as mid-1935.[1] At that time, saxophonist Jackie Kelso was a devout Lunceford fan. But that changed:

> I became totally disinterested during the war. Oh yeah. They had lost their total character. It got to be so heartbreaking, I just wouldn't listen to the band, because the playing was rough. And it almost got to the point where—a lot of bands now, they play things faster than they should be playing. And Lunceford's band _never_ felt like it was playing the wrong tempo. But after the Lunceford band lost the key men and they lost their real character, they began to play things that sounded rough and too fast. Tempos can get so fast that

the musicians have a hard time executing. And then it doesn't sound too good. And I think sometimes that's what happened to the second Jimmie Lunceford band. They were attempting to be exciting with material that couldn't be executed slowly.

Frank Bonitto, Jimmie's friend from the days of the first large-scale tours, held a similar view. "There's a lot of Lunceford in that era—I don't even buy it. Cause it's not the Lunceford band, the real Lunceford band that we know."

So how did the Jimmie Lunceford Orchestra really develop? From its initial records one can conclude that by the early 1930s the band had already reached high levels of musical proficiency and personality. The 1933 test recordings for ARC prove that at that stage it had both a recognizable style and a remarkable degree of cohesion and professionalism. If the band did not belong in the top league already, it was getting close. By the same token, it can not be maintained that all of its early recordings belonged in the five-star category. The overall level very gradually rose until by 1940 the orchestra had attained a standard comparable only to Duke Ellington. Then after Gerald Wilson and Snooky Young joined, the trumpet section became snappier and more powerful, resulting in a finer internal balance in the band. The orchestra acquired a new polish, which emphasized its machine-like character. From 1942 on, with the departure of some of its key members, and the arrival of new arrangers and musicians, the band lost some of its personal handwriting, some of the subtlety and transparency that had characterized the smaller 1930s outfit. It remained, however, an extremely exciting outfit. Four years later, when the postwar depression had set in, the orchestra suffered an artistic and economic low. Between 1944 and 1947, George Duvivier rewrote part of the prewar library to accommodate the eight to nine brass, five reeds (six sometimes, with the leader added), and four rhythm.[2] Then in early 1947, the band was regaining momentum, and the future once again looked bright.

Just prior to the war, Sy Oliver, Eddie Durham, Gerald Wilson, and Billy Moore Jr. from time to time had submitted arrangements that might be considered cutting edge. Tadd Dameron, a kindred spirit who worked out of Harold Oxley's office in New York, complained in *Jazz Masters of the Forties* that some of his arrangements were attributed to Sy, and others, which he judged "very good," remained unrecorded. Gerald Wilson questioned Dameron's claim, stating that Sy at that point had truly arrived, and did not need anybody else's work to prove his abilities. "He was trying to write like Sy Oliver when he joined our band! He was no bebopper then! No no, he was no bebopper yet. Oh, he was a good arranger, he was quite an arranger. But he was not into bebop, you know. But as I said, Sy Oliver would have no need to play any of his arrangements." In the same book, Dameron acknowledged Oliver's influence. One of his first assignments had been for Zack Whyte's orchestra, shortly after Oliver had left that band, "and I heard all these arrangements. I was writing just like Sy."[3]

"Did we record *(I Like New York in June) How About You?*" Wilson wondered (they didn't). "Tadd had an arrangement on it in the band, it was a very good arrangement. There were some others, yeah." A most remarkable Lunceford chart that rests in the Smithsonian Archives is an uncredited *Fine and Dandy*. Judging from the meandering reed parts, this might be Dameron's very first "bop" arrangement. If so, Lunceford was actually playing bebop in 1942! (The first time the new music was documented was probably on February 15, 1943, when Dizzy Gillespie, Charlie Parker, and Oscar Pettiford gathered in Room 305 of Chicago's Savoy Hotel and recorded *Sweet Georgia Brown* on a portable Silvertone machine.) Dameron did not travel with the Jimmie Lunceford orchestra, though sometimes the leader sent for him to rehearse the ensemble.

The Lunceford musicians rehearsed on a daily basis, provided the itinerary permitted them. Their sight-reading facilities were tested when they played the *Jubilee* shows in California. These shows were staged at either the Hollywood NBC studio, Sunset and Vine, or the Casa Mañana, in nearby Culver City. The *Jubilees* were live radio programs, emceed by Ernie "Bubbles" Whitman, dubbed "The stomach that walks like a man," a hip, jive-talking actor. The *Jubilee* audience mainly consisted of black GIs. The weekly programs were pressed on sixteen-inch vinylite disks, which were shipped to the various theaters of war. The shows were a project of the Armed Forces Radio Service, an agency that during World War II produced entertainment programs for the troops. Major Mann Holiner, a former Broadway and CBS producer, had developed the idea, and he unveiled his first *Jubilee* show in October 1942, starring Ethel Waters, Eddie "Rochester" Anderson, the Hall Johnson Choir, and the Duke Ellington Orchestra. The Lunceford band made its debut on the eighth edition, where the leader met an old acquaintance: screen star Hattie McDaniel, who in the 1920s had been the singer with the George Morrison Jazz Orchestra, emceed this show.

The *Jubilees* were designed as the black "answer" to popular programs like *Command Performance* and *Mail Call*, directed at white servicemen. Heavily sponsored, the black shows featured the top bands of the nation, along with the best singers and vaudeville performers. By mid-1943, the half-hour programs were transmitted to both the East and West Coasts and the European theater of war by short-wave radio. The series ended in 1952, but by that time its original format was already history.

In the period between 1942 and 1945 the Jimmie Lunceford Orchestra headlined no less than twelve *Jubilee* shows. This might be seen as a proof of its undiminished popularity, since only Benny Carter's L.A.-based band was busier.[4] Jimmie's trumpet star Russell Green recalled, "Sometimes we'd do these *Jubilees;* you didn't have time to rehearse. So Jimmie would just pass it [the sheet music] out, and he said, 'I give you the tempo, read what you see.'" Most of the time this proved to be no problem. Most of the time the listeners did not even notice that the performance they heard was unrehearsed.

The war years were extremely difficult for both the big bands and the dance halls. Even before Pearl Harbor, the Selective Service draft had begun to take away many young musicians fit to battle—or to play in a military band. From the very beginning in Memphis, Jimmie had always kept lists of promising musicians he ran across, in case he needed replacements. But now his new recruits were either veterans or younger, inexperienced musicians, schoolboys sometimes, who, because of scarcity, began to command outrageous salaries. By the end of the war, salaries had tripled, so ballrooms were forced to double admittance prices. The demand for entertainment was still substantial, even increasing, and the wartime economy had stuffed the pockets of the workers with bundles of dollars. While in 1940 one could hire a name band like Lunceford's for anything between five hundred and a thousand dollars a night,[5] Tommy Dorsey had to ask fifteen thousand dollars in 1945 to meet the payroll and other expenses of his string-laden orchestra.

All along the West Coast blackout regulations were in force, for fear of a Japanese attack, resulting in the cancellation or postponing of dances. From early 1942 on everybody had to deal with traveling restrictions. First, the government imposed a general speed limit of 35 mph in order to save gasoline and tires. In March, gas and rubber were rationed. Many dance orchestras became dependent on loyal fans who supplied them with spare ration stamps for the purchase of gasoline. "Youngsters no longer take the

family car and drive 30 or 40 miles to hear a band," *Down Beat* reported.
"They stay home and play records, or gather in roadhouses to dance to juke
music. Colleges which usually fatten a bandleader's take by paying from
$1,500 to $2,500 for two-night engagements of name bands are now playing
local orchestras, or canceling parties altogether."[6]

For a while, buses were confiscated by the military, and the few buses
that remained were often dilapidated. Bands had to journey long stretches
in overcrowded trains, and had to commit themselves to perform at least
twice a week at U.S.O. (United Service Organization) canteens, war bond
rally stages, or army camps, if they were to get travel permits at all. In the
fall of 1942, the Lunceford orchestra traveled a distance of five hundred
miles by train. Except for two seats, it was standing room only.[7] In early
October even train travel became "frozen." If Oxley was lucky, he could
arrange an Army Air Force C-47 to fly the band to the next base, in
exchange for one or more free performances. Due to the wartime traveling
restrictions, Oxley decided to fully concentrate on his number one attraction again, the Lunceford orchestra, dropping his other acts, including the
Tommy Reynolds band.

All in all, the touring did not diminish. Russell Green, who replaced
Paul Webster in the middle of the war, boasted, "We could do as many
one-nighters as there were days in the month. I've seen a time when we
would do thirty in thirty-one nights. Well, that one day was traveling! We
had a reputation of being the greatest one-night band in the country. It was
a pleasure to play for him, although you couldn't make the right kind of
money."

The musicians were always glad when summertime came, because they
knew they were going to California to work for about a month, or longer,
at the Casa Mañana in Culver City. From 1938 on, Oxley had been working with independent booker Reginald Marshall in California. Marshall
booked Lunceford and Edgar Hayes on the coast, while Oxley handled
Marshall's roster (whose main asset was the Floyd Ray Orchestra) in the
East.[8]

A favorite place in Los Angeles for traveling bands was the Orpheum
Theater, where Lunceford would perform every year. The Club Plantation
in Watts was also an important location on the West Coast. At his stage, the
musicians' wives were permitted to travel with the band—if they could
keep up with the pace and the conditions, and the sidemen used to bring
their wives when they toured California. But Jock Carruthers's wife, for

instance, wasn't cut out for it: she used to turn green on the bus. "And I guess that made some problems, too," added lead trumpeter Joe Wilder, who served in the postwar edition of the band. "Because there were a lot of guys who, you know, were not being very faithful. And at some point, when the other wives and things were traveling, they would find this out. This would be just a matter of, I guess, of happenstance. But when they found it out, of course, word would get back, and they cause a lot of dissension, I guess. That was another problem they had."

In a later stage of the war, 1944, the cabaret tax was introduced: any venue that featured dancing or singing, either on stage or on the floor, had to add an extra 20 percent—and eventually 30 percent—war tax on the receipts. Officials defined the locations that qualified: "a place which furnishes a public performance for profit, including every public vaudeville or other performance of diversion in the way of acting, singing, declamation or dancing either with or without instrumental, or other music, conducted by professionals, amateurs or patrons, under the auspices of the management in connection with the serving of food or other refreshment or merchandise." Juke joints were exempted, provided there was no singing or dancing to the box.[9] To the horror of both ballroom operators and bandleaders, this tax was not lifted when the war was over, which was the coup de grâce for many a ballroom and, consequently, for a large number of dance bands. Finally, the midnight curfew ordered by the government during the winter of 1944–45 further affected the vanishing dance culture. These regulations were a major assault on America's popular dance culture, and kids virtually stopped dancing until the advent of rock and roll, ten years later.

From 1942 on, musicians started to drift in and out of the Lunceford band. The first one to hand in his notice was arranger Roger Segure, who had two reasons for quitting the band: he did not like the idea that Stan Kenton, Woody Herman, and all kinds of other bands capitalized on Lunceford's style; and he also had the idea that he had been ripped-off by Lunceford and Oxley. Usually he got twenty-five dollars, sometimes fifty, for an arrangement. When *Back Door Stuff* became a hit, two years after Segure had left the Lunceford organization, he received a check from Decca Records, who handled the publishing rights of the piece, for over two thousand.[10] Oxley signed young Tadd Dameron as Segure's replacement.

Trumpet player, bandleader, songwriter, and producer Dave Bartholomew, a key figure in New Orleans rhythm and blues since the mid-1940s, remembered with relish how he was asked to sub for an ailing Snooky Young. This was in early 1942, when the orchestra passed through New Orleans. Jimmie inquired whether there were any musicians available who could play first trumpet and was told to look for Bartholomew, who had gained experience working with pianist Fats Pichon, the leader of one of the hottest dance orchestras in the city. One of the young trumpeter's characteristics was his power, his strong sound. But since Dave had just married, he did not really want to travel with Lunceford, though he thought it a great honor—"the biggest pleasure I have ever had in my life"—to be asked to play in the band he considered the greatest in the world. So he ended up working just a couple of weekends. But the famous producer later spoke with awe of this experience: "Those guys were playing, man, that was a trip. I wish they had one like that now. It would be a thrill to play in it and the people would actually enjoy it, because it was all music. It's a shame the economy won't allow us to have that type of music now. Things are so high, you couldn't pay a band like that. But if possible, it would be a pleasure, and the people would come out and have a real evening of good fun." Gerald Wilson remembered the nights in New Orleans: "He was a good reader. He could read, he did all right, I know that. He was a good trumpet player, yes he was."

The absence of Lunceford's regular lead trumpeter gave other young players a chance to gain experience working with the Harlem Express. "I followed Snooky in Jimmie Lunceford's band. It's a strange story," Russell Jacquet said,

> I was in Wiley College in the college band. So here's the weekend, you know, college boys never have any money. But I was determined to go hear Jimmie Lunceford. I hitchhiked along the highway to Longview. That's twenty-five miles from Marshall, Texas. I don't know how I got in there. I was determined to get in. I want to hear that band.
>
> And when I groped my way, this crowd that just—people were just standing next to each other. I don't know how I went there, just magic, I found myself in front of the stage—and Jimmie Lunceford did this [signals] to me. I did not know him, but I had seen the band several times. But word gets around, you know that. So I went backstage, to see what he wanted, I thought he was gonna put me out. I

hated to go in there, because I didn't have any money. And he says, "Where's your horn?" I said, "Where is my horn?! I thought you were going to put me out." He says, "I want you to sit in with the band." I said, "Well, I don't have my horn with me." He say, "I'll get you a horn." The problem was, they had a great trumpet player who couldn't read at sight and didn't have time for rehearsal. So he was not doing a good job. We replaced mouthpieces. I went there perhaps five or six days, in that little territory. This was '42.

Lunceford continued to ride high. An advertisement for Conn instruments claimed, "His much-copied style, requiring musicianship of a high order, sells millions of Decca records."[11] That may have been an exaggeration, but in March of that year, Lunceford did break Andy Kirk's attendance record at the Sunset Terrace, in Indianapolis. The band was asked back in April.[12] In a popularity poll, conducted by Patterson, New Jersey, radio station WPAT, Basie gathered 14,267 votes, and was crowned "Sepia King of Swing," while Lunceford had to content himself with 4,285 votes and second place.[13] A pool room owner in Boston apparently knew exactly what his clientele liked, and stuffed his jukebox with records by Lunceford and Basie only.[14] In 1944 the *Chicago Defender* commented, in an announcement of two dances at the local White City Ballroom, featuring Lionel Hampton and Jimmie Lunceford respectively, "In bringing Hampton and Lunceford to Chicago in one week [promoter Otis] Thomas is scoring a grand slam. No other bands in the business will outdraw either."[15] Yet in September of that year the William Morris Agency proudly announced that Billy Eckstine's big band, featuring Dizzy Gillespie and Sarah Vaughan, had outstripped Basie, Lunceford, and Ellington in that city.[16] That same year, *Song Hits* magazine, the largest music publication in the States and Canada, presented Lunceford with its Award of Merit.[17] All this adds up to the conclusion that it was quite busy at the top, with Basie, Ellington, Lunceford, Hampton, and Eckstine all vying for the limelight.

In Europe, critics such as Frenchman Hugues Panassié had always been champions for the Lunceford approach. Sometimes, Old World adoration took on an ethereal form of worship. Toni Del Renzio's appraisal of *I'm Gonna Move to the Outskirts of Town* would have suited a spiritualist séance by Madame Blavatsky. Ed Wilcox arranged this Casey Bill Weldon song, made famous by Louis Jordan. Here, the vocalist was Dan Grissom, who by this time was singing better, less sugary, than in the early days. The review appeared in the first issue of the British publication *Jazz Forum*.

With this perspective, instrument of feeling as much as of intellect, we are able to apprehend *actively* the blues in all its glorious mutations. Of these, recently perhaps the loveliest and most inspiring is that wrought by the Jimmie Lunceford Band weaving their sonorous ectoplasm *On The Outskirts Of Town*. Dissatisfied with the picturesque folk-material that has so often served to hide the blues even from devoted and earnest admirers, this band has not eschewed any limiting and inhibiting factors. Skillfully they have avoided, however, destroying the quintessential jazz which alone, like an elixir, can prevent a pitiful Ellingtonian collapse into the negation and sterile hues of beige, brown-pink, primrose yellow.

On the outskirts of town we learn to appreciate the fiery flow of jazz as distinct from the watery flow of the great fatheads, Brahms, Beethoven . . . apocalyptic, the blues light up the future and its promises. On the outskirts of town man and woman[,] each so long entertaining the germ of the other, melt qualitatively into the whole circle of light and dark where the intended and the unexpected are reconciled, the arranged and the improvised in the music of Lunceford.[18]

The *Jazz Forum* did not last long.

To blues guitarist T-Bone Walker, Lunceford's rendition of the Louis Jordan hit lacked soul. He pointed out that Jordan "plays good blues and he sings them like they were originally sung, too." The difference with Grissom was that the latter "sings sweet but the blues aren't sweet. You've gotta feel the blues to make them right."[19] Yet Grissom had a direct influence on younger blues singers such as Charles Brown.

Lunceford's blues definitely had a different hue—and a different beat. With his "rippling rhythm" gimmick—he used to start his radio shows blowing bubbles through a straw—bandleader Shep Fields had built a large audience during the 1930s. In 1941 he surprised the dance band business with a mammoth thirty-five-piece saxophone orchestra. Since Fields used arrangers of the caliber of Glenn Osser, the resulting sound was rich and varied. The bandleader obviously had listened closely to the Lunceford band. After stating that the Dorseys, Les Brown, and Sonny Dunham led "the swing to Lunceford stylings," his analysis for *Down Beat* magazine went on:

> A lot of bands haven't succeeded in copying Lunceford well, but have gotten a heavy, overphrased style that lags instead of jumping lightly, politely but not slightly. The reason's simple: they thought that by having the rhythm play two beats unaccented and by over-phrasing the sax licks, you'd get that terrific subtle kick that Jimmie's men do.
>
> That isn't the case. That light beat comes only with hours of rehearsal, lead men with Willie Smith's talent for phrasing, and con-stant work to keep the band from bogging down in its own phrases.[20]

By now, three months after Pearl Harbor, the musicians began receiving draft cards. Unlike most of his sidemen, Lunceford, thirty-nine, was too old to be inducted. The first ones to feel the draft were Gerald Wilson and Snooky Young. The trumpeters parted the same night at the Graystone Ballroom in Detroit, in mid-April 1942. At the time, the music fraternity buzzed with suggestions of a conspiracy, since Wilson had been instrumen-tal in getting Young into the band, in late 1939. But both men left because they had received their draft card, and were classified 1-A: fit for combat and any kind of military service. So they knew their time was running out.

The buzzing was partly triggered by a puzzling press release in May. According to Oxley,

> A few prima donnas had developed in the ranks of the band in recent years and a general realignment has been under consideration for some time. Moses Allen, bass; Snookie Young and Joe Wilson trum-pets; Ted Buckner, sax; Elmer Crumbley, trombone; and Dan Gris-som, sax and vocalist are the six men given notice. . . . Replacements for all the departing musicians have been made, according to Lunce-ford, but names of only two of the new men were available at press time. These were Freddie Webster, trumpet man from Cleveland, recently with Lucky Millinder, and Peewee Jackson, trumpet player from the Earl Hines band. James "Trummie" Young, trombonist who took a leave of absence recently and who, it was rumored, planned to organize his own band, has returned to the Lunceford

fold and has indicated his intention of remaining.

"Joe" protested: Snooky and he were no prima donnas; they were the youngest members in the band. And Ted Buckner and Elmer Crumbley were the quietest, most friendly human beings one might wish to encounter. Nevertheless, in addition to Oxley's memorandum, the band-leader said that if any of his musicians "are dissatisfied with their jobs, now is the time to walk."[21] That same month the next two replacements were announced, Benny Waters for Buckner and Fernando "Chico" Arbello for Crumbley.

After the six "fired" men, Willie Smith followed their example and then "Trummy Young left, which was a big blow," said Gerald Wilson. "Because Trummy did a lot of singing, he contributed a lot of compositions to the band, like *'Tain't What You Do,* he sang *Twenty-Four Robbers.*" One of the reasons Trummy Young finally left Lunceford in March 1943 on short notice, to join Charlie Barnet, was a fifty-dollars-a-week difference in salary. Furthermore, Young was tired of the road, and since the Basie band was constantly traveling he had also turned down an offer from Count Basie. Oxley was not pleased with his sudden departure, and took up the matter with the union.[22]

Willie Smith had left in July 1942 and joined trumpeter Charlie Spivak's reeds. Willie cried the last night he was with the band. He did not really want to leave, but by now he could command much more by playing lead alto in other big bands. For too long, Lunceford had treated his men like the schoolboys of the Chickasaw days. Too late he realized they were grown men now, and consequently their financial needs had changed. Not long before his death the leader confided to a journalist that his one big mistake had been a serious lack of concern about his musicians' financial welfare.

Finding a suitable first alto was a tough job. Lunceford called Russell Procope in New York. But Procope did not want to leave his job with the John Kirby Band: "I liked what we were doing and wanted to be in New York as much as possible."[23] Young Jerome Richardson was considered. Two years ago he had jammed with Willie and other members of the orchestra, and he was kind of their mascot: "I stood behind the saxophones all the time. During the time that they were there and playing, Lunceford used to let me hold that big flute he had. I didn't know what it was. Of course, it was an alto flute." Would he be willing to give it a try? "I would have paid them to let me play!" he exclaimed.

It so happened that Willie Smith left when the band was in Oakland, California. And that's where I'm from originally. I knew some of the guys in the band, so they mentioned that Willie was going. I said, "Well, can I audition?" So they brought me up to Lunceford. Lunceford said, "Can you play loud?" I said, "Yeah." "You like Willie Smith?" I said, "Yeah." In the meantime he didn't know—I don't think he realized—that every year that they would come, I was the first one in the hall and the last one out. And I had memorized all the saxophone things and everything. So he asked me to come and play at the Oakland Auditorium. So I came and played and kept asking for *Chopin Prelude*. Well, they sort of didn't want to . . . and I kept asking. They said, "Well, we lost the first part." I said, "Play it." And I played with them. I played it from memory. I was gonna make sure I got this gig. Of course, he wanted me to be in the band.

So anyway, to make a long story short, I was with the band for about a week and a half, two weeks, and that was during the war years. Before he gave me a uniform he said, "What draft status are you?" I said, "Uh-oh, 1-A." He said, "I'm sorry. As soon as I give you a uniform, they'll call you." Sure enough, I stayed with him two weeks and two weeks later they called me.[24]

Next, the bandleader checked Kirtland Bradford, who played in Cee Pee Johnson's band. Lunceford liked what he heard, but Bradford had other commitments. The band left the coast and traveled east. In Houston, Lunceford tried Conrad Johnson. In the 1950s Connie developed into a busy session man for rhythm-and-blues dates, and later he got a name as one of the city's most revered teachers. In 1942 he was an aspiring alto man. "I got a chance to play with him, one or two engagements. *Whoo!* It took a little effort. You didn't just walk in and play that book without any provocation, you had to put some time in. *Whoo, yeah!* I sure did enjoy that short stay when they were in Texas."

Next stop was St. Louis, and still the band was without a regular first alto. Though St. Louis had always been noted for its fine trumpet players, it produced excellent, highly original alto men as well. Tab Smith, Don Stovall, Oliver Nelson, and Lunceford's own Ted Buckner come to mind, and one of the local talents in the early 1940s was Clyde Higgins. Higgins played in Eddie Randle's Blue Devils, one of the top dance bands in town. Miles Davis was in their trumpet section. The Blue Devils were an exceptionally clean band, which could play very nice and soft, and then suddenly shout it out. It was a tactic that worked well in band battles. "My father made you really work," said Eddie Randle Jr., the bandleader's son.

When Higgins auditioned, he astonished everybody. On *I'm Walking through Heaven with You*, even *Flight of the Jitterbug*, he played the most difficult charts effortlessly. Yet he did not get the job—because he was a small man, and his complexion was too dark. St. Louis musicians criticized this example of "discrimination against our own people." Considering Lunceford's well-known stance in racial matters, this case of bias is remarkable, to say the least.

Eugene Porter, who was a fair musician, but not in Higgins's class, was chosen instead. He had a lighter skin and was already a seasoned veteran. Porter had played with local bands in Chicago as early as 1928, and had gained experience working with the top bands of New Orleans and St. Louis. He had made his name in Don Redman's 1937 reed section. Gene Porter played all the saxophones, plus clarinet, flute, and violin. The tenor sax was his main instrument; he had a simple, "booting" style and a huge, dark, raw sound, not unlike Joe Thomas's. He could tell a story too. His clarinet was pure quicksilver, but it had a delightful New Orleans sonority in the bottom register. Omer Simeon had been his teacher—he, coincidentally, would replace Benny Waters in the band, a couple of months later. Porter toured with the Lunceford orchestra during the remainder of the summer of 1942.

Lunceford had no luck either when he asked trumpeter Miles Davis for his band. Davis, sixteen at the time, had to decline the offer, "because I was too young and my mother was having a fit."[25] This was the first time Davis heard and met Freddie Webster, and they remained friends. "My real main man during those first days was Freddie Webster," Miles Davis later stated. "He had a big, singing sound, a big warm, mellow sound. I used to try to play like him."[26]

In October nineteen thousand swing fans, who had paid from $1.10 to $2.50 a seat, gathered in New York's Madison Square Garden to watch the combined Lunceford, Harry James, and Casa Loma Bands play *Two O'Clock Jump*, *For Dancers Only*, and *I Got Rhythm*. *Down Beat* called it "a strict Superman kick." After the show, the orchestras swapped arrangements, and the James men were especially delighted with *For Dancers Only*, a score they had always wanted. The Harry James Orchestra was currently appearing at the Hotel Lincoln, and *Down Beat* reported that "there's still a roof over the place but nobody is taking bets on how long it will last with the James aggregation riding high every night on the Lunceford special."[27]

The level of performance stayed high, in spite of the massive walkout. Later that year, George Simon, *Metronome*'s critic, saw Lunceford at the Apollo, and remembered, "I was so thrilled that I sat through several shows, just as one would sit through several sets if the band were playing in a regular spot—something it was doing distressingly seldom during those days. Some more new members impressed me too: Freddy Webster, a brilliant young trumpeter, and Truck Parham, a stronger bassist than Mose Allen had ever been, though no bassist could match Mose for contagious spirit."[28]

Down Beat was the first to point out a gradual decline. Reviewing a November 1942 show at Chicago's Regal Theater, it said,

> The arrangements are the sore spot for us in the new setup, though. While they are musically close to perfection, there is too much emphasis on production and not enough on the real Lunceford style. Compare such things as the very productionish *Blues In The Night* and *Outskirts Of Town* with the fine old things like *Battle Axe, Annie Laurie, Cheatin' On Me, I'm Nuts About Screwy Music,* etc. The new arrangements have none of that trick rhythm, fine odd voicings, light rhythm and fast intricate sax passages, none of those wonderful fast dynamics. Yes, the band is a wonderful band but, doggone, we miss that fine old Lunceford that used to top our list.

By now Dan Grissom played first alto, and Joe Thomas was temporarily replaced by Teddy McRae, which did little to enhance the performance of the reeds. According to *Down Beat*, the saxes were at "their lowest ebb." McRae knew how to start a solo, "but following that, excitement and inspiration fall flat." This was partly compensated by the brass, "with the trumpets still the most amazing section in the business. How they can possibly stay so thoroughly high throughout the entire evening is beyond comprehension."[29]

Altoist Chauncey Jarrett led the reeds for a while, but in July 1943, after the leader himself had played alto in his orchestra, Lunceford finally settled for Kirtland Bradford. At the time, Kirt was working with Benny Carter's orchestra at the Casa Mañana in Culver City, and this time the saxophonist and Lunceford reached an agreement. Bradford, a little man with a big, gorgeous sound, joined the band with an attitude: here comes the world's greatest alto saxophonist. He climbed down when he had to play Willie's parts and his solos. Maybe he wasn't as lightning-fast as his predecessor, but after he had acquired a long, narrow custom-built mouthpiece with a very small chamber from a specialist in Tucson, Arizona, the reed section sounded just like in the old days. Well, almost: in the upper register, the new man had a more piercing sound. Bradford's features were lush ballads like *Alone Together* and *Meditation*, from Jules Massenet's opera *Thaïs*.

Yet, nobody could deny that by now, the orchestra had changed drastically. "We were people who really loved the band," Gerald Wilson stated in a warm voice.

> Snooky and I loved the Lunceford band. And he hired two wonderful trumpet players, but they didn't love the band. They didn't try to play like the Lunceford band played. They had come over from Earl Hines's band. Pee Wee Jackson was a good trumpet player, and you *know* what Freddie Webster was: a *beautiful* trumpet. But they were not meant for the Lunceford band. Their intonation was not of the Lunceford band. Their phrasing was not of the Lunceford band.

It was a view shared by Sy Oliver: the new men sometimes were better musicians than the ones they replaced, but they did not possess the spirit of the classic Lunceford organization. The original orchestra had been greater than the sum of its members. On the other hand, as with Ellington, "The Lunceford band got its individuality from the individual members," maintained Buddy DeFranco. "Each member of the band had input into that style. They created that style. The Lunceford band was more subtle than the others. It's almost impossible to put together a band now and make it sound like Lunceford. The individual's personality, putting their stamp and molding that. Each person in the band had something to say, and put it together, and gave it a character. But it was much more subtle."

The leader did his utmost to fill the open spaces in his orchestra with the best or most promising musicians available, but received harsh criticism nevertheless. One time, even Wilcox, his pianist, his main writer, and his confidant, was sure he'd get called up. The band was playing in Montreal, where Lunceford heard a seventeen-year-old piano prodigy called Oscar Peterson. The leader asked him to join his band, which, of course, was very tempting to the youngster. In an interview, the master pianist recalled,

"Well, it isn't that it didn't tempt me! I was ready to go, believe it or not, but I was still in school, my parents were a little concerned about me. [They] didn't think it was wise at that time to just go and burst into that environment."[30] When impresario Norman Granz approached him seven years later, Peterson was ready.

Though from early 1942 on the personnel was changing rapidly, the band managed to retain its flair and sense of showmanship. Dexter Gordon in another three years would be a major force on the tenor saxophone. He remembered how Freddie Webster, small in stature but gigantic as a balladeer, for dramatic effect pointed his trumpet toward the wings when he started his solo. Webster was an exceptional ballad player, sensitive yet strong, especially in the lower register of the horn. He was also able to make the whole trumpet section sparkle: he dominated it, and one could actually recognize a Webster-led trumpet group. Young trumpeters used to go to dances, or listed to Lunceford's broadcasts, just to hear Freddie Webster play *Yesterdays* or *Embraceable You*.

Sadly, Freddie Webster left but a small legacy on records, since he insisted his solos be paid by the bar. He knew what he was worth. When he was supposed to join the Basie band, in 1947, the leader asked him what his price was. "After you've paid the rest of those guys, you and I split 50–50!" was the answer.[31] Basie did not get along with this scheme. Webster would rather just jam someplace with friends than be on the road.

Like Webster, trumpeter Benny Bailey came from Cleveland, and "Webs" was his idol. Bailey did not hear Webster when the latter was with Lunceford. He first met him in Cleveland, before Webster moved to New York. Bailey was afraid to talk to him, because Freddie was seen as a god in Cleveland. "But he actually played for us; [it] was me and another trumpet player. We were playing in a guy's house, the guy's bedroom. Freddie just played, you know, ballads, with no accompaniment. And that's something I'll never forget."

Benny Bailey agreed that Webster was fastidious about jobs; he only worked high-paid jobs.

And everybody wanted him, because he had that hell of a sound. Even Dizzy's band, all the bands. When Dizzy was off one night, I think, and then he hired Freddie to play, take over the band, and he played this number *I Should Care*. Well, the story is that after he played that, Dizzy tore it up, he never played it again. It was a trumpet feature. And after Freddie played it, well, that was it. Well, you can imagine with Freddie, he'd just play the fucking melody, would be so beautiful, everybody would cry. That's what I did when I heard him. Man, it was so beautiful, I never heard something like that. He used to put perfume on his handkerchief when he went out to play, you know, to put him in a good mood. He was a very strange guy. He could touch his nose with his tongue. Yeah, he used to do that. They're still talking about Freddie Webster in Cleveland.

Freddie Webster made just a handful of studio recordings with the Lunceford band. In 1942 the American Federation of Musicians Unions, concerned with the rapidly growing number of jukeboxes in the country, and therefore afraid that musicians would lose jobs, called for a ban on recording. By 1939, slot machines had become responsible for the consumption of about thirty million records yearly, and the amounts continued to rise. In 1940 recording artists such as Artie Shaw had their singles in close to four hundred thousand jukeboxes nationwide. For a couple of years, the federation had been watching with suspicion the rise of "canned music," and considered the advance of the coin-operated machines a serious threat to live music. It was true: jukeboxes were popular with entrepreneurs because they were cheaper and less quarrelsome than musicians, and some were convinced their customers preferred the recorded music of Glenn Miller in good sound quality to live local combos. Apparently, James Petrillo, the unions' dictator, was deaf to the argument that entertainers needed the jukebox as an important means of promotion. *Metronome* criticized Petrillo and "the vain, the clumsy, the tyrannical attempt . . . to fight technological progress." The trade press argued that swing musicians were underrepresented at the AFM convention at which the recording ban was discussed and decided. The ban, observers argued, would mainly benefit the older, less mobile members, whose jobs were in radio and studio orchestras. The union leader even ignored President Roosevelt's personal plea to retain the music boxes as morale boosters. At the same time, the AFM felt that radio, too, had become a threat to live music, with its growing number of disc jockeys and their "platters" replacing house bands.

The recording ban went into effect on the first of August. Ironically, by this time the production of jukeboxes had come to a standstill. In December 1941, Donald M. Nelson, priorities director of the Office of Production Management, had ordered a 75 percent curtail on the manufacture of these machines, to be effective February 1, since materials and production capacity were needed for the war effort. In another two or three months, Rock-Ola was making preparations to start assembly lines for rifles and ammunition boxes, and Wurlitzer went into the production of aircraft and tank parts.[32]

The Lunceford band did not record commercially between July 14, 1942, and February 8, 1944. Its live recordings from air checks prove that the 1942–43 unit remained a violently swinging and perfectly balanced big band. These recordings showcase, for instance, trumpeter Russell Green's versatility. He had everything, was an exciting soloist, an expressive growler, an ear-splitting high-note man, and a sensitive, big-toned balladeer ("I could play a melody, make you cry"), second only to Freddie Webster. Kirtland Bradford developed into a distinguished alto stylist with a beautiful, voluptuous sound. Audience reactions indicate the band continued to be appreciated by substantial numbers of music and dance lovers.

In Dallas, John Carter and his friend Charles Moffett, as youngsters of thirteen and fourteen respectively, "saw the Lunceford band through the window of a big ballroom. That was the only time I saw them." Being minors, they were not allowed in places where liquor was being served. To Carter's mind, Jimmie Lunceford was

very fascinating. I can remember the beautiful uniforms, shiny horns, the vocal group on the side. Very impressive to me. That sticks on in my mind, that band and the Lucky Millinder band, which we saw in a package show, with the Ink Spots and Peg Leg Bates, and the Lucky Millinder band.

But the thing that was impressive to me was not the music so much, because I was not able at that point to digest what they were doing, and make the big decisions about was this good music. What it did was good to me, and I was impressed with it. Just the drama of it all, you know, the big sound of the shiny horns, the diamond rings, the musicians. This is a big impression on a thirteen-year-old. So I can remember . . . instances like that, seeing things, that made me know that I wanted to be a musician.

During the 1970s John Carter established his name as one of the leading clarinet players in jazz; his friend Charles Moffett gained fame as drummer with composer and alto player Ornette Coleman and other vanguard musicians.

Around the time Carter and Moffett first saw the Lunceford orchestra, in the spring of 1942, sax man Benny Waters joined the band. He already was a veteran with twenty years of experience in big bands. He always told everybody that to his mind, Lunceford's was the greatest band he ever worked with. In 1940–41 Waters had played in Claude Hopkins's orchestra: "He had a good band also. I worked with trumpeter Hot Lips Page; we had a nice little group also. I worked with Fletcher Henderson and Charlie Johnson. Charlie Johnson's band was better than all those bands, but not better than Jimmie." To his mind, Johnson and Lunceford were a match for each other—in the strictly musical sense. The latter's entertainment gave him the edge.

Until the end of his long and illustrious career, Benny Waters remained a first-rate soloist. In the Harlem Express, however, the distribution of solo spots was fixed. Among the reeds, Willie Smith and Joe Thomas had always been the most prominent soloists.

I was playing alto, clarinet, and tenor. Mostly alto, because I took Teddy Buckner's place, see. I had the whole three horns in one case, I was called "utility man." I didn't have many solos. Willie Smith took all the solos on alto. And Joe Thomas took *all* the solos on tenor. I said, "I can play tenor too." So I get to thinking, I'm gonna make an arrangement, on I don't know what. For me, a solo for me. I'm gonna give the trombones, the only guys I liked in the band, I give the trombones a little bit. Who else? I didn't give no saxophone, nobody but me, see. Jimmie ate it up, crazy about this arrangement. I played my little tenor solo, two choruses, and the coda in the end. [Waters hummed a cascade of notes, emphasizing them with gestures.] I could arrange. I made six of those arrangements with Charlie Johnson's band, released on Victor. Benny Carter made two and I made the rest.

In California we had a three-days-a-week program, radio program, each week, good for publicity. Jimmie used to play it often, every once a week he played it at least one time. Joe Thomas says, "Hey, I'm supposed to be the tenor saxophone player, why do you play so-and-so?" Jimmie told him that the man at the station asked for it. Joe never did know that I was listening to that. I don't know if the man requested at all, see—that's what Jimmie said. He had to say *something*, you know.

The same saxophonist recalled the problems with other bookers:

I was down in New Orleans, man, and Joe Glaser booked Louis Armstrong the same night in New Orleans as Jimmie Lunceford. It had to be sabotage. Because any two agents are not gonna book no two big stars in the same town at the same night if they have no idea of competition, huh? That's obvious. New Orleans is the home of Louis Armstrong. Okay, they both lost money. Jimmie lost money, and so did Louis. After that, they never did that again. The guy who booked Louis Armstrong thought he'd gonna wash Jimmie out. Not so. The crowd was split. No one had no big crowd.

We were drawing a minimum of two and three thousand people a night. And very often four to six thousand people. Dance halls. Only black people, yeah—no, no, not exactly: we worked in the Biltmore Hotel in Chicago. Generally the South, yeah, that's where the money is. Not in the North, always the money has been in the South. Negroes, they pay, you know.

Joe Houston added: "Lunceford was playing a lot of little houses. He was playing places that Duke and Basie didn't play. Yeah, the South, little places, you know. Duke and them stayed back East."

Ben Waters also remembered a completely different engagement at the plush Biltmore Hotel in Chicago, the only big white hotel he played while he was in the band.

The Biltmore was an old, classy establishment, on top of a hill. This is where Waters discovered that the band was in the possession of a completely "new" book. At the usual dances, the orchestra catered to a black clientele that was used to loud, riff-heavy stuff. But this big hotel required a different approach. "The only arrangement that we played at Negro dances [and played at the Biltmore] was *Margie*. And the only reason for that was because that wasn't so noisy." But other than that, and ballads like *Stardust*, it was more than 50 percent muted brass and clarinets. Waters thought it was typical for Jimmie, the former schoolteacher, to be prepared for occasions such as this one.

In the meantime, wartime challenges kept mounting. The transportation difficulties were getting more complicated by the month, and in January 1943 manager Oxley prophesied that the "wartime emergency will knock out grade B and C names by summer."[33]

It wasn't just the "little houses" that Lunceford played, though. From the engagement at the New York Paramount Theater on, in August–September of 1939, the band could regularly be spotted on the country's major stages. A 1943 performance at Loew's State Theater in New York, for instance, prompted *Down Beat* to comment: "The show that Lunceford put on at the State was by no means inferior. Like most stage presentations, it concentrated on over-voluble sax solos, flashy drumming, and time-tested tunes, all guaranteed to keep the kids in the upper balcony rocking. But beyond that, it was as solid an hour of entertainment as you're apt to hear in several months' coverage of theaters." *Down Beat*'s reviewer did acknowledge, of course, the influence of the draft: "Any leader who manages to keep a fixed band for as long as two weeks is a lucky leader indeed," but he urged his readers to "take a listen to what Jimmie's doing with his present set-up, because it ain't bad, Jack, it ain't bad."[34]

At the time the review was published, Jimmy Crawford, tired of the constant traveling and dissatisfied with the lack of new arrangements, had left the band. He had given his notice in February 1943, and stayed another ten days to help his successor Joe Marshall get used to the particulars the job required. Nineteen-year-old Marshall had been with Milt Larkin's band. After a short-lived stint at the shipyards, Crawford learned that Specs Powell was leaving tenor man Ben Webster's group, which was working on New York's Fifty-second Street. Specs was hired by the CBS studios (probably the first black drummer there), so Crawford got his job. After a decade and a half of powerhouse chopping, this was quite an adjustment: Webster had a quartet, and it took Jimmy Crawford a full week to fit in with the combo.[35]

Ironically, though by now hundreds of thousands of young Americans were sent overseas, fighting, as wartime propaganda used to phrase it, for democracy and against racial abuse, the situation for black people at home remained unchanged. (It is ironic that segregation also was standard in the army and navy.) Over the years, Lunceford had learned to deal with flagrant racism. The leader fought segregation as much as he could, and he wasn't willing to buckle down. In June 1943 the band played a successful engagement at the Trianon Ballroom in Los Angeles. Every night, parts of the show were broadcast live by station KHJ and the Mutual Network. The Basie band was appearing elsewhere in town, and Lunceford had invited Snooky Young, who now led Basie's trumpet section, to drop by. The doorman, however, refused to admit Snooky, who had brought along his colleague Harry Edison. Lunceford was called, and he explained that both musicians were his guests, all to no avail. He was advised that he did not have a say, since he only *worked* at the place. The band was hired for six weeks, but Lunceford went to the manager and told him he was willing to work for the rest of the week and then would pull out. "An unprecedented move," reported *Billboard* in awe.[36]

{14}

DOWNHILL—AND UP

They'd fill the hall; they still had the drawing power.
—Joe Wilder

When Russell "Shakey" Green joined the trumpet section in late 1943, the average salary was ninety-seven dollars a week. As he was used to more than two hundred dollars a week, working in the pit and, occasionally, on the stage of the Paradise Theater in Detroit, he considered this "no money." Lunceford had come down to the Paradise and, peeking from behind a curtain, had checked him out. The bandleader was looking for a replacement for Paul Webster. Lunceford pointed Green out to Lanky Bowman, the leader of the pit band. "As a matter of fact when he hired me, he hadn't heard my solo work. He heard my tone quality. I could solo and I enjoyed soloing, and he was very glad to hear that," recalled the trumpeter.[1] At first, Green had been reluctant. "I didn't wanna go. I was making good money. Then also, I did want a little reputation, too, and that's all where you could get it." He decided that it would be wise to make some sacrifices. But first he had to come to terms about the money, and he bargained with Lunceford. "I said, 'I have an idea.' I said, '$155 a week.' Work or no work, I still get paid."

The bandleader and his new first trumpeter agreed, but pretty soon a new argument developed about the costs of a uniform. "I said, 'I didn't come in this band to buy uniforms. So you want a uniform—*you* pay for it.' So that tells you I was a stickler in business, man. So he told me one day— he gave me a two-year contract—and he said, he called me Youngster, he said, 'Youngster, I like a businessman.' That tells you. On the stage I did my debut with a piece called *Boulevard of Broken Dreams*. It should have been recorded."

Green proved to be an iron-jawed leader of the trumpets. Another new face in the trumpet section was Bob Mitchell, who sang and who could play the high notes just as Green could. A little later, Paul Webster came back, followed by Trummy Young. Trummy no longer traveled with the orchestra, but just played a recording session.

For the wartime recording ban had been lifted. The biggest labels, RCA and Columbia, resisted the union until November 1944, but over a year earlier, Decca had signed a contract with the AFM that committed the company to include a fixed fee on all recordings sold, to be put in a fund for unemployed musicians. The band's first 78 rpm single that Decca put out was the two-sider *Back Door Stuff*. *Down Beat* was elated:

> It's great to hear this famous organization again, especially after such a long dry spell. Maybe a good many of the original men are gone, maybe Sy Oliver is an irreplaceable loss, but Jimmie still sounds better than most of the bands of today. This disc has just about everything a Lunceford fan could ask, a tricky arrangement well played and some solo passages of lasting interest. An instrumental is doubly welcome in this day of the vocalist, and this is it![2]

The orchestra continued to play occasional band battles. The most devastating one, by all accounts, was the battle against the new and still unknown Billy Eckstine Orchestra, in the summer of 1944 at the Brooklyn Armory in New York. Lunceford at the time was still strong, but somehow his band didn't have its day. The Eckstine crew, on the other hand, consisted of young and eager musicians, and was hip to the bone. The first big band to attract attention with the new bebop music, it featured such luminaries as Dizzy Gillespie, Charlie Parker, and Lucky Thompson. Ironically, Eckstine relied heavily on Tadd Dameron's charts, who had come to New York a little over two years earlier with Lunceford and had been working as the latter's staff arranger. Dameron's knack for peculiar, atmospheric voicings, using for instance the baritone saxophone as the lead voice, had developed during his time with Lunceford.

Jimmie Lunceford opened the dance. Naturally, the audience stood and danced at his side of the stage. Eckstine followed and the people moved over to the other side. But as the evening progressed, the audience stopped shifting from band to band and stuck with Billy Eckstine's side. It became a victory for Mr. B, and a victory for the new music as well. Eckstine remembered the event: "It's long since over, and I can say, now, that there was no comparison. It was like night and day. That band was asked to really play . . . a battle between the old and the new. And let me tell you, it was a night to remember! You never heard a sound like that in *any* big unit." Lunceford's trumpet star Freddie Webster wrote a letter to a friend, simply stating, "B and his band, life," and in very small letters, "Lunceford and us, death."[3]

In December, Jimmie Lunceford made a bold decision when he hired Bill Darnell, a white singer, for a recording session. Darnell had worked with the Red Nichols and Bob Chester bands, and though he had sung with Edgar Hayes as early as in 1937, seven years later it was still a rarity to find a white vocalist with a black band. The other way around was more accepted socially, as exemplified by George "Bon Bon" Tunnell with Jan Savitt's Top Hatters, Billie Holiday with Artie Shaw, or June Richmond with Jimmy Dorsey. Likewise, Lunceford's earlier decision to add white men to his roster of arrangers had been considered unusual in the music trade. Though Fletcher Henderson had worked with white arrangers, Lunceford's decision to put works by Will Hudson and, later, Roger Segure, Bud Estes, and Lonnie Wilfong in his book raised a few eyebrows.

The band remained a top-flight swing orchestra. Critic Bob Kreider rated the reeds "the best section in the band. It is one of the best saxophone sections one can hear in dance bands. Pushed by the two veterans Joe Thomas and Earl Carruthers it generates an astonishing swing, inspiring the rest of the orchestra."[4]

Lunceford's orchestra worked highly efficiently. A standard recording session took three hours. In this three-hour span, a band or a vocal act was supposed to record four tunes. The early Basie band needed four to five hours for four sides: the musicians "dressed" their head arrangements on the spot, which naturally required more time. In two days in February 1944, the Harlem Express recorded a total of twenty titles for World Transcriptions. And on October 3, 1945, the orchestra went into NBC Studio 8-H in New York and under the supervision of George T. Simon recorded six tunes—in just one hour![5] They were released on V-Discs, twelve-inch 78 rpm records that were shipped to U.S. Army and Navy bases all over the world.

Wartime restrictions and the rise of the vocalists resulted in the band business going down during the last year of the war. Lunceford and Oxley, manager of the Harlem Express for twelve prosperous years, parted ways. Harold Oxley had signed pianist and singer Joe Liggins and His Honeydrippers, who had hit the jackpot with their eponymous hit. Oxley knew the road and he knew the ropes. He set up office in Hollywood and in due time built up an impressive roster of rhythm-and-blues pioneers, including T-Bone Walker, Wynonie "Mr. Blues" Harris, Cecil Gant, aka "The G.I. Sing-Sation," Big Jay McNeely, Fats Domino, former Lunceford singer Dan Grissom, and Liggins. Oxley in October 1946 signed a deal with Ben Bart's newly formed Universal Attractions in New York. From then on, Universal Attractions represented Oxley's artists in the East, while the latter booked Bart's talent on the West Coast. Harold Oxley continued to manage black talent until his death in 1952, at the age of fifty-four. His clients always spoke of him as an honest and loyal man, who had no hidden agendas.[6]

As we have noted, around 1946 the band lost some of its characteristic dynamics, its individuality, its signature style. The frequent changes in personnel from 1942 on, and its growth from twelve pieces in 1933 to seventeen, ten years later, partly accounted for this change. The orchestra's lineup continued to be in flux: tenorist Ernest Purce, who had joined in late 1943, was replaced by William Horner, and Earl Hardy and James Williams left the trombone section, while Russell Bowles returned.

During the 1940s the style of the band gradually shifted toward the emerging rhythm-and-blues music. It was not alone in developing this way, since other black orchestras such as the ones led by Lucky Millinder, Erskine Hawkins, and Buddy Johnson all started to feature blues tunes, honking saxophones, and shouters or blues crooners. Lunceford began playing songs popularized by Louis Jordan, the most influential rhythm-and-blues musician of the time, plus covers of tunes made famous by Tiny Bradshaw, Helen Humes, Slim Gaillard, Nat Cole, and Jack McVea.

Lunceford's 1945 version of *The Honeydripper,* originally by Joe Liggins, warrants special mention. It turned out to be Lunceford's last big hit, climbing to the number one slot of the Harlem Hit Parade, and becoming one of the ten best-selling records in the United States.

For a while in 1947, the trumpet section consisted of Paul Webster, Reunald Jones, Joe Wilder, Bob Mitchell, and Russell Green. "In fact," Green recalled, "with our band Jimmie made a statement: that was the best brass section he ever had." "Oh yeah, there's no question about it," Joe Wilder agreed, who had replaced Chiefty Scott—whose main task had been to copy parts. "I came in the band to play lead, and Reunald Jones was also there, was a very reliable lead player. It was really a nice trumpet section." It was, no doubt, one of the few trumpet sections in the business whose members were all good soloists and good lead men.

"He was just one beautiful man, Jimmie was," summarized Green.

> There was a pride there, yes. In other words, to play with Jimmie Lunceford gave you a lot of pride, because of the way that he conducted his business and his band. You couldn't come in there half-shy. You couldn't just be anybody, you had to be straight, or he wouldn't accept you. When he did accept you, you could say to yourself, I must be all right. He was that kind of a person. Oh, everything I can say about Jimmie was just beautiful. It was a pleasure to be with him.

Lunceford carefully selected his singers. Dan Grissom left the organization in late 1942, while the band played an engagement at the Royal Theater in Baltimore, and then, after having thought it over, he came back and stayed until July 1943.[7] In the meantime, Lunceford had hired two new singers: Ted Smith, who had worked in Chicago, in the Grand Terrace floorshow, and Bob Mitchell, who also played trumpet, and stayed in the band until after the leader had passed. Crooner Duke Groner was next, but he, too, stayed for just a couple of months.

In early 1944 Oxley hired Claude Trenier, who had started singing at Alabama State College, in Montgomery, to become the band's new balladeer. The bandleader used to introduce him as "The Sepia Sinatra." One year later twin brother Clifford joined, and together they recorded the song *Buzz-Buzz-Buzz.* Toward the end of that year they left the organization and formed The Treniers, an electrifying rhythm-and-blues act that eventually incorporated five jumping and singing brothers, and became a big attraction in Las Vegas and Atlantic City.

Though the Lunceford style during the 1940s roughly developed parallel to the rhythm-and-blues trend, the orchestra continued to play more adventurous charts as well. In 1945 the band recorded its first boppish arrangement, written by Wilcox. At the time, Decca decided not to issue *I've Got Those Carolina Blues*—because it was too modern? The company did not record bebop artists. Though it is a regular blues ballad, sung by Nick Brooks, in *Carolina Blues* the trumpets play typical bebop licks. The orchestra had always featured arrangements that used to attract young musicians and music fans. But by the mid-1940s, other big bands, attuned to the new music, were vying for attention. The most successful ones were led by Stan Kenton, Billy Eckstine, and Woody Herman, but other adventurous orchestras, such as Dizzy Gillespie's and Boyd Raeburn's, did not do nearly as well. While in the 1930s aspiring musicians and young jazz fans had dug Duke and Lunceford, the new generation now was flocking to hear Gillespie and Kenton.

In late 1945 and 1946 the band suffered from a decrease in bookings and, consequently, a series of layoffs. This was partly due to the postwar economic depression. During the boom caused by the war effort, ballroom operators were able to pay just about any price a booker asked. When the defense contracts ran out and consequently the bottom of the entertainment business fell out, bandleaders were faced with the dilemma of either decreasing their groups in size or lowering their prices—or disbanding altogether. Salaries that had peaked during the war now shrank to prewar levels, or even less. In some cases the large booking offices had to advance money to pay the musicians and transportation costs, and orchestras accordingly began to accumulate heavy debts. When these bands failed to pay back the advances, the agencies started to demand shares of the organizations as security. The big band scene that had been so healthy just one or two years before, now turned out to be very shaky.

For a while the Jimmie Lunceford band functioned as a telephone orchestra, which meant that whenever a gig turned up, the agency started calling the musicians. Gradually more substitutes, not familiar with the book, began to move in. This resulted in rather uninspired performances and recordings during 1946 and into 1947. *Down Beat*, in a review of Majestic 1077 (the tunes *Shut Out* and *Them Who Has-Gets*) noted, "Lunceford desperately needs a rhythm section that plays lighter than his present one."[8]

Band Leaders and Radio Review, another trade magazine, wrote in February 1947 that the musicians excelled in monotony. Joe Wilder elaborated,

> He was still building. There were a couple of people who were let go, not long after I was in the band. I had nothing to do with it, but I mean, there were some people who Jimmie just felt weren't quite up to what he wanted, and they were released. When Jimmie died in 1947, the band had been pretty well consolidated then. I mean, he wasn't changing personnel. The band was really beginning to click, and everybody was happy.

Billy Shaw of the William Morris Agency had become the band's new business guide in 1945, and managed to secure dance dates at the most prominent university campuses in the country. *Down Beat* heralded the news with the headline "Lunceford Stock Goes Up, Up, Up." As early as 1933, the band had become an attraction at white colleges across the nation. Under the new management, the orchestra played at Massachusetts Institute of Technology, William and Mary College, Cornell, Duke, Purdue, the University of Texas, Clemson, Kansas State, and Notre Dame. It was, again, the first black band to play at this latter university's spring prom, in May 1946. (Tommy Dorsey, Glenn Miller, Artie Shaw, and Guy Lombardo had supplied the music at earlier spring proms.)[9] Among college students, Jimmie's recording of *The Honeydripper* was a favorite, a nationwide survey concluded. The band really put its mark that year: no other dance orchestra had played so many gala proms at top colleges and universities.

Though he probably welcomed this apparently expanding market, the leader developed mixed feelings about his new management. Joe Wilder recalled that Jimmie expected more work, but soon found out that his new agency sold him to roughly the same venues where he had been playing anyway for the last ten or twelve years. Another disadvantage was that sometimes Billy Shaw would sell the orchestra to a dance hall on the condition that the hall would also take a different, lesser-known act, on a different date (usually one or two weeks before the major attraction). This happened to many top acts, and it was not advantageous to them, to be used as battering rams. Wilder explained, "So he didn't like that. He had an agreement by which they could call off the contractual agreement that they had made, if either or the other was dissatisfied with it. That was the end of that. Didn't last long."

The popularity of the 1946–47 band could still be called substantial: "They'd fill the hall; they still had the drawing power," Joe Wilder remembered. The *New York Age* called the band's three-week engagement at the Club Riviera, in St. Louis, "sensational."[10]

In March 1946, the orchestra secured a promising engagement as the house band of the Royal Roost, a spacious chicken restaurant at 1674 Broadway, between West Forty-seventh and Forty-eighth Streets in Manhattan. On opening night one of the worst blizzards that New York had seen in years hit the city. Fewer than fifty people showed up—on a Saturday night, so that was the end of that. A couple of weeks later, the Roost organized a bebop session on a Tuesday night, with Fats Navarro, Miles Davis, Allen Eager, Dexter Gordon, Charlie Parker, and Tadd Dameron all taking turns. It attracted seven hundred people, and the restaurant was jam-packed. Manager Ralph Watkins even had to call the cops.[11] After that legendary night, the Roost became a regular haven for the modernists, and was advertised as The House that Bop Built.

"It did go down some," commented trombonist Al Cobbs on the band's quality at the time. In mid-1946 he had switched from Louis Armstrong's big band to the Luncefordeans. "When I joined the band, it had gone quite a ways down. And then, when different ones of us came back into the band, then it started building up again. It was trumpeter Joe Wilder from Philadelphia to join and a few others, a couple of trombone players. Al Grey'd come in."

Cobbs stressed the fact that during this period, not enough new quality arrangements were coming in. More and more, the musicians had to be content with tried-and-true warhorses and inferior new compositions. Lunceford's new recordings of *Margie* and *Four or Five Times* for Majestic had caused a stir in the business: one wasn't supposed to rerecord one's previous hits when one changed labels. But according to a new union rule, artists were entitled to record new versions of their old songs under a new contract, provided five years had elapsed since the original recording. Dusting off the old tunes can be seen as a deliberate, but futile attempt to restore the band's luck. By coincidence, the "new" version of *Margie* hit the market at the same time that Decca put out a reissue of the 1938 original. *Down Beat* was quick to note the differences.

> 1937 [actually, 1938] Lunceford was light, swinging and possessed of a powerful back beat. 1947 Lunceford is heavy, with bad intonation and an uncertain attack.

John Hammond, now Majestic recording director, used to tell me that the old Lunceford band was a machine that never played good jazz. Mebbe so, but I wish there were more machines around like that today. There has never been a band that played more complicated arrangements with better taste and sense of humor. Tommy Dorsey has been trying to copy it for eight years and still doesn't have it down.[12]

Generally speaking, the new arrangements lacked original ideas and common goals. Consequently, the Lunceford style was watered down. Cobbs pointed out how the situation in the recording studios began to change:

See, what happened in that era, when we go to record, we go down the studio. The man say, "Okay, Jimmie, what you got?" "Okay, I got this number, I got that number." "Good, let's record it." Now those were numbers that we had played on the road, and numbers that we had gotten any good response to. New numbers, you know what I mean. So there we knew just what the public liked, what they wanted, and we're goin' record that.

And then one time, we came in, and same thing: "Well, what you got?" "Well, we got this, we got that." "Good," he said, "but now here try this." Now we looked at that and we went, "What is this?" Now you see, what was creeping into the thing was politics. So now here is somebody that his son wrote something, and he owns a record company. Or he's got this X amount of money, you know what I mean, so he gives it to the company, said, "Get this recorded, it's my son's tune." And we looked at it and . . . we know it's nothing. So there we are trying to make an arrangement on this nothing. And consequently the music business went down. And then a lot of people came into the business that didn't know A from B.

Al Cobbs must have been referring to the tune *Water Faucet,* recorded in May 1947 for Majestic. Based on the familiar *I Got Rhythm* changes, it featured a Slim Gaillard–inspired lyric that was only mildly funny. The record label lists Bennett and Tepper as the composers; Bennett may or may not have been George J. Bennett, who in the late 1940s as A&R (Artists and Repertoire) man was involved in a string of small independent record firms.

For a while, Lunceford even considered retiring altogether. It was rumored that Joe Thomas was to take over leadership. But gradually the leader managed to restore the quality of the orchestra, when new musicians strengthened the band.

Joe Wilder, dissatisfied with the conditions in Lionel Hampton's orchestra ("I unfortunately didn't get along very well with him, and Gladys, she was even worse"), was hired as lead and solo trumpeter, and recalled that he once took a trip with his new boss that stood engraved in his memory over half a century later.

The first time I ever flew in an airplane, it was with him. Wilcox was the co-pilot, and I was the only passenger, because a lot of the guys were afraid to fly. I had never flown in my life, and I flew from New York to Boston with him. That was the Cessna, was a five-passenger Cessna. And you know, when we left here, we were up in West-chester Airport, and the sky overhead was cloudy. You couldn't see anything. I had always thought, when you see the clouds, the over-laying clouds, that that was it. From where that started up into the everywhere, you know. That's how silly I was about it, I mean, I was just that naive. And when we took off, and we flew in the clouds for a while, and all of a sudden we came through the clouds and there was the sky as blue as it could be, the sun was shining bright. And I remembered what I said to myself: this is the closest I have ever been to God. I mean, not as a joke, I really felt seriously that this was something special.

And when we came back, we came back to land at Westchester Airport, and we were coming in for the landing, and all of a sudden Wilcox started screaming: "Jimmie, pull up, pull up, pull up!" And when he pulled up, the wheels that were down for landing had just touched the tops of some trees. This was how close we probably came to see our last moments there. But he pulled it up. He pulled it up, and we went around and came in and made a perfect landing, But—*ough!* You didn't have a chance to be afraid, because it was happening so quickly.

Al Grey joined the brass that same year, 1946, and recalled the personnel. He pointed out that Kirtland Bradford became known as Mustapha Hashim after he converted to the Islamic faith. By now, there were two white faces in the trombone section: Porky Cohen, who had worked with Charlie Barnet, and Freddy Zito, from Stan Kenton's orchestra. This was another first for Jimmie Lunceford. No other traveling black band had ever included white musicians. Back in 1937 Benny Carter had fronted a racially mixed big band, but that had been in Europe.

A little later that same year Al Cobbs joined the trombones, and after him, Al Brown and Buster Scott, who would change his name to Abdul Hamid. In the summer of 1947 Elmer Crumbley returned, in the last stage of the original Lunceford organization. Grey admitted he did not pay close attention to Elmer Crumbley at the time, who handled the plunger mute. Al had taken Trummy's chair, and was supposed to just re-create his predecessor's solos as faithfully as possible. Later, of course, Grey would develop into one of the foremost plunger specialists in jazz. He pointed out that the main reason for the band's decline lay in the constant shifting in the personnel. It was not easy to regain the orchestra's original level of performance. "See, well, in the industry it just started back and recurred. So it's all over—it's hard-ground floors to get into."

As noted before, the late 1940s was a difficult time for big bands. Many name bands broke up, if only temporarily. Quite often, bandleaders started new outfits within a few months, with less expensive—and less experienced—musicians. The promoters and booking agencies had started to take away the star soloists and the vocal attractions from the large orchestras and were busy crafting solo careers. On top of that, crime waves stopped audiences from going out late at night. Television started to rear its head, and urban renewal programs drove part of the population into suburbia and deprived the inner cities of their entertainment strips. So the bands lost their dancers. The East Coast was hit harder than the middle part of the country. In the Midwest and the Southwest, a modest big band dance scene existed well into the 1960s.

Against the tide, Lunceford was rebuilding the band, and observers noticed it was coming back strong. The reception it got at theaters and dances was stimulating, but it took some time before the orchestra had regained its former power, cohesion, and brilliance. Al Cobbs explained,

> The band was coming back up again, but it had dropped quite a bit. I don't know whether it was arrangement-wise. You see, the music that Lunceford had, it called for a certain caliber of musicians. Now most—a lot of—musicians can play right on the beat, see what I mean? Like studio musicians, symphony musicians. But the way you

had to time with Lunceford, made you fall out your chair backward, you know. But that's the way they played it. [The trombonist demonstrated this with a typical lick:] *Bit-bit-bit-tiee.* So that means that everything was way back. And a lot of musicians just could not get that particular feeling. But then after we brought in these other musicians, and they began to get the feeling, then it begin to come back up.

George Duvivier had no problems with the rhythmic requirements. After his discharge from the army, in 1945, Lunceford hired him—primarily as an arranger, not as a bass player. He witnessed the demise of the band first-hand, but stated that by 1947 "that band was absolutely roaring!"[13]

Alas, no recorded broadcasts from the last months have come to light. Judging from the material waxed by the 1948 band, however, it then definitely was a spirited band that took no prisoners. This final edition was comparable to the 1945 ensemble in every way.

In the meantime, the orchestra's influence on other big bands hardly diminished. Count Basie, who had started out in a completely different, loose, four-four style, playing mostly "head" riffs and emphasizing solos over ensemble, during the 1940s gradually moved into a fuller, more compact approach that resembled Lunceford's. For a while, Gerald Wilson worked in Basie's band, and he also contributed to the book. He revealed that the Count definitely wanted an ensemble sound comparable to Lunceford's. So Wilson stayed at Basie's home for nine weeks, with Catherine Basie and their child Diane. Basie wanted to make sure he got that work done. He did not want anybody bothering Gerald. "And he wanted those ensembles like Lunceford played, you know, played real soft—and then shout it out."

For the Jimmie Lunceford Orchestra the future looked bright again. One eyewitness confirmed that the band played better than it had done during the preceding years. "From the first bars on, one feels the orchestra is full of self-confidence." He added that the leader was aware that his ensemble in time would carry his name to the very top once more, and concluded that the present band must be reckoned to be among the best black orchestras currently on the road.[14] Lunceford had the idea to gather most of the men from his mid-1930s orchestra and once again build a top outfit.

For the fall, the agency planned a European tour—again. In fact, this was an idea the bandleader had been toying with since VE Day. Jimmie had heard about the triumphant concerts Don Redman's orchestra had played overseas, and his ensemble wasn't even a regular band: it had been hastily assembled in New York, just prior to the tour. Europe, after years of *Marschmusik,* was craving for good solid American jazz. In Europe, Lunceford's name apparently had lost little of its glory: the English Decca company was busy reissuing many of his old successes.

Jimmie's head buzzed with ideas. Early in 1946, he had gotten his commercial pilot's license, which entitled him to fly airliners. He had also invested in a new coast-to-coast airline, run by former Army Air Force pilots and mechanics.[15] In March of that year, he had flown his band across Texas in a C-47 Skytrain, playing one-nighters. The aircraft was on loan from the AAF, in exchange for a couple of free concerts at Army camps and USO canteens.[16]

From the vast surplus dumps of the air force one could obtain an airworthy and fully equipped C-47 at a bargain price. Lunceford was already in the middle of negotiations for the purchase of a Skytrain (better known as Dakota) for touring purposes. He was going to fly his band to Europe, by way of Canada, Greenland, and Iceland. Jimmie Lunceford and the Harlem Express were going to tour the Old World in style—in their own airplane.

{15}

SUNSET IN SEASIDE

What do you mean, you can't serve us?!
—Jimmie Lunceford

Outside, the blazing sun soaked up the colors till the Coast Ranges looked like a faded 8 mm movie. Inside, twenty men sat sprawled in their seats. It was a quiet, uneventful bus trip. That Saturday, July 12, 1947, they had boarded in Portland. From Portland to Seaside was less than one hundred miles, so this hop was a piece of cake. The only sound was the steady buzz of the air-conditioning, a noise one never completely got used to, least of all if one was a musician with sensitive ears. Consequently, some of the men had put in earplugs while trying to catch some sleep. Others dug the wild landscape with the snow-capped mountaintops speeding across the windows, or sat reading. A novel or a comic book here, a sports magazine or *Metronome* there. Two men tried their hands at crosswords puzzles. In the back, in front of the costume trunks, a young musician was eagerly drinking in advice from a seasoned veteran on matters of embouchure and intonation.

230

The hostile reaction at a Portland restaurant, the other day, was still on their minds. At the restaurant across the street from the ballroom the band had been refused service. Some six decades later, Joe Wilder still had a clear picture of what had happened.

We just went in and took seats. There were other customers in there. Of course, they thought it was great they were in the same place with the Lunceford band. We sat there for about, at least ten minutes, fifteen, twenty minutes, and none of the waitresses or the people working came anywhere near us. So we said, "Can we have some service or something?" And the woman who owned the place said, "We don't serve people." So we said, "Well, wait a minute, this is Oregon, you're supposed to serve anybody, anywhere." In the meantime we didn't leave. We just said, "We'll wait," you know. And she went to the phone and she called the cops. She told them she had a bunch of blacks in there who were threatening her or something, and these guys came. There were four cops and they came in in their usual fashion, with their hands resting on the pistols—they hadn't picked them out of the holsters—wanting to know what was going on. "What did they do?" and whatever. They were less than friendly when they first arrived—like, if anybody makes a move, we gonna shoot him. I said, "This is Oregon. Aren't they supposed to serve people in any place, in these public restaurants, in that state?" And they did have a law that said they had to. We said, "Well, she refuses to serve us." And some of the people who were patrons in the restaurant were saying, "Those fellows haven't done anything at all. They just came in and asked to be served." And the cops then turned their anger towards the woman. So the guy in charge said to the woman, "If you're not going to serve, you'll have to be closed." And she said, "Well, I'm closed." And she went over and pulled the curtain down that was on the door, and on this side that she pulled down it said *Closed*. That was on the street side. And that was it—she didn't serve us and we didn't eat in there.

As a matter of fact, we had spent the whole intermission in there arguing with this idiot to see if we could get some food. But nothing ever happened. I don't even remember the name of the restaurant, unfortunately—and I don't know whether it's unfortunate; we all tried to erase it from our memory. It was such an unpleasant experience. The people for whom we were playing in the ballroom, they were nice people, you know. It was just that the woman who owned the restaurant was . . . . And we went back and finished playing the dance.

The musicians were surprised by the restaurant owner's reaction. The band frequently played the South, where "you could in some ways avoid that. But then when you got to places like Oregon, where you always thought that they were too far removed from that kind of a thing, it was kind of a little devastating when you ran into it," said Wilder. "Even when I think of it now, I get very annoyed by it, because it came as a shock."

Russell Green recalled that, probably due to the hot weather, the band's breakfast had been rather flimsy as well. "Before we left Portland, Oregon, I had gone down to the corner and picked up a pint of ice cream and he [Lunceford] asked me, he said, 'Youngster, where'd you get the ice cream.' I said, 'Down at the corner. You want me to get you some?' He said, 'Yes.' So I ran down and found him a pint of ice cream."[1]

In the bus, Wilcox, who had served with the organization since 1929, when the Chickasaw Syncopators school orchestra was transformed into a professional unit, had swapped seats with trombone player Al Cobbs. Cobbs was now seated next to the leader. Last month the former had written a couple of new arrangements for the band, some originals and some on standards. He had taught himself to write in 1935 by copying Lunceford charts from the records, and consequently when he joined the band, he already knew most of the arrangements. "I sat on the book the whole time I was with the band," he used to boast later.[2]

The boss wanted to talk business. "Cobbs, when we leave Seaside, and when we'll come back to Los Angeles, we'll record five of your numbers." "Wow, five of my tunes," the trombonist repeated under his breath, blushing in spite of himself. "My first songs out." Five years earlier, he had written one or two things for the Les Hite Orchestra, but even though this band had to repeat his *Three Bones* three times when it appeared at the Apollo Theater, nothing was recorded.

As he gazed out the window, they were entering the outskirts of Seaside, where they were scheduled for the next show of this short northwestern tour that had started one week ago in Portland. Soon they would be back in Los Angeles, their second home, after New York. As a rule, the band would spend six to sixteen weeks annually on the West Coast. Some of the musicians had their regular boarding rooms in Watts, the black section of Los Angeles.

It was around five o'clock in the afternoon when the bus slowly ground to a halt at 304 Broadway, on the corner of East Downing, in front of a big wooden building that looked like a barn. A rectangular sign, accentuated by a green neon tube, said "DANCE." This was the Bungalow, the dance hall where the Jimmie Lunceford Orchestra was scheduled to play that night. The place housed a medium-sized skating-rink under a thirty-five-foot decorated ceiling. During the weekends the rink was converted into a ballroom, with a capacity of about five hundred dancers. There were no tables or any other furniture; the place was just one big dance floor. It was always crowded, and because of the high ceiling, the acoustics were pretty bad, but this was remedied to some extent by the PA system. Outside, in a corner, Fabre's Siberian Ice Cream stand served soft ice, a novelty for Seaside. Fabre's had a counter on the dance hall side as well, so music patrons could be served ice cream, soda, and sandwiches.

To the local teenagers, the Bungalow was heaven, and in fact it was one of the top locations on the West Coast. In the summer, during the early years of the swing craze, the twelve-piece Johnny Busch Band from Oregon State College had been the resident dance orchestra. Nowadays name bands played the Bungalow every Saturday night, all through the year, which meant the locals did not have to drive to Portland to see their favorites. It was not just the white bands that worked at the Seaside dance hall. Older dancers still remembered the show that Les Hite and his Famous Cotton Club Orchestra and Revue had staged in 1936. Lionel Hampton had brought his then brand-new big band to the Bungalow, Cab Calloway and Duke Ellington had played here, Fats Waller, and, more recently, Ernie Fields. Isham Jones, Glen Gray and the Casa Loma Band, Jack Teagarden, Jan Savitt and his Top Hatters, Tommy Tucker, Phil Harris, Ted Fio Rito, Georgie Auld, Gus Arnheim, all the top bands played the Bungalow. The dancers' parents could have told you that they had taken lessons with Mr. and Mrs. Glenn Oswald's Dancing Class at the Bungalow, thirty years earlier. The dance hall was the heart of the community: a large part of the yearly Fourth of July celebration took place at the rink, including the introduction of the candidates for the Miss Northwest election, the Queen's Ball, and the Carnival Dance. The echoes of the festivities were still reverberating in the hall, so to speak, this Saturday, July 12.

"Ooh, this leg of mine is aching," Lunceford moaned as he rose. "I hope nothing's wrong with it." "Maybe you'd better see a doctor," Al Cobbs suggested, a little concerned. "You know, you've been on the road now for how long? Twenty years? Well, you never missed a single gig as far as I know." "Uh-huh, soon as we get back to L.A. Maybe. We'll see." Al Cobbs vaguely remembered that a few days ago the boss had also complained that he was not feeling well. What he did not know was that Lunceford had been suffering from high blood pressure for a while. A doctor friend had helped him reduce it to get his pilot's license renewed.

He didn't tell anybody, but the leader was not just worrying about his own health. His mother, sixty-four, had just been hospitalized at the Cleveland Clinic Hospital. The bandleader had arranged it. This was the second time she had to go to the clinic to be examined. Jimmie was very close to his parents. Even though because of his busy itinerary he rarely saw them, he always kept contact. The last time he had spent time with his family had been last October, when the band had played a one-nighter at Warren, Ohio's Robins Theater. He already had made arrangements to go visit his mother on August 1.

One by one the musicians left the bus, squeezing their eyes against the sun, flexing their muscles and shaking their legs after the two-hour drive, lighting a cigarette. Jock Carruthers did a little impromptu dance.

Seaside was exactly what its name implied, a resort town crammed with bars and restaurants, where young people from the surrounding region gathered during the summer months, to swim, sunbathe, drink, date, and generally, to raise hell. The streets were full of tourists. We might draw a pretty nice crowd tonight, Al thought.

A couple of musicians were wandering off, looking for the manager of the hall. The short tour had been successful: the band had drawn once again very well. The audiences in the ballrooms on this northwestern tour, however, had consisted almost exclusively of whites. Therefore, the musicians had called a few friends and relatives in Portland and Seattle to come over. Trombone player Al Grey had found the manager, Charles Niemi. "Sir, would you be so kind as to putting a couple of our friends on the guest list," he had asked. The man had looked at him disapprovingly, muttering that he was trying to run a business, not a playground, and that he would consider taking up the matter with the bandleader. Grey had come across this kind of reaction before—but that had been in the South.

The musicians soon learned that this was to be a segregated dance, something they resented very much, as it was completely contrary to their policy. There were hardly any black families living in Seaside, anyway. Jimmie Lunceford's name was so big his management as a rule was able to be fastidious about the venues where the band was scheduled to play. "We tried to avoid it," explained Joe Wilder. "Jimmie tried to avoid it. Jimmie was a very dignified man. Very well educated, and a very proud man. He demanded that the guys in the band deport themselves in a certain way, and people respected us for it. I don't know that he was able to enforce it completely, but he let the people for whom we were working know that he would be on the side of integrating the dances." Russell Green was even more specific: "We did demand that. We did a lot for the integration of races, things a lot of people wouldn't dream. But we wouldn't accept anything, so he wasn't forced to pay us. A voluntary thing the members of the band went along with."[3]

In the meantime, the valet had started hauling the band's stands and instruments into the ballroom. At a different entrance, people were coming up to buy tickets for the dance. Admission was $1.50. The last time a big name band had played the Bungalow, May 11, the tickets had been $2.00. But that dance had featured Les Brown's Band of Renown, and they were still riding high on their 1945 million-seller *Sentimental Journey*. The regular admission price at the Bungalow was $1.50.

Today, some of the customers were black, so the people who ran the ballroom called the valet, Lunceford's valet, and offered him fifty dollars if he would stand out front and discourage the black couples who came to purchase tickets from buying, "by telling them, 'Hey,' you know, a buddy-buddy kind of a thing, 'They don't want to sell tickets to people like us,' or something like this," Joe Wilder explained. Of course, the valet told the band, and the first reaction of several musicians, including first trumpeter Wilder, was, "Let's not play."

What happened next is unclear. The band had become hungry, and according to Joe Wilder, the musicians had to content themselves with strawberry pie, "which none of us had eaten before. Rhubarb pie was popular, but this was a strawberry pie and it was exceptionally good. And we just went crazy, I mean, most of us ate at least two slices of it and Jimmie did likewise. And I think he caught what I thought was indigestion. And then he ended up with a headache."

Truck Parham remembered it differently. He thought the band members ate at a restaurant at 10 Downing, close to the Bungalow. In Parham's mind's eye, the musicians strolled to this restaurant, only to be offended by the staff. "Can't serve you," the waitress bluntly answered when they were seated and asked for the menu. "We don't have no food." The leader got angry. To the musicians across the table it looked scary: they never saw their leader lose his temper. He never even raised his voice. As a rule, their employer was a model of self-control, every inch a gentleman. But now he pounded the table with his fists and cursed. He was furious. Truck Parham remembered that the leader cried, "What the hell do you mean, you can't serve us?!" Lunceford explained that his band was scheduled to play at the Bungalow that night. He repeated, "What do you mean, you can't serve us? Call the manager!"

The waitress panicked. She hurried to the back and consulted the manager. After a minute or two she came back and said that the men could order after all. The guys ordered hamburgers. "No, I'm sorry," she said, "but we don't have nothing but beef sandwiches, hot beef sandwiches." The grumbling musicians ordered beef sandwiches, with the exception of Truck Parham. Truck had seen this movie before.

Well, I'd had that experience with Roy Eldridge, and it taught me. We were on our way from Chicago to New York. And we had stopped in Pennsylvania. Used to have to go over the mountains, now the Mellon Highway goes through. Any ten miles you'd see a sign: Eat at Bill's Place! We were in cars, with Roy. We just left the Three Deuces, on our way to New York, to play the Savoy Ballroom. And we stopped there, we ordered, you know. "We don't have it!" People eating around. "No, we don't have it." We all had soup, since they didn't wanna serve us. We go about five miles down the road, everybody had to stop the car and get out and shit all over the road, man. Vomited. That taught me: never eat in a place where they refuse to serve you. Never insist that they serve you.

Parham didn't eat the food. "The rest of the band ate it. Lunceford had it. He's sitting right here, and I'm sitting over here."

After the makeshift meal, the men returned to the hall and the band-leader again complained—this time to Russell Green—that he was tired and wasn't feeling well. He told his trumpeter that he wanted to take a little rest on a bench. Russell said, "Okay, I'm going to do the same thing. Why don't you see a doctor, have him take a look at you. He might give you a shot, and maybe you better go to a little booster shop or something like that." Lunceford answered, "I'll be all right, I gotta go across the street here and autograph some records at this record place." The trumpeter shrugged and said, "Well, all right then," citing the title of one of their famous themes.

"There was something peculiar about it," Joe Wilder added, "because there was some headache powder, it used to come in little packages, and he had a severe headache or something. And he had taken a couple of these BC powders, I think they called them, to ward off the headache that he had. He took a double dose."

After half an hour the bandleader got up and went across the street, to Callahan's Radio and Record Shop at 411 Broadway, next to the Broadway Cafe. Brass players Joe Wilder and Al Cobbs accompanied him. They were just strolling, enjoying the fine weather. "The owner of the record shop had asked him if he would come over early in the afternoon, or even in the morning, and autograph some albums, for some of his customers," remembered Wilder. "And that's what Jimmie did. He was there autographing albums and suddenly he spun around and keeled over and fell."

At the Bungalow, the rest of the band had assembled outside, beside the bus, put on their "bop glasses," and proceeded to take it easy. A couple of them had started shooting dice. Truck Parham and Omer Simeon stood looking and laughing and cheered them on. Pretty soon, the men were shooting quite seriously, hollering and betting and urging one another to put in more money. Russell Green was the cashier. "With Jimmie Lunceford's orchestra I had a business," he said in a low conspiratory voice. "And guess what it was . . . hahahaha! Loan shark. That's it. See, I made enough money out in California to take care of my bills and everything, and I was sending money all the time to my wife."

Omer Simeon, the veteran in the band, who had played with Jelly Roll Morton's Red Hot Peppers even before the establishment of the Chickasaw Syncopators, had the nasty habit of cracking his knuckles. He was standing there, looking and laughing and pulling, *crack, crack, crack*. And just when some of the guys started to get annoyed with the sound, a little black kid came dashing in. "Uh-huh," he panted, and after he had caught his breath, he cried, "One of your drum beaters got sick downtown. Record store, drum beater! The drum beater got sick down that store." "Drum beater— who?" wondered Parham. The guys looked around, Joe Marshall, their "drum beater" was sitting right there. "Jimmie, he's the only one down," said Joe. Cobbs and Wilder had returned in the meantime. No, they hadn't noticed anything unusual. The leader had been signing records and they had gone back to the Bungalow after he had warned them it was about time to get ready for the dance.

It was getting close to six-thirty. The dance was supposed to start at seven, and the band members went to the dressing room to put on their uniforms, still wondering what the little fellow had meant. It was agreed that Omer Simeon would go over to the store to see if anything was wrong. At a quarter to seven the orchestra was seated, waiting for their leader to tune up and check the balance. Ten to seven, no leader. He was never late, ever. "Maybe he's out there in the back, hassling with the manager over the guest list," a musician suggested.

After ten or fifteen minutes Simeon returned, looking concerned. "He's sick," he reported. "He was laying down there on the floor, water out his mouth. I don't know what happened. They told me he had asked for a glass of water, and then he fell down and went into convulsions and passed out. I stayed down there until the ambulance came to take him to the hospital." According to the shop's owners, Lunceford was about to autograph a wall they reserved for names of musical celebrities, when they noticed that he looked weak and ill. The next moment, Jimmie fainted and fell. The customers in the store thought the bandleader had just lost his balance, but it didn't take long before they realized it looked like a heart attack. In the meantime and without telling anybody, an anxious Eddie Rosenberg, the band's manager, ran to the record store to see what had happened.

When he returned, he did not say a word about Lunceford's condition, but began arguing with the promoter, who wanted to start the dance. For thirty or forty minutes the worried musicians refused to begin, claiming they wanted to make sure nothing serious had happened. In addition, there still was the question of the segregation on the floor. Rosenberg, backed by Wilcox, persuaded the musicians, "Well, you know, if Jimmie were here, he probably wouldn't play either. But you know, the contract will be null and void unless we play and fulfill the obligations of the contract." Finally the management gave in and decided to admit the black customers. Joe Wilder recalled, "And so with that we finally decided, okay, we'll play whatever time is left of the dancing. And that's what we did." Reluctantly, the musicians pulled out the music. In the meantime, the seventeen-piece Van Armitage Band from Portland, hired as the intermission attraction, did the honors and played a half-hour set of its custom arrangements and stocks.

The Lunceford band always opened with a flag-waver, to break the ice, so to speak. During the 1930s the introduction usually had been the fast-paced *Jazznocracy*, their first hit and their flamboyant signature tune, or *For Dancers Only*, their showpiece. This night, however, after a few bars of their current theme song, *Uptown Blues*, the band burst into a frantic *Jeep Rhythm*, a Horace Henderson arrangement, based upon the well-known Gershwin piece *I Got Rhythm*. In the original 1944 studio recording, the fast two-beat intro had sounded a little awkward, but by now the band had tackled the tune often, and everything sounded more relaxed, yet very exciting. Russell Green growled, Joe Thomas roared, the band shouted, and the capacity crowd responded with enthusiastic screams and whistles. Outside, behind the big-screened windows, left open on hot nights like this one, underage kids with their parents and youngsters who could not afford the admission price were looking on and shouted their approval as well. When you were standing there, it was as if you were inside the hall. A constant stream of old and newer tunes followed. The orchestra entertained and enthralled its audience, as it had done for twenty years. The joint, as Fats Waller used to put it so eloquently, was really jumpin'.

Come intermission—still no Jimmie. Rosenberg had not uttered a single word yet. The musicians filed back to their dressing room, quite worried by now. "Hey Kirt," Truck called, "you got a nickel? Go on and call and see how Jimmie is, man." Kirtland Bradford went across the dance floor to the phone. After a few minutes he returned. The small, dignified-looking man with the shiny processed hair was white as a sheet. He looked horrified and had to brace himself. "Oh my God, something is terribly wrong," gasped Truck as Kirt stumbled into the room. And as everybody looked on and listened in disbelief, Kirt told them the news. "Well, I called the hospital," his voice was almost choking, "I talked to the nurse, I said, 'I just wanna know how the fellow is who took sick at the record store.' She said, 'Oh, Jimmie Lunceford, he's dead. He just died a few minutes ago, at 8:45.'" The saxophonist clearly was in a shock. He did not seem to understand his own words, and repeated, "Can you imagine the way she talked to me: 'Oh, Jimmie Lunceford, he's dead.'"[4]

Everybody was shattered. For a moment, nobody said a word. Realizing that the manager had not told them about Jimmie's condition, some of the musicians were ready to hit him. Truck got so mad he had to be restrained from jumping on Eddie Rosenberg. "They almost had to nail him down," said Wilder. "He was so disgusted with it. The rest of us were, too." "This must be a joke, man, this is sick," somebody whispered. It wasn't.

James Melvin Lunceford, known to the black community as the leader of one of the nation's best-loved swing bands, winner of both *Orchestra World*'s and *Metronome*'s black popularity polls, in addition to New York Paramount Theater's polls, icon of African American culture, model and inspiration for countless bandleaders and musicians, had passed.[5] He had turned forty-five only last month.

It was hard to understand. Here was a perfectly healthy man, who had boxed, run track, and played softball, who flew his own airplanes, who last year had gotten his commercial license. Joe Wilder emphasized, "The week that he died, he was in L.A., and he had to go in for his—every hundred hours that you've flown, or something, you're supposed to go in and have a physical. And he had the physical in Los Angeles, and was given a clean bill of health." As a matter of fact, the leader had flown his Cessna to the West Coast for this particular tour. Furthermore, Lunceford was a teetotaler with no demons haunting him. "It was one of the saddest days in my life," Joe Wilder said.

With tears streaming down their faces, the musicians made it back to the stage. Joe Thomas announced the leader's death and proceeded to lead the orchestra through the second set. "So we started playing but everybody just broke down and cried like babies," recalled Russell Green. "We got on the stage to do our job and I don't think we had ever sounded as good as we sounded that night because we were actually playing for him—and because of those people that they didn't want to come in at first."[6] But it wasn't long before the performance turned into near disaster. One musician after the other could be heard shouting, "Man, I gotta jump off, I gotta go to the bathroom." "Everybody went lined up getting in the restroom, vomiting and shitting," Parham remembered. "I'm the only one that didn't get sick. Botulism, you know."

It was, no doubt, a very confusing and emotional night, but remarkably, the band managed to finish the dance. Significantly, Parham was not the only one who did not get sick. Joe Wilder was a vegetarian at the time, and he did not experience the effects of the beef sandwiches. He thought the BC powder Lunceford had taken earlier might have had something to do with his sudden death. But Wilder, too, remembered that some of the band members got sick later, during the dance. Russell Green, on the other hand, believed that Lunceford hadn't had any food at all. Green may not have been present when the rest of the band had its hot beef sandwiches. At any rate, Lunceford was not feeling well once the orchestra arrived at the ballroom. If he did already have blood pressure problems—as had come to light when he was about to renew his flying license—then the effect of consuming the contaminated meat could have given his system the fatal extra blow. The convulsions noted by Simeon, who saw Lunceford lying in the record store, are consistent with the neurological effects of toxic botulism (produced by *Clostridium botulinium,* a microbe). Importantly, Lunceford suffered these symptoms within the time frame typical for botulism infections. (It should be noted that in the 1940s the mortality rate for botulism still was about 60 percent.)

To add injustice to incredibility, July 12 happened to be payday. Lunceford had carried the payroll in his pocket, and owed his management a certain amount of money. But mysteriously, the money had vanished. "All he had on him," said Carruthers, "was a couple of $100 bills autographed by Joe Louis and Glenn Miller."[7] Depressingly, the band had to play an extra seven performances before it had covered the debt plus the fare back to New York. The original tour schedule had called for a total of twelve more one-nighters. Joe Wilder recalled the musicians's feelings:

All of us, we just wanted to cancel the rest of the tour and come home. Eddie had us continue to play some of the dances between the time that we learned of Jimmie's death and his funeral. He said, well, it would be better if we'd finish out the engagements that we had on our way back to New York, and we would probably get back in time for Jimmie's funeral. And it was unfortunate, because what we should have done when we finished that night in Seaside, we should have packed up and come back to New York, cancel the other jobs. We did not. So we didn't get back to New York until after his funeral was over. It was all over and done with. None of us were able to attend the funeral or anything. It was kind of cruel, actually. And in fact it was an affront to Jimmie's stature for us to do it. There were a lot of ill feelings about that. It was very sad. . . . That was a sad day for me, I remember it well. Like the end of the world, couldn't believe it. I was very fond of Jimmie. He was awfully kind to me, a nice man. And I think that at that time he and his wife were separated. I mean, they were still living in the same house, and I'm not sure, I don't know if they were in the process of getting ready to get a divorce or something. But there was some friction there, and it kind of put a damper on the funeral service itself, from what I heard.

At the request of Crystal Lunceford, Lunceford's body was flown to New York City on July 14 for the funeral service. The leader was buried in Memphis, at Elmwood Cemetery, where the Lunceford family owned a plot.

Eddie Rosenberg had announced a memorial concert for Wednesday night at Rockaway Beach, Oregon. After that performance, the Jimmie Lunceford Orchestra was to be permanently disbanded. But this was before the road manager had learned of the financial problems, caused by the disappearance of the money.

"Heart attack," read the verdict of County Coroner William R. Thompson, who had examined the body in the Seaside Hughes-Ransom mortuary, adding that there was no suspicion of foul play in connection with Lunceford's death. On arrival at the Seaside Hospital, Lunceford had been pronounced dead of unknown causes. An autopsy performed by Dr. Alton Alderman disclosed that the bandleader had died of "coronary occlusion, due to Thrombosis of anterior coronary artery, due to Arteriosclerosis." (In other words, Lunceford had died of a heart attack, caused by a blockage, resulting from a clot in one of the arteries of the heart, which was preceded by hardening of the arteries.) The physician concluded that the death was due to natural causes.[8]

Pretty soon rumors started to drift around the music community. A plane crash: he did mess up his Bellanca, didn't he? Hadn't he always prophesied, jokingly, of course, that he would die in an airplane, and "there won't be enough pieces to pick up." Others maintained it was a cerebral hemorrhage. Still others knew it had been a case of eating too many stuffed sweet peppers. Writer Dave Dexter stated that Lunceford "ate a double portion of chili con carne in a small Oregon restaurant while on tour and died almost immediately."[9] In their book *Heart and Soul*, Bob Merlis and Davin Seay more recently suggested that the bandleader was shot by a gangster.

Before long, the myth surrounding Lunceford's death was in full swing. Yet it is not too far-fetched to maintain that Jimmie Lunceford was poisoned for being the proud black man that he was.

{16}

THE BOUNCE GOES ON—FOR A WHILE

The music still sounds good, and it still inspires me.
—Horace Silver

After Jimmie's death, Crystal Tulli Lunceford moved from 162 South Road, White Plains, New York, where the couple had been living during the last five years, to Nashville, where she got a teaching assignment. She remarried and became Crystal Tulli Haines. Crystal ended up in Florida. Joe Wilder commented, "You know, we never got really to know her. I think I met her once."

The management decided to keep the band together for the time being, if only to play the dates already scheduled for the current tour. Rosenberg appointed Joe Thomas as temporary front man—but Wilcox called the numbers. They were to work in Seattle, July 14 and 15, 1947, then on to Victoria and Bremerton and back to their West Coast headquarters in Los Angeles.[1] But when the group returned to New York, it was ready to disband. The critics agreed: it was no use trying to keep the Jimmie Lunceford Orchestra alive without its leader. However, according to the *Defender*, when Eddie Wilcox entered his home, "He found the living room looking like Manhattan's main post office." Hundreds of letters, telegrams, and petitions littered the floor, all urging him to continue with the band. Members of the Jimmie Lunceford Fan Club in South Carolina had pooled their savings and traveled to New York, with the same plea.[2]

For a moment, the Gale Agency considered trombonist and arranger Blip Tompkins for a new front man, but he preferred to go back to Houston to start his own band, which in the event turned out to be very successful. Russell Green was another one who quit. "When Jimmie died, Wilcox, they want to cut my pay, give me a hard time. I said, 'I don't need you.' Eddie Rosenberg, who was our road manager, begged me to try to come back with the band. I told them no. I wasn't about to give in because I got too many things I can do. The band was still good, but see how long it lasted after that? About two years."

Old hands Ed Wilcox, Earl Carruthers, and Joe Thomas jointly became the new leaders of the Lunceford orchestra, but this arrangement did not work, and they decided to divide the work between Thomas and Wilcox. Since Joe Thomas had been the star soloist, he would front the band, and Wilcox would do the arranging and handle the behind-scenes business, such as the contacts with the agency. In actual practice, Wilcox also did most of the cueing. The band was billed as the Jimmie Lunceford Orchestra under the Direction of Eddie Wilcox and Joe Thomas.

Gale, Wilcox, and Crystal Tulli agreed that the widow would get fifty dollars a week for the use of the Lunceford name. After six months, this figure would rise to seventy-five dollars a week, again for six months. Then after that first year, Crystal was to receive five thousand dollars a year for the next two years, and from then on the figure would be seventy-five hundred dollars yearly.[3]

Any doubts anybody still might have had about the viability of the enterprise were erased when the newly assembled band on August 29 made its gala debut at the recently refurbished Apollo Theater. Billy Eckstine, who had turned over his own, groundbreaking orchestra recently to trumpeter King Kolax—the singer had lent his ear to certain people in the business who told him this was better for his career—was the headliner of the show. The sophisticated dancing team of Honi Coles and Cholly Atkins plus comedian Pigmeat Markham were also on the bill. It was standing room only for two full weeks. A beaming Wilcox commented dryly that there simply was not enough room left for any "jazz experts," because of the amount of fans at the Apollo during these two weeks.[4] Such was their success that the band was asked back in December, this time on a bill with the Eddie Vinson Orchestra and the vocal group the Ravens. The *Age* wrote, "Indeed it could be truthfully said that the new and fresher ideas inserted into the band's arrangements by the capable youngsters have improved the band immeasurably."[5]

Four months later, when the band played the Royal Roost, *Down Beat* noted that the brass had been cut back from eight to six pieces, and that the band had revived a lot of the 1930s book.

> Not in years has the Lunceford band sounded as much as the band we knew ten to fifteen years ago, the one that gained the late maestro such wide acclaim. Any Lunceford fan is due for a nostalgic treat in witnessing the resurrection of this great organization. The trunks have been opened and the old arrangements restored to their rightful places on the music racks. It is unfortunate that this wasn't done by Jimmie himself before he passed on.

The magazine praised the men for their courage at "challenging the famous old Lunceford band for supremacy in its own field," but noticed "some rough edges in the outfit." The report ended with a sigh: "We've been too long without this kind of music in the flesh."[6]

Reviewing the single *Whatcha Gonna Do/One for the Book* (Manor 1120) later that year, *Down Beat*'s critic remarked, "*Do* bears the closest resemblance to the old band with a score that could easily have been knocked out by Sy Oliver, a sax section that sounds like Willie Smith was sparking it, and a four-four rhythm section that is probably one of the last of the swing band–styled sections."[7]

In 1948 the orchestra embarked on a four-month "Lunceford Memorial Dance" tour. It was organized jointly by Eddie Rosenberg and Billy Shaw, and all profits, except musicians's salaries, were set apart for Mrs. Lunceford. Russell Green, who was about to leave for Atlantic City to hook up with Count Basie's orchestra, dropped the Basie job and rejoined the Wilcox-Thomas aggregation. Young tenor man Billy Mitchell, who later would make his name as a soloist with the Basie band, was hired to battle Joe Thomas. Tenor battles, after the furor created by Lionel Hampton's orchestra, by now were considered a must. A problem was, the bulk of the old book was written for one tenor. Mitchell got the job because he was able to transpose the book at sight. There was no time to write a second tenor part. "That ain't hard. After you look at it two or three times, you memorize it—and after you play it night after night for two months," the saxophonist laughed. "You don't even look at the music anymore, you know."

"We went to Memphis, Tennessee where he [Lunceford] was buried and I remember the press came out," said Green. "We took pictures at the grave site and we proceeded along with our tour."[8]

Sitting next to the originals, next to Joe Thomas, Omer Simeon, and Jock Carruthers was a blessing, Billy Mitchell thought. "You know, those were great names when I was a kid. I was twenty-one years old, but I was in awe. But you know, *the spirit* was gone," the former kid musician explained.

> Everybody knew that it was not working. People weren't coming to see. I tell you something: people don't come out to see the band if the bandleader is not there. Count Basie had a heart attack about 1976, '77. I was teaching at the University of Michigan at the time. And they were playing at this little town, in Flint, Michigan. So one of the teachers said, "Come on, let's go see Basie." I said, "Oh, of course, you know I'm gonna see them, but you know Basie is not there." I say, "I'm just going and see the fellows, because you know that night ain't gonna be anybody there." He say, "Oh yes," he says, "when the band comes here, everybody turns out, regardless of whether Count's there." *Not so.*

Al Grey was in the band a little longer and remembered it differently. "We stayed, and the band was tremendous and we had a drawing power. Lunceford was popular enough where they thought maybe the people wouldn't come, because he's not there any longer. Which was different: it was seldom the people didn't come."

The Wilcox-Thomas orchestra recorded for Manor Records, a small New York firm. One of the best-sellers in the Manor catalog was *Saxology*. Wryly, its writer, Al Cobbs, admitted that this was the tune that taught him the nature of the music business, because he learned later that he should have received considerably more than the forty dollars he got from Manor. His reward should have been closer to four thousand dollars: the tune sold very well. "And then, what the man did, he closed up shop, closed the business down, and went down South and bought an orange grove. With my money," Cobbs explained. After so many years, the trombonist-turned-composer could laugh about his misfortune.

Wilcox's idea was to revamp the orchestra and eventually reduce it in size, signing young, energetic musicians and writing new material. Then, in October 1948, problems arose about the percentages. Al Grey explained,

> It was formed to be a cooperative band. And everybody took a salary breakdown. Wherever we would play they were supposed to pay us percentages, all [the money] over so many [musicians]. And they run into a lot of percentages cuts. But we got into political difficulties; a dispute started over the finances. It was designated that we go on tour, and when we get back to New York, we would count whatever percentage they had, and you'd get your money. But it never took place. They kept shamming with that, so the guys got very tired of it. And up one day, five of them left. That's the end of it. This mother's been counting in New York, with percentage and everything, and no one's got a penny out of it. Band broke up, couldn't survive.

At this point, it is not clear what exactly happened. Probably because of contractual and organizational reasons, the co-leadership remained nominally intact for another four or five months. But before it had run out, Joe Thomas effectively left the fold, taking with him Bob Mitchell and Johnny Grimes, trumpet, Dickie Harris, trombone, George Duvivier, bass, and Joe Marshall, drums, and formed an octet, the Jimmie Lunceford All-Stars.

Mitchell and Thomas handled the vocals, and with the addition of Grimes and Harris were able to harmonize in the best Sy Oliver tradition. The right to use the Lunceford name had been granted them by Crystal Tulli, who was now suing Wilcox and his agency, Gale, who apparently had failed to adhere to their original contract with her. One year later Crystal won the ten-thousand-dollar suit for the use of her late husband's name by the ghost band.

George Duvivier, Lonnie Wilfong, Joe Benjamin, Ruben Phillips, and Al Mockler started writing the Lunceford All-Stars' book. Their booking office, Ben Bart's Universal Attractions, arranged tours through the Northeast: Washington, DC, New York, New Jersey, Philadelphia. Meanwhile, Universal was putting pressure on Thomas to adjust himself to the fast-growing rhythm-and-blues market. The All-Stars went on tour with singer

Dinah Washington[9] and recorded several exciting jump tunes for the King label, of which *Lavender Coffin* and *Tearin' Hair* attracted some attention, which was enough to keep the band on the road for six months. Alto saxophone screamer Earl Bostic, who was riding the rhythm-and-blues waves at the time, complained to his office about the competition Joe Thomas and the Lunceford All-Stars had given him. He instructed his agency to never again book him opposite the Lunceford men. Ironically, Willie Smith's flights of fancy on the alto had been Bostic's main inspiration when the latter was just starting out.

However, this raw, simple rhythm-and-blues stuff was not where the band's heart was. Duvivier wrote a couple of ballads, beautifully scored for the five horns. Stylistically, they were a mix of Lunceford, Ellington, and Kenton.

During the early 1950s, Joe Thomas expanded his combo to big band size, named the Jimmie Lunceford Band under the Direction of Joe Thomas. The Lunceford-Thomas orchestra drew well for about six months. Between 1952 and 1954 Thomas experienced a series of bad bookings, and the departure of pianist George Rhodes was the final blow. The leader dissolved the band and retreated to Kansas City, where his in-laws owned property and ran a funeral parlor. There was no lack of lavender coffins. He ended up making a good living off the dead, very seldom getting his tenor out of its case. His business card read "Watkins Brothers Funeral Parlor," and on the other side "Music for All Occasions."

In 1957 Thomas was one of the alumni who recorded the album *Jimmie Lunceford in Hi-Fi* for Capitol, along with Trummy Young, Willie Smith, and Dan Grissom. Billy May, who had always been an admirer (to his mind, the Lunceford band was "the greatest all-around outfit ever"), ran the session. Since everybody assumed the original book was lost, May had painstakingly re-created the arrangements from the original recordings. "It was really a labor of love and I enjoyed doing it," he told writer Stanley Dance. Billy May was notorious for arriving at recording dates with the scores still wet—or unfinished. This time, everything was well prepared. May had the arrangements and the timing letter-perfect, down to the original almost imperceptible violin solo by Al Norris in *My Blue Heaven,* which was re-created by Benny Gill. Willie Smith played baritone sax, next to his familiar alto—for the first time since 1939. Trumpeters Pete Candoli and Ollie Mitchell proved to be worthy successors to Tommy Stevenson and

Paul Webster. But it was the original Lunceford singers who put a final stamp of authenticity on this project.

After the session, the musicians gathered in a bar below the Capitol studio. The session leader remembered his conversation with Thomas:

> Joe: I can't wait till those records come out!
> Billy: Why?
> Joe: You really got the music down right well. But when I get the records I'm going to take them down in my cellar and get the arrangements out.
> Billy: What! You mean you've got those old arrangements?
> Joe: Yes, I got 'em.[10]

Six years after this recording session producer George Wein had Thomas flown in for a sensational guest appearance with the Basie band at the Newport Jazz Festival, where they played *Cheatin' on Me* and *For Dancers Only* for a crowd of ten thousand, who showed their appreciation in no uncertain terms. "He is a genuine jazz singer and he remains—though he is now an undertaker—one of the best graduates of Coleman Hawkins's academy," noted critic Whitney Balliett.

It was not before the late 1970s that Joe Thomas was rediscovered by producer Robert Sunenblick. The tenor man, affectionately known as Old Gal during his Lunceford days, made his first long-playing album for the lo-fi Uptown label. The production of *Raw Meat* was rather sloppy, and one could hear that Thomas's tenor had been gathering dust for a couple of decades. The sequel *Blowin' In from K.C.* offered more interesting material: arranger Don Sickler had restored Duvivier's old charts from 1949–51, and original sidemen Dickie Harris, Johnny Grimes, and Duvivier were on hand, and played as if no thirty years had elapsed since the days of the All-Stars. George Duvivier had dropped a Frank Sinatra gig in order to be able to make this session.[11]

Thomas's end was not pleasant. Joe Wilder related,

> I saw Joe before he died, I guess six months, almost a year. He was here in New Jersey in a recording session, and he was so sick, I didn't even recognize him. I walked into the studio, and I knew it was supposed to be with him, and some of the other musicians were

there. I saw this frail fellow sitting on a chair, and I sort of looked at him, near him and I didn't even . . . And then I suddenly started: that's Joe Thomas! And I walked over and said hello to him. And I couldn't *believe* that he was that frail. You know, he used to be very hefty, and I would say that [now] Joe must have weighed about, maybe 130 pounds or something like that. He was quite small. And he could only play, maybe at the most four bars at a time, and they were trying to put together a piece that he was playing on. It was almost impossible; he finally gave up. It was never released. He could not play enough to finish a whole chorus of anything.

You know, he had a mishap, somebody hit him in the face with a brick, in some club he was playing. And it wasn't a provocation, it was just somebody who was envious of him, and just decided he would try to harm him. Knocked out some of his teeth, and he had a bridge in, and, oh, it was horrible. And I think from that he became ill and psychologically just went down the drain. He was a nice man, good-hearted guy.

Aaron Bell is well known for his long stint as Duke Ellington's bass player. But as a youngster, he idolized Lunceford's band. When he studied at Xavier University in New Orleans, Lunceford played the Blue Note, and Aaron went down to hear him. "I loved that band! I think I listened to them more than Duke, in that period."

Bell was delighted when one of his first jobs with a name band turned out to be with the Lunceford ghost orchestra, directed by Wilcox. In November 1948 the latter had been forced to drop Lunceford's name from the title, and from then on billed it as the Eddie Wilcox Orchestra. Bell traveled and recorded with the band. New York remained its home base. "Our main job was the Savoy Ballroom. That was our steady job. We stayed there, I think we did maybe twenty, thirty weeks a year right there." The Apollo Theater also remained a regular venue for the band. And then there were the one-nighters, mainly in the northeastern part of the country. At the time when the bassist joined, the Lunceford ghost orchestra still contained several of the original members, such as Paul Webster, Elmer Crumbley, Russell Bowles, Omer Simeon, and of course Wilcox. The leader tried to keep the big band working, but times had become even leaner for large jazz ensembles. He experienced long periods of inactivity, and cut the ensemble down to twelve pieces. The last known advertisement for the band appeared in the *New York Amsterdam News* of Saturday, April 7, 1951, announcing the Third Annual Dance of the Fur Union Veterans, at the City Center Casino, 135 West Fifty-fifth Street.[12]

Two months later Edwin accepted a job as producer and arranger for Derby Records. By now, Lunceford veterans Paul Webster, Reunald Jones, Russell Bowles (after twenty-one years!), Omer Simeon, and Al Norris had left. Elmer Crumbley was the only one from the old fold who worked with Wilcox right until the end. Backing vocalists Bette McLaurin and Sunny Gale, the orchestra managed to score two final hits: *The Masquerade Is Over* and *The Wheel of Fortune*. However, in these tunes the band played backgrounds only. In instrumentals such as the thundering *Shuffle Express* the orchestra showed it could still hold its own against Buddy Johnson or any other blazing rhythm-and-blues big band. During the last stage of the band Wilcox had two powerful and highly original tenor stylists in Lucky Thompson and Freddy Mitchell, but this did not save the enterprise. The hits did help the leader to pay off the debts his orchestra had accumulated. Still later, he abandoned the band altogether and started working with trios and set up shop as a vocal coach.

Lunceford's style continued to inspire other bandleaders, perhaps on an even larger scale than it had done when he was still alive, though the popularity of big band music in general gradually declined. Sonny Burke, George Williams, Sonny Dunham, Georgie Auld, and Ray Anthony—before he jumped on the bandwagon of his former boss Glenn Miller—not to mention studio orchestras all over the world, continued the tradition of tight, dynamic, swinging arrangements, and screaming trumpets, played with great precision.

During the middle and late 1940s, trumpeter Randy Brooks led an underrated big band that sounded just like Lunceford turned on to bebop. A little later, Billy May fronted a successful orchestra, with as trademark slurring saxophones, that clearly caricatured Lunceford's reeds, to a comical effect. Willie Smith was the leader of his saxophone section.

In the 1980s John Lewis, pianist, composer, and longtime leader of the Modern Jazz Quartet, attempted to re-create Lunceford's music. At the time he was leading the American Jazz Orchestra, a band made up of top musicians, dedicated to perform America's orchestral jazz music. Lewis later confided that he had had no trouble re-creating other swing compositions, including works by Benny Carter, Duke Ellington, and Fletcher Henderson, but that Lunceford was way beyond their ability. The American Jazz Orchestra's weakness lay in its rhythm section, which "simply does not have the necessary snap at these tempos, and too often abandons Lunceford's trademark bounce entirely for a more modernized and, in this context, nondescript swing," reviewer Bob Blumenthal judged.[13] Writer Gary Giddins was involved with the project, and his verdict was, "Lunceford is ultimately untouchable."[14]

Clarinetist Buddy DeFranco was positive: "I do know that all the bands that I can remember, trying to emulate Lunceford, were not successful. They simulated. You know, you can tell. Glenn Miller—the live thing wasn't there. They did a good job, playing together, and executing the notes and all that. It's hard, though, to put your finger on it."

Most of the Harlem Express's influence came in an indirect, more diffuse way: its standard of precision, the power and range of its brass, the richness of its harmonies, the originality of the scores, full of little surprises, those were qualities that were disseminated in many big bands of the 1950s.

Thad Jones in New York and Francy Boland and Kenny Clarke in Paris opted for contemporary variations on the Lunceford repertoire. In the number *Tip Toe*, Jones used typical "double feel" figures, suggesting a transient speeding up of the tempo, borrowed from Sy Oliver's *Stomp It Off*. The saxophone serpentines in *The Groove Merchant* sound like they could have been written by Wilcox. In fact, the tune was a composition by former Lunceford man Jerome Richardson.

Sy Oliver's big band, which was predominantly a studio enterprise, but toured as well, obviously showed Lunceford traces. He was the first, in 1950, to record a tribute album, titled *The Original Arrangements of Jimmie Lunceford in Hi-Fi*. It was one of Decca's very first twelve-inch 33 rpm jazz albums ("A New World of Sound"). Sy, who was notorious for "improving" his charts constantly, had embellished his original arrangements with little decorations, and the sound of his eight brass and five reeds was definitely heavier than that of the 1930s Lunceford band. From a "camp" point of view, the most remarkable re-creation was *I'm Walking through Heaven with You*, sung by Joe Bailey, who managed to out-Grissom Dan Grissom.

The orchestra that most convincingly modernized Lunceford's sound was Gerald Wilson's. After his discharge from the navy in 1945, Wilson started his own big band, a group that was amazingly advanced, yet also unusually successful. The Gerald Wilson orchestra sounded warm and rich, but it could hit hard the very next minute. There were traces of both

Lunceford and Ellington, and the bottom sound, dominated by baritone saxophonist Maurice Simon, definitely had an Eckstine flavor. In 1946, the band appeared at the Apollo ("and played to standing room only"), appropriately sandwiched between Duke's and Jimmie's stints at the theater.

Gerald Wilson is the only one left of the original Luncefordeans to still lead a jazz orchestra. And yes—he can still send shivers down your spine with his renditions of *Hi Spook* and *Yard Dog Mazurka*. He no longer throws his trumpet in the air, though. He doesn't even play the trumpet anymore, but concentrates on writing, conducting, and teaching.

Swing big bands, first, and all kinds of rhythm-and-blues groups, later, carried on the visual tradition of the Harlem Express. His eyes sparkling, pianist Gerald Wiggins heartily agreed with writer Ralph Gleason, who once remarked that to his mind, the Lunceford band was tailor-made for television. Wiggins remembered seeing the orchestra at the Apollo.

> I was there, every Saturday morning. Lunceford had a thing going: the guys would sing, they did all that, throwing their instruments in the air. If you could get a band that would do that today, they would make a great video and make him a fortune. But everybody today is too hip. You can't be bothered, they sit and play, you know, and that's it. They put their horns down, they sit and look like statues.

"I never hear anything about Lunceford," Snooky Young stated, with a trace of disappointment in his voice. "And a lot of people, the young people, even musicians, when you mention Jimmie Lunceford, they don't even know who he was. Can you imagine anything like that? And they don't never play his music on the air. That's a shame, that's really sad. That's a shame." Joe Wilder concurred: "It's funny, you hear occasionally a radio program where they play some records of the older bands. They don't play Lunceford, they don't play the John Kirby band. Louis Prima's another one who was exciting at that time, you know. Now they're gone. I mean, it's like, 'Hey, why waste time playing that music, it doesn't mean anything anymore.' It means a lot, actually!"

Some years ago, Beale Street, the famous entertainment strip in Memphis, was tidied up after decades of neglect. The city fathers had decided there was money in Beale Street's history. Part of the rejuvenation process was the installation of a Beale Street Walk of Fame, where all the singers and entertainers who had played a part in the city's rich musical past got their "note." All of them—save for Jimmie Lunceford. Former music teacher Emerson Able tried to rectify the situation. "I have written in to the paper—oh, man! No, no, no, it's not 'too long ago.' W. C. Handy was older than Mr. Lunceford—they got him! I think it was ignorance. He stayed here long enough to get his group together."

"I think certainly that it did not play for enough people, while it was in existence," is how Buddy DeFranco explained the fading of the Harlem Express. "It was a big name, but he didn't play for enough of the core of the big band listeners and dancers." He added that Lunceford's hit records sold in smaller quantities than those by Miller, Shaw, Tommy Dorsey, Goodman, or even Basie. "Then again, there's a question of nobody carrying the banner."

The Smithsonian Institution in Washington, DC, hosts Eddie Wilcox's book, some three hundred scores, dating back to 1934. Sy Oliver's heritage, 1,545 arrangements, including many, but far from all, of the Lunceford classics, rests in the New York Public Library.

Young Horace Silver was turned on when he first heard these Lunceford classics, on that hot night in Norwalk, Connecticut. They showed him the way, as a pianist and as a composer. He still cherishes his collection of Lunceford records.

> Oh yeah. I got most of their old 78 rpm recordings, and I transferred them to tape. Every now and then I listen, and the music still sounds good, and it still inspires me, you know. I just think that band had everything. It was just one helluva band.

Maybe the Jimmie Lunceford Orchestra represented swing music's final stage. Its finesse and feeling of oneness could not be duplicated, let alone be topped. Buddy DeFranco agreed: "I don't think anybody could. That was the product. That was it, you know. That's why the imitations don't really sound. . . . What can you possibly do?"

When Decca in 1949 released an album of mid-1930s favorites, *Down Beat*'s reviewer judged, "In my humble opinion, this is the greatest dance album I have ever heard, and certainly at the very top of the list of Band Jazz groupings too."[15]

Dizzy Gillespie once stated that in the end the records will provide the evidence that everything has really happened. He was talking about creative musicians in general, but he might have thought of the music of the

Jimmie Lunceford Orchestra in particular. Its records could be found in Harlem jukeboxes throughout the 1950s. They are the documents of a group of gifted musicians, who enjoyed their moment of fame during a time when excellent music was the rule, rather than the exception, on the floor and in the polls. Remarkably, unlike most of the popular music from the 1930s and 1940s, Lunceford does not sound dated: he can still excite young people.

A final word from Snooky Young: "I know the biggest thrill that I ever had was when I went to the neighbors, told 'em—I was a kid—that I went with the first band I ever played with. But I got the biggest kick out of playing with Lunceford."

NOTES

Quotations in the text not otherwise documented are taken from the following interviews, conducted by the author.

Emerson Able Jr. Telephone, Groningen-Memphis, October 26, 2004, and November 26, 2004.
Rashied Ali. Leeuwarden, The Netherlands, March 3, 1995.
Benny Bailey. Telephone, Groningen-Amsterdam, June 23, 2004.
Butch Ballard. Hilversum, The Netherlands, October 28, 1999.
Dave Bartholomew. Amsterdam, March 14, 1978.
Aaron Bell. The Hague, July 15, 1989.
Art Blakey. Oud Loosdrecht, The Netherlands, July 22, 1984.
Frank Bonitto. Telephone, Groningen–Cambridge, MA, December 18, 2003, January 18, 2004, and February 9, 2004.
John Carter. Groningen, March 31, 1984.
Arnett Cobb. Groningen, April 5, 1987.
Al Cobbs. Groningen, May 1, 1979.
Honi Coles. Groningen, October 19, 1979.
Buddy Collette. The Hague, July 10, 1984.
Buddy DeFranco. The Hague, July 10, 2005.
Von Freeman. Groningen, March 25, 2005.
Babs Gonzales. Groningen, ca. late July 1975.
Russell Green. Detroit, September 19, 1992.
Al Grey. The Hague, July 16, 1982.
Val Don Hickerson. Telephone, Groningen–Bandon, OR, May 5, 2005.
Joe Houston. The Hague, July 9, 1987, and Utrecht, November 13, 2004.
Russell Jacquet. Groningen, November 5, 1982.
Conrad Johnson. Houston, October 28, 1992.
Hank Jones. The Hague, July 9, 2004.
Jonah Jones. The Hague, July 1978.
George Kelly. Groningen, October 30, 1977.

Jackie Kelso. The Hague, July 11–12, 1999.

Freddie Kohlman. Oud Annerveen, The Netherlands, November 19–20, 1979.

Milt Larkin. Houston, October 23, 1992.

Jim Leigh. Hilversum, June 14, 1988.

Al Lunceford. Telephone, Groningen–Warren, OH, January 28, 2005, and Febrary 12, 2005.

Bertil Lyttkens. Telephone, Groningen–Halmstad, Sweden, January 25, 2005, and February 20, 2005.

Billy Mitchell. Veendam, The Netherlands, April 29, 1982.

Willie Mitchell. Between Haarlem and Tilburg, October 17, 1990.

Jimmy Oliver. Philadelphia, September 6, 1992.

Chuck Parham. Chicago, September 27, 1992.

Kathryn Perry Thomas. Telephone, Groningen-Memphis, November 25, 2004.

Bobby Plater. The Hague, July 16, 1978.

Eddie Randle Jr. St. Louis, MO, April 4, 2005.

Red Richards. The Hague, July 16, 1995.

Jerome Richardson. The Hague, July 9, 1994.

James Flash Riley. Groningen, November 5, 1981.

Little Jimmy Scott. The Hague, July 15, 1995.

Horace Silver. Telephone, Groningen–Malibu, CA, April 7, 2003.

Sun Ra. Groningen, August 6, 1984.

Sir Charles Thompson. The Hague, July 18, 1976.

Robert Veen. Telephone, Groningen–The Hague, February 26, 2005.

Earle Warren. Amsterdam, August 7, 1980.

Benny Waters. The Hague, July 12, 1980.

Frank Wess. Veendam, The Netherlands, March 28, 1984.

Gerald Wiggins. The Hague, July 9, 1988.

Joe Wilder. Telephone, Groningen–New York, February 19, 2003, February 16, 2004, February 23, 2004, September 4, 2004, and October 3, 2004.

Don Wilkerson. Utrecht, November 28, 1992.

Gerald Wilson. The Hague, July 14, 1990, and July 8, 1999. Telephone, Groningen–Los Angeles, February 16, 2004, and January 11, 2005.

Snooky Young. The Hague, July 13, 1979.

ABBREVIATIONS USED IN NOTES

AM   Albert McCarthy, *Big Band Jazz*, 1974

BAA   *Baltimore Afro American*

BK   Burt Korall, liner notes for *The Original Arrangements of Jimmie Lunceford in Hi-Fi* (Decca DL 8636), 1950

CB	Count Basie and Albert Murray, *Good Morning Blues*, 1985
CD	*Chicago Defender*
CEL	Eric Lincoln, *The Negro Pilgrimage in America*, 1969
CM	Claude McKay, *A Long Way from Home*, 1985
DB	*Down Beat*
DD	Dave Dexter, liner notes for *Jimmie Lunceford in Hi-Fi* (Capitol TAO924), 1957
DG	Dizzy Gillespie and Al Fraser, *To Be or Not to Bop*, 1979
DJ	*De Jazzwereld*
DL	David Levering Lewis, *When Harlem Was in Vogue*, 1981
DS	David W. Stone, *Swing Changes*, 1994
DT	Dempsey J. Travis, *An Autobiography of Black Jazz*, 1984
EB	Edward Berger, *Bassically Speaking*, 1993
EJB	Ernie Andrews, ed., *Esquire's 1947 Jazz Book*, 1947
GG	Gary Giddins, *Visions of Jazz*, 1998
GSEJ	Gunther Schuller, *Early Jazz*, 1968
GSSE	Gunther Schuller, *The Swing Era*, 1989
GTS	George T. Simon, *The Big Bands*, 1974
HPCM	Hugues Panassié, *Cinq Mois à New-York*, 1947
HPJH	Hugues Panassié, *Jazz Hot*
HPRJ	Hugues Panassié, *The Real Jazz*, 1943
HR	Bob Kreider, *Hot-Revue*
IC	Ian Crosbie, *Jazz Journal*
IG	Ira Gitler, *Jazz Masters of the Forties*, 1966
JH	Jim Haskins, *The Cotton Club*, 1977
JK	Jim Krivine, *Juke Box Saturday Night*, 1977
KS	Klaus Stratemann, *Negro Bands on Film*, vol. 1, 1981
LE	Lewis A. Erenberg, *Swingin' the Dream*, 1998
LW	Leo Walker, *The Wonderful Era of the Great Dance Bands*, 1964
MJ	Max Jones, *Talking Jazz*, 1988
MM	Mezz Mezzrow and Bernard Wolfe, *Really the Blues*, 1957
MS	Marshall Stearns, *Jazz Dance*, 1979
NYA	*New York Age*
NYAN	*New York Amsterdam News*
NYT	*New York Times*
OJNH	Nils Hellström, *Orkester Journalen*
OJNL	Niels Lynberg (Lars Westin), *Orkester Journalen*
PC	*Pittsburgh Courier*
PL	Peter J. Levinson, *Tommy Dorsey*, 2005
RG	Russell Green, WDET-FM interview, conducted by Jim Gallert, 1984
RJ	Robert Gottlieb, ed., *Reading Jazz*, 1997
SDWS	Stanley Dance, *The World of Swing*, 1974

SDCB   Stanley Dance, *The World of Count Basie*, 1980
SDDE   Stanley Dance, *The World of Duke Ellington*, 1981
WA   Walter C. Allen, *Hendersonia*, 1974
WD   W. E. B. DuBois, *The Souls of Black Folk*, 1961
WTC   *Warren Tribune Chronicle*
ZK   Zane Knaus, *Conversations with Jazz Musicians*, 1977

CHAPTER 1

1. Lynchings: CEL, 81.

2. Jimmie Lunceford's ancestry: www.afrigeneas.com/forum/index.cgi? noframes; read=20788.

3. Music scene Oklahoma: Charles N. Gould, *Travels through Oklahoma* (1928), 157; George O. Carney and Hugh W. Foley, *Oklahoma Music Guide* (2003), xi; and Hugh W. Foley, *Oklahoma Route 66 Music Guide* (2005), 24–25.

4. Jimmie Lunceford on brother Junior: *DJ*, September 1939, 2.

5. Reconstruction era: WD, 38–39, 127–37, and 150; and CEL, 78.

6. Circulation and influence of *The Crisis:* DL, 7.

7. Profile W. E. B. DuBois: Nick Aaron Ford, ed., *Black Insights* (1971), 18; and Rosey E. Pool and Paul Breman, eds., *Ik zag hoe Zwart ik was* (1958), 183–84.

8. "Castle is an acquired taste": Cecil Smith, *Musical Comedy in America* (1950), 166.

9. Castle House School of Dancing: MS, 97–98; AM, 11; and www.central-home.com/ballroomcountry/foxtrot.htm.

10. Wilberforce Whiteman on jazz: www.hometownsource.com/2004/November/8wood.html.

11. Denver music scene: George Hoefer, *DB*, September 24, 1964, 35; GSEJ, 365–69; Andy Kirk and Amy Lee, *Twenty Years on Wheels* (1989), 43–50; and OJNL, June 2002, 23.

12. "I trained him": GSEJ, 369.

13. See note 11 above.

14. George Morrison on Art Hickman: GSEJ, 365.

15. Repertoire and arrangements: GSEJ, 360, 362, and 365.

16. Waltzes and rumbas: *San Antonio Register*, March 22, 1946, 6.

17. George Morrison on rodeo trips: GSEJ, 363.

CHAPTER 2

1. Ku Klux Klan affiliation: *Orkester Journalen*, Stockholm, June 2002, 23.

2. James Lunceford Sr. in Warren: *WTC*, June 20, 1956, 4.

3. Fisk University and the Fisk Jubilee Singers: Reavis L. Mitchell and Haywood Farrar, Fisk University (1866–), www.tnstate.edu/library/digital/FISKU.HTM, www.pbs.org/wnet/jimcrow/stories_events_fisk.html; DL, 45, 89–90, 159–60; Ate van Delden, ed., *Doctor Jazz Magazine*, September 1978, 13–23; and Viv Broughton, *Black Gospel* (1985), 12–13.

4. DuBois on education: WD, 78, 80.

5. Sociology curriculum: *Fisk University News*, 1922, 74–76, www.learningto-give.org/papers/people/mary_richmond.html, and cepa.newschool.edu/het/profiles/bowley.htm.

6. Music curriculum: *Fisk University News*, 1922, 63–65, library.indstate.edu/level1.dir/cml/rbsc/walker/walker-f.html, and www.assumption.edu/ahc/1920s/Eugenics/DoesJazzPuttheSin.html.

7. Stage fright: Ken Evans, *DJ*, September 1939, 2.

8. Air Meet: Roger D. Launius and Jessie L. Embry, "The Los Angeles Air Show," *Southern California Quarterly*, 77, 329–46.

9. Sports at Fisk: All in the *Greater Fisk Herald:* Hardeway, December 1925, 10; Charles S. Lewis, January 1926, 19; Walter P. Adkins, February 1926, 19 and March 1926, 29; John Leary, April–May 1926, 27; and Walter P. Adkins, June 1926.

10. Yolande DuBois romance: David Levering Lewis, *W.E.B. Du Bois*, part 2 (2001), 107–8 and 222.

11. W. E. B. DuBois on *Home to Harlem:* Jervis Anderson, *This Was Harlem* (1983), 222–23.

12. Claude McKay on W. E. B. DuBois: CM, 110.

13. DuBois's beard guard: Buck Clayton and Nancy Miller Elliott, *Buck Clayton's Jazz World* (1986), 14.

14. Marriage Yolande DuBois: David Levering Lewis, *W.E.B. Du Bois*, part 2 (2001), 212.

15. Civic Club Gathering: DL, 89 and 93–94.

16. "We were shown off": Arna Bontemps, *The Harlem Renaissance Remembered*, (1984), 18–19.

17. "I do not care a damn": W. E. B. DuBois, *The Crisis*, March 1926.

18. "Each one wanted to be": CM, 322.

CHAPTER 3

1. Elmer Snowden at Bamville Club: AM, 46–47.

2. Arrival in Memphis: MJ, 185.

3. Lunceford on Memphis scene: *EJB*, 46–47.

4. Alphonso Trent Orchestra: EYJ, Ross Russell, *Jazz Style in Kansas City and the Southwest* (1973), 61–64; Sammy Price, *What Do They Want?* (1989), 20–21; and JJ, March 1959.

5. "Our local musicians": *EJB*, 47.

6. Mátyás Seiber's Jazz Class: www.dra.de/dok_1204.htm.

7. Courses in swing music: DS, 28–29.

8. Annie 'Baby' White and the International Sweethearts of Rhythm: D. Antoinette Handy, *The International Sweethearts of Rhythm* (1983), 103.

9. "He would do some arranging": David Earl Jackson, *Downtowner*, December 1997, 26.

10. Size Chickasaw Syncopators: *EJB*, 47.

11. Jimmy Crawford profile: SDWS, 119–24; and BK.

12. Barry Ulanov on rhythm: IC, 5.

13. "Breathing pure oxygen": EB, 67.

14. "I could tell": Stanley Dance, liner notes for *Jimmie Lunceford 1939–40*, CBS 666421, 1981.

15. "The Chickasaw Syncopators ply their art": *CD*, February 4, 1930.

16. Willie Smith profile: SDWS, 95–105.

17. Parents Willie Smith: Stanley Dance, *DB*, May 18, 1967, 21.

18. Sound Willie Smith: HPJH, February–March 1939; and HPRJ, 109 and 190.

19. Johnny Hodges on Willie Smith: SDDE, 93.

20. Position of reeds: Alain Gerber, liner notes for *Blues in the Night*, M.C.A. 510.040.

21. "No modern 'Super Sax' group": GSSE, 210–11.

22. Edwin Wilcox profile: Kirk Silsbee, *DB*, January 2006, 50; Sharon A. Pease, *DB*, February 1, 1943, 18; and SDWS, 111–15.

23. Beale Street Hour: *EJB*, 47.

24. W.C. Handy and the Chickasaw Syncopators: W. C. Handy and Arna Bontemps, *Father of the Blues* (1970), 245–46.

25. First national tours: LE, 27.

26. Cleveland winter: SDWS, 97.

27. Booking practice: *EJB*, 46.

28. "The unity of direction": BK.

29. Cohesion band: HPJH, February–March 1939.

30. Gospel influence: SDCB, 275.

31. "We didn't return": *EJB*, 47.

CHAPTER 4

1. "Lunceford And Bunch Sensation": *PC*, October 4, 1930, 8.

2. Speed Webb band battle: AM, 123–24.

3. Handling liquor: IC, 2.

4. Departure Jonah Jones: *DB*, April 3, 1958.

5. Willie Smith on Eddie Tompkins: Stanley Dance, *DB*, May 18, 1967, 22.

6. Joe Thomas profile: John Chilton, *Who's Who of Jazz* (1972), 376; and SDWS, 115.

7. "That is a night we'll never forget": DD.

8. Gyrations band: MBS-WOR broadcast, Fiesta Danceteria, New York, June 16, 1940.

9. "His only rival": *RJ*, 497.

10. Visual effects by Tommy Stevenson: GTS, 333.

11. Tommy Stevenson as junkie: DG, 283.

12. "Ensemble spirit": Barry Ulanov, *A Handbook of Jazz* (1958), 27.

13. Sy Oliver profile: SDWS, 125–34; ZK, 159; DT, 435–46; and MJ, 170–74.

14. Sy Oliver recommended by Edwin Wilcox: SDWS, 115.

15. Arranging principle: ZK, 157–58.

16. See note 13 above.

17. Sy Oliver arrangements for Zack Whythe: SDWS, 225–27.

18. See note 13 above.

19. "He had a powerful sense": Albert McCarthy, *Jazz Monthly*, November 1955.

20. "Though Sy frequently orchestrates": HPRJ, 186.

21. Arranging as creative art: ZK, 156.

22. Management Harold Oxley: *Billboard*, February 2, 1952; LW, 257; OJNL, June 2002, 27; and DD.

23. Unemployment in New York: I. A. Hirschmann, *Nation*, November 15, 1933.

CHAPTER 5

1. Debut at Lafayette Theater: ad, *NYAN*, September 27, 1933; CB, 126–27; and Stanley Dance, *DB*, May 18, 1967, 22.

2. Glee club: DT, 440.

3. Tempo White Heat: Gene Ferrett, *A Thousand Golden Horns* (1966), 82.

4. Cotton Club: JH, 29–33, 44, 62–64, 70, 97–101, 107, and 110; MS, 274–75; *CD*, March 17, 1934; *NYAN*, June 16, 1934; and SDDE, 48.

5. Cotton Club on Parade: ad, *NYAN*, June 9, 1934.

6. See note 4 above.

7. Rehearsal room: MM, 208; Robert Goffin, *Le Roi du Jazz: Jazz from the Congo to the Metropolitan* (1944), and EB, 65.

8. Dispute with Irving Mills: WA, 297.

9. "Could never explain": ZK, 163.

10. Debut at Renaissance Casino: ad, *NYA*, December 30, 1933, 9.

11. Henry Wells at Renaissance: *DB*, July 30, 1947, 12.

12. Willie Smith on Renaissance: Stanley Dance, *DB*, June 1, 1967, 26.

13. Bert Hall Rhythm Club: WA, 328.

14. Attendance record Renaissance: *DJ*, September 1939, 2.

15. Last appearance at Renaissance: ad, *NYAN*, April 9, 1947, 21.

16. Debut at Apollo Theater: ad, *PC*, May 19, 1934; and *NYA*, June 2, 1934.

17. Friendship Bill Robinson: *WTC*, December 24, 1941, 15.

18. Engagements at Apollo Theater: *DJ*, September 1939, 2; and SDWS, 408–15.

19. Character Lunceford band: *RJ*, 496.

20. *Stratosphere* too far out: GSSE, 209.

21. Repertory Swedish tour: souvenir program, Soirée Dansante Berns, March 9, 1937.

22. "The band is winning favor": *PC*, November 3, 1934.

23. Attendance record Old Orchard: *PC*, March 28, 1936, 7.

24. Success *Rhythm Is Our Business: PC*, August 31, 1935, 7; and Frank Driggs and Harris Lewine: *Black Beauty, White Heat* (1982), 283.

25. Background Dave Clark: Lawrence N. Redd, *Rock is Rhythm and Blues* (1974), 125.

26. Tactics Dave Clark: Nelson George, *The Death of Rhythm & Blues* (1988), 17–18.

27. Popularity "Make Believe Ballroom": Elliott Grennard, *New Masses*, September 9, 1941, 26–27.

28. Fats Waller at Soldier Field: George Avakian, liner notes for *Satch Plays Fats*, CBS 52804, 1970.

29. Harlem Express tour: *CD*, January 19, 1935, 7; *CD*, March 23, 1935, 8; ad, *NYAN*, May 18, 1935, 10; *WTC*, July 13, 1935, 7; *Fisk News*, Spring 1935; and SDCB, 275.

CHAPTER 6

1. 1920/1921 baby boom: www.census.gov/population/estimates/nation/pop-clockest.txt.

2. Rise of the juke-box: JK, 11, 38, and 54–58.

3. Increase ballrooms: Barry Kernfeld. ed., *The New Grove Dictionary of Jazz*, vol. 2 (1988), 193–241.

4. Unifying effect swing culture: LE, 39–40.

5. Saluting ceremony: RG.

6. "That was all novelty": SDCB, 66.

7. Eddie Tompkins as straw boss: SDWS, 116.

8. Jesse Owens with Skeets Tolbert: John Clement, liner notes for *Skeets Tolbert and His Gentlemen of Swing*, Everybodys 3001, 1983.

9. "To the average person": Edward Stein, *Metronome*, May 1936, 26.

10. Truckin' Show: JH, 107.

11. "They walked": *RJ*, 497.

12. Reviews Will G. Gilbert: *DJ*, November 1936, 12, and August 1937, 11.

13. Horns playing rhythm: PL, 106.

14. Amplified guitar: SDCB, 63–64.

15. Elks Grand Ball: ad, *BAA*, August 8, 1938.

16. See note 14 above.

17. Stranded in Smithville: Alice Dunn-Jensen, *Reminisce*, undated.

CHAPTER 7

1. Lunceford's dimensions and preferences: OJNH, March 1935; and unidentified newspaper clipping, probably July 14, 1947.

2. Lunceford's intellectual capacity: *DJ*, September 1939, 2.

3. The Ballet: Louis Cantor, *Wheelin' on Beale* (1992), 38–39.

4. Black Fred Waring: Robert Sunenblick, liner notes for *Raw Meat*, Uptown UP 27.01, 1979.

5. See note 1 above.

6. Sy Oliver's perception of Lunceford: DT, 444–46; and Bill Coss, *Metronome*, November 1960.

7. Boxing match: RG.

8. "He was consistent": GTS, 330.

9. "He was a very gentle man": *Jazz Journal*, April 1963.

10. Lunceford on softball: Jimmie Lunceford AFRS Downbeat interview, probably late 1943.

11. Sponsorship: *WTC*, May 29, 1937, 7; and *BAA*, July 19, 1947, 6.

12. Larchmont Casino: SDWS, 103.

13. Broadcasts from Larchmont: *CD*, August 1, 1936, 11.

14. Jamboree for Spain: ad, *NYAN*, November 19, 1938, 20.

15. Membership NAACP: *PC*, November 10, 1945.

16. Crescendo Club: WA, 382.

17. "I'm not surprised": HPCM, 71.

18. "On my lucky day": Bill Treadwell, ed., *Big Book of Swing* (1946), 55.

CHAPTER 8

1. Army Pictorial Service film: OJNL, November 2002, 24.

2. Vitaphone short: www.imbd.com/name/nm0376221/; and KS, 67.

3. Popularity at colleges: H. W. Wind, *Variety*, January 22, 1936, 52; Walter J. Dodd Jr., *Variety*, January 29, 1936, 45; and *Billboard Band Year Book*, September 24, 1942.

4. Ellington criticism: John Hammond, *DB*, November 1935, 1; and OJNL, July–August 2002, 28.

5. "Duke and Lunceford lead in Poll": *NYAN*, August 15, 1936, 10.

6. Sy Oliver system: DT, 442–44.

7. "They could swing a band": Garvin Bushell and Mark Tucker, *Jazz from the Beginning* (1998), 101.

8. Larry Clinton battle: GTS, 129.

9. Temptation of Willie Smith: SDWS, 103.

10. *For Dancers Only* at Apollo: EB, 67.

11. "His four trumpet players": SDWS, 342.

12. "Grinding down the blues-ish sound": *RJ*, 496, 498.

13. Bob Crosby version of *For Dancers Only:* John Chilton, *Stomp Off, Let's Go!* (1983), 116.

14. Tempos: HPCM, 76; and GG, 168.

15. Descending chord: *RJ*, 500.

16. Streamliners: www.forums.railfan.net/forums.cgi?board=PassengerTrains ;action=display;num=1079.

CHAPTER 9

1. Influence on Snub Mosley and Louis Jordan: John Chilton, *Let the Good Times Roll* (1992), 71.

2. Influence on Erroll Garner: Arthur Taylor, *Notes and Tones*, 1977, 99; and Arnold Shaw, *52nd St: The Street of Jazz* (1977), 292.

3. Planning Scandinavian tour: *DB*, February 1937, 5; OJNL, July–August 2002, 30–31; *PC*, February 13, 1937, 18; and ad, *NYA*, February 6, 1937, 9.

4. Farewell show Apollo: Andy Gray, *DJ*, September 1939, 2.

5. Crosby-Lunceford battle: *DB*, March 1937, 14.

6. Scandinavian tour: OJNH, March 1937, 10; OJNH, April 1937, 8–9; and OJNL, July–August 2002, 31.

7. Reviews Swedish press: Bertil Lyttkens, *Svart och Vitt* (1998), 87–89.

8. Impact Lunceford on Swedish musicians: OJNL, October 2002, 26; and *Fick-Journalen*, January 1957.

9. Resistance British Musicians Union: *CD*, April 7, 1937.

10. Easter Sunday Dance: ad, *NYA*, March 27, 1937; and Clyde Bernhardt and Sheldon Harris, *I Remember* (1986), 127–28.

11. Count Basie battle: SDCB, 67, 106–7; CB, 195–96; GG, 169; and IC, March 1972, 28.

12. Addition of Trummy Young: SDDE, 136.

13. "Apart from Duke": JH, February–March 1939.

CHAPTER 10

1. Box office record: *CD*, October 9, 1941.

2. Record-breaking tour: *CD*, March 27, 1943.

3. Union scale: LE, 168.

4. Chicago ball: *BAA*, October 7, 1939, 14.

5. Reception band: EB, 66.

6. Duke Ellington's *Concert of Sacred Music: DB*, January 12, 1967, 11.

7. Whites at Washington dance: Tom Scanlan, *The Joy of Jazz*, (1996), 63.

8. Appreciation by musicians and blacks: HPCM, 53.

9. Cancellation European tour: *BAA*, June 18, 1938, 11.

10. Itinerary 1938: *BAA*, June 18, 1938, 11.

11. Wear and tear: *BAA*, January 1, 1939, 11.

12. Review George T. Simon: *Metronome*, September 1938.

13. Lunceford bounce: GTS, 329; and HPRJ, 39 and 189.

14. Conversion of Paul Gonsalves: SDDE, 169.

15. "In front of the band": *RJ*, 496–97.

16. Planning dance set: *RJ*, 498.

17. New band uniforms: *BAA*, June 18, 1938, 11.

18. Poisoning at Band Box: HPCM, 91–93; and MM, 294.

19. Review Hugues Panassié: HPJH, November–December 1937.

20. "Jimmie Lunceford, undoubtedly": *BAA*, August 20, 1938, 10.

21. Sonny Greer on Lunceford: SDDE, 70.

22. Duke Ellington battle: SDDE, 76–77 and 89–90; HPCM, 119–20; and HPJH, April–May 1939.

23. *Lunceford Suite:* www.blackbird.vcu.edu/v2n2/features/hummer_tr_021404 /hummer_tr_text.htm.

24. Tour with Billie Holiday: John Chilton, *Billie's Blues* (1977), 35.

25. Performances with Bessie Smith: ad, *BAA*, November 21, 1936.

26. "Though annexing trios": Will Friedwald, *Jazz Singing* (1991), 179–80.

27. Trio singing: ZK, 151.

28. Departure Sy Oliver: SDWS, 125–27.

29. Rehearsal Dorsey band: Herb Sanford, *Tommy and Jimmie: The Dorsey Years* (1972), 164.

30. Bill Finegan arrangement: PL, 103–4.

31. Dorsey band studying Lunceford: PL, 105–6.

32. Gerald Wilson joins: *DB*, January 2006, 50.

33. George Duvivier and Royal Barons: EB, 32–35, 37, 65–66, and 70; A. B. Spell-man, *Black Music* (1973), 157; and Herbie Nichols, liner notes for *Herbie Nichols Trio*, Blue Note 5C 038.98578S, 1977.

34. Introduction Billy Moore Jr.: OJNL, October 2002, 22.

35. Lunceford as co-composer: *DB*, July 30, 1947, 12.

36. Lunceford and New York musicians: DG, 133.

37. Planning European tour: *DJ*, October 1939, 1.

38. "Where they, too": *CD*, July 1, 1939, 11.

39. Details European tour: *Estrad*, August 1939, 4.

40. Lineup Paramount: ad, *NYT*, August 23, 1939, 19.

41. Genesis *Uptown Blues: DB*, January 17, 1963, 41.
42. Review *Uptown Blues: Jazz Information*, January 12, 1940.
43. "One of the first 'casualties' ": *NYA*, September 16, 1939, 7.
44. GIs in Germany: *DB*, July 30, 1947, 12.

CHAPTER 11

1. Verdict John Hammond: *Tempo*, June 1937; and Stanley Dance, liner notes for *Teddy Wilson and His All-Stars*, CBS 67289, 1973.
2. Recording plans: *NYAN*, December 30, 1939, 21.
3. San Antonio appearance: *San Antonio Register*, February 2, 1940, 6.
4. Popularity Lunceford in Los Angeles: Steven Isoardi, ed., *Central Avenue Sounds* (1998), 327–28; and CB, 243.
5. Jimmie Lunceford Swingaroo: DS, 31.
6. Itinerary West Coast: ad, *CD*, February 24, 1940, 10.
7. "I personally wish": LW, 262.
8. Bill Perkins on Ellington and Lunceford: Bruce Crowther and Mike Pinfold, *The Big Band Years* (1988), 126.
9. Wilson's first arrangements: Kirk Silsbee, *DB*, January 2006, 50.
10. Snooky Young joins: Jon Faddis, *DB*, May 2005, 44.
11. Teddy Wilson battle: *NYA*, December 12, 1939, 4; and *DB*, July 27, 1955.
12. Erskine Hawkins battle: SDWS, 210.
13. Battle of the bands: WA, 386; *Metronome*, December 1940; and George T. Simon, *Glenn Miller* (1974), 241.
14. New Year's gala revue: *NYAN*, December 30, 1939, 21; ad, *NYA*, December 30, 1939; and *NYA*, April 7, 1945.
15. Number of records sold: IC, 26.
16. BMI versus ASCAP: *DB*, November 1, 1940, 1 and 16; and DS, 110–12.

CHAPTER 12

1. Bellanca crash: *WTC*, September 10, 1941; and *DB*, October 15, 1941, 4.
2. Flying trip George Duvivier: EB, 72.
3. Refusal Mary Lou Williams: MJ, 186.
4. Rickenbacker bass: www.fredsmusic.com/.rickenbacker/rick_hist.html.
5. *Blues in the Night* movie: BAA, August 2, 1941, 14; *WTC*, August 7, 1941; and KS, 68.
6. Reviews *Blues in the Night*: *NYT*, December 12, 1941, 35; and *DB*, November 15, 1941, 12.
7. Verdict *Down Beat: DB*, February 1, 1942.

8. Chamber Music Society of America: *NYT*, October 28, 1941, 29; and *DB*, December 1, 1941, 6.

9. "All aboard for the Harlem Express!": ad, *CD*, October 31, 1942, 11.

10. "Jumpin' with jive and joy!": ad, *CD*, April 18, 1942. 11.

11. San Francisco jam session: David F. Selvin, *Jazz Information*, March 1, 1940.

12. Criticism Bill Russo and Albert McCarthy: Martin Williams, ed., *Jazz Panorama* (1965), 132–38.

13. "That tune": Stanley Dance, *Jazz Journal International*, May 1982, 6.

14. Bands copying Lunceford: *DB*, June 15, 1941, 8.

CHAPTER 13

1. Deterioration of band: GSSE, 212.

2. Rewriting library: EB, 67.

3. Tadd Dameron and Sy Oliver: IG, 263 and 265.

4. *Jubilee* shows: Richard S. Sears, Rainer E. Lotz, Ulrich Neuert, and Carl A. Hällström, *AFRS Jubilee*, privately published, 2005.

5. Fee Lunceford: Leo Walker, *The Big Band Almanac* (1989), 269.

6. "Youngsters no longer take the family car": *DB*, March 14, 1942, 1.

7. Train trip: LW, 278.

8. Bookings on the West Coast: *PC*, March 5, 1938, 20.

9. Cabaret Tax: *DB*, May 1, 1944, 1.

10. Departure Roger Segure: Ted Hallock, *Melody Maker*, August 28, 1954.

11. "His much-copied style": ad, *DB*, March 1, 1942, 7.

12. Attendance record: *DB*, April 15, 1942, 13, and May 1, 1942, 6.

13. 1942 Popularity Poll: *CD*, May 2, 1942, 13.

14. Boston pool room: LE, 45.

15. "In bringing Hampton and Lunceford": *CD*, August 26, 1944, 9.

16. Success Billy Eckstine: *NYA*, September 23, 1944.

17. Award of Merit: *NYA*, December 30, 1944.

18. Review in *Jazz Forum*: Jim Godbolt, *A History of Jazz in Britain, 1919–50* (1984), 165–66.

19. T-Bone Walker on Dan Grissom: Nat Shapiro and Nat Hentoff, eds., *Hear Me Talkin' to Ya* (1966), 250.

20. Analysis Shep Fields: *DB*, July 1, 1942, 17.

21. Press release Oxley: www.swingmusic.net/Big-Band-Music-Biography-Jimmie–Lunceford.html.

22. Departure Trummy Young: *DB*, March 15, 1943, 3; and Scott DeVeaux, *The Birth of Bebop* (1997), 257.

23. Departure Willie Smith: SDWS, 117; and SDDE, 162.

24. Audition Jerome Richardson: Bob Bernotas, *Saxophone Journal*, March–April 1995, 31.

25. "Because I was too young": *Encore,* July 21–28, 1975.

26. Meeting Miles Davis–Freddie Webster: www.cleveland.oh.us/wmv_news/jazz22.htm.

27. Show Madison Square Garden: *DB,* October 15, 1942, 2.

28. At Apollo: GTS, 334.

29. At Regal: *DB,* November 15, 1942, 12.

30. Encounter with Oscar Peterson: Peterson BBC Radio 3 interview, conducted by Peter Clayton, April 12, 1974.

31. Freddie Webster and Count Basie: see note 26 above.

32. AFM Record Ban: *NYT,* December 11, 1941; *Metronome,* August 1943, 4; JK, 74; and Christopher Pearce, *Honderd Jaar Jukebox* (1989), 40–41.

33. "Wartime emergency": *DB,* February 1, 1943, 1.

34. At Loew's State: *DB,* October 15, 1943, 17.

35. Jimmy Crawford with Ben Webster: SDWS, 122–23.

36. Incident Trianon Ballroom: Arnold Shaw, *Honkers and Shouters* (1978), 124.

CHAPTER 14

1. Hiring Russell Green: RG.

2. Review *Back Door Stuff: DB,* April 1, 1944, 8.

3. Battle Billy Eckstine: Ira Gitler, *Swing to Bop* (1985), 127; and Stan Britt, *Long Tall Dexter* (1989), 56–57.

4. "The best section in the band": *HR,* 1945.

5. V-Discs: GTS, 335.

6. Oxley's West Coast agency: *Billboard,* January 13, 1951, and February 2, 1952.

7. Departure Dan Grissom: *DB,* March 1, 1943, 3, and August 1, 1943, 3.

8. *Down Beat* review: *DB,* September 23, 1946, 2.

9. Change in management: *PC,* December 1, 1945, 16, and April 27, 1946, 11; and *NYA,* February 2, 1946, 10.

10. Club Riviera engagement: *NYA,* March 9, 1946, 10.

11. Royal Roost opening: IG, 269.

12. Review *Margie: DB,* February 12, 1947, 19.

13. "That band was absolutely roaring": EB, 70.

14. "From the first bars on": *HR,* 1945.

15. Airline investment: *NYA,* February 23, 1946.

16. Texas trip: *CD,* March 30, 1946, 25.

CHAPTER 15

1. Portland breakfast: RG.

2. Al Cobbs as arranger: John S. Wilson, *NYT,* February 24, 1979.

3. Integration policy: RG.

4. Message Kirt Bradford: RG.

5. Popularity polls: *BAA*, July 19, 1947, 6.

6. Second set: RG.

7. "All he had on him": Barry Ulanov, *The Swing Era, 1939–1940* (1971), 42.

8. Cause of death: Frederick J. Spencer, MD, MPH, *IAJRC Journal*, Summer–Fall 2003, 21–23.

9. "Ate a double portion": IC, 28.

CHAPTER 16

1. Itinerary West Coast: *NYAN*, July 5 and 12, 1947.

2. Reaction fans: *CD*, October 9, 1947.

3. Contract Crystal Tulli: *San Antonio Register*, December 30, 1949, 5.

4. Debut Wilcox-Thomas band: *NYA*, August 30, 1947, 10.

5. "Indeed it could be truthfully said": *NYA*, December 13, 1947, 5.

6. At Royal Roost: *DB*, April 7, 1948, 7.

7. Review *Whatcha Gonna Do: DB*, July 28, 1948, 13.

8. Memorial tour: RG and *DB*, July 30, 1947, 1.

9. Departure Joe Thomas: *Billboard*, October 30 and December 4, 1948; *DB*, December 29, 1948, 14; and SDDE, 180.

10. Billy May session: *Jazz Journal International*, May 1982, 7.

11. Frank Sinatra date: Robert Sunenblick, liner notes for *Blowin' in from K.C.*, Uptown UP 27.12, 1983.

12. Fur Union Veterans Dance: ad, *NYAN*, April 7, 1951, 22.

13. "Simply does not have": Bob Blumenthal, *Boston Globe*, February 1992.

14. Verdict Gary Giddins: www.jerryjazzmusician.com/mainHTML.cfm?page= giddins-underrated4.html.

15. "In my humble opinion": *DB*, May 20, 1949, 15.

DISCOGRAPHY

In compiling this list I have consulted Bertil Lyttkens, The Jimmie Lunceford Legacy on Records, 1996; Frank Dutton, Matrix 66–67, 86, and 95; Richard S. Sears, Rainer E. Lotz, Ulrich Neuert, and Carl A. Hällström, *AFRS Jubilee* (privately published, 2005); *Micrography* 42 (Autumn 1976); Richard S. Sears, *V-Discs: A History and Discography* (1980); Joe Wilder; and Gerald Wilson.

Note: from Lunceford's commercial studio recordings, only the original 78 rpm records and the reissues on CD are included. The live recordings and radio broadcasts are listed in CD or mp3 format, when available; the remainder in their LP form.

ABBREVIATIONS

Instruments

as	alto saxophone
b	bass
bars	baritone saxophone
bj	banjo
cel	celeste
cl	clarinet
d	drums
ens	ensemble
fl	flute
g	guitar
p	piano
tb	trombone
tp	trumpet
ts	tenor saxophone
tu	tuba

vib   vibraphone
vo   vocal

Arrangers

[WB]	Will Beines
[LC]	Leon Carr
[AC]	Al Cobbs
[ED]	Eddie Durham
[GD]	George Duvivier
[TD]	Tadd Dameron
[BE]	Buford "Bud" Estes
[RH]	Ray Heindorf
[HH]	Horace Henderson
[EH]	Elton Hill
[WH]	Will Hudson
[EI]	Edward Inge
[HJ]	Harry "Pee Wee" Jackson
[JL]	Jimmie Lunceford
[BM]	Billy Moore Jr.
[?P]	? Peters
[SO]	Sy Oliver
[DR]	Don Redman
[JS]	Jesse Stone
[RS]	Roger Segure
[WS]	Willie Smith
[TW]	Tom Whaley
[CW]	Chappie Willett
[EW]	Edwin Wilcox
[EWa]	Earle Warren
[LW]	Lonnie Wilfong
[GW]	Gerald Wilson

The discography lists the following:
BILLING OF THE BAND ON LABEL
Personnel
Place and date of recording
Matrix number with suffix indicating number of take; *Title*, (vocalist); [Arranger]; original 78 rpm issue
Reissues on CD, (mp3), or (LP).

CHICKASAW SYNCOPATORS

Charlie Douglas, Henry Clay (tp), H. B. Hall (tb), Allen Williams (cl, ss, as), George Clarke (cl, ts), Jimmie Lunceford (ss, as), Christopher Johnson (as, bars), Bobbie Brown (p), Alfred Kahn (bj), Mose Allen (tu, vo), Jimmy Crawford (d)

Memphis, December 13, 1927

W 145.373-2 *Chickasaw Stomp* (ma vo) [JL] Columbia 14301-D

Masters of Jazz MJCD 12, Frog DGF 31, Alpha CD 47

W 145.374-3 *Memphis Rag* [JL] Columbia 14301-D

Masters of Jazz MJCD 12, Frog DGF 31, Memphis Archives MA 7005, Alpha CD 47

JIMMIE LUNCEFORD AND HIS CHICKASAW SYNCOPATORS

Probably Melvin "Sy" Oliver, Douglas, Clay (tp), Henry Wells (tb), Lunceford (as), Willie Smith (cl, as), Johnson (as, bars), Clarke (cl, ts), Edwin Wilcox (p), Alfred Kahn (bj), Allen (tu, vo), Crawford (d)

Memphis, June 6, 1930

62599-2 *In Dat Mornin'* (ma vo) [JL] Victor V38141

Classics 501, Masters of Jazz MJCD 12, Living Era CDAJA5031, Frog DGF 24, ABC 836188-2, BBC 647, Legends of Jazz 18032-2, Alpha CD 47

62600-1 *Sweet Rhythm* [EW] Victor V38141

Classics 501, Masters of Jazz MJCD 12, Living Era CDAJA5031, Frog DGF 24, ABC 836188-2, ASV 5031, Membrane 221999-300, Alpha CD 47

JIMMIE LUNCEFORD AND HIS ORCHESTRA

Clay or Eddie Tompkins, Tommy "Steve" Stevenson, William "Sleepy" Tomlin (tp), Wells (tb, vo), Russell Bowles (tb), Lunceford (as?), Smith (cl, as), Joe Thomas (cl, ts), Earl Carruthers (cl, as, ts, bars), Wilcox (p), Al Norris (g), Allen (b), Crawford (d, vib, bells)

New York, May 15, 1933

TO-1299-PA *Flaming Reeds and Screaming Brass* [EW] ARC test

Classics 501, Masters of Jazz MJCD 12, Drive 3516, ASV 5091, KAZ CD 317, Membran 221999-306, Acrobat ACRCD 165

TO-1300-PA *While Love Lasts* [EW] ARC test

Classics 501, Masters of Jazz MJCD 12, Drive 3516, ASV 5091, Membran 221999-306

Note: original coda of Flaming Reeds and Screaming Brass *missing. Complete tune on Columbia CL 2715 (LP).*

Oliver (tp, vo) replaces Tomlin; Tompkins (tp) replaces Clay; Smith also (bars); Tompkins, Oliver, Smith (trio vo)

New York, January 26, 1934

BS 81324-1 *White Heat* [WH] Victor 24586

Classics 501, Masters of Jazz MJCD 12, Drive 3516, Bluebird 9583-2-RB, KAZ CD 317, Membran 221999-306, Time-Life STBB-15, Music Memoria MM 393422, Alpha CD 47, Acrobat ACRCD 165

BS 81325-1 *Jazznocracy* [WH] Victor 24522

Classics 501, Masters of Jazz MJCD 12, Drive 3516, Intersound 1040, Jasmine JASCD 423, Jasmine JASCD 391, KAZ CD 317, Membran 221999-306, Music Memoria Mm 393422, Alpha CD 47, Acrobat ACRCD 165

BS 81326-1 *Chillun, Get Up* Victor 24522

Classics 501, Masters of Jazz MJCD 12, Drive 3516, Alpha CD 47

BS 81327-1 *Leaving Me* Victor 24586

Classics 501, Masters of Jazz MJCD 12, Drive 3516, Alpha CD 47

Will Hudson (vo)
New York, March 20, 1934
BS 82218-1 *Swingin' Uptown* [SO] Victor 10119
BS 82218-2 *Swingin' Uptown* [SO] Victor 24669

Classics 501, Masters of Jazz MJCD 12, Drive 3516, Best of Jazz 4002, Bluebird 9583-2-RB, RCA Victor 66746, RCA Victor 68509, BMG BSP 48492, KAZ CD 317, Membran 221999-306, Alpha CD 47

BS 82219-2 *Breakfast Ball* (wh, ens vo) [SO] Victor 24601

Classics 501, Masters of Jazz MJCD 12, Drive 3516, Membran 221999-306, Gallerie 455, Alpha CD 47

BS 82220-1 *Here Goes (a Fool)* (hw vo) [TW] Victor 24601

Classics 501, Masters of Jazz MJCD 12, Drive 3516, Alpha CD 47

BS 82220-2 *Here Goes (a Fool)* (hw vo) [TW]

Classics (F) 501, Masters of Jazz MJCD 12, Drive 3516, Alpha CD 47

BS 82221-1 *Remember When* (hw vo) [WH] Victor 10119

Classics 501, Masters of Jazz MJCD 12, Alpha CD 47

BS 82221-2 *Remember When* (hw vo) [WH] Victor 24669

Drive 3516, Best of Jazz 4002

LaForest Dent (cl, as) added; Crawford also timpani (1)
New York, September 4, 1934
38531-A *Sophisticated Lady* [WS] Decca 129

Classics 501, Masters of Jazz MJCD 12, Drive 3516, Decca 608-2, ASV 5091, Empress 897, Charly 1118, Living Era CDAJA5091, Membran 221999-306

38532-A *Mood Indigo* [WS] Brunswick A505154

Classics 501, Masters of Jazz MJCD 12, Charlie 1118, KAZ CD 317, Membran 221999-306, Alphs CD 47, Acrobat ACRCD 165

38532-B *Mood Indigo* [WS] Decca 131

Drive 3516, Masters of Jazz MJCD 12, Decca 608-2

38533-A *Rose Room (in Sunny Roseland)* [WS] Decca 131

Drive 3516, Masters of Jazz MJCD 12, Decca 608-2, GRP9923, Classics 501, Empress

897, Jasmine JASCD 391, KAZ CD 317, Membran 221999-306, Alpa CD 47, Acrobat ACRCD 165

38534-A *Black and Tan Fantasy* [SO] Decca 453

Drive 3516, Masters of Jazz MJCD 12, Decca 608-2, Classics 502, ASV 5091, Charlie 118, Big Band Era 2601812, Black & Blue BLE59241-2, Living Era CDAJA5091, Membran 221999-306

38535-A *Stratosphere* (1) [JL/EW] Decca 299

Drive 3516, Masters of Jazz MJCD 12, Decca 608-2, GRP9923, Charlie 1118, Legends of Jazz 18032/2, Past Perfect PPCD 78111, BBC REB590, Topaz TPZ 1005, ABC 836182, Jasmine JASCD 391, KAZ CD 317, Membran 221999-306, Smithsonian RD 030 2, Acrobat ACRCD 165

New York, September 5, 1934

38541-A *Nana* (hw vo) [SO] Decca 130

Drive 3516, Masters of Jazz MJCD 18, Classics 501, Jasmine JASCD 391

38542-A *Miss Otis Regrets (She's Unable to Lunch Today)* (so vo) [EW] Decca 130

Drive 3516, Masters of Jazz MJCD 18, Classics 501, Decca GRD609-2, GRP9923, Empress 897, Conifer CHD132, Membran 221999-306

38543-A *Unsophisticated Sue* (trio vo) [SO] Decca 129

Drive 2516, Masters of Jazz MJCD 18, Classics 501, Fremeaux & Associés 212, Past Perfect PPCD 78111, Phontastic PHONTCD 7653, Legends of Jazz 18032-2, Jasmine JASCD 391, Membran 221999-306

38544-A *Stardust* (hw voc) [EW] Decca 369

Masters of Jazz MJCD 18, Decca GRD608-2

38544-B *Stardust* (hw vo) [EW] Decca 369

Masters of Jazz MJCD 18, Classics 501

New York, October 29, 1934

38915-A *Dream of You* (so vo) [SO] Decca 765

Masters of Jazz MJCD 18, Classics 501, Decca GRD608-2, GRD9923, Fremeaux & Associés 212, Best of Jazz 4002, Jasmine JASCD 391, KAZ CD 317, Time-Life STBB-27, Saga Jazz 066-4612, Alpha CD 47

38916-A *Shake Your Head (from Side to Side)* [SO] Brunswick 02815

38917-A *Stomp It Off* [SO] Decca 712

Masters of Jazz MJCD 18, Classics 501, Decca GRD608-2, GRD9923, Fremeaux & Associés 212, EMP Jazz Archives 158242, KAZ CD 317, Time-Life STBB-27, Alpha CD 47, Acrobat ACRCD 165

38918-A *Call It Anything (It Wasn't Love)* (hw vo) [EW] Decca 572

Masters of Jazz MJCD 18, Classics 501

Allen (tu, 1), Lunceford (as, 1)

New York, November 7, 1934

38967-A *Because You're You* (hw vo) [SO] Decca 415

Masters of Jazz MJCD 18, Classics 501, Conifer CHD132

38967-B *Because You're You* (hw vo) [SO] Decca 415

Masters of Jazz MJCD 18

38968-B *Chillun, Get Up* (hw, trio vo) [SO] Decca 02601

Masters of Jazz MJCD 18, Classics 505, Conifer CHD 132

38969-A *Solitude* (1, hw vo) [SO] Decca 299

Masters of Jazz MJCD 18, Classics 505, Decca GRD608-2, Membran 221999-306

New York, December 17, 1934

39169-A *Rain* (trio vo) [SO] Decca 415

Masters of Jazz MJCD 18, Classics 505, Fremeaux & Associés 212, Conifer CHD132, Big Band Era 201812, Alpha CD 47

39170-A *Since My Best Gal Turned Me Down* (trio vo) [SO] Decca 453

Masters of Jazz MJCD 18, Classics 505, Fremeaux & Associés 212, Conifer CHD132, Empress 897, Living Era CDAJA5091, Alpha CD 47

39171-A *Jealous* (hw vo) [EW] Decca 788

Masters of Jazz MJCD 18, Classics 505, Fremeaux & Associés 212, Big Band Era 260181, Alpha CD 47

New York, December 18, 1934

38916-C *Shake Your Head (from Side to Side)* [SO] Brunswick 02815

Masters of Jazz MJCD 18, Classics 505, Conifer CHD132, Living Era CDAJA5091, Time-Life STBB-27, Alpha CD 47

39172-A *Rhythm Is Our Business* (ws, ens vo) [EW] Decca 369

Masters of Jazz MJCD 18, Classics 505, Living Era CDAJA5091, Best of Jazz 4002, Charlie 1118, FMP 158284, Past Perfect PPCD 78111, Decca GRD608-2, GRP9923, Legends of Jazz 18032-2, Topaz TPZ 1005, Topaz TPZ 1030, CBS RPCD611, Phontastic PHONTCD 7653, Affinity CDAFS1036-4, Fremeaux & Associés 212, GRP99242, Columbia 1201, KAZ CD 31710, Jasmine JASCD 391, Membran 221999-306, Acrobat 4076, Time-Life STBB-27, Music Memoria MM 393422, Saga Jazz 066-4612, HNRCS 8005, Alpha CD 47, HNRSC 8005, Acrobat ACRCD 165

39172-B *Rhythm Is Our Business* (ws, ens vo) [EW] Decca 369

Masters of Jazz MJCD 18, Decca GRD608-2

39173-A *I'm Walking through Heaven with You* (hw vo) [EW] Decca 682

39173-B *I'm Walking through Heaven with You* (hw vo) [EW] Decca 682

Masters of Jazz MJCD 18, Classics 505

Paul Webster (tp), Tompkins, Oliver (tp, vo), Elmer Crumbley, Bowles (tb), Eddie Durham (tb, g), Smith (cl, as, bars, vo), Dent (as), Dan Grissom (cl, as, vo), Thomas (cl, ts, vo), Carruthers (cl, as, bars), Wilcox (p), Norris (g), Allen (b), Crawford (d, vib, bells)

Lunceford replaces Grissom, as (1)

New York, May 29, 1935

39551-A *Sleepy Time Gal* (1) [EW] Decca 908
Classics 505, Masters of Jazz MJCD 57, Decca GRD608-2, Living Era CDAJA 5091, EMP Jazz Archives 158242, Fremeaux & Associés 212, Topaz TPZ1005, Jasmine JASCD 391, KAZ CD 317, Membran 221999-306, Music Memoria MM 393422, Saga Jazz 066-4612, Alpha CD 47, Acrobat ACRCD 165

39552-A *Bird of Paradise* [ED] Decca 639
Classics 505, Masters of Jazz MJCD 57, Decca GRD608-2, Past Perfect PPCD 78111, Legends of Jazz 18032-2, Membran 221999-306, Alpha CD 47

39553-A *Rhapsody Junior* [ED] Decca 693
Classics 505, Masters of Jazz MJCD 57, Decca GRD608-2, Membran 221999-306

39554-A *Runnin' Wild* [WS] Decca 503
Classics 505, Masters of Jazz MJCD 57, Decca GRD608-2, GRP9923, Fremeaux & Associés 212, Topaz TPZ 1005, Membran 221999-306, Music Memoria MM 393422

39555-A *Four or Five Times* (so vo) [SO] Decca M30878
Topaz TPZ 1005

39556-A *Four or Five Times* (so vo) [SO] Decca 503
Classics 505, Masters of Jazz MJCD 57, Living Era CDAJA 5091, Jazz Portrait 14531, EMP Jazz Archives 158242, Black & Blue BLE59241-2, Past Perfect PPCD 78111, Joan 7147, GRP9923, Jasmine JASCD 391, History 2.1913-HI, Membran 221999-306, Saga Jazz 066-4612, Verve Spiegel CD 83178

39556-B *Four or Five Times* (so vo) [SO] Decca 503
Classics 505, Masters of Jazz MJCD 57, Empress 897, Past Perfect 204358-303, Jazz after Hours 200025, Decca GRD608-2

39557-A *(If I Had) Rhythm in My Nursery Rhymes* (ws vo) [EW] Decca 572
Classics 505, Masters of Jazz MJCD 57, Empress 897, Conifer CHD132

New York, September 23, 1935
39996-A *Babs* (trio vo) [SO] Decca 576
Classics 505, Masters of Jazz MJCD 57, Fremeaux & Associés 212, Conifer CHD132, Quad Jazz 80007UAR1U

39996-D *Babs* (trio vo) [SO] Decca 576

39997-A *Swanee River* [SO] Decca 688
Classics 505, Masters of Jazz MJCD 57, EMP Jazz Archives 158242, Decca GRD645, Fremeaux & Associés 212, Black & Blue BLE54241-2, Past Perfect PPCD 78111, Conifer CHD132, MCA GRP9923, Legends of Jazz 18032-2, West Hill WH-4017(9), Membran 221999-306, Acrobat 4076, Saga Jazz 066-4612, Quad Jazz 80007UAR1U

39998-A *Thunder* (dg vo) [EW] Decca 576
Classics 505, Masters of Jazz MJCD 57, Quad Jazz 80007UAR1U

39999-A *Oh Boy* [ED] Decca 628
Classics 505, Masters of Jazz MJCD 57, Decca GRD645, Fremeaux & Associés 212, Black & Blue BLE54241-2, Past Perfect PPCD 78111, Conifer CHD132, MCA GRP 9923, Legends of Jazz 18032-2, Quad Jazz 80007UAR1U

New York, late September 1935

60000 *Charmaine* (dg vo) [SO]

Conifer CHD132

60001 *Hittin' the Bottle* (so vo) [ED]

Topaz TPZ 1005

New York, September 30, 1935

60013-A (*You Take the East, Take the West, Take the North) I'll Take The South* (so, trio vo) [SO] Decca 805

Classics 505, Masters of Jazz MJCD 57, Decca GRD645, Empress 897, Past Perfect PPCD 78111, Conifer CHD132, TP 115, Quad Jazz 80007UAR1U

60014-A *Avalon* [ED] Decca 668

Classics 505, Masters of Jazz MJCD 57, Decca GRD645, Fremeaux & Associés 212, EMP Jazz Archives 158242, Black & Blue BLE59241-2, Topaz TPZ 1005, GRP GRD2-629, MCA GRP9923, Jasmine JASCD 391, Time-Life STBB-27, Quad Jazz 80007UAR1U

60015-A *Charmaine* (dg vo) [SO] Decca 628

Classics 505, Masters of Jazz MJCD 57, Decca GRD645, Quad Jazz 80007UAR1U

60016-A *Hittin' the Bottle* (so vo) [ED] Decca 765

Classics 505, Masters of Jazz MJCD 57, Decca GRD645, Living Era CDAJA5091, Past Perfect PPCD 78111, Topaz TPZ 1005, MCA GRP 9923, Legends of Jazz 18032-2, Jasmine JASCD 391, Quad Jazz 80007UAR1U, Pearl 7095

Norris also vln (1)

New York, December 23, 1935

60274-A *My Blue Heaven* (1, trio vo) [SO] Decca 712

Classics 510, Masters of Jazz MJCD 57, Decca GRD645, MCA GRP9923, Empress 897, EMP Jazz Archives 158242, Living Era CDAJA5091, Living Era CDAJA5151, Living Era CDAJA5309, Living Era CDAJA5280, Best of Jazz 4002, Legends of Jazz 18032-2, ASV 239, Phontastic PHONTCD 7657, Membran 221999-306, Time-Life STBB-27, Quad Jazz 80007UAR1U, Gallerie 445

60274-B *My Blue Heaven* (1, trio vo) [SO] Decca 3520 unissued

60275-A *I'm Nuts about Screwy Music* (ws vo) [EW] Decca DL79238

MCA 1305, MCA 510018, Brunswick 87582, Coral COPS3452

60275-B *I'm Nuts About Screwy Music* (ws vo) [EW] Decca 682

Classics 510, Masters of Jazz MJCD 57, Decca GRD645, MCA GRP9923, Fremeaux & Associés 212, Conifer CHD132, Jasmine JASCD 391, Quad Jazz 80007UAR1U

60276-A *The Best Things in Life Are Free* (dg vo) [EW] Decca 788

Classics 510, Masters of Jazz MJCD 57, Past Perfect PPCD 78111, Conifer CHD132, Legends of Jazz 18032-2, Quad Jazz 80007UAR1U

60277-A *The Melody Man* (so vo) [SO] Decca 805

Classics 510, Masters of Jazz MJCD 57, Past Perfect PPCD 78111, Conifer CHD132,

GRP GRD642, Jasmine JASCD 391, Membran 221999-306, Quad Jazz 80007UAR1U

60277-B *The Melody Man* (so vo) [SO] Decca 805

Masters of Jazz MJCD 57

Ed Brown (as, ts, cl) replaces Dent; Oliver, Tompkins also percussion (1); Myra Johnson, vo

New York, ca. July 1936

Jazznocracy (part) [WH]

Masters of Jazz MJCD 57, Jazz Hour 3004 New Sound Planet JU 325, Gallerie 455

It's Rhythm Coming to Life Again (? vo) [EW]

Masters of Jazz MJCD 57, Jazz Hour 3004, New Sound Planet JU 325, Gallerie 445

Rhythm Is Our Business (ws, ens vo) [EW]

Masters of Jazz MJCD 57, Jazz Hour 3004, New Sound Planet JU 325

You Can't Pull the Wool Over My Eyes (mj vo) [SO]

Masters of Jazz MJCD 57, Jazz Hour 3004, New Sound Planet JU 325

Moonlight on the Ganges [EW]

Masters of Jazz MJCD 57, Jazz Hour 3004, New Sound Planet JU 325

Nagasaki (1) (et, ens vo) [SO]

Masters of Jazz MJCD 57, Jazz Hour 3004, New Sound Planet JU 325

Note: this is the soundtrack of the Vitaphone short "Jimmie Lunceford and His Dance Orchestra."

Wilcox also cel (1)

New York, August 31, 1936

61246-A *Organ Grinder's Swing* (1) [SO] Decca 908

Classics 510, Masters of Jazz MJCD 71, Decca GRD645, Empress 897, Fremeaux & Associés 212, EMP Jazz Archives 158242, Past Perfect 204358-203, Charly 1118, Charly CD DIG 15, Living Era CDAJA5091, Jazz after Hours 200025, Black & Blue BLE59241-2, Jazz Portrait 14531, MCA GRP9923, Affinity CDAFS1036-4, Jazz Roots CD 56013, Topaz TPZ 1005, Topaz TPZ 1030, GRP99242, Joan 7147, Jasmine JASCD 391, Phontastic PHONTCD 7658, KAZ CD 317, History 2.1913-HI, Membran 221999-306, Properbox 76, Acrobat 4076, Time-Life STBB-27, Music Memoria MM 393422, Saga Jazz 066-4612, Quad Jazz 80007UAR1U

New York, September 1, 1936

61247-A *On the Beach at Bali Bali* (so vo) [SO] Decca 915

Classics 505, Masters of Jazz MJCD 71, Decca GRD645, Empress 897, Conifer CHD132, Quad Jazz 80007UAR1U

61248-A *Me and the Moon* (trio vo) [SO] Decca 915

Classics 505, Masters of Jazz MJCD 71, Quad Jazz 80007UAR1U

61249-A *Living from Day to Day* (dg vo) [SO] Decca 960

Classics 505, Masters of Jazz MJCD 71, Quad Jazz 80007UAR1U

61250-A *'Tain't Good (Like a Nickel Made of Wood)* (1, trio vo) [SO] Decca 960

Classics 505, Masters of Jazz MJCD 71, Decca GRD646, Phontastic PHONTCD 7658, Acrobat 4076, Quad Jazz 80007UAR1U

Smith, Oliver, Norris (trio vo)

New York, October 14, 1936

61323-A *Muddy Water (a Mississippi Moan)* (trio vo) [SO] Decca 1219

Classics 505, Masters of Jazz MJCD 71, Decca GRD646, Conifer CHD123, Past Perfect PPCD 78111, Past Perfect PPCD 78130, Legends of Jazz 18032-2, Membran 221999-306, Quad Jazz 80007UAR1U

61324-A *I Can't Escape from You* (dg vo) [SO] Decca 980

Classics 505, Masters of Jazz MJCD 71, Quad Jazz 80007UAR1U

61325-A *Harlem Shout* [ED] Decca 980

Classics 505, Masters of Jazz MJCD 71, Decca GRD646, MCA GRP9923, Jazz after Hours 200025, Black & Blue BLE59241-2, Jazz Portrait 14531, Avid AVC532, Topaz TPZ 1005, Legends of Jazz 18032-2, Joan 7147, PLATCD479, Living Era CD AJA 5504, Jasmine JASCD 391, KAZ CD 317, History 2.1913-HI, Membran 221999-306, Time-Life STBB-27, Quad Jazz 80007UAR1U, Acrobat ACRCD 165

New York, October 26, 1936

61345-A *(This Is) My Last Affair* (dg vo) [SO] Decca 1035

Classics 505, Masters of Jazz MJCD 71, Decca GRD646, Acrobat 4076, Quad Jazz 80007UAR1U

61346-A *Running a Temperature* (so vo) [ED] Decca 1035

Classics 505, Masters of Jazz MJCD 71, Decca GRD646, Fremeaux & Associés 212, Charlie 1118, Jasmine JASCD 391, Quad Jazz 80007UAR1U

New York, January 18, 1937

61531-B *Honey, Keep Your Mind on Me* (dg vo) [ED]

Masters of Jazz MJCD 71

61532-A *Count Me Out* (dg vo) [ED] Decca 1229

Masters of Jazz MJCD 71, Classics 510, Quad Jazz 80007UAR1U

New York, January 20, 1937

61533-A *I'll See You in My Dreams* (dg vo) [EW] Decca 1318

Masters of Jazz MJCD 71, Classics 510, Black & Blue BLE59241-2, Quad Jazz 80007UAR1U

New York, January 26, 1937

61550-A *He Ain't Got Rhythm* (jt vo) [SO] Decca 1128

Masters of Jazz MJCD 71, Classics 510, Decca GRD645, MCA GRP9923, Past Perfect PPCD 78111, Jasmine JASCD 391, Quad Jazz 80007UAR1U

61551-A *Linger Awhile* (dg vo) [SO] Decca 1229

Masters of Jazz MJCD 71, Classics 510, Quad Jazz 80007UAR1U

61552-A *Honest and Truly* (dg vo) [EW] Decca 1219

Masters of Jazz MJCD 71, Classics 510, Quad Jazz 80007UAR1U

61552-B *Honest and Truly* (dg vo) [EW] Decca DL79239

MCA 1307, MCA 510032, Ajazz C1601

61553-A *Slumming on Park Avenue* (trio vo) [SO] Decca 1128

Masters of Jazz MJCD 71, Classics 510, Past Perfect PPCD 78111, Past Perfect PPCD
    78127, Best of Jazz 4002, Legends of Jazz 18032-2, Jasmine JASCD 391, Acrobat
    4076, Quad Jazz 80007UAR1U

Smith, Oliver, Tompkins (trio vo)

Broadcast, Konserthuset, Göteborg, Sweden, March 13, 1937

Sophisticated Lady [WS]

My Blue Heaven (trio vo) (part) [SO]

Rose Room (part) [WS]

Stratosphere (part) [JL/EW]

Durham (tb, g) probably replaced by unknown

New York, June 15, 1937

62259-A *Coquette* (dg vo) [SO] Decca 1340

Masters of Jazz MJCD 71, Classics 510, Fremeaux & Associés 212, Charly 1118, Topaz
    TPZ 1005, Time Life R960-20, Decca GRD641, Membran 221999-306, Time-Life
    STBB-27, Quad Jazz 80007UAR1U

62260-A *The Merry-Go-Round Broke Down* (so, ens vo) [SO] Decca 1318

Masters of Jazz MJCD 71, Classics 510, Decca GRD645, EMP Jazz Archives 158242,
    Jasmine JASCD 391, Membran 221999-306, Acrobat 4076, Music Memoria MM
    393422, Quad Jazz 80007UAR1U

62260-B *The Merry-Go-Round Broke Down* (so, ens vo) [SO] Decca 1318

Masters of Jazz MJCD 71

62261-A *Ragging the Scale* [SO] Decca 1364

Masters of Jazz MJCD 71, Classics 510, Best of Jazz 4002, EMP Jazz Archives 159982,
    Black & Blue BLE59241-2, Quad Jazz 80007UAR1U

62261-B *Ragging the Scale* [SO]

Decca GRD645, MCA GRP 16452

62262-A *Hell's Bells* Decca 1506

Masters of Jazz MJCD 71, Classics 520, Decca GRD645, Past Perfect PPCD 78111,
    Best of Jazz 18032-2, Jasmine JASCD 391

62263-A *For Dancers Only* Decca 1340

Masters of Jazz MJCD 71, Classics 520, Decca GRD645, Past Perfect PPCD 78111,
    Past Perfect PPCD 78104, Past Perfect 204358-203, MCA GRP99242, GRP9923,
    Hindsight HCD413, Black & Blue BLE59241-2, Fremeaux & Associés 212, Jazz
    Roots CD56013, Best of Jazz 4002, Prism PLATCD 971, Prism PLATBX 183, Liv-

ing Era CDAJA5091, Jazz after Hours 200025, Charly 1118, Jazz Portrait 14531, Topaz TPZ1005, Time-Life STBB-27, Time Life R960-20, Legends of Jazz 18032-2, Joan 7147, Golden Stars 5308, Jasmine JASCD 391, KAZ CD 317, History 2.1913-HI, Acrobat 4076, Music Memoria MM 393422, Saga Jazz 066-4612, Verve Ken Burns CD 2

New York, July 8, 1937

62344-A *Posin'* (ws, ens vo) [SO] Decca 1355
Masters of Jazz MJCD 84, Classics 520, EMP Jazz Archives 159982, Black & Blue BLE59241-2, Charly 1118, Phontastic PHONTCD 7663, Past Perfect PPCD 78111, Intersound 1446, Acrobat 4076, Quad Jazz 80007UAR1U

62345-A *The First Time I Saw You* (dg vo) [EW] Decca 1364
Masters of Jazz MJCD 84, Classics 520, Empress 897, Acrobat 4076, Quad Jazz 80007UAR1U

62346-A *Honey, Keep Your Mind on Me* (dg vo) [ED] Decca 1355
Masters of Jazz MJCD 84, Classics 520, Quad Jazz 80007UAR1U

62347-A *Put On Your Old Grey Bonnet* (et, jt vo) [WS] Decca 1508
Masters of Jazz MJCD 84, Classics 520, Black & Blue BLE59241-2, P-Vine PCD 5777, Acrobat 4076, Music Memoria MM 393422, Quad Jazz 80007UAR1U

Tompkins, Oliver (tp, vo), Webster (tp), Crumbley, Bowles (tb), James "Trummy" Young (tb, vo), Smith (cl, as, bars, vo), Ted Buckner (as), Grissom (cl, as, vo), Thomas (cl, ts, vo), Carruthers (cl, as, bars), Wilcox (p), Norris (g), Allen (b), Crawford (d, bells)

Los Angeles, November 5, 1937

DLA1010-A *Pigeon Walk* [ED] Decca 1659
Masters of Jazz MJCD 84, Classics 520, EMP Jazz Archives 158242, Living Era CDAJA5091, Topaz TPZ 1005, Black & Blue BLE59241-2, Jasmine JASCD 391, Music Memoria MM 393422, Quad Jazz 80007UAR1U

DLA1010-C *Pigeon Walk* [ED] test pressing, unissued

DLA1011-A *Like a Ship at Sea* (dg vo) [EW] Decca 1617
Masters of Jazz MJCD 84, Classics 520, Best of Jazz 4002, Quad Jazz 80007UAR1U

DLA1012-A *Teasin' Tessie Brown* (et, ens voc) [SO] Decca 1734
Masters of Jazz MJCD 84, Classics 520, Quad Jazz 80007UAR1U

DLA1013-A *Annie Laurie* [SO] Decca 1569
Masters of Jazz MJCD 84, Classics 520, Fremeaux & Associés 212, EMP Jazz Archives 158242, Best of Jazz 4002, Time Life R960-20, Time-Life STBB-27, Black & Blue BLE59241-2, Charly 1118, Jasmine JASCD 391, Music Memoria MM 393422, Saga Jazz 066-4612, Quad Jazz 80007UAR1U

DLA1014-A *Frisco Fog* [LC] Decca 1569
Masters of Jazz MJCD 84, Classics 520, Past Perfect PPCD 78111, Past Perfect PPCD 78129, Legends of Jazz 18032-2, Jasmine JASCD 391, Quad Jazz 80007UAR1U

New York, January 6, 1938

63133-A *Margie* (ty vo) [SO] Decca 1617

Masters of Jazz MJCD 84, Classics 520, Past Perfect PPCD 78111, Past Perfect 204358-
203, Legends of Jazz 18032-2, Black & Blue BLE59241-2, Jazz after Hours 200025,
Charly 1118, EMP Jazz Archives 158242, Jazz Portrait 14531, Topaz TPZ 1005,
Time Life R960-20, Time-Life STBB-27, Living Era CDAJA5091, Living Era
CDAJA5466, Best of Jazz 4002, Jazz Roots 56013, Phontastic PHONTCD 7665,
Joan 7147, Columbia 120103, Jazz Archives 159972, Jasmine JASCD 391, KAZ CD
317, History 2.1913-HI, Music Memoria MM 393422, Saga Jazz 066 4612, Quad Jazz
80007UAR1U, Acrobat ACRCD 165

63134-A *The Love Nest* (dg vo) [SO] Decca 1734

Masters of Jazz MJCD 84, Classics 520, Quad Jazz 80007UAR1U

63135-A *I'm Laughing Up My Sleeve (Ha-ha-ha-ha-ha)* (so vo) [SO] Decca 1659

Masters of Jazz MJCD 84, Classics 520, Quad Jazz 80007UAR1U

New York, April 12, 1938

63585-A *Down by the Old Mill Stream* (dg vo) [SO] Decca 1927

Masters of Jazz MJCD 84, Classics 520, Quad Jazz 80007UAR1U

63586-A *My Melancholy Baby* (dg vo) [EW] Decca 1808

Masters of Jazz MJCD 84, Classics 520, Quad Jazz 80007UAR1U

63587-A *Sweet Sue, Just You* (so vo) [SO] Decca 1927

Masters of Jazz MJCD 84, Classics 520, Jasmine JASCD 391, Quad Jazz 80007UAR1U

63588-A *By the River Sainte Marie* (dg vo) [SO] Decca 1808

Masters of Jazz MJCD 84, Classics 520, Fremeaux & Associés 212, Time-Life R960-
20, Time-Life STBB-27, Saga Jazz 066-4612, Quad Jazz 80007UAR1U, Soundies
SCD 4132

Broadcast "America Dances," CBS Studio, New York, October 21, 1938

Jazznocracy [WH]

Charmaine (dg vo) [SO]

Margie (ty vo) (part) [SO]

Organ Grinder's Swing [SO]

Put On Your Old Grey Bonnet (et, jt, ens vo) [WS]

Four or Five Times (so vo) [SO]

For Dancers Only (part) [SO]

My Blue Heaven (trio vo) [SO]

Avalon (part) [ED]

Rhythm Is Our Business (so, ens vo) (part) [EW]

New York, January 3, 1939

23904-1 *Rainin'* (dg vo) [SO] Vocalion/OKeh 4595

Masters of Jazz MJCD 84, Classics 520, Quad Jazz 80007UAR1U

23904-2 *Rainin'* (dg vo) [SO] Odeon A2360

23905-1 *'Tain't What You Do (It's the Way That You Do It)* (ty, ens vo) [SO] Vocalion/OKeh 4582

Masters of Jazz MJCD 84, Classics 520, Fremeaux & Associés 212, EMP Jazz Archives 158242, Columbia 503283 2, Columbia CK45143, Columbia C2K52454-2, Arcade 2004580, Past Perfect 204358-203, Charly CD DIG 2, Jazz Portrait 14531, Jazz after Hours 200025, Jazz Roots 56013, Topaz TPZ 1005, Topaz TPZ 1030, Best of Jazz 4002, Living Era CDAJA5091, Phontastic PHONTCD 7667, Joan 7147, PLATCD479, Jasmine JASCD 391, KAZ CD 317, History 2.1913-HI, New Sound NSTD 215, P-Vine PCD 5777, Acrobat 4076, Acrobat ACRCD 165, Time-Life STBB-27, Music Memoria MM 393422, Saga Jazz 066-4612, Quad Jazz 80007UAR1U, Castle Pulse PLSMC 419

23905-2 *'Tain't What You Do (It's the Way That You Do It)* (ty, ens vo) [SO] Vocalion/OKeh 4595

23906-1 *Cheatin' on Me* (ty, trio vo) [SO] Vocalion/OKeh 4595

Masters of Jazz MJCD 84, Classics 520, Fremeaux & Associés 212, EMP Jazz Archives 158242, Jazz Portrait 14531, Best of Jazz 4002, Time Life R960-20, Time-Life STBB-27, Jazz Roots CD56013, Past Perfect 204358-203, Jazz after Hours 200025, Topaz TPZ 1005, Joan 7147, History 2.1913-HI, Saga Jazz 066-4612, Quad Jazz 80007UAR1U

23906-2 *Cheatin' on Me* (ty, trio vo) [SO] Vocalion/OKeh 4595

Masters of Jazz MJCD 84

2397-1 *Le Jazz Hot* [SO] Vocalion/OKeh 4595

Masters of Jazz MJCD 84, Classics 520, Living Era CDAJA5091, Columbia 503283 2, Jazz Portrait 14531, Past Perfect 04358-203, Jazz after Hours 200025, Black & Blue BLE59241-2, Joan 7147, KAZ CD 317, History 2.1913-HI, Music Memoria MM 393422, Quad Jazz 80007UAR1U, Acrobat ACRCD 165

23907-2 *Le Jazz Hot* [SO] Vocalion/OKeh 4595

Masters of Jazz MJCD 94

23908-1 *Time's A-Wastin'* (so vo) [SO] Vocalion/OKeh 4887

Masters of Jazz MJCD 84, Classics 520, Living Era CDAJA5091, Fremeaux & Associés 212, Time-Life R960-20, Time-Life STBB-27, Jasmine JASCD 391, Quad Jazz 80007UAR1U, Castle Pulse PLSMC 419

23908-2 *Time's A-Wastin'* (so vo) [SO] Vocalion/OKeh 4887

Masters of Jazz MJCD 84

CBS broadcast, "Saturday Night Swing Club" No. 129, New York, January 28, 1939

Cheatin' On Me (ty, trio voc) [SO]

Jazz Hour 3004

'Tain't What You Do (It's the Way That You Do it) (ty, ens vo) (part) [SO]

Jazz Hour 3004

New York, January 31, 1939

24051-1 *Baby, Won't You Please Come Home?* (jt vo) [SO]

Masters of Jazz MJCD 98

24051-2 *Baby, Won't You Please Come Home?* (jt vo) [SO] Vocalion/OKeh 4667

Classics 532, Masters of Jazz MJCD 98, Columbia 503283 2, Past Perfect 204358-203, EMP Jazz Archives 159982, Living Era CDAJA 5091, Jazz after Hours 200025, EMP Jazz Archives 158242, Fremeaux & Associés 212, Jazz Roots CD56013, Black & Blue BLE59241-2, Jazz Portrait 14531, Joan 7147, Tring GRF086, History 2.1913-HI, Music Memoria MM 393422, Saga Jazz 066 4612, Quad Jazz 80007UAR1U, Castle Pulse PLSMC 419

24051-3 *Baby, Won't You Please Come Home?* (jt vo) [SO] Armed Forces Radio Service H-12-538

24052-2 *You're Just a Dream* (dg vo) [SO] Vocalion/OKeh 4754

Classics 532, Masters of Jazz MJCD 98, Tring GRF086, Castle Pulse PLSMC 419 391

24053-1 *The Lonesome Road* (ty voc) [SO] Vocalion/OKeh 4831

Classics 532, Masters of Jazz MJCD 98, Columbia 503283 2, Columbia 120104, Columbia 120109, Columbia 220114, Past Perfect 204358-203, Best of Jazz 4002, Jazz after Hours 200025, Jazz Portrait 14531, Fremeaux & Associés 212, Jazz Roots CD56013, Joan 7147, Tring GRF086, KAZ CD 317, History 2.1913-HI, Saga Jazz 066 4612, Quad Jazz 80007UAR1U, Acrobat ACRCD 165

24054-2 *You Set Me On Fire* (dg vo) [SO] Vocalion/OKeh 4712

Classics 532, Masters of Jazz MJCD 98, Tring GRF086, Castle Pulse PLSMC 419

24055-1 *I've Only Myself to Blame* (dg vo) [SO] Vocalion/OKeh 4754

Classics 532, Masters of Jazz MJCD 98, Tring GRF086

New York, February 7, 1939

24083-1 *What Is This Thing Called Swing* (jt vo) [SO] Vocalion/OKeh 4875

Classics 532, Masters of Jazz MJCD 98, Legends of Jazz 18032-2, Past Perfect PPCD 78111, Jasmine JASCD, Castle Pulse PLSMC 419 391, Tring GRF086

24083-2 *What Is This Thing Called Swing* (jt vo) [SO]

Masters of Jazz MJCD 98

24084-1 *Mixup* [SO] Columbia 35919

Classics 532, Masters of Jazz MJCD 98, Tring GRF086

24085-1 *Shoemaker's Holiday* [SO] Vocalion/OKeh 4712

Classics 532, Masters of Jazz MJCD 98, Columbia 503283 2, Tring GRF086, Castle Pulse PLSMC 419 391

24086-1 *Blue Blazes* [SO] Vocalion/OKeh 4667

Classics 532, Masters of Jazz MJCD 98, Columbia 503283 2 Best of Jazz 4002, Black & Blue BLE59241-2, Tring GRF086

CBS broadcast, "Saturday Night Swing Club," New York, ca. March 1939

Well, All Right Then (ens vo) [head]
Jazz Hour 3004

New York, April 7, 1939
24350-A *Mandy (Make Up Your Mind)* [SO] Vocalion/OKeh 4831
Classics 532, Masters of Jazz MJCD 98, Columbia 503283 2, Jazz Portrait 14531, Past
   Perfect 204358-203, Jazz after Hours 200025, Jazz Roots CD55013, Joan 7147, Tring
   GRF086, History 2.1913-HI, Quad Jazz 80007UAR1U, Castle Pulse PLSMC 419
   391
24351-A *Easter Parade* (ty vo) [SO] Columbia 35484
Classics 532, Masters of Jazz MJCD 98, Fremeaux & Associés 212, Jasmine JASCD
   391, Tring GRF086, Castle Pulse PLSMC 419 391
24352-A *Ain't She Sweet?* (ty, trio vo) [SO] Vocalion/OKeh 4875
Classics 532, Masters of Jazz MJCD 98, Fremeaux & Associés 212, Sony Columbia
   50328 2, l'Art Vocal 8, Jazz Roots CD56013, Best of Jazz 4002, Time-Life R960-20,
   Time-Life STBB-27, Columbia 503283 2, Jazz after Hours 200025, Past Perfect
   PPCD 78111, Phontastic PHONTCD56013, Legends of Jazz 18032-2, Tring
   GRF086, KAZ CD 317, History 2.1913-HI, Saga Jazz 066-4612, Quad Jazz
   80007UAR1U, Castle Pulse PLSMC 419 391, Acrobat ACRCD 165
24353-A *White Heat* [WH] Vocalion/OKeh 5156
Classics 532, Masters of Jazz MJCD 98, Columbia 503283 2, Avid AVC540, Tring
   GRF086, Castle Pulse PLSMC 419

New York, May 17, 1939
24643-B *Oh Why, Oh Why* (dg vo) [SO] Vocalion/OKeh 4979
Classics 532, Masters of Jazz MJCD 98, Tring GRF086
24644-A *Well, All Right Then* (ens vo) [head] Vocalion/OKeh 4887
Classics 532, Masters of Jazz MJCD 98, Columbia 503283 2, Jazz Portrait 14531,
   Start/Parade PAR 2012, Fremeaux & Associés 212, Time-Life R960-20, Time-Life
   STBB-27, Jazz Roots CD56013, Jasmine JASCD 391, Tring GRF086, History
   2.1913-HI, Quad Jazz 80007UAR1U
24644-B *Well, All Right Then* (ens vo) [head]
Masters of Jazz MJCD 98
24645-A *You Let Me Down* (dg vo) [SO]
Masters of Jazz MJCD 98, Classics 53
224645-B *You Let Me Down* (dg vo) [SO] unissued
24646-A *I Love You* (dg vo) [SO] Columbia 38097 dj copies only
24646-B *I Love You* (dg vo) [SO] Vocalion/OKeh 4979
Masters of Jazz 98, Classics 532, Tring GRF086

Broadcast, unknown location and date, 1939
Up a Lazy River [RS]
Song of the Islands [EW]

Tompkins, Gerald Wilson, Webster (tp), Crumbley, Bowles (tb), Young (tb, vo), Smith (cl, as, vo), Buckner (fl, cl, as), Grissom (cl, as, ts, vo), Thomas (fl, cl, ts, vo), Carruthers (cl, as, bars), Wilcox (p), Norris (g), Allen (b), Crawford (d)

New York, August 2, 1939

24965-A *Who Did You Meet Last Night?* (dg vo) [WB] Vocalion/OKeh 5116

Masters of Jazz MJCD 98, Classics 532, Tring GRF086

24966-A *You Let Me Down* (dg vo) [SO] Vocalion/OKeh 5033

Masters of Jazz MJCD 98, Classics 532, Start/Parade PAR 2012, Tring GRF086

24967-A *Sassin' the Boss* (ens, ws vo) [JS] Vocalion/OKeh 5116

Masters of Jazz MJCD 98, Classics 532, Tring GRF086

24968-A *I Want the Waiter (with the Water)* (ty, ens vo) [SO] Vocalion/OKeh 5033

Masters of Jazz MJCD 98, Classics 532, Start/Parade PAR 2012, Columbia 503283-A, Tring GRF086

24969-A *I Used to Love You (but It's All Over Now)* (jt vo) [EH] Vocalion/OKeh 5276

Masters of Jazz MJCD 98, Classics 532, Start/Parade PAR 2012, EMP Jazz Archives 159982, Jasmine JASCD 391, Tring GRF086

Lunceford, Buckner, and Thomas also fl (1)

New York, September 14, 1939

26066-A *Belgium Stomp (Dutch Kitchen Stomp/State and Tioga Stomp)* [BM] Vocalion/OKeh 5207

Masters of Jazz MJCD 147, Classics 532, Start/Parade PAR 2012, Fremeaux & Associés 212, Living Era CDAJA 5091, Jasmine JASCD 391, Tring GRF086

26067-A *You Can Fool Some of the People (Some of the Time)* (ty vo) [BM] Vocalion/OKeh 5156

Masters of Jazz MJCD 147, Classics 532, Tring GRF086

26068-A *Think of Me, Little Daddy* (ty vo) [EI] Vocalion/OKeh 5207

Masters of Jazz MJCD 147, Classics 532, Start/Parade PAR 2012, Best of Jazz 4002, Time-Life R960-20, Time-Life STBB-27, Jasmine JASCD 391, Tring GRF086

26069-A *Liza (All the Clouds'll Roll Away)* (1) [EI] Vocalion/OKeh 5276

Masters of Jazz MJCD 147, Classics 532, Start/Parade PAR 2012, Tring GRF086, Past Perfect PPCD 78131

Note: Trummy Young sings "Think of me, little mama."

Eugene "Snooky" Young (tp) replaces Tompkins

New York, December 14, 1939

25749-1 *Put It Away* (ws, ens vo) [WB] Vocalion/OKeh 5362

Masters of Jazz MJCD 147, Classics 565, Black & Blue BLE59241-2

25750-1 *I'm Alone with You* [BE] Columbia 35484

Masters of Jazz MJCD 147, Classics 565, Living Era CDAJA5091, KAZ CD 317, Acrobat ACRCD 165

25751-1 *Rock It for Me* (jt vo) [BM] Columbia 35860

Masters of Jazz MJCD 147, Classics 565, Living Era CDAJA5091, Start/Parade PAR 2012, Columbia 503283-2, KAZ CD 317, Castle Pulse PLSMC 419, Acrobat ACRCD 165

25752-1 *I'm in an Awful Mood* (ty vo) [BM] Vocalion/OKeh 5395
Masters of Jazz MJCD 147, Classics 565, Start/Parade PAR 2012

25752-2 *I'm in an Awful Mood* (ty vo) [BM]
Masters of Jazz MJCD 147, EMP Jazz Archives 159982, EMP Jazz Archives 159802

25753-1 *Wham (Re-Bop-Boom-Bam)* (ws, ens vo) [ED] Vocalion/OKeh 5326
Masters of Jazz MJCD 147, Classics 565, Columbia 503283 2, Fremeaux & Associés 212, EMP Jazz Archives 158242, Hindsight HCD413, Black & Blue BLE59241-2, Saga Jazz 066-4612

25753-2 *Wham (Re-Bop-Boom-Bam)* (ws, ens vo) [ED]
Masters of Jazz MJCD 147

25754-1 *Pretty Eyes* (dg vo) [BM] Vocalion/OKeh 5430
Masters of Jazz MJCD 147, Classics 565

25755-1 *Uptown Blues (Marilyn Comes On)* [head] Vocalion/OKeh 5362
Masters of Jazz MJCD 147, Classics 565, Columbia 503283 2, Fremeaux & Associés 212, EMP Jazz Archives 158242, Best of Jazz 4002, Jazz Roots CD56002, Jazz Roots 56013, Start/Parade PAR 2012, Memoir CDMOIR507, Past Perfect 204358-203, Living Era CDAJA 5091, Jazz after Hours 200025, Time-Life R960-20, Time-Life STBB-27, Jazz Portrait 14531, Topaz TPZ 1005, RST 91566-2, Columbia CK40651, Black & Blue BLE59241-2, Joan 7147, Jasmine JASCD 391, KAZ CD 317, History 2.1913-HI, Music Memoria MM 393422, Saga Jazz 066-4612, Quad Jazz 80007UAR1U, Castle Pulse PLSCD 546, Acrobat ACRCD 165

25756-1 *Lunceford Special* [ED] Vocalion/OKeh 5326
Masters of Jazz MJCD 147, Classics 565, Columbia 503283 2, Fremeaux & Associés 212, EMP Jazz Archives 158242, Start/Parade PAR 2012, Sony A24382, Black & Blue BLE59241-2, Jasmine JASCD 391, KAZ CD 317, Music Memoria MM 393422, Saga Jazz 066-4612, Castle Pulse PLSMC 419, Acrobat ACRCD 165

New York, January 5, 1940
26397-A *Bugs Parade* [BM] Columbia 35547
Masters of Jazz MJCD 147, Classics 565, Start/Parade PAR 2012, EMP Jazz Archives 159982, Abrams CD221

26398-A *Blues in the Groove* [ED] Vocalion/OKeh 5395
Masters of Jazz MJCD 147, Classics 565, Start/Parade PAR 2012, Castle Pulse PLSMC 419

26399-A *I Wanta Hear Swing Songs* (ty vo) [BM] Columbia 35453
Masters of Jazz MJCD 147, Classics 565, Fremeaux & Associés 212

26400-A *It's Time to Jump and Shout* [ED] Vocalion/OKeh 5430
Masters of Jazz MJCD 147, Classics 565, Columbia 503283 2

Unidentified broadcast, New York, January 7, 1940
Sonata by Ludwig van Beethoven "Pathétique" Opus 13 [CW]

Los Angeles, February 28, 1940
LA2163-C *What's Your Story, Morning Glory?* [BM] Columbia 35510
Masters of Jazz MJCD 147, Classics 565, Columbia 503283 2, Living Era CDAJA 5091,
    Fremeaux & Associés 212, Music Memoria MM 393422, Saga Jazz 066-4612
LA2164-C *Dinah pt 1* [SO] Columbia 36054
Masters of Jazz MJCD 147, Classics 565, Columbia 503283 2
LA2165-C *Dinah pt 2* (jt vo) [SO] Columbia 36054
Masters of Jazz MJCD 147, Classics 565, Columbia 503283 2
LA2166-A *Sonata by Ludwig van Beethoven "Pathétique" Opus 13* [CW]
Columbia P3-16175
LA2166-C *Sonata by Ludwig van Beethoven "Pathétique" Opus 13* [CW] Columbia
    35453
Masters of Jazz MJCD 147, Classics 565

Chicago, May 9, 1940
WC3067-A *I Got It* (ty voc) [BM] Columbia 35510
Masters of Jazz MJCD 160, Classics 565, Start/Parade PAR 2012, Jasmine JASCD
    391, Castle Pulse PLSMC 419
WC3068-A *Chopin's Prelude No. 7* [RS] Columbia 35547
Masters of Jazz MJCD 160, Classics 565, Start/Parade PAR 2012, Saga Jazz 066-4612,
    Castle Pulse PLSMC 419
WC3068-C *Chopin's Prelude No. 7* [RS]
Columbia P3-16175
WC3069-A *Swingin' on C* [ED] Columbia 35725
Masters of Jazz MJCD 160, Classics 565, Start/Parade PAR 2012, Columbia 503283,
    EMP Jazz Archives 158242, Castle Pulse PLSMC 419
WC3069-B *Swingin' On C* [ED]
Masters of Jazz MJCD 160
WC3070-A *Let's Try Again* (dg vo) [BM] Columbia 35725
Masters of Jazz MJCD 160, Classics 565, Start/Parade PAR 2012, Castle Pulse
    PLSMC 419
WC3070-B *Let's Try Again* (dg vo) [BM] Columbia 35725
Jazum 46 (LP)
WC3071-A *Monotony in Four Flats* [BM] Columbia 35567
Masters of Jazz MJCD 160, Classics 565, Start/Parade PAR 2012, Saga Jazz 066-4612

MBS-WOR/CBS-WABC broadcast, Fiesta Danceteria, New York, June 7, 1940
Jazznocracy [WH]
Jazz Hour 3004

Swingin' On C [ED]
Jazz Hour 3004
Chopin's Prelude no. 7 [RS]
Jazz Hour 3004
Lunceford Special (part) [ED]
Let's Try Again (dg vo) [BM]
Alamac QSR 2422 (LP)
Blah-Blah-Blah! [EW]

Note: broadcast actually started at midnight.

CBS-WABC broadcast, Fiesta Danceteria, New York, June 8, 1940
My Melancholy Baby [EW]
Jazz Hour 3004
Lunceford Special (part) [ED]
Jazz Hour 3004

Note: broadcast actually started at midnight.

CBS broadcast, Fiesta Danceteria, New York, June 12, 1940
Barefoot Blues (ws vo) (part) [BM]
Privateer PRV 103 (LP)
By the River Sainte Marie (dg vo) (part) [SO]
Privateer PRV 103 (LP)
Isn't That Everything (dg vo) [RS]
Up a Lazy River [RS]
Song of the Islands [EW]
Body and Soul [EW]
Wham (Re Bop Boom Bam) (ws, ens vo) [ED]
Privateer PRV 103 (LP)
Uptown Blues [head] (part)

CBS-WABC broadcast, Fiesta Danceteria, New York, June 13, 1940
In the Shade of the Old Apple Tree [EW]
Everybodys EV-3006 (LP)
Make Believe [BE]
Jazz Hour 3004
The Lonesome Road (ty vo) [SO]

Philco broadcast, New York, June 1940
P27895-1 *Jazznocracy* (part) [WH], Lunceford talking
Columbia-Philco 8-B

Monotony in Four Flats [BM]

Smith, Trummy Young, Wilson (trio vo)
MBS-WOR broadcast, Fiesta Danceteria, New York, June 16, 1940
What's Your Story Morning Glory [BM]
Alamac QSR 2422 (LP)
My Blue Heaven (trio vo) [SO]
Le Jazz Hot [SO]
Ti-pi-tin (part) (ens vo) [SO]
Pavanne (part) [RS]
Alamac QSR 2422 (LP)
I Can't Believe That You're in Love with Me [BE]
Charmaine [RS]
Uptown Blues [head]

Dandridge Sisters (vo)
New York, June 19, 1940
26936-A *Barefoot Blues* (ws vo) [BM] Columbia 35860
Masters of Jazz MJCD 160, Classics 565, Start/Parade PAR 2012, Living Era CDAJA 5091
26937-A *Minnie The Moocher Is Dead* (ds vo) [RS] Columbia 35700
Masters of Jazz MJCD 160, Classics 565, Start/Parade PAR 2012
26938-A *I Ain't Gonna Study War No More* (ds, ens vo) [RS] Columbia 35567
Masters of Jazz MJCD 160, Classics 565, Milan RNCD-1302
26939-A *Pavanne* [RS] Columbia 35700
Masters of Jazz MJCD 160, Classics 565, Castle Pulse PLSMC 419

MBS-WOR broadcast, Fiesta Danceteria, New York, June 20, 1940
My Blue Heaven (trio vo) [SO]
Jazz Hour 3004
Monotony in Four Flats [BM]
Jazz Hour 3004
For Dancers Only [SO]
Privateer PRV 103 (LP)

Note: broadcast actually started after midnight.

Broadcast, Fiesta Danceteria, New York, June 22, 1940
I Used to Love You (but It's All Over Now) (jt vo) [EH]
Alanac QSR 2422 (LP)
Stardust [EW]

Please Say the Word (dg vo) [LW]

Coquette (dg vo) [SO]

CBS-WABC broadcast, Fiesta Danceteria, New York, June 25, 1940

Jazznocracy [WH]

Privateer PRV 103 (LP)

In the Shade of the Old Apple Tree [EW]

Take It [SO]

The Lonesome Road (ty vo) [SO]

Uptown Blues [head]

Broadcast, Fiesta Danceteria, New York, June 28, 1940

By the River Sainte Marie (dg vo) [SO]

Broadcast, Fiesta Danceteria, New York, June or July 1940

Just You [BE]

Privateer PRV 103 (LP)

Impromptu [EW]

Alamac QSR 2422 (LP)

Body and Soul/Stardust (part) [EW]

Alamac QSR 2422 (LP)

Unidentified broadcast(s), 1940

Uptown Blues [head]

First Time 2501, Onward to Yesterday 2501 (LPs)

I'm Walking through Heaven with You (dg vo) [EW]

Carruthers (vo)

New York, July 9, 1940

WC 3070-C *Let's Try Again* (dg vo) [BM]

Masters of Jazz MJCD 160

28005-A *Whatcha Know, Joe?* (ty, ens vo) [RS] Columbia 35625

Masters of Jazz MJCD 160, Classics 622

28006-A *Red Wagon* (ds, ec vo) [RS] Columbia 35782

Masters of Jazz MJCD 160, Classics 622

28007-A *You Ain't Nowhere* (ds, ens vo) [RS] Columbia 35782

Masters of Jazz MJCD 160, Classics 622, Gallerie 445

28008-A *Please Say the Word* (dg vo) [LW] Columbia 35625

Masters of Jazz MJCD 160, Classics 622

28008-B *Please Say the Word* (dg vo) [LW] unissued

Broadcast, probably Panther Room, Chicago, July 1940
What's Your Story Morning Glory [BM]
Honeysuckle Rose [GW]
Jazz Hour 3004
The Morning After (dg vo) [EW]
Wham (Re Bop Boom Bam) (ws, ens vo) [ED]
Rhythm Is Our Business (ws vo) [EW]
Uptown Blues (part) [head]

Lang-Worth Transcriptions, New York, November 12, 1940
LW 36 *State and Tioga Stomp (Belgium Stomp)* [BM]
Circle CCD11, Delta 11088, Hindsight HCD221
LW 33 *I Had a Premonition* (dg vo) [BM]
Circle CCD11, Delta 11088, Hindsight HCD221
Annie Laurie [SO]
Circle CCD11, Delta 11088, Hindsight HCD221
There I Go (dg vo) [EW]
Circle CCD11, Hindsight HCD221
LW 33 *My Heart Is a Helpless Thing* (dg vo) [EW]
Circle CCD11, Hindsight HCD221
I'm a Heck of a Guy (jt vo) [BM]
Circle CCD11, Hindsight HCD221
LW 34 *Blue Afterglow* (dg vo) [RS]
Circle CCD11, Delta 1088, Hindsight HCD221
I Heard My Heart (dg vo) [BM]
Circle CCD11. Hindsight HCD221

Lang-Worth Transcriptions, New York, December 11, 1940
LW 36 *Moonlight and Music* [BE]
Circle CCD11, Delta 11088, Soundscape 679
LW 36 *Battle Axe* [BM]
Circle CCD11, Delta 11088, Hindsight HCD221
LW 34 *The Morning After* (dg vo) [EW]
Circle CCD11, Delta 11088, Hindsight HCD221
LW 34 *Isn't That Everything* (dg vo) [RS]
Circle CCD11, Hindsight HCD221
Like a Ship at Sea (dg vo) [EW]
Circle CCD11, Delta 11088, Hindsight HCD221
LW 33 *Just You* [BE]
Circle CCD11, Delta 11088, Hindsight HCD221, Soundscape 679
I'm Walking through Heaven with You (dg vo) [EW]

Circle CCD11, Delta 11088, Hindsight HCD221
LW 36 *Okay for Baby* [LW]
Circle CCD11, Delta 11088, Hindsight HCD221, Soundscape 679

Broadcast, unknown location, probably late 1940
I'm Alone with You [BE]
Now I Lay Me Down to Dream (dg vo) [BE]
Put It Away (ws, ens vo) [WB]
Flight of the Jitterbug [DR]
Please Say the Word (dg vo) (part) [LW]

New York, December 23, 1940
29293-A *Okay for Baby* [LW] Columbia 35967
Classics 622, Masters of Jazz MJCD 160, Phontastic PHONTCD7668, Music Memo-
    ria MM 393422, Castle Pulse PLSMC 419
29294-A *Flight of the Jitterbug* [DR] Columbia 35967
Classics 622, Masters of Jazz MJCD 160
29295-A *Blue Afterglow* (dg vo) [RS] Columbia 35919
Classics 622, Masters of Jazz MJCD 160

New York, March 26, 1941
68874-A *Blue Prelude* (dg vo) [RS] Decca 3892
Classics 622, Masters of Jazz MJCD 160, Charly 1118, Empress 897
68875-A *I Had a Premonition* (dg vo) [BM] Decca 3718
Classics 622, Masters of Jazz MJCD 160, Jasmine JASCD 391
68876-A *Twenty-Four Robbers* (ty, ens vo) [RS] Decca 3892
Classics 622, Masters of Jazz MJCD 160, Charlie 1118, Jazz Portrait 14531, Jazz Roots
    CD56013, Past Perfect 204358-203, Jazz after Hours 200025, Joan 7147, Jasmine
    JASCD 391, History 2.1913-HI, Quad Jazz 80007UAR1U
68877-A *Battle Axe* [BM] Decca 3807
Classics 622, Masters of Jazz MJCD 160, Jasmine JASCD 391

New York, April 22, 1941
69035-A *Peace and Love for All (Prayer for Moderns)* (dg vo) [RS] Decca 3892
Classics 622, Masters of Jazz MJCD 160
69036-A *Chocolate* [RS] Decca 3807
Classics 622, Masters of Jazz MJCD 160, Jasmine JASCD 391
69036-B *Chocolate* [RS] unissued

Los Angeles, June 23, 1941
DLA2447-A *I'm Walking through Heaven with You* (dg vo) [EW] Decca 25016
Classics 622

DLA2448-A *You're Always in My Dreams* (dg vo) [EW] Decca 18534
Classics 622
DLA2449-A *Flamingo* (dg vo) [RS] Decca 3931
Classics 622, Jasmine JASCD 391
DLA2450-A *Siesta at the Fiesta* [head] Decca 3931
Classics 622, Best of Jazz 4002, Charly 1118, Jasmine JASCD 391
DLA2450-D *Siesta at the Fiesta* [head] Decca F-8053 unissued

Broadcast, Casa Mañana, Culver City, July 19, 1941
Up a Lazy River [RS]
Jazz Hour 3004

add Santo Pecora (tb), Stan Wrightsman (p)
Hollywood, ca. August 1941
Hang On to Your Lids Kids [RS] unissued
Blues In the Night (William Gillespie, Edward Barley chorus vo) [GW, WS, RH]
Rhino R2 75287, Rhino R2 79805

Note: this is the soundtrack of the Warner Brothers movie Blues in the Night.

omit Pecora and Wrightsman; Charles "Chuck" Parham (b) replaces Allen
New York, August 26, 1941
69680-A *Gone* (dg vo) [RS] Decca 4083
Classics 622
69681-A *Hi Spook* [GW] Decca 4032
Classics 622, Empress 897, Topaz TPZ 1005, Jasmine JASCD 391, KAZ CD 317
69682-A *Yard Dog Mazurka* [GW] Decca 4033
Classics 622, Empress 897, Best of Jazz 4002, Charly 1118, Fremeaux & Associés 212,
    Topaz TPZ 1005, KAZ CD 317, Saga Jazz 066-4612
69683-A *Impromptu* [EW] Decca 4083
Classics 622, Topaz TPZ 1005, Jasmine JASCD 391, Saga Jazz 066-4512

CBS Pabst Blue Ribbon broadcast, New York, November 13, 1941
Impromptu [EW]
Gone (dg vo) [RS]
My Blue Heaven (trio vo) [SO]
Jersey Bounce [GW]
Uptown Blues [head]

Wilcox (vo)
New York, December 22, 1941
70093-A *Blues in the Night pt 1* (ens vo) [GW, WS, RH] Decca 4125

Classics 622, Topaz TPZ 1005, Best of Jazz 4002, Empress 897, Charly 1118, Jazz Portrait 14531, EMP Jazz Archives 158242, Jazz after Hours 200025, Hindsight HCD413, Time-Life R960-20, Time-Life STBB-27, Jazz Roots CD56013, Jazz Roots CD56002, Joan 7147, Jasmine JASCD 382, Jasmine JASCD 391, History 2.1913-HI, Acrobat 4076, Music Memoria MM 393422, DBMCD 3001, Prism PLATBX 183, Quad Jazz 80007UAR1U

70094-A *Blues In the Night pt 2* (ens, ew, jt vo) [GW, WS, RH] Decca 4125

Classics 622, Topaz TPZ 1005, Best of Jazz 4002, Empress 897, Charly 1118, Jazz Portrait 14531, EMP Jazz Archives 158242, Jazz after Hours 200025, Hindsight HCD413, Time-Life R960-20, Time-Life STBB-27, Jazz Roots CD56013, Jazz Roots CD56002, Joan 7147, Jasmine JASCD 382, Jasmine JASCD 391, History 2.1913-HI, Acrobat 4076, Music Memoria MM3g3422, DBMCD 3001, Prism PLATBX 183, Quad Jazz 80007UAR1U

New York, December 23, 1941

70095-A *I'm Losing My Mind (Because of You)* (dg vo) [RS] Decca 4289

Classics 862, Jazz after Hours 200025, History 2.1913-HI, Membran 221999-306, Quad Jazz 80007UAR1U

70096-A *Life Is Fine* (ty, ens vo) [EWa] Decca 4289

Classics 862, Jazz after Hours 200025, Past Perfect PPCD 78111, History 2.1913-HI, Membran 221999-306, Acrobat 4076, Ceraton CT7003, Quad Jazz 80007UAR1U

Broadcast, New York, ca 1941–1942

Fatigue [EW]

Big Band Archives 2204-1 (LP)

Yard Dog Mazurka [GW]

Smith, Trummy Young, Thomas, Wilson (quartet vo)

New York, April 14, 1942

70654-A *It Had to Be You* (quartet vo) [TD] Decca 18504

Classics 862, History 2.1913-HI, Membran 221999-306, Acrobat 4076, Quad Jazz 80007UAR1U

70655-A *I'm Gonna Move to the Outskirts of Town pt 1* (dg vo) [EW] Decca 18324

Classics 862, Jazz after Hours 200025, Past Perfect 204358-203, Charly 1118, Jazz Portrait 14531, Joan 7147, History 2.1913-HI, Acrobat 4076, Prism PLATBX 183, Quad Jazz 80007UAR1U

70656-A *I'm Gonna Move to the Outskirts of Town pt 2* (dg vo) [EW] Decca 18324

Classics 862, Jazz after Hours 200025, Past Perfect 204358-203, Charly 1118, Jazz Portrait 14531, Joan 7147, History 2.1913-HI, Acrobat 4076, Prism PLATBX 183, Quad Jazz 80007UAR1U

Freddie Webster and Harry "Pee Wee" Jackson (tp) replace Snooky Young and Wilson; Fernando "Chico" Arbello (tb) replaces Crumbley, and Benny Waters (as) replaces Buckner

Broadcast, New York, mid-1942
Yard Dog Mazurka [GW]

Los Angeles, June 26, 1942
L3063-A *Strictly Instrumental* [GW] Decca 18463
Classics 862, Jazz after Hours 200025, EMP Jazz Archives 159982, Charly 1118, Topaz
    TPZ 1005, Jasmine JASCD 391, History 2.1913-HI, Quad Jazz 80007UAR1U
L3064-A *This Is My Confession (to You)* (dg vo) [EW]
Jazz after Hours 200025
L3065-A *Knock Me a Kiss* (ws vo) [EW] Decca 18463
Classics 862, Jazz after Hours 200025, EMP Jazz Archives 159982, Charly 1118, Topaz
    TPZ 1005, History 2.1913-HI, Quad Jazz 80007UAR1U
L3066-A *Keep Smilin', Keep Laughin', Be Happy* (jt vo) [HJ] Decca 18504
Classics 862, Jazz after Hours 200025, EMP Jazz Archives 159982, Best of Jazz 4002,
    EMP Jazz Archives 158242, FD Music 152052, History 2.1913-HI, Membran 221999-
    306, Quad Jazz 80007UAR1U

Broadcast, Trianon Ballroom, South Gate, June 1942
Jersey Bounce [GW]
IAJRC 17 (LP)

Bob Mitchell (tp)
Broadcast, Los Angeles, ca July 1942
LR-3007 *When the Swallows Come Back to Capistrano pt 1* (dg vo) [EW]
Classics 1151
LR-3008 *When the Swallows Come Back to Capistrano pt 2* [EW]
Classics 1151

*Note: the poor intonation of the trombones suggests that this recording may not be by the reg-
ular Lunceford orchestra.*

Los Angeles, July 14, 1942
L3096-A *I Dream a Lot about You* (dg vo) [TD] Decca 18618
Classics 862, History 2.1913-HI, Membran 221999-306, Acrobat 4076, Quad Jazz
    80007UAR1U
L3097-B *Easy Street* (ty vo) [EW] Decca 18534
Classics 862, Jazz after Hours 200025, History 2.1913-HI, Membran 221999-306, Quad
    Jazz 80007UAR1U

Chauncey Jarrett (as) and Omer Simeon (cl, as) replace Smith
Unknown location, early October 1942
G.I. Jive [unknown]

Jarrett out; Teddy McRae (ts) replaces Thomas; Maxine Sullivan (vo)

Armed Forces Radio Service Transcriptions, NBC Studio, Hollywood, December
1942
Jubilee 8 *Short 'n Sweet but Hard* [unknown]
Jubilee 8 *Loch Lomond* (ms vo) [unknown]
Jubilee 8 *At Last* (ens vo) [SO]
Jubilee 8 *Cow Cow Boogie* (ms vo) [unknown]
Jubilee 8 *'Tain't What You Do (It's the Way That You Do It)* (part) [SO]

Waters out; Lunceford (ss, as) added; John "Streamline" Ewing (tb) replaces Young;
    Joe Thomas (cl, ts, voc) replaces McRae; Joe Marshall (d) replaces Crawford;
    Dolores Williams (vo)
AFSR Transcriptions, NBC Studio, Hollywood, May—June 1943
Jubilee 29, 263 *Blues in the Night* (jt, ens vo) [GW, WS, RH]
Hindsight HBCD504
Jubilee 29 *Happiness Is Just a Thing Called Joe* (dw vo) [unknown]
Jubilee 29 *Chocolate* [RS]
Polydor 236524
Jubilee 29 *Do I Know What I'm Doing?* (dw voc) [unknown]

Note: additional Jubilee number indicates later re-broadcast of this selection.

Velma Middleton (vo)
Armed Forces Radio Service Transcriptions, NBC Studio, Hollywood, May—June
    1943
Jubilee 31 Unknown title
Jubilee 31 Unknown title (vm vo)
Jubilee 31 Unknown title
Jubilee 31 Unknown title
Jubilee 31 Unknown title

Ada Brown (vo)
Armed Forces Radio Service Transcriptions, NBC Studio, Hollywood, June–July
    1943
Jubilee 33 *Uptown Blues* [head]
Cicala 8016, Festival 146, First Time 1506 (LPs)
Jubilee 33, 49, 133, 263 *Hallelujah* [EW]
Jazz Hour 3004, Soundscape 679, Otrcat Jubilee! Disk 1 (mp3)
Jubilee 33, 49, 133, 263 *Yesterdays* [EW]
Hindsight HBCD 504, Otrcat Jubilee! Disk 1 (mp3)
Jubilee 33 *Hip Hip Hooray* (ab vo) [unknown]
Otrcat Jubilee! Disk 1 (mp3)
Jubilee 33, 133, 263 *Wham (Re-Bop-Boom-Bam)* (ec, ens vo) [ED]

Jazz Hour 3004, Otrcat Jubilee! Disk 1 (mp 3)
Jubilee 33, 123, 263 *For Dancers Only* (part) [SO]
Jazz Hour 3004, Otrcat Jubilee! Disk 1 (mp 3)

Charles Stewart, Mitchell, William "Chiefty" Scott, Russell "Shakey" Green (tp), Arbello, Bowles, Earl Hardy, Ewing (tb), Simeon (cl, as), Kirtland Bradford (as), Thomas (cl, ts, vo), William Horner (ts), Carruthers (cl, as, bars, vo), Wilcox (p), Norris (g), Parham (b), Marshall (d)
Unknown Armed Forces Radio Service Transcriptions, "Down Beat," New York, probably late 1943
For Dancers Only (part) [SO]
Bandstand BS-7128 (LP)
Wham (Re Bop Boom Bam) (ens, ec vo) [ED]
Holiday for Strings [EW]
Alone Together [EW]
Keep Smilin', Keep Laughin', Be Happy (jt vo) [HJ]
Estrellita [EW]
'Tain't What You Do (It's the Way That You Do It) (jt, ens vo) [SO]
Bandstand BS-7128, Privateer PRV 103 (LPs)
For Dancers Only [SO]

Note: Lunceford announces Trummy Young, but it is Thomas who sings 'Tain't What You Do.

Melvin Moore (tp) replaces Stewart; Ernest Purce (ts) replaces Horner, Claude Trenier (vo)
New York, February 8, 1944 (Decca and World Transcriptions)
71756/W200-6269 *Back Door Stuff pt 1* [RS] Decca 18594
Classics 862, Empress 987, Past Perfect 204358-203, Jazz after Hours 200025, Jazz Portrait 14531, Jazz Roots 56013, Joan 7147, Jasmine JASCD 391, History 2.1913-HI, Acrobat 4076, Quad Jazz 80007UAR1U
71757/W200-6270 *Back Door Stuff pt 2* [RS] Decca 18594
Classics 862, Empress 987, Past Perfect 204358-203, Jazz after Hours 200025, Jazz Portrait 14531, Jazz Roots 56013, Joan 7147, Jasmine JASCD 391, History 2.1913-HI, Acrobat 4076, Quad Jazz 80007UAR1U
W300-6271 *Down by the Old Mill Stream* (ct vo) [SO]
Circle CLP-92 (LP)
71758/W300-6272 *The Goon Came On* (jt vo) [BM]
Circle CLP-92, Privateer PRV 103, JRC C1433 (lps)
71759 *Just Once Too Often* (ct vo) [EW]
Circle CLP-92 (LP)

71760 *Jeep Rhythm* [HH] Decca 18618
Classics 862, Hindsight HCD413, EMP Jazz Archives 159982, Golden Stars 5308, History 2.1913-HI, Quad Jazz 80007UAR1U
N-1627-2 *Jeep Rhythm* [HH]
Circle CLP-92 (LP)
W 300-6602 *Charmaine* (ct vo) [SO]
Circle CLP-92, Hits 1002, Privateer PRV 103 (part) (LPs)
Solitude [SO]
Circle CLP-92 (LP)
Like a Ship at Sea (ct vo) [EW]
Circle CLP-92 (LP)
For Dancers Only [SO]
Circle CLP-92, Hits 1002, Privateer PRV 103, RCA RC330, JRC C1433, Golden Era 15056, Purple Heart 163, Joyce LP-5006 (LPs)

World Transcriptions, New York, February 9, 1944
1640 *(The Chicks That I Pick Are) Slender, Tender and Tall* (ct vo) [EW] unissued
1641 *Platonic* [?P]
1642 *By the River Sainte Marie* (ct voc) [SO]
JRC C1433 (LP)
1643 *Limehouse Blues* [unknown]
1644 *Pretty Eyes* (ct voc) [BM] unissued
1645 *Margie* (ct voc) [SO]
Circle CLP-92 (LP)
1646 *Sleepy Time Gal* [EW]
Circle CLP-92 (LP)
1647 *I Got It* [BM]
1648 *I'm Alone with You* [BE]
1649 *My Melancholy Baby* [EW]
JRC C1433 (LP)
1650 *Sophisticated Lady* [WS]
1651 *Whatcha Know, Joe?* [RS]

Armed Forces Radio Service Transcriptions, unknown date and location, probably spring 1944
BML 173 *Estrellita* [EW]
Hindsight HCD221

John Mitchell (g) replaces Norris
Armed Forces Radio Service Transcriptions, NBC Studio, Hollywood, June 1944
Jubilee 85 *One O'Clock Jump* (part) [EW]
Otrcat Jubilee! Disk 1 (mp3)
Jubilee 85, BML P-138 *Little John* [EW]

Soundscape 679, Otrcat Jubilee! Disk 1 (mp3)
Jubilee 85, BML P-138 *The Goon Came On* (jt vo) [BM]
Otrcat Jubilee! Disk 1 (mp3)
Jubilee 85, BML P-138 *Alone Together* [EW]
Soundscape 679, Otrcat Jubilee! Disk 1 (mp3)
Jubilee 85 *One O'Clock Jump* (part) [EW]
Otrcat Jubilee! Disk 1 (mp3)

Lunceford (fl-1); Sullivan, Carruthers (vo)
Armed Forces Radio Service Transcriptions, NBC Studio, Hollywood, June 1944
Jubilee 86 *One O'Clock Jump* (part) [EW]
Otrcat Jubilee! Disk 1 (mp 3)
Jubilee 86 *Holiday for Strings* (1) [EW]
Hindsight HCD221, Otrcat Jubilee! Disk 1 (mp3)
Jubilee 86 *Molly Malone* (ms vo) [unknown]
Otrcat Jubilee! Disk 1 (mp3)
Jubilee 86, 123 *Keep Smiling, Keep Laughing, Be Happy* (jt vo) [HJ]
Hindsight HCD221, Otrcat Jubilee! Disk 1 (mp3)
Jubilee 86 *Milkman Keep Those Bottles Quiet* (ms vo) [unknown]
Otrcat Jubilee! Disk 1 (mp3)
Jubilee 86 *Wham (Re-Bop-Boom-Bam)* (ec, ens vo) [ED]
Otrcat Jubilee! Disk 1 (mp3)
Jubilee 86 *One O'Clock Jump* (part) [EW]
Otrcat Jubilee! Disk 1 (mp3)

Lena Horne (vo)
Armed Forces Radio Service Transcriptions, NBC Studio, Hollywood, July 1944
Jubilee 89 *One O'Clock Jump* [EW]
Otrcat Jubilee! Disk 1 (mp3)
Jubilee 89 *Hallelujah* [EW]
Otrcat Jubilee! Disk 1 (mp3)
Jubilee 89 *Between the Devil and the Deep Blue Sea* (lh vo) [unknown]
Otrcat Jubilee! Disk 1 (mp3)
Jubilee 89 *I'll Walk Alone* (lh vo) [unknown]
Otrcat Jubilee! Disk 1 (mp3)
Jubilee 89 *Pistol Packin' Mama* (ens vo) [EW]
Soundscape 679, Otrcat Jubilee! Disk 1 (mp3)
Jubilee 89 *One O'Clock Jump* (part) [EW]
Otrcat Jubilee! Disk 1 (mp3)

Effie Smith (vo)
Armed Forces Radio Service Transcriptions, Hollywood, 1944
BML P-27 *(The Chicks That I Pick Are) Slender, Tender and Tall (es vo)* [EW]

Privateer PRV 103 (LP)
BML P-27 *Give, Baby, Give* (es vo) [unknown]
JRC C1408 (cassette)
BML P-27 *'Tain't What You Do (It's the Way That You Do It)* (jt, ens vo) [SO]
JRC C1408 (cassette)

Note: Effie Smith sings "The gates that I date are slender, tender, and tall."

Moore, Ralph Griffin, Scott or Mitchell, Green (tp), Arbello, Hardy, Ewing, Bowles (tb),
     Simeon (cl, as), Bradford (as), Thomas (cl, ts, vo), Purce (ts), Carruthers (cl, as, bars),
     Wilcox (p), Mitchell (g), Parham (b), Marshall (d), Bill Darnell, Trenier (vo)
New York, December 27, 1944 (Decca and World Transcriptions)
72655 *I'm Gonna See My Baby* (ens vo) [EW] Decca 18655
Classics 862, Jazz after Hours 200025, History 2.1913-HI, Quad Jazz 80007UAR1U
72656 *That Someone Must Be You* (ct vo) [EW] Decca 18655
Classics 862, Jazz after Hours 200025, History 2.1913-HI, Membran 221999-306, Quad
     Jazz 80007UAR1U
72657 *A Lover's Lullaby* (ct vo) [EW] World 6830
JRC C1433
72658 *Oh Gee, Oh Gosh, Oh Pshaw* (jt vo) [EW]
Classics 1082
72659 *I'm in a Jam with Baby* (bd vo) [LW] Coral 60041
Classics 862, History 2.1913-HI, Membran 221999-306, Quad Jazz 80007UAR1U
What a Difference a Day Made [EW]
Soundies SCD4132

Rostelle Reese and Les Current (tpt) replace Moore, Griffin, and Current; Joe
     Williams (tb) replaces Ewing
Unknown Armed Forces Radio Service broadcast, NBC Studio, Hollywood, 1945 or
     earlier
Jubilee? *Bust Out* [EW]

Trenier Twins (vo)
New York, February 27, 1945
72748 *I Passed through Memphis Last Night* (ct vo) [EW]
Classics 1082
72749 *Buzz-Buzz-Buzz* (tt, ens vo) [JL] Coral 60041
Classics 862, Jazz after Hours 200025, History 2.1913-HI, Membran 221999-306,
     Acrobat 4076, Quad Jazz 80007UAR1U
72750 *This Is My Confession (to You)* (ct vo) [LW] Decca 24254
Classics 862, History 2.1913-HI, Quad Jazz 80007UAR1U
72751 *I Need a Lift* (ens vo) [EW]
Classics 1082

Broadcast, Apollo Theater, New York, April 4, 1945
Yard Dog Mazurka [GW]
Everybodys EV-3003 (LP)

Moore and Scott (tp) replace Reese and Current; Ewing (tb) replaces Williams;
   George Duvivier (b) replaces Parham, Garry Moore, Effie Smith (vo)
Armed Forces Radio Service broadcast, Hollywood, early June 1945
Jubilee 137, 213 *One O'Clock Jump* (part) [EW]
RST JUBCD 1010-2, Otrcat Jubilee! Disk 2 (mp3)
Jubilee 137, 213 *Bust Out* [EW]
RST JUBCD 1010-2, Soundscape 679, Otrcat Jubilee! Disk 2 (mp3)
Jubilee 137, 213 *The Honeydripper* (es vo) [EW]
RST JUBCD 1010-2, Otrcat Jubilee! Disk 2 (mp3)
Jubilee 137, 213 *I'm Beginning to See the Light* (es vo) [EW]
RST JUBCD 1010-2
Jubilee 137, 213 *Meditation From "Thais"* [EW]
RST JUBCD 1010-2, Otrcat Jubilee! Disk 2 (mp3)
Jubilee 137, 213 *In the Good Old Summertime* (gm vo) [unknown]
RST JUBCD 1010-2, Otrcat Jubilee! Disk 2 (mp3)
Jubilee 137, 213 *I'm Gonna See My Baby* (ens vo) [EW]
Otrcat Jubilee! Disk 2 (mp3)

Parham (b) replaces Duvivier, Alvino Rey (el steel g-1), Tina Dixon, The Town
   Criers (vo)
Armed Forces Radio Service broadcast, Casa Mañana, Culver City, June 1945
Jubilee 138 *One O'Clock Jump* [EW]
Otrcat Jubilee! Disk 1 (mp3)
Jubilee 138 *Little John* [EW]
Soundscape 679, Otrcat Jubilee! Disk 1 (mp3)
Jubilee 138 *Ee-ba-ba-lee-ba* (td, ens vo) [EW]
Otrcat Jubilee! Disk 1 (mp3)
Jubilee 138 *Idaho* (ttc vo) [EW]
Otrcat Jubilee! Disk 1 (mp3)
Jubilee 138 *Please No Squeeze da Banana* (ttc vo) [EW]
Otrcat Jubilee! Disk 1 (mp3)
Jubilee 138 *Body and Soul* (1) [EW]
Otrcat Jubilee! Disk 1 (mp3)

Dixon, Timmie Rogers (vo)
Armed Forces Radio Service Transcriptions, NBC Studio, Hollywood, June 1945
Jubilee 139 *One O'Clock Jump* (part) [EW]
RST JUBCD 1003 2, Otrcat Jubilee! Disk 1 (mp3)

Jubilee 139 *Jeep Rhythm* [HH]
RST JUBCD 1003 2, Otrcat Jubilee! Disk 1 (mp3)
Jubilee 139 *Stuff Like That There* (td vo) [unknown]
RST JUBCD 1003 2, Otrcat Jubilee! Disk 1 (mp3)
Jubilee 139 *The Jimmies* [EW]
RST JUBCD 1003 2, Otrcat Jubilee! Disk 1 (mp3)
Jubilee 139 *The Old Music Master* (tr vo) [unknown]
RST JUBCD 1003 2, Otrcat Jubilee! Disk 1 (mp3)
Jubilee 139 *Song of the Islands* [EW]
RST JUBCD 1003 2, Otrcat Jubilee! Disk 1 (mp3)
Jubilee 139 *One O'Clock Jump* (part) [EW]
RST JUBCD 1003 2, Otrcat Jubilee! Disk 1 (mp3)

Herb Shriner (harmonica-1); Lunceford (vo)
Armed Forces Radio Service broadcast, NBC Studio, Hollywood, July 1945
Jubilee 144 *One O'Clock Jump* (part) [EW]
Jubilee 144 *Minor Riff* [EW]
Extreme Rarities LP 1007, First Heard FH-15, Polydor 236524, Musidisc 302A 5200,
    Golden Era GE 15058, Connoisseur Rarities CR 521 (LPs)
Jubilee 144 *Alexander's Ragtime Band* (1) [SO] unissued
Jubilee 144 *The Honeydripper* (jl, ens vo) [EW]
First Heard FH-15, Connoisseur Rarities CR521 (LPs)
Jubilee 144 *For Dancers Only* [so]
Extreme Rarities LP 1007, First Heard FH-15, Polydor 236524 (LPs)
Jubilee 144 *One O'Clock Jump* (part) [EW]

Joe Williams (tb) replaces Ewing and Bowles; Nick Brooks (vo)
Armed Forces Radio Service broadcast "One Night Stand" No. 720, Casa Mañana,
    Culver City, August 4, 1945
ONS 720 *I Need a Lift* (ens vo) [EW]
Joyce LP1103 (LP)
ONS 720 *What a Difference a Day Made* [EW]
Soundscape 679
ONS 720 *By the River Sainte Marie* (nb vo) [SO]
Joyce LP1103 (LP)
ONS 720 *Like a Ship at Sea* (nb vo) [EW] unissued
ONS 720 *Mandy* [SO]
Joyce LP1103, Palm POM-1, Musidisc 30 JA 5200, Extreme Rarities LP1007 (LPs)
ONS 720 *Sentimental Journey* (nb vo) [unknown] unissued
ONS 720 *Caldonia* (jt, ens vo) [EW]
Palm POM-1 (LP)
ONS 720 *Sophisticated Lady* [WS]

Charles "Chuck" Stewart replaces Moore; Bob Mitchell also vo; Delta Rhythm Boys,
    Brooks (vo)
Los Angeles, August 9, 1945
L3906-A *Baby, Are You Kiddin'?* (drb vo) [EW] Decca 23451
Classics 862, History 2.1913-HI, Membran 221999-306, Acrobat 4076, Quad Jazz
    80007UAR1U
L3907 *Where's the Melody* (bm? ens vo) [EW]
Classics 1082
L3908-A *The Honeydripper* (drb voc) [EW] Decca 23451
Classics 862, Jasmine JASCD 391, History 2.1913-HI, Membran 221999-306, Acrobat
    4076, Quad Jazz 80007UAR1U
L3909 *I've Got Those Carolina Blues* (nb vo) [EW]
Classics 1082

Armed Forces Radio Service broadcast, "One Night Stand" No. 694, Casa Mañana,
    Culver City, September 8, 1945
ONS 694 *Uptown Blues* (part) [head]
First Heard FH-15, Joyce LP 1103 (LPs)
ONS 694 *Little John* [EW]
First Heard FH-15, Joyce LP1103 (LPs)
ONS 694 *Fascinating Rhythm* [unknown]
Joyce LP1103 (LP)
ONS 694 *Like a Ship at Sea* (nb vo) [EW]
Joyce LP1103 (LP)
ONS 694 *Caldonia* (ens, jt vo) [EW]
ONS 694 *Sophisticated Lady* [WS/EW]
ONS 694 *Dreams* (nb vo) [HH]
Joyce LP1103 (LP)
ONS 694 *I Got It* (nb vo) [BM]
Joyce LP1103 (LP)
ONS 694 *Sentimental Journey* (nb vo) [unknown]
Joyce LP1103 (LP)
ONS 694 *For Dancers Only* (part)
Joyce LP1103, First Heard FH-15 (LPs)

New York, October 2, 1945
For Dancers Only [SO]
IAJRC 51 (LP)

New York, October 3, 1945
VP-1590 *The Jimmies* [EW] V-Disc 568-A
Classics 1082, RST 91566-2

VP-1590 *I Need a Lift* (ens vo) [EW] V-Disc 568-A
Classics 1082, RST 91566-2
VP-1598 *For Dancers Only* [SO] V-Disc 586-A
Classics 1082, Time-Life OPCD4538
For Dancers Only (part) [SO]
VP-1598 *What to Do* [EW] V-Disc 586-A
Classics 1082, EMP Jazz Archives 159982
Wham (Re-Bop-Boom-Bam) (ec, ens vo) [ED] unissued
You Ain't Nowhere [RS] V-Disc 882-A
Bast 7128

The Quintones (vo)
Armed Forces Radio Service broadcast "Spotlight Bands" No. 772, Jefferson Bar-
    racks, Missouri, November 23, 1945
Coke 925 *Theme*
Aircheck No. 8, Musidisc 30 JA 5200 (LPs)
Coke 925 *Uptown Blues (Marylin Comes On)* (part) [head]
Hindsight HCD221
Coke 925 *Jeep Rhythm* [HH]
Hindsight HCD221, Hindsight HCD413, Jazzterdays 102401, Soundscape 679, AET
    CD 50172
Coke 925 *Blues in the Night* (ens vo) [GW, WS, RH]
Hindsight HCD221, Hindsight HCD 413, Jazzterdays 102401, Soundscape 679, AET
    CD 50172
Coke 925 *What to Do* [EW]
Hindsight HCD221, Jazzterdays 102401, Soundscape 679, AET CD 50172
Coke 925 *Baby, Are You Kiddin'?* (q vo) [EW]
Hindsight HCD221, Jazzterdays 102401, Soundscape 679, AET CD 50172
Coke 925 *Holiday for Strings* [RS]
Hindsight HCD221, Soundcsape 679
Coke 925 *Keep Smiling, Keep Laughing, Be Happy* (jt vo) [HJ]
Hindsight HCD221
Coke 925 *Wham (Re-Bop-Boom-Bam)* (ens vo) [ED]
Hindsight HCD221, Hindsight HCD413, Soundscape 679
Coke 925 *Estrellita* [EW]
Hindsight HCD221, Soundscape 679
Coke 925 *Meditation from "Thais"* [EW]
AET CD 50172
Coke 925 *The Honeydripper* (q vo) [EW]
Soundscape 679, AET CD 50172
Coke 925 *For Dancers Only* [SO]
Hindsight HCD413, Jazzterdays 102401, Soundscape 679, AET CD 50172

Coke 925 *Uptown Blues* (part) [head]
Aircheck No. 8 (LP)
Coke 925 *Theme*
Aircheck No. 8 (LP)

Add Roy Eldridge (tp)
Broadcast, British Forces Network, New York, February 9, 1946
I Surrender, Dear [unknown]

omit Eldridge
Willie "Blip" Tompkins and Alfonso King (tb) replace Hardy and Williams; William
   Horner (ts) replaces Purce; Brooks, Thomas Carruthers, Wilcox (quartet vo)
New York, April 25, 1946
T716 *Cement Mixer* (jt, quartet vo) [GD] Majestic 1045
Classics 1082, Savoy ZDS 1209, Acrobat 4076
T717 *Just Once Too Often* (nb vo) [EW] Majestic 1045
Classics 1082, Savoy ZDS 1209
T718 *Jay Gee* [GD] Majestic 1053
l 1082, Savoy ZDS 1209, Delta 11088
T719 *Sit Back and Ree-lax* (quartet vo) [EW] Majestic 1053
Classics 1082, Savoy ZDS 1209
T720 *The Jimmies* [EW] Majestic 1060
Classics 1082, Savoy ZDS 1209
T721 *I Need a Lift* (ens vo) [EW] Majestic 1060
Classics 1082, Savoy ZDS 1209, P-Vine PCD 5800

Reunald Jones (tp) replaces Stewart; Trummy Young (tb, vo) replaces Arbello; Al
   Cobbs (tb) replaces Tompkins and King
New York, August 28, 1946
T879 *Them Who Has Gets* (jt vo) [GD] Majestic 1077
Classics 1082, Savoy ZDS 1209
T880 *Margie* (ty vo) [SO] Majestic 1103
Classics 1082, Savoy ZDS 1209, Delta 11088
T881 *Four or Five Times* (jt vo) [SO] Majestic 1103
Classics 1082, Savoy ZDS 1209, Delta 11088
T882-4 *Shut-out (Close-out)* [GD] Majestic 1077
Classics 1082, Savoy ZDS 1209, Delta 11088, Metro METRDCD540
T882-6 *Close Out* [GD]
Halo 50223

Joe Wilder (tp) replaces Scott; Al Grey (tb) replaces Young; Lee Howard (ts) replaces
Horner; Lunceford (vo); Mitchell, Thomas, Carruthers, Wilcox (quartet vo)

New York, May 17, 1947
T1102 *Call the Police* (jl, jt, ens vo) [EW] Majestic 1122
Classics 1082, Savoy ZDS 1209, Delta 11088, Metro METRDCD540, P-Vine PCD
    5800, Acrobat 4076
T1103 *Water Faucet* (quartet vo) [GD] Majestic 1122
Classics 1082, Savoy ZDS 1209, Delta 11088
Open the Door Richard (ec vo) [unknown] unissued
One O'Clock Jump [EW]
Classics 1082, Savoy ZDS 1209

JIMMIE LUNCEFORD ORCHESTRA UNDER THE DIRECTION OF
EDDIE WILCOX AND JOE THOMAS

Willie Cook and Paul Webster (tp) replace Jones, Wilder, and Green; Elmer Crumb-
    ley (tb) replaces Al Grey; Othis "Hashim" Hicks replaces Bradford; Ed Sneed (b)
    replaces Parham
New York, early 1948
A1573 *Scratch My Back* (jt, ens vo) [EW] Manor 1110
Classics 1151
A1574 *Saxology* [AC] Manor 1110
Classics 1151
A1575 *What'cha Gonna Do?* (jt vo) [EW] Manor 1120
Classics 1151
A1576 *One for the Book* [EW] Manor 1120
Classics 1151
A1577 *Sneaky Pete* (jt, ens vo) [GD] Manor 1111
Classics 1151
A1578 *Moonbeams* [EW] Manor 1111
Classics 1151

Rostelle Reese, Tommy Simms, Paul Webster (tp), Mitchell (tp, vo), Crumbley,
    Bowles, Arnett Sparrow (tb), Simeon (cl, as), Curby Alexander (as), Thomas (cl, ts,
    vo), Slim Henderson (ts), Carruthers (cl, as, bars), Wilcox (p), Norris (g), Sneed
    (b), Danny Farrar (d); Freddy Bryant (vo)
Armed Forces Radio Service broadcast, "Magic Carpet," Royal Roost, New York,
    March 20, 1948
Uptown Blues [head]
What Else But If We're On (jt vo) [SO]
I Love You (fb vo) [unknown]
White Heat [WH]
Robbins' Nest [unknown]
A Kiss in the Dark [EW]

Savannah Churchill (vo)
New York, early 1949
A1661 *Ooh, That's What I Like* (fb vo) [EW] Manor 1187
Classics 1151
A1662 *Fatigue* [EW]
Classics 1151
A1663 *Midriff* [EW]
Classics 1151
A1664 *At Sundown* [EW]
Classics 1151
A1665 *A Study in Blue* (sc vo) [EW]
Classics 1151

New York, early 1949
A1690 *Jackie* (jt vo) [EW] Manor 1161
Classics 1151
A1691 *Arleen* (bm vo) [EW] Manor 1138
Classics 1151
A1693 *Gug Mug (Grazing)* [EW] Manor 1138
Classics 1151

Note: Gug Mug *identical to* Midriff.

New York, early 1949
The Worm [EW]
Classics 1151
My Baby and Me (jt vo) [EW]
Classics 1151
That's the Way You Fall in Love (bm vo) [EW]
Classics 1151
Magic of You [EW]
Classics 1151

Note: MCA GRD 2-629-2 identical to MCA GRP 26292
MCA GRD 608-2 identical to MCA GRP 16082
MCA GRD 645 identical to MCA GRD 16452
Columbia 65647 identical to Columbia 503283 2
Parade PAR 2012 identical to Trace 040 16 22
Soundscape 679 identical to Sounds of Yester Year DSOY679
Membran 221999-306 identical to CJA 221999

INDEX

Balliett, Whitney, 249

Bamville Club (New York, NY), 26

Band Box (New York, NY), 152, 162, 179

A Band of Negro Minstrels Who Call Themselves Colored Christian Singers (Fisk Jubilee Singers), 14

Banks, Ristina, 65

Barker, John, 79

Barnes, George, 98

Barnet, Charlie, 28, 82, 131, 165, 205, 226–27

Barnett, Cliff, 57

Bart, Ben, 220, 247

Bartholomew, Dave, 200–201

Basie, Catherine, 228

Basie, Bill "Count," 26, 28, 35, 48, 51, 61, 66, 73, 77, 89, 91, 103, 106, 110, 121, 125, 129–30, 139–40, 144, 150, 152–53, 157, 167, 170, 175–76, 178–79, 181, 202, 205, 210, 214–15, 219, 228, 245–46, 249, 254

Basie, Diane, 228

Baskette, Jimmie, 132

Bates, "Peg Leg," 212

Battle Axe, 177, 208

Battle Hymn of the Republic (John Brown's Body), 14

Bauduc, Ray, 133

Beale Street Auditorium (Memphis, TN), 42, 144

Beauchamp, George, 185

Because You're You, 62

Bechet, Sidney, 162, 170

Beethoven, Ludwig Van, 167, 174, 203

Behrman, Sam, 71

Beiderbecke, Leon "Bix." *See* Bix

Belgium Stomp (State and Tioga Stomp/Dutch Kitchen Stomp), 164, 166, 173

Bell, Aaron, 250

Bells, The, 15

Benford, Tommy, 26

Benjamin, Joe, 247

Bennett, George J., 225

Bennett Hall Orchestra, 19

Berkeley, Busby "Buzz," 52

Berkowski, Captain, 133

Berlin, Ellin, 71

Berlin, Irving, 71

Bernhardt, Clyde, 138

Berns Salonger (Stockholm, Sweden), 134–35, 137

Berry, Leon "Chu," 124, 176

Bestor, Don, 71

Best Things in Life Are Free, The, 95

Bigard, Barney, 36, 54–55, 154

Biltmore Hotel (Chicago, IL), 214

Bix, 152

Bird of Paradise, 78, 97

Birmingham Breakdown, 54

Black and Tan Fantasy, 54, 69–71, 78

Blackman, Teddy, 63

Blake, Eubie, 111

Blake, Jimmy, 161

Blakey, Art "Bu," 35

Blanke, Henry, 186

Blavatsky, Helena, 202

Block, Martin, 80–81, 131, 179

Blue Blazes, 162

Blue Devils, 3

Blue Note (New Orleans, LA), 250

Blue Ribbon Syncopators of Buffalo, 49, 128

Blues in the Night, 67, 125, 181, 186–88, 191, 194, 208

Blumenthal, Bob, 252

Body and Soul, 171, 176, 193

Boland, Francy, 252

Bonitto, Frank, 76, 83–84, 102, 179, 186–87, 196

Bontemps, Arna, 22–23

Bostic, Earl, 38, 98, 122, 248

Boulevard of Broken Dreams, 218

Bowles, Russell, 48, 96, 126, 139, 141, 220, 250–51

(Chicks That I Pick Are) Slender, Tender and Tall, 129
Chillun, Get Up, 68, 70–71, 159
Chilton, John, 129
Chinatown, My Chinatown, 132
Chisca Hotel (Memphis, TN), 35
Chopin's Prelude No. 7, 173, 206
Christian, Charlie, 99
Christopher Columbus, 124
City Center Casino (New York, NY), 251
Civic Auditorium (Memphis, TN), 45
Clark, Dave, 79–80
Clark, Sam C., 184
Clarke, George, 31, 45, 50, 166
Clarke, Kenny "Klook," 32, 252
Clark Park Auditorium (Memphis, TN), 46
Clay, Henry, 31
Clay, Otis, 108
Clay, William "Sonny," 10
Clayton, Wilbur "Buck," 21
Clementine, 58
Clinton, Larry, 122
Club Afrique (New York, NY), 129
Club Alabam (San Francisco, CA), 189
Club DeLuxe (New York, NY), 69
Club Harlem (Buffalo, NY), 50
Club Riviera (St. Louis, MO), 224
Cobb, Arnett, 51, 120, 171, 176–78, 193
Cobbs, Al, 224–25, 227, 232, 234, 237, 246–47
Cohen, "Porky," 226
Cole, Nat "King," 220
Coleman, Ornette, 212
Coles, Charles "Honi," 64, 244
College Inn (Chicago, IL), 68
Collette, William "Buddy," 121
Colonial Theater (New York, NY), 70
Coltrane, John "Trane," 157
Concert of Sacred Music, 146
Connelly, Bobby, 70
Connie's Inn (New York, NY), 64

Conrad, Joseph, 105
Continental, The, 67
Cooper, Al, 129–30
Cooper, Ralph, 76
Coquette, 94
Cotton Club (Austin, TX), 38, 193
Cotton Club (New York, NY), 37, 49, 56, 64, 67–74, 81, 83–84, 86–87, 92–94, 109, 131, 145, 163
Count Me Out, 97
Cravath, Erastus M., 13
Crawford, Jimmy "Craw," 26, 31–35, 42, 44, 52, 66, 72–73, 106, 116, 119, 121, 126, 134, 136, 149, 158, 166, 190–91, 215
Crosby, Bing, 77, 92, 169
Crosby, Bob, 125, 132–33
Crow, Dr., 35
Crumbley, Elmer "Klinkertop," 82, 92, 94, 96, 141, 204–5, 227, 250–51
Cullen, Countee, 22

Dallas Blues, The, 4
Dameron, Tadd, 126, 163, 189, 196–97, 200, 219, 224
Dance, Stanley, 34–35, 41, 57, 248
Dancer, Maurice, 76
Dandridge Sisters, 158–59, 177
D'Angelo (Michael Archer), 92
Danish Radio Jazz Orchestra, 165
Dardanella, 9
Darktown Strutters' Ball, 9
Darnell, Bill, 219
Davis, Joe, 124
Davis, Leo, 11
Davis, Miles, 206–7, 224
Davis, "Wild" Bill, 176
Dawn Club (San Francisco, CA), 188
De Bann, Steve, 132
Debussy, Claude, 181
DeFranco, Boniface "Buddy," 33, 147, 161, 191, 209, 252, 254
De Gaston, Gallie, 65

239–40, 243–50
Thomas, Kathryn Perry, 31
Thomas, Otis, 202
Thomas, Rufus, 104
Thompson, Eli "Lucky," 218, 251
Thompson, "Sir" Charles, 153
Thompson, William R., 242
Thompson Band, 108
Three Bones, 232
Three Brown Jacks, The, 116
Three Deuces, The (Chicago, IL), 236
Thunder, 97
Tiger Rag, 134, 154, 192
Time's A Wastin', 156
Tip Toe, 252
Tiptoe through the Tulips, 31
Tolbert, Campbell "Skeets," 93
Tompkins, Eddie, 49–50, 53–54, 92–93,
    96, 116, 135, 158–59, 163, 167, 173,
    175
Tompkins, Willie "Blip," 244
Top, The (Chicago, IL), 68
Travis, Dempsey J., 119
Trenier, Claude, 221
Trenier, Clifford, 221
Treniers, The, 221
Trent, Alphonso, 10, 28–29, 32, 41,
    53–54, 58, 129
Trianon Ballroom (Los Angeles, CA),
    186, 215
Truckin', 93
Tucker, Tommy, 233
Tunnell, George "Bon Bon," 219
Twenty-Four Robbers, 173, 191, 205
Two O'Clock Jump, 207

Ulanov, Barry, 34, 54
Uptown Blues, 68, 168, 171, 182, 239

Valentine, Gerald, 129
Vallee, Rudy, 30
Van Vechten, Carl, 63
Vaughan, Sarah "Sassy," 202

Vendome Hotel (Buffalo, NY), 45,
    48–50
Venuti, Joe, 131
Vernon, Frank, 131, 133
Vieuxtemps, Henri, 9
Vinson, Eddie "Cleanhead," 177, 245
Vodery, Will, 111

Wagner, Richard, 169
Waldorf Astoria Hotel (New York,
    NY), 187
Walker, Aaron "T-Bone," 203, 220
Walker, Nelson, 13
Walking by the River, 70
Waller, Thomas "Fats," 8, 41, 76, 81, 83,
    86–87, 89, 94, 110–11, 118, 142, 233,
    239
Wallis, Hal, 186
Wand, Hart A., 4
Ward, Aida, 69
Ward, Lester, 16
Waring, Fred, 71, 81, 104–5
Warren, Earle, 85, 89
Washington, Booker, 34
Washington, Dinah "The Queen," 248
Water Faucet, 225
Waters, Benny, 53, 92, 103, 106, 151, 205,
    207, 213–14
Waters, Ethel "Sweet Mama String-
    bean," 76, 197
Watkins, Ralph, 224
Watkins Brothers, 248
Watters, Lu, 189
Webb, Elida, 70
Webb, Lawrence "Speed," 48
Webb, William "Chick," 28, 32, 64, 76,
    89, 121, 131, 141, 153, 158–59, 169,
    176
Webster, Ben "Frog," 51, 146, 215
Webster, Freddie "Webs," 171, 204,
    207–12, 219
Webster, Paul, 48, 50, 82, 96, 98, 116,
    124, 127, 135, 166, 199, 217–18, 221,

Text design by Jillian Downey
Typesetting by Delmastype, Ann Arbor, Michigan
Text font: Fournier MT
Display font: Newport Classic SG

In 1924, Monotype based Fournier MT on types cut by Pierre Simon Fournier circa 1742. These types were some of the most influential designs of the eighteenth century, being among the earliest of the "transitional" style of typeface, and were a stepping stone to the more severe "modern" style made popular by Bodoni later in the century.
                                                    —Courtesy www.adobe.com

Newport Classic SG is based on the Newport typeface, which was designed by Willard T. Sniffin for American Type Founders in 1932.
                              —Courtesy www.myfonts.com and www.identifont.com